LEARNING TO HEAL

LEARNING TO HEAL

The Development
of American
Medical Education

KENNETH M. LUDMERER

Basic Books, Inc., Publishers   New York

Two chapters in this book are revised versions of previously published material. Chapter 8 appeared in *Bulletin of the History of Medicine* 57(1983):218–29, © 1983 by The Johns Hopkins University Press. Chapter 12 appeared in *Journal of the History of Medicine and Allied Sciences* 38(1983):389–414, © 1983 by the *Journal of the History of Medicine and Allied Sciences*. The following have generously given permission to use quotations from archival materials: Medical Archives, New York Hospital-Cornell Medical Center, New York; Department of Rare Books and Special Collections, The University of Rochester Library, Rochester, N.Y.; Special Collections, Bowdoin College Library, Brunswick, Me.; and Yale University Archives, New Haven, Conn.

Library of Congress Cataloging-in-Publication Data
Ludmerer, Kenneth M.
   Learning to heal.
   Bibliographic notes: p. 281
   Includes index.
   1. Medical education—United States—History.
I. Title. [DNLM: 1. Education, Medical—history—
United States. W 18 L945L]
R745.L84 1985   610'.7'1173   85–47554
ISBN 0–465–03880–8 (cloth)
ISBN 0–465–03881–6 (paper)

To Donald Fleming and Lloyd Stevenson

Contents

Contents

Preface

THIS BOOK BEGAN one summer afternoon as I was reading several essays written in the 1870s by John Shaw Billings, a prominent nineteenth-century medical educator, about how medical students should be taught at the proposed Johns Hopkins Medical School. I was stunned, because Billings was advancing the same ideas about how learning should proceed as those of John Dewey a generation later. Suddenly the meaning of the Johns Hopkins Medical School—and modern medical education—became clear to me: it was Dewey's "progressive education" in a medical setting. After further study, however, I found that much more was involved in the development of American medical education than a revolution in the methods of teaching. For the new educational approaches to be implemented, the modern medical school had to be created, and the medical profession had to be transformed into its present sociological form. To relate the story of these interconnected events is the objective of this book.

As any physician will recognize, learning to heal is a lifelong process that only begins with what one learns in medical school. Why, then, should the medical school be the focus of a book on medical education, as distinct from internship, residency, fellowship, or the continuing education that every physician undergoes while in practice? The answer lies in the question. It is during the four years of formal medical study that students are prepared to be lifelong learners. Basic principles and skills are taught; methods and approaches for acquiring and assessing information are imparted; a common framework of knowledge is transmitted; and students are sometimes lured into careers in teaching and research. This period of "undergraduate" medical education involves the formation of a new intellectual orientation and the complete transformation of a student's character, personality, and outlook. Understanding this experience is central to understanding every other aspect of learning medicine.

The notes at the end of the book will serve as a guide to the primary sources I used and to the secondary literature to which I owe so much. My most important sources, as readers will discover, were unpublished records of medical schools, hospitals, foundations, and private individuals. During the research stages of the project, I visited more than thirty cities and was able to locate documents pertaining to all types of medical schools—weak institutions as well as strong; schools that became extinct as well as those that are still alive; and schools in every region of the country (though predominantly the Northeast, middle Atlantic coast, Great Lakes states, and Midwest, thus reflecting the distribution of medical schools in the late nineteenth and early twentieth centuries). More than once I found archival records that revealed a story much different from that presented in the medical journals and the publications of the state and county medical societies, the sources traditionally used in the study of the history of medical education. The notes to the book are purposely long so that all of the pertinent archival documentation could be included. However, the notes should not be a distraction, and the book may be read without referring to them.

The development of our present system of medical education was a magnificent achievement—one that seems even more impressive when viewed in the context of the lowly state of medical education and practice from which it arose. Yet the system was not achieved without costs—either to doctors or to the public. As the system developed, so did many of the problems that continue to plague medical education and medical practice today. Because these problems are becoming more severe, Americans will soon have to make difficult decisions about the future of their medical schools and their health-care system. These decisions can best be made only with an understanding of the process of how the problems arose. My hope is that the analysis contained in the following pages will help provide the framework for doing so.

Acknowledgments

UPON THE COMPLETION OF A BOOK, it is a great joy to thank the many persons whose ideas, encouragement, and support were so helpful along the way. Words are never sufficient to convey the gratitude an author feels. Nevertheless, it is a pleasure to acknowledge my deep appreciation to the many friends who have so unstintingly given their assistance to this project.

This book began during the summer of 1976, when, as a postdoctoral fellow in the Department of Medicine at Washington University, I spent a year-long sabbatical at the Department of the History of Science at Harvard University. In Cambridge, Everett Mendelsohn and Barbara Rosenkrantz were gracious hosts, and they were always available for discussions and musings. My work has continued to benefit from their ongoing interest and assistance. The book was formulated that year in the course of dozens of conversations with Jon Roberts and Robert Silverman, who have remained valued supporters of the project and friends of the author. In Cambridge I also profited from conversations with many other persons, especially Donald Fleming, Oscar Handlin, Paul Starr, and Richard Wolfe.

The book was written in St. Louis, where I enjoyed the support and suggestions of numerous colleagues, past and present, in the internal medicine and history departments of Washington University. I would particularly like to thank Mark Frisse, Lewis Chase, Gerald Perkoff, Peter Tuteur, John Vavra, David Konig, Glen Holt, Mark Leff, Henry Berger, Michael Weinberg, Donald Bellomy, Robert Williams, Ralph Morrow, and Richard Walter. I am also exceedingly grateful to Professors Morrow and Walter for the trust they placed in me by allowing my unusual interfaculty appointment. Garland Allen of the biology department at Washington University was another who gave freely of his ideas and opinions throughout the course of the project.

Acknowledgments

The research for the book proved an imposing task, and I would not have been able to conduct it without the generous assistance of many dozens of librarians and archivists throughout the country. The notes will serve as an index to the staffs that proved so friendly and helpful. I am especially indebted to librarians Estelle Brodman and Susan Crawford and the rest of the staff of the Washington University Medical Library, particularly Christopher Hoolihan and Paul Anderson. I am also very grateful to the Rockefeller Archive Center for a travel grant that allowed a month of research in their magnificent holdings.

Several colleagues took time from their own valuable work to read an earlier version of the manuscript. I would like to thank Donald Fleming, Mark Frisse, David Konig, Mark Leff, Sol Ludmerer, Ralph Morrow, Robert Silverman, and August Swanson for their many helpful criticisms and suggestions. Laurence Veysey offered some very useful comments on an earlier version of chapter 2; Regina Markell Morantz kindly verified the accuracy of my remarks on women's medical education. I am also extremely grateful to Debi Katz for the expert technical assistance she provided in typing the manuscript, and to Sandra Dhols of Basic Books for her skill in guiding the manuscript to publication.

To a few friends I would like to express my special thanks. From the beginning the Ludmerer family was a source of ideas. Even more important was the morale-boosting they provided when the future looked bleakest. Jon Roberts and Robert Silverman were perpetual sources of sage advice and good humor, and their innumerable suggestions have enriched the entire book. Mark Frisse unselfishly interrupted his own important work to discuss the project with me too often to keep count. Only he understands how valuable his comments have been and how much he served as a mood lifter when my spirits were flagging. For several years Martin Kessler of Basic Books has been a true friend to the author. His advice proved immensely helpful as I was deciding how to organize the material, and the last chapter owes much to his critical suggestions. Lloyd Stevenson was a valuable source of ideas and encouragement; I often visited him in Baltimore to profit from his insights into the history of medicine. Donald Fleming repeatedly shared with me his unusual understanding of history, and his brilliance, high standards, and encouragement inspired me at every moment of the project. His influence pervades each page of the book.

My greatest debt is to David Kipnis, who had the trust and confidence in me to allow the history of medicine to be my "clinical science" in the Department of Medicine at Washington University. He provided every conceivable type of support and encouragement, and he made certain that the

Acknowledgments

limiting factor in this project was my ability and determination, not the conditions of work. I am equally grateful to the American College of Physicians for supporting me as a Teaching and Research Scholar, and to the Henry J. Kaiser Family Foundation for selecting me as a Faculty Scholar in General Internal Medicine. Both the College and the Kaiser Foundation, like David Kipnis, accepted the idea that research in the history of medicine is a legitimate scholarly pursuit for an academic internist. My hope is that they will feel that their trust has been justified, and my dream is that other academic clinicians may soon receive the same opportunities to pursue the history of medicine as their clinical science.

LEARNING TO HEAL

Introduction

A CENTURY AGO, being a medical student in America was easy. No one worried about admission, for entrance requirements were lower than they were for a good high school. Instruction was superficial and brief. The terms lasted only sixteen weeks, and after the second term the M.D. degree was automatically given, regardless of a student's academic performance. Teaching was by lecture alone. Thus, students were spared the onerous chores of attending laboratories, clinics, and hospital wards. Indeed, except for the enterprising and affluent few who would bribe patients into submitting to an examination, students would often graduate without ever having touched a patient.

If this mode of medical teaching seems foreign to contemporary eyes, the organization and structure of the medical school are equally unrecognizable. In the post-Civil War era the typical faculty consisted of only seven or eight instructors. The schools were owned by the professors, who operated them for profit. For that reason medical schools were called "proprietary schools." Medical teaching was a part-time activity, a side business to one's private practice. Since laboratories and hospital facilities were not utilized in medical education, only modest resources were needed to run a medical school. A second floor above a corner drug store would do; a school that had a building of its own was richly endowed. Very few schools had university affiliations or were connected with teaching hospitals, and medical research was almost nonexistent.

American medical education has changed dramatically in the last century. Medical training has ceased to be a casual and superficial experience. Quite the contrary—it has become arduous, long, and demanding. Students are no longer taught by lectures alone. Instead, through laboratory instruction and clinical clerkships, they are made active participants in their own learning process. The schools—with their immense plants, sophisticated laboratories, capacious teaching hospitals, and large, full-time faculties—have become factories for the production of well-trained doctors and the pursuit of medical research. American medical education, once subservient to European medical education, has become the best in the world. To explain the emergence of this country's present system of medical education is the first purpose of this book. To describe the importance of these events to the sociological development of the medical profession, and to demonstrate how these events gave rise to the challenges facing medical education and practice today, is the second.

The story begins in the mid-nineteenth century. Amid the informal conditions of medical education described above, events were underway that were to transform the system. A revolution in experimental medicine was proceeding in Europe; a cadre of American doctors was traveling to Europe to learn laboratory methods; the modern university in America was emerging; the system of mass public education was developing; and some very rich industrialists were starting to cultivate a habit of philantrophy. These developments were to provide the infrastructure of the American system of medical education that would later appear. By 1910, when Abraham Flexner published his landmark survey of the conditions in American and Canadian medical schools (the "Flexner report"), the system in its main outline was already in place. The widely held view that the era of modern medical education began with the Flexner report is a myth—one of the many myths about American medical education that needs to be destroyed.

Medical education is always changing, and for that reason the story related in this book continues to the present. The most recent trends and issues in medical education are explored in the last chapter. Yet, as important as these developments have been, they must not obscure a fundamental insight: that by the 1920s the country's system of medical education was mature, both in the methods of teaching and in the structure and organization of the medical school. Recent trends have represented developments within that system, not changes in the system itself. The strengths of American medical education today—as well as the challenges facing it—are legacies from how the system came into being.

The maturation of American medical education was a complex process —one that spanned two continents and occurred over a century and a half. Some of the many events that shaped it are familiar to medical historians, such as the development of experimental medicine and the rise of clinical science. Others at first glance might seem out of place in a history of medicine: the emergence of the modern university, the growth of this country's system of

4

public education, the muckraking reforms of the Progressive Era, the assumption of new regulatory authority by state and federal government, and the rise of American philanthropy.[1] The creation of the present system involved the highest educational idealism among some doctors. Others perceived the reform of medical education as a way to alleviate their professional and economic insecurities. The medical profession was never united in its view of how the medical school should be changed. Indeed, fierce disputes among various factions of physicians continually threatened to tear the profession apart—and many of these tensions persist today. Amid this broad canvas of time, geography, cultural influences, and personal motivations, it would be helpful to identify the main themes for the reader to keep in focus.

At its root, the development of American medical education involved a conceptual revolution in how medical students should be taught. With the introduction of laboratory and hospital work, students were expected to be active participants in their learning process, and the new goal of medical training was to foster critical thinking, not merely the memorization of facts. These were the same educational ideas as those associated with the progressive education movement. Medical teachers began advocating these concepts a generation before leaders of elementary and high schools did so, and it was in the medical schools that progressive education was to have its most enduring impact in America. Indeed, the goal of producing critical thinkers remains the primary objective of medical educators today. This ideal has always been very difficult to achieve in practice, but in an era of medical specialization and rampant medical technology, it has become more important than ever.

Learning to heal, like every other type of learning, is profoundly influenced by the institutional framework in which instruction is carried out. For the new educational ideals to be implemented, an institutional revolution was required as well: the proprietary school had to be abandoned, and in its place had to be created the modern university medical school. Between 1885 and 1925 this transition occurred. Large sums of money were raised, new laboratories and facilities were constructed, teaching hospitals were acquired, an army of full-time faculty was assembled, and a bureaucratic administrative structure appeared. By the 1920s medical schools had assumed a corporate form. The result was a system of medical education that has been constant for the past sixty years, even though there have been many changes in the content of medical knowledge and the patterns of medical practice.

These changes in medical education were interrelated with changes in the medical profession. Before the Civil War, there were only private practitioners in America, and all medical teaching was provided by practitioners as a sideline to their medical practices. In the mid-nineteenth century, this situation began to change. As the growth of medical knowledge accelerated, the production, assessment, and transmission of knowledge became a full-time activity. Accordingly, a new class of doctors—the full-time professor—took responsibility for those functions. By the late nineteenth century, academic medicine was a powerful force on the American medical scene, and the medical scholar had assumed an identity distinct from that of the ordinary practitioner. Even at the beginning, academic medicine was never monolithic —it always contained many specialties and factions within, and feuds among academic physicians were to shape much of the later development of American medical education. However, by the 1890s the distinction between scholarship and practice had come to represent the most important division of labor within the field of medicine. All prospective doctors had to decide whether they wanted careers as professors or practitioners of medicine; very few could do both.

Recognition of these internal distinctions within the medical profession is crucial, for the leaders of the educational reform movement were not private practitioners worried about their low income and status—as most accounts of American medical education have maintained—but full-time medical scientists and educators. Academic medicine did not emerge from the modern system of American medical education; it was the force that created the system. Prominent medical educators—William Welch, Franklin Mall, Henry Bowditch, Simon Flexner, Frank Billings, and hundreds of others—were not only outstanding teachers and investigators but skillful entrepreneurs and institution-builders. In the late nineteenth and early twentieth centuries they created the system of medical education that continues today. These individuals were driven by a single overriding purpose: to make academic medicine a secure career in America. Few medical scientists even cared about how much money the average doctor in practice made. Their goals were similar to those of enterprising institution-builders in other scientific fields, who were likewise struggling at that time to "professionalize" their disciplines.

As academic medicine rose to power, medical scientists began to dominate U.S. medical schools. Private practitioners did not surrender control of the schools without a struggle, however, and many bitter conflicts erupted between the two groups that continue to flare even today. In this struggle, private practitioners were the losers. Control of medical education was seized from them by the academic establishment. Prestige, authority, and influence within the profession became a matter of academic accomplishment, not income. Yet, hostility between the groups gradually abated as the achievements of medical research and the creation of a strong system of medical education allowed practitioners to enjoy higher incomes and increased social

6

status—benefits that had eluded them throughout the nineteenth century. By World War I an accommodation had been reached. There was seen to be enough room in the medical profession for both professors and practitioners. As a result of how medical education developed, the American medical profession evolved into its present sociological form.

The dominance of academic physicians in these events explains two of the most conspicuous features of the development of American medical education: the rise of medical research, and the movement of medical education to the universities. Academic physicians were medical scholars. They not only wanted to have full-time careers in medical teaching; they wanted to advance medical knowledge, just as medical professors in Germany were doing. Ultimately, research became as much a function of the modern medical school as good teaching was—some would say it even became the primary function. In America the natural milieu for advanced scholarship was the university. As medical scientists struggled to professionalize their field, their greatest allies were university presidents, who saw that the prestige of their respective universities would be enhanced if they controlled strong medical schools. The rise of academic medicine, the development of American medical research, and the movement of medical education into the universities proceeded hand-in-hand.

Contrary to popular perception, neither Abraham Flexner nor the American Medical Association (AMA) participated in the creation of modern American medical education. Both played important roles in its later development, but by that time the conceptual revolution in how medicine should be taught had already taken place and the university medical school had already appeared. Nevertheless, both Flexner and the AMA profoundly influenced the final form that the system took. Each insisted that only research-oriented university schools should be permitted to exist. In their minds, there was no room for "practical" schools—schools run by private practitioners where up-to-date teaching methods were employed but research was not promoted. Largely because of their influence, American medical education developed much differently than did legal education, where the university law school became the dominant educational institution but where lower tiers of independent schools, night schools, and correspondence schools continued to flourish. In legal education there had been a similar impulse to create a system consisting only of university law schools, but that effort failed.[2]

It should be made clear to the reader that American medical education did not develop along an inevitable path. At every point there were roads taken or not taken. The enthronement of research and the elimination of the "practical" schools represented but two of the innumerable choices that were made, choices that were made not only by academic physicians and university leaders, but by the public as well. Research would not have prospered had the public not been willing to help finance its medical schools; "practical" schools would not have been eliminated had the public not supported the state licensing laws that exterminated them. The public would do well to remember its own influence as it assesses the current condition of medical education and practice.

As the system of medical education evolved, so did many familiar problems of education and practice, and today these problems have become so pressing that they can no longer be ignored. It is to these issues that the last chapter turns. It would be naive to expect history to provide the solutions to the social and political problems that face medicine today. The question of the relative importance of teaching and research, or of how generously to support the medical schools, or of whether anyone who needs a highly expensive procedure, such as a heart transplant, should receive it, are issues of cultural values and social priorities, not of historical fact. However, insofar as a historical analysis can elucidate the nature of the choices that confront us, it can be invaluable in resolving our present dilemmas. Only by understanding the choices can decisions about the future be sensibly made.

1 American Medical Education in the Mid-Nineteenth Century

Medical Education at Mid-Century

The Civil War was a medical as well as a human tragedy. In this conflict, the bloodiest in the history of the United States, disease was an even more formidable enemy of the soldier than was battle. One authority has estimated that 110,000 Union soldiers died from wounds while 225,000 perished from disease. For the Confederate forces, there were about 50,000 deaths from fighting, 150,000 from illness.[1] Soldiers of both sides—ill fed, inadequately clothed, and subjected to the harshest exposures and most squalid sanitary conditions—were ravaged by dysentery, malaria, measles, typhoid fever, small-pox, tuberculosis, pneumonia, bronchitis, scarlet fever, and scurvy. "Minor" problems, such as colds, scabies, and a host of gastrointestinal illnesses, were endemic. Each year nearly three-quarters of the Union troops were plagued by severe diarrhea, which earned the nickname "Tennessee quickstep" and caused soldiers to joke grimly that in the army bowels were more important than brains.[2] For the wounded it was more difficult to find humor in their afflictions. Wartime hospitals provided a haven for such fulminating infections

9

as gangrene, septicemia, tetanus, and erysipelas. Septicemia (then called "pyemia")—poisoning of the blood by microorganisms—was the most virulent infection of all. After torturing its victims with fevers, chills, profuse sweating, jaundice, bleeding, and multiple abscesses, it would commence its almost inevitable progression to death.

Amid this grisly horror of disease and suffering, American physicians stood virtually helpless. Although physicians were beginning to recognize the importance of proper sanitation and hygiene in preventing disease—indeed, the United States Sanitary Commission implemented several innovative public health measures during the war—doctors were virtually powerless once disease or injury had struck. Only chloroform and ether to induce anesthesia and quinine to treat malaria were effective among the drugs in use. Other drugs were useless and many were extremely harmful. Amputation was the standard treatment for severely injured limbs, and no existing surgical techniques could reliably correct major hemorrhage, which led to death in three out of five cases. Among Union troops, penetrating chest wounds incurred a 62 percent mortality, and abdominal wounds carried an 87 percent death rate. In contrast, during World War II only about 3 percent of injured American soldiers failed to survive.[3] With Civil War surgeons still laboring under the ancient concept of "laudable pus," the idea that suppuration represented a natural part of the healing process, wound infection was rampant. The importance of clean hands and sterilized equipment was not understood; thus, physicians themselves propagated much of the infection by probing wounds with fingers wiped on pus-stained aprons and towels. Maggots were the most effective infection-fighters of the war. Infesting wounds of injured soldiers, they fortuitously served as wound debriders, eating only diseased tissue and leaving behind the healthy part of the wound so that it could heal more quickly.[4]

The Civil War made painfully clear the deficiencies of mid-nineteenth century American medical education. The training and skills of the average doctor were hopelessly inadequate, even based on existing standards of the day. Elementary techniques of physical examination, such as measuring temperature and percussing the chest, were performed only by a small portion of Civil War physicians. Thermometers, stethoscopes, ophthalmoscopes, hypodermic syringes, and other simple instruments were rarely employed by military practitioners, even though their use was already strongly advocated by the leading medical schools of Europe. Pain was frequently treated by the useless technique of applying opiate powders to wounds topically rather than by administering the drugs through hypodermic injections. Military physicians continued to purge their patients with dangerous doses of potent laxatives and emetics long after French medical scientists had convincingly demonstrated that these traditional "heroic" therapies were not only unbeneficial but often harmful. When a brave Union surgeon general, William Alexander Hammond, banned the use of two toxic drugs, calomel and tartar emetic, because of their severe side effects (profuse salivation and putrid gangrene of the gums, mouth, and face), he was court-martialed and condemned by the AMA.[5] Army doctors, untrained in operative techniques in medical school, entered the war totally unqualified to perform surgery. Most gained their first surgical experience treating gunshot wounds and other trauma during battle. Delusions of an erudite medical profession were shattered by the results of the written examinations of the military medical boards, which showed that the typical physician expressed "vague and confused" ideas in "barbarous English" that was "at defiance with all rules of grammar."[6] To the chagrin of the fledgling AMA, the military medical services were opened to a host of practitioners of the various medical cults, and patients seemed none the worse for that decision. No one could deny that American medical education had failed to meet the demands that the war had placed upon it.

The practices of Civil War physicians were a result of their education. The typical American physician of the 1860s had received his training at one of the country's several dozen "proprietary" medical schools.[7] These schools were originally created as a supplement to the apprenticeship system, which had been the primary mode of medical instruction during the colonial period. However, because they could more readily provide systematic teaching, by the middle of the nineteenth century proprietary schools had superseded apprenticeship as the dominant vehicle of medical education in America. In 1800 only three medical schools existed—at the University of Pennsylvania, at Harvard, and at King's College. Between 1810 and 1840, twenty-six new schools were established, and between 1840 and 1876, forty-seven more.[8] The Civil War only temporarily retarded this process, for in the decades that followed schools continued to sprout up at an even more rapid rate.

The standard course of instruction at the nation's medical schools in the mid-nineteenth century consisted of two four-month terms of lectures during the winter season, with the second term identical to the first. The curriculum generally consisted of seven courses: anatomy; physiology and pathology; materia medica, therapeutics, and pharmacy; chemistry and medical jurisprudence; theory and practice of medicine; principles and practice of surgery; and obstetrics and the diseases of women and children. Scientific subjects received scant attention, the emphasis being placed on topics considered of "practical" value. (So ignorant of recent developments in medical science was Harvard's professor of pathologic anatomy that in 1871 he confessed his inability to use the microscope.[9]) At no school was there any gradation of studies (the sequencing of courses so that subjects would be taken in logical order), nor were there written examinations. To receive the M.D. degree, students merely needed to pass a brief set of casual, perfunctory oral questions. A minimum age of twenty-one was generally required for graduation, but in practice this requirement was frequently overlooked. Licensing of physicians by the state did not exist; the medical school diploma itself served as a license to practice. Armed with his diploma, then, the graduate was free to practice medicine anywhere in the country.

Instruction at the schools was almost wholly didactic. The main teaching device was the lecture, given before an entire student body assembled in a large amphitheater. Students endured six to eight hours of lectures daily, supplemented by textbook readings and occasional recitations. Except for anatomy at the better schools, where the opportunity for dissection was sometimes provided, the scientific subjects were taught without the use of laboratories. Clinical subjects were similarly taught without providing students any practical experience. Students would graduate without having attended a delivery, without having witnessed an operation, and often without having examined a patient. All emphasis was on committing to rote the onerous detail of the lectures. The inevitable result of the system: "physical and mental dyspepsia,"[10] according to critics on the University of Pennsylvania faculty, for the material was too vast to be assimilated in such a short time even by the keenest and best-organized minds. In the mid-nineteenth-century medical school the didactic lecture was the product of an educational philosophy similar to that of "mental discipline" in the American college of that period, which led to the collegiate curriculum's emphasis on the classics, logic, mathematics, and philosophy.[11] Teaching in both medical schools and colleges was all too often literal-minded and uninspired.

Other than the ability to pay the fees, entrance requirements to medical school were essentially nonexistent. Indeed, literacy was not required for admission, and stories abound concerning the lack of intellectual achievements of mid-nineteenth-century medical students. One of the most famous incidents occurred at Harvard Medical School in 1871. Charles Eliot, the president of Harvard University, had proposed that written examinations be required for graduation from the medical school. Henry Jacob Bigelow, the professor of surgery, vigorously objected, stating that over half of Harvard's medical students could barely write.[12] What is clear is that merely a handful of students entering medical school had college preparation—at the University of Michigan in 1871, for instance, only fourteen of 350 medical students held college degrees[13]—and those who did have college degrees tended to be academically inferior, since the better students generally chose careers in teaching, law, or the clergy.[14] Most medical students had completed elementary school only, and many were illiterate. With great accuracy Eliot pointed out that "an American physician or surgeon may be, and often is, a coarse and uncultivated person, devoid of intellectual interests outside of his calling, and quite unable to either speak or write his mother tongue with accuracy."[15]

Whereas entrance requirements to medical schools were universally low, in some instances they approached criminal laxity. A standard but often ignored requirement was that the student provide written evidence testifying to his good moral character. In the rush to expand enrollment and increase revenues it was pointed out that "professors have been known to visit city prisons to become bondsmen for students who have violated the common decencies of life, and within a few days thereafter affix their names to the diplomas of these men."[16] If diplomas could not be earned, they could be bought. Ranking high among the notorious scandals of the Gilded Age were the widely publicized diploma mill scandals of 1880–81. Unscrupulous businessmen, for an appropriate price, would sell anyone a diploma from the "college" of his choice. The most infamous was John Buchanon, whose clients included two-year-old children. Buchanon later confessed to having sold 60,000 diplomas at prices as high as $200.[17] Clearly an M.D. diploma did not guarantee the competency of its possessor.

With such lax admission standards, it should be no surprise that student discipline posed a major problem. Medical schools in America, of course, have never experienced a period devoid of student pranks, particularly in the anatomy room. For example, during World War I, long after Western Reserve had become a modern scientific medical school, the faculty had to reprimand a student for throwing pieces of human cadavers from the dissecting room windows at various passersby, including a policeman.[18] Nevertheless, all evidence suggests that the typical level of classroom comportment in the 1860s and 1870s was such that teaching was continually in danger of being compromised. In 1876 at the Medical School of Maine, for example, a student who had frequently been intoxicated in class became so disruptive while in a state of extreme drunkenness that he had to be forcibly removed from the room by his fellow students.[19] A graduate of Western Reserve's class of 1870 recalled that it was difficult to pay attention during lectures because his classmates were accustomed to throwing objects at one another in the classroom.[20] Such comportment went beyond even the notoriously perverse humor of medical students and became destructive of effective teaching. Professors at mid-nineteenth century American colleges, who expended so much time and energy subduing the rebellious spirits of the undergraduates, could sympathize with the disciplinary problems confronting the medical faculties.[21]

Whereas admission to medical school frequently involved no more than the ability to pay the fees, these relaxed standards applied only to white males. Blacks and women faced much greater obstacles that mirrored the problems they encountered elsewhere in nineteenth-century American life. Before the Civil War, physicians in the North openly denied blacks entrance to the profession. In the South, blacks were sometimes permitted to practice folk and herbal remedies on fellow slaves but were not allowed to receive formal medical instruction.[22] The first black medical college, Howard University Medical College, was not organized until 1869. For the next century the black medical school served as the predominant vehicle of medical education for members of that race.

The obstacles confronting women were also severe, though less so than those faced by blacks. In 1849 Elizabeth Blackwell became the first woman to graduate from an American medical school, the Geneva Medical College in Geneva, New York. Thereafter women were usually admitted to medical schools, but it took an especially strong and determined person to combat the enormous barriers to entering a traditionally male bastion. In 1848 the Boston Female Medical School, the nation's first women's medical college, was founded, and in subsequent decades other women's medical schools were opened. Like the black medical schools of the latter nineteenth century, these schools were severely lacking in resources.[23] At every school where women studied, female medical students faced all the prejudices of male-dominated Victorian society. Alfred Stillé, the president of the AMA, asserted in 1871 that women are "unfitted by nature" to become physicians because of their "uncertainty of rational judgment, capriciousness of sentiment, fickleness of purpose, and indecision of action, which totally unfit [women] for professional pursuits."[24] Stillé's successor as president, D. W. Yandell, could not find a biological justification of why women might not be suited for medicine, but he expressed the hope that women would "never embarrass us by a personal application for seats in this Association."[25] At Harvard Medical School in the 1860s, one faculty member vigorously advocated reform of the educational curriculum, yet could not bring himself to support the admission of women to the school.[26]

The proprietary schools of mid-nineteenth century America were independent institutions, existing without the university or hospital affiliations that later came to characterize medical schools of the modern period. University affiliations, in the few cases in which they existed, were nominal. Medical schools operated on a separate calendar, assumed responsibility for their own

14

finances, and used the association largely to justify affixing the name of the affiliated university to the medical diploma. Hospital affiliations, when they existed, were equally casual. A few schools gave clinical lectures in hospital amphitheaters or occasionally took students on tours of the wards or clinics, but at no medical school was hospital training a central part of its teaching program.

The faculties of mid-century medical schools typically consisted of six to eight professors. A commercial spirit pervaded the schools, for the professors shared the spoils of what was left of student fees after expenses. Faculties desired to maximize enrollments, since with large classes profits increased far more rapidly than did operating costs. Medical schools were thus businesses rather than educational enterprises; they measured their success on the basis of their output (the number of graduates) and profitability. "The reputation of a medical school in this country depends in great measure on its size,"[27] Harvard's Henry Jacob Bigelow wrote in 1862. Accordingly, in what became a fierce competition to attract students, few medical schools dared to endanger their enrollments by introducing more rigorous standards. "No [medical] school has thought proper to risk large existing classes and large receipts in attempting a more thorough education,"[28] stated Bigelow. Indeed, the few that tried invariably found that prolonging the length of the term or raising entrance requirements met with a swift decline in enrollment.[29]

This concern for profits led to some of the most unseemly episodes in the history of American medical education. Even the lax requirement of four-month terms was frequently violated as many schools granted credit to paid-up students for a mere four or six weeks' attendance.[30] In the competition for students and prestige, medical professors engaged in bitter controversies and disputations. One historian of the early American medical schools wrote: "Characters were dissected and reputations ravished. While pioneers fought Indians and subdued the wilderness, medical professors dissipated intellectual energy and professional dignity in vituperative attacks on each other."[31] Such rampant commercialism led to the bad name that came to characterize proprietary schools in subsequent generations. They "lay like a blight on the medical profession,"[32] the famed Johns Hopkins professor of medicine, William Osler, said of them in 1905.

With all due allowance for rhetorical exaggerations of the deplorable condition of the country's medical schools by critics, there can be no doubt that medical education in the 1860s was terribly deficient. The United States government tacitly acknowledged this fact during the Civil War by imposing compulsory examinations for a physician to be admitted to the army or navy's medical service—an examination that could be passed by only a quarter of the country's medical graduates who took the examination, even those with degrees fresh in hand.[33] James B. Angell, the president of the University of Michigan, bemoaned: "On no educational subject is an awakening of interest more needed. The present state of education in the profession is as disgraceful to the practitioners as it is dangerous to the patients."[34] Yet, despite its deficiencies, nineteenth-century American medical education gave rise to such luminaries as William Pepper, S. Weir Mitchell, John Shaw Billings, Oliver Wendell Holmes, J. Marion Sims, and William Gerhard. As William Welch put it, "The results were better than the system."[35] This was the case not because of chance, but because a certain number of nineteenth-century physicians were able to bypass the system and receive quality training by pursuing one or more of the several alternative paths of medical education that existed to supplement the mediocre training provided at the proprietary schools.

One important alternative, particularly in the early 1800s, was the apprenticeship. The apprenticeship system survived well into the nineteenth century, even though medical schools had already begun to grow in number and importance. The educational quality of apprenticeships varied enormously. Under John Redman of Philadelphia—one of the great early preceptors—students could be assured of a valuable educational experience. Redman provided his apprentices meaningful work in an active medical practice, close supervision, and the opportunity to discuss their questions with a dedicated mentor who was knowledgeable in all aspects of medicine.[36] Examples abound, however, of physicians complaining about the poor education they received during their apprenticeship. Few preceptors made any effort to provide systematic instruction to their trainees, and even when they did, their efforts were usually hindered by the lack of books, equipment, and clinical resources, as well as by their unfamiliarity with recent developments in medical knowledge. Many apprentices spent more time performing menial household chores for their preceptors than learning medicine. "Private pupilage, as it is now generally conducted, is worse than useless," one group of critics complained in 1867. "It is, in fact, simply a waste of time and money, without one solitary compensating advantage."[37] Until after the Civil War, evidence that a student had spent time, usually three years, with a preceptor remained a standard condition to receiving the M.D. degree. By mid-century, however, this requirement had largely become a formality, since certificates of apprenticeship were routinely issued to any student who merely registered with a physician, even if he had received no instruction or practical experience. "The relations of students and preceptors have become merely nominal,"[38] wrote the prominent medical educator Nathan Smith Davis in 1877. Of all the alternative educational pathways, the apprenticeship was the least reliable.

A second alternative was provided by nondegree-granting medical schools —the extramural private medical schools that operated during summer vacations when the degree-granting institutions were not in session. Created to supplement the didactic instruction of the regular sessions, their very existence stood as a testimony to the inadequacy of conventional medical education. The extramural schools provided the hands-on clinical experience that could not be obtained in medical schools during the winter lectures. The emphasis was on physical diagnosis: techniques of percussion, auscultation, and palpation, as well as the use of new diagnostic instruments such as the opthalmoscope and otoscope. Some schools provided opportunities for dissection as well as experience in bandaging wounds and performing minor surgical procedures. Such training, though not at all comparable to the extensive clinical experience afforded by the clerkship in a later era of clinical training, was far superior to the purely didactic teaching of the winter sessions. The extramural schools numbered far fewer than the degree-granting schools, and they attracted only modest numbers of students—those with both the ambition to further their education and the financial means not to have to work during the summer. Nevertheless, they provided the ambitious and fortunate student much better training than could be obtained from the conventional course of education alone.[39]

Serving in a hospital as a "house pupil," either before or after receiving the M.D. degree, was another method of supplementing one's medical education. A handful of students, usually selected by competitive examination, would reside in a hospital and assume responsibility for managing cases, much as medical students and house officers do today. The experience at the Cincinnati Hospital was typical in this regard:

> In aid of the staff, six under-graduates are selected, after a competitive examination, whose designations are "Resident Physicians." Entering upon duty, they are distributed to different wards, where they remain two months; they then exchange places, so that each one, during the year, has an opportunity of witnessing the practice of the entire Hospital. They accompany the staff in their daily visits to the sick, receive their orders, keep a record of the cases and their treatment, report all violations of medical discipline, and have a general supervision over their respective wards.[40]

The house pupil experience emerged as a feature of American medical education in the 1820s and 1830s and slowly grew more popular through mid-century. Cincinnati Hospital, for instance, appointed its first house pupil in 1830, and for the next dozen years it selected only one house pupil per year.[41] In the 1850s and 1860s the duties of house pupils became much more demanding, largely as a result of the growing amount of surgery performed in hospitals following the introduction of anesthesia. By the 1880s and 1890s, the work of house pupils had become tantamount to that of present-day interns, overworked and overstressed. In 1892, members of the surgical staff at the Massachusetts General Hospital pleaded with the trustees to increase the number of house officers. The responsibilities of the house staff had become so great that "few men finish the hospital curriculum without some illness, plainly due to the weight they have been carrying."[42]

There has been some confusion about the house pupil system because it went by different names at different places. In mid-century the terms "house pupil," "intern," and "resident" were often used interchangeably to describe the same experience. Adding to the confusion, house pupils before the Civil War were usually medical students, whereas after the war, hospitals generally limited their positions to medical school graduates. In the early 1880s, Cincinnati Hospital used the term "resident" for positions filled by medical students, whereas the Massachusetts General Hospital still retained the older term "house pupil," even though all of its positions by then were being filled by medical graduates. Terminology aside, the important point is that a fortunate few—some during medical school; others, after graduation—had the opportunity to receive intensive clinical training at the bedside. Many former house pupils would later become leaders of the movement to upgrade clinical teaching in America.

The fourth major alternative was European study, usually upon completion of the regular course of medical lectures. Although Americans journeyed to many countries, in the early and mid-nineteenth century the unchallenged mecca of foreign medical study was France. Between 1820 and 1861 nearly seven hundred Americans studied medicine in Paris, at least sixty-seven of whom became professors in medical schools in the United States.[43] This left a distinct French mark on American medical education and practice. In Paris, American physicians studied pathology, physical diagnosis, and the "numerical" (statistical) method of clinical research. Many of them obtained personalized instruction in private courses taught by professors or hospital interns seeking to enhance their incomes. Parisian study provided extremely valuable postgraduate training. Those who undertook it comprised a mid-century elite among American doctors.[44]

Thus, the results of American medical education were better than the system because many could supplement the standard medical school training through any or all of the four alternative paths. The same fluidity and multiplicity of paths that characterized medical education in America at mid-century characterized all formal education as well. Yet it must be kept in mind that these additional educational avenues were taken by only a few. The best training of the day was not obtained by the average physician. For the great majority, without the financial means to study abroad or in extramural schools, and without the good fortune to win a position as house pupil, the education provided by the proprietary schools had to suffice.

It is easy to be overly harsh in evaluating the mid-century medical schools. We must recognize that during the first two-thirds of the nineteenth century, the proprietary schools had served the public satisfactorily. With an expanding national domain and a growing population, there was a real shortage of medical personnel. Under frontier conditions a little training was better than none. Medical knowledge was still relatively sparse, and the extension of the curriculum at that time would have resulted primarily in the teaching of speculative theories that later would have had to be unlearned. Some of the major scientific advances of that era, most of them emanating from France, had shown the lack of efficacy of a majority of the conventional medical treatments. Accordingly, the American public was very skeptical of doctors, and many persons chose to consult sectarian practitioners rather than physicians for their medical needs.

Moreover, although much attention has traditionally been focused on the greed of the early medical professors, a more balanced view indicates that rampant commercialism, though not uncommon, was the exception rather than the rule. The annals of early American medical history are replete with examples of "proprietary schools" that made genuine efforts to serve the educational needs of their day.[45] Popular images to the contrary, no medical professor (con men excluded) became rich from teaching, with $250 being considered a large income for the year. Even at the University of Pennsylvania, where the professor of anatomy earned an average of $2,600 between 1855 and 1859, by 1859 the Pennsylvania medical faculty had expended in the aggregate more than $30,000 of their own funds to illustrate their lectures and classes.[46] Many dedicated professors at other schools made little or no money at all, choosing instead to relinquish their profits and support the work of the school.[47]

Although the proprietary school may have served its purpose adequately earlier in the century, by the 1860s it was clearly no longer sufficient to meet the needs of modern medical education. The revolution in medical science was already underway in Europe; a striking contrast had emerged between the education and practice of the average American physician and the important work in progress in medical research abroad. As one sign of the problem, Americans flocked to Europe for medical study, but Europeans did not flock to America. "Who ever heard of a gentleman leaving the schools of Paris or London for a more thorough education in America?"[48] one observer asked. To the knowledgeable few—those Americans who had studied in Europe or had kept abreast of the developments abroad—the reform of American medical education had become an imperative.

Early Efforts at Reform

The deficiencies of American medical education did not go unnoticed during the mid-nineteenth century. From the 1820s onward, concern over the problem led to many calls to reform the medical curriculum. Examples included the Northampton, Massachusetts, convention of New England medical colleges and societies in 1827, Daniel Drake's famous essays on medical education in 1832, and the AMA's pronouncements on medical education that started in 1847.[49] Here and there in the 1840s, 1850s, and 1860s, an occasional medical school would heed the cry, lengthening its course to six months in an effort to provide more thorough instruction.

Discussions concerning the reform of medical education during this period were monotonously similar. The standard plea called for lengthening the period of instruction from four months to six, establishing the requirement that medical students should have adequate preliminary education, and making certain that all students had completed an apprenticeship with a qualified preceptor. These recommendations were made by virtually all who spoke on the subject, including the most ardent advocate of educational reform of all, the AMA. As such, cries for reform contemplated no fundamental innovations in the system of instruction but merely a propping up of the system already in place. "It is reform, not revolution, that is contemplated,"[50] explained one president of the AMA. Reformers concerned themselves much more with the trappings of medical education than with the substantive issues of what should be taught, or how.

There were exceptions, however. Two schools at mid-century distinguished themselves from the others by instituting genuinely innovative changes in their respective curricula. In 1859 the Medical Department of Lind University in Chicago, led by Nathan S. Davis, became the first school in the United States to establish a graded curriculum, with subjects being taught sequentially and in logical order over two five-month terms.[51] This school, a forerunner of Northwestern University Medical School, thereby anticipated similar changes at Harvard, Pennsylvania, and the University of Michigan in the 1870s.

Around 1857 the New Orleans School of Medicine introduced even more radical changes into its clinical teaching. Inspired by the plan of clinical instruction employed in Paris, Vienna, and Dublin, Erasmus Darwin Fenner, the professor of medicine and dean of the school, introduced a system in which students were assigned individual patients to follow for their entire hospital course, from admission to discharge. Students would take detailed histories, perform complete physical examinations, and present their findings to the professor, who would discuss the case and make recommendations for management. Students would follow the daily progress of their patients, making progress reports and presenting the previous day's events to the professor each morning on rounds. If the patient died, an autopsy was performed before the class after the professor and student had first predicted the pathological findings that would be found. The New Orleans school thus pioneered the clinical clerkship in America, the modern method of clinical instruction that later came to be adopted by all American medical schools. The New Orleans School of Medicine quickly became the best medical school in the country before falling victim to the Civil War.[52] It remained for Johns Hopkins in the 1890s to finally establish the clerkship as a permanent part of the medical scene.

The Medical Department of Lind University and the New Orleans School of Medicine were distinctly unusual. During the middle third of the nineteenth century few schools made any attempt to improve their programs, and those that did were content to expand the lecture terms to six months without addressing the more fundamental educational issues of subject matter and teaching methods. Complaints about the low standards of medical education in America greatly outnumbered the concrete efforts to remedy the situation. As the eminent Philadelphia surgeon W. W. Keen recalled, medical education during this period was characterized by "bushels of talk and thimblefuls of action."[53]

That there was resistance to reform should be no surprise. Talk of expanding the lecture terms to six months carried little weight when it was unclear that a longer period of instruction could be filled up with clinically useful information. At this time higher entrance requirements and more course work might have resulted in a more erudite profession, but the additional knowledge imparted would have had little beneficial effect on the outcome of patient care. At mid-century the lack of substantive knowledge in clinical medicine was tacitly recognized by the abandonment of licensing laws in the various states and by the popularity of the Thomsonian movement, a sectarian movement based on the concept that the principles of medicine were simple enough to be comprehended by everyone, so that any person could be his or her own physician.[54] As a result, students flocked to schools where requirements were lax and degrees could easily be obtained. Professors, dependent on large enrollments for both reputation and income, were reluctant to introduce more rigid requirements for fear of losing students. In 1862, Henry Jacob Bigelow of Harvard thus objected to introducing any major changes into his school's methods of teaching and examination for fear that the students, particularly the less adept ones, would become alarmed.[55]

Besides the dependence of medical professors on student fees, there was a further obstacle to reform at mid-century. With few exceptions, American physicians did not yet appreciate the importance of experimental science to medical questions. This attitude could be found even among the best-educated physicians of the period. Hence, almost all discussions of educational "reform" dealt with the trappings of the educational system rather than with more substantive educational issues. A modern philosophy of medical education had not yet emerged.

To understand this point it is necessary to understand the impact of French medical science during the first half of the nineteenth century.[56] The role of the Paris clinical school in ushering in the era of modern medicine cannot be underestimated. Making the hospital the center of medical education and research, Parisian physicians pioneered the development of pathologic anatomy, physical diagnosis, and the study of the natural history of disease and of therapeutics by the use of the "numerical" (statistical) method. The French method of medical inquiry was exclusively empirical: observing and analyzing the facts carefully, and letting the facts speak for themselves without creating explanatory theories. Such an antitheoretical bias stood as a welcome and needed tonic to the outlandish theories and speculative abuses that had dominated medical thought through the early nineteenth century.

Whereas French medical science was characterized by keen observation, it did not make use of experimentation—the manipulation of nature—which later came to be associated with German medical research. Understanding the difference between the two approaches is crucial. As the great physiologist Walter Cannon has explained, there are two ways to obtain knowledge of nature's secrets:

> We may merely watch natural events as they occur or we may arrange conditions so that the events will appear, disappear, or be modified as we decide. For example, the growth of wheat may be studied carefully in different native surroundings or, on the other hand, the wheat may be grown where the effects

on it of heat and cold, sunlight and darkness, wind, gravity, drought, and the chemicals of the soil can be examined individually as these various agencies affect its growth and productiveness. The former method is purely observational, the latter is experimental. The experimental method, in which the conditions to be observed are held under control, is in the main the distinguishing feature of modern science.[57]

The French clinical workers were observers, not experimenters. They felt that medical knowledge resulted from chance clinical observation, not from the conscious manipulation of nature through experimental design. Secrets were stumbled upon by luck rather than wrested from nature by experimentation. The great clinician R. T. H. Laennec illustrated the skeptical attitude of the French toward experimental research when he called his discovery of the stethoscope an accident. "In general," he stated, "the really useful things are thus given to us, and not conquered by efforts."[58] To French clinicians, the causes of disease were unknowable, and the fundamental sciences were not relevant to medical issues. In this context it can be understood how the great names of French medical science—Louis Pasteur, Claude Bernard, Xavier Bichat, François Magendie—never held professorships in a medical school.[59]

American medicine through the Civil War predominantly reflected the French influence. American physicians, bearing the indelible impact of their French mentors, commonly distrusted the laboratory sciences. Medical discovery, they felt, resulted from careful clinical observation, not from experimental investigation. Thus, in 1832, some of the ablest Americans who had studied in France founded the Society for Medical Observation (in contrast to the German-influenced physicians in 1908 who created the American Society for Clinical Investigation). Skepticism toward the value of experimental research in medicine persisted through the end of the century and helped explain why some of the most eminent members of the profession between 1860 and 1880 did not accept the germ theory of disease and in the last three decades of the century opposed animal vivisection.[60] Throughout most of the century American medical research—what little there was of it—concerned itself mainly with the description and classification of disease, not with the elucidation of fundamental disease mechanisms.

Such attitudes toward medical research could be found among almost all leading medical professors at mid-century and had great bearing on the type of medical training they offered. At Harvard, for instance, the faculty recognized the gross deficiencies in medical knowledge of the period, but they saw no way of rectifying those deficiencies, except by chance observations that might be made by astute clinical observers. "We must not expect too much from 'science' as distinguished from common experience. . . . Accident is the great chemist and toxicologist,"[61] warned Oliver Wendell Holmes of the

Harvard faculty in 1867, himself one of the few great nineteenth-century American contributors to the medical literature. Accordingly, the Harvard faculty, like the rest of the country's medical faculties, regarded medical schools as trade schools whose function it was to provide students with the facts they needed for clinical practice, without cluttering their minds with irrelevant information. For that reason, the Harvard faculty in 1849 decided not to prolong its lecture terms to six months. They felt that such a change would be "wearisome, or irksome, or exhausting"[62] for the students without providing them material of value. According to Holmes, "The business of a school like this is to make useful working physicians, and to succeed in this it is almost as important not to overcrowd the mind of the pupil with merely curious knowledge as it is to store it with useful information."[63] At a time when laboratory investigation was only beginning to clarify and expand the theoretical framework and practical usefulness of medicine, such a viewpoint did not seem unjustified. Many in responsible positions were convinced that a thorough scientific education was simply not needed in medicine.

Thus, at mid-century there was a major intellectual constraint on reforming American medical education. At a time when the relation of experimental science to medical knowledge and practice was not entirely clear, no great imperative existed to reform the medical curriculum. Most doctors—including the best members of the profession—distrusted the laboratory. Their concern arose only in part from the fear of the potential dehumanizing aspects of science, and not at all because of any fear of increasing medical costs or of creating an imbalance between specialists and generalists—fears that were later to accompany the intrusion of science into clinical medicine. Rather, at this time experimental science was subject to the worst criticism of all—the charge that it was not relevant to medicine. What was needed to change medical education was not simply more knowledge, but a new attitude among the leaders of American medicine who controlled the medical schools and hospitals toward how medical knowledge could best be acquired.

A Profession in Disarray

One further aspect of American medical education at the time of the Civil War merits emphasis. At no medical school in the 1860s did original research constitute a part of a faculty member's responsibilities. Professors lectured and tended to various administrative duties of the school. On their own time they engaged in medical practice, performed consultations, and occasionally wrote textbooks. However, few faculty members felt they had the responsibility to promote the gathering of new knowledge. The rare medical professor who tried to conduct research, such as Charles E. Brown-Séquard at Harvard in the mid-1860s, did so on his own time and at his own expense.[64] No medical school supported or encouraged such work.

The difficulties encountered in pursuing medical investigation as a full-time activity were nowhere more strikingly illustrated than in the case of S. Weir Mitchell, the founder of the American Physiological Society and the leading experimental physiologist of his generation. During the Civil War, Mitchell discovered that his interests lay with research rather than practice. He poignantly wrote his sister that he dreaded any distraction "removing me from the time or power to search for new truths that lie about me so thick."[65] Unfortunately, his colleagues did not share his enthusiasm for research. Twice at Jefferson Medical College (in 1863 and 1868) and once at the University of Pennsylvania (in 1868) Mitchell was denied the chair of physiology, despite having made vigorous efforts to secure the positions. Ironically, Mitchell had already established his reputation as a physiologist, having already begun his pioneering experiments on snake venom that later became a foundation stone of modern immunology. The eminent naturalist, Louis Agassiz of Harvard, commiserated with Mitchell. "You should not be disappointed," he told Mitchell, "if your very eminence in the field of your investigations should be an impediment to your worldly success."[66] Simply stated, Mitchell's prowess in physiological research stood in the way of his receiving a professorship of physiology at the two medical schools.

Mitchell was not alone in his inability to secure a position in full-time research and teaching. Particularly after the Civil War, as Americans started returning from postgraduate study in Germany, a whole generation of young, highly trained physicians encountered almost insurmountable obstacles to achieving their dreams of professional careers in medical research. Even in the 1870s and 1880s laboratory positions were very scarce, and the few that did exist intimidated all but the hardiest spirits by their inadequate salaries, substandard facilities, decrepit working conditions, and, perhaps most importantly, lack of collegial support and encouragement. In 1878, William Welch, the great Johns Hopkins pathologist and a beneficiary of European study, told his sister: "I was often asked in Germany how it is that no scientific work in medicine is done in this country, how it is that many good men who do well in Germany and show evident talent there are never heard of and never do any good work when they come back here. The answer is that there is no opportunity for, no appreciation of, no demand for that kind of work here."[67]

The above discussion is not to suggest that American doctors in the first two-thirds of the nineteenth century made no contributions to medical research. William Beaumont's classic studies on the physiology of digestion; William Gerhard's brilliant distinction between typhoid and typhus; Oliver Wendell Holmes's discovery of the mode of transmission of puerperal fever; Jacob Bigelow's famous essay on self-limited disease; and the discovery of anesthesia by William Morton (and other claimants)—all represented scientific achievements of the first magnitude that gained wide recognition in Europe as well as in the United States.

However, these investigations were as exceptional as they were brilliant. Throughout the century American medical research lagged profoundly behind that of Europe. Little investigative work was undertaken, and that which was done tended to be derivative and confirmatory. As in most other areas of culture, American medicine was dependent on the products of European creativity. "The great danger seems to be," one alarmed group of observers in 1848 said of medical research in the country, "that in place of the genuine culture of our own fields, the creative energy of the country shall manifest itself in generating a race of *curculios* to revel in voracious indolence upon the products of a foreign soil!"[68] In this regard medical research was no different from research in other scientific fields. Nineteenth-century Americans distinguished themselves for their inventions and technologic innovations, but, with rare exceptions, not for the originality and importance of their work in pure science.[69]

Medical research in America during most of the nineteenth century was impeded by many obstacles. The country was still developing culturally and economically—fundamental prerequisites to supporting any consistently productive scientific enterprise. The same spirit of practicality—some would say anti-intellectualism—that pervaded other aspects of life in a country still expanding its borders and conquering its terrain penetrated the medical profession as well. As a result, the country did not possess the institutions and organizations necessary to support medical research adequately. Even at the medical schools, professors earned the bulk of their income from consultations and private practice. Nowhere in the United States could anyone make a living by pursuing medical research and teaching as a full-time career. Medical investigation was not a viable profession but merely a part-time avocation pursued by a devoted few.

America's indifference to research extended far beyond medicine. Other mid-nineteenth century American scientists who wished to turn scientific research into a professional enterprise encountered the same obstacles. In the 1850s the "Lazzaroni"—an elite group of scientists belonging to the American Association for the Advancement of Science—struggled incessantly against public apathy to legitimize science as a respectable career and promote the development of scientific institutions for the support of research. They achieved some success, but they fell far short of their hopes and expectations.[70] Few aspiring investigators in any field found full-time opportunities to work.

Even within the medical profession aspiring medical scientists were not the only group of frustrated physicians. Many practitioners, dismayed at the low status to which the medical profession in America had sunk, were equally unhappy. Evaluation of the status of a profession or occupation is always fraught with hazard, but all indications suggest that the medical profession at mid-century stood very low in terms of prestige, income, and authority.[71] Certainly, doctors themselves perceived low status to be a major problem afflicting the profession, a concern that led a group of physicians in 1847 to organize the AMA. At the group's first annual meeting its president declared: "The profession to which we belong, once venerated on account of its antiquity,—its various and profound science—its elegant literature—its polite accomplishments—its virtues,—has become corrupt, and degenerate, to the forfeiture of its social position, and with it, of the homage it formerly received spontaneously and universally."[72] A quarter of a century later the situation had not noticeably changed. In 1871 another Association president was still complaining about "the present depressed measure of professional standing in our country."[73]

To the AMA, which worried more about the perceived decline in status of the profession than any other group, the culprit was clear: defective medical education. An AMA committee declared, "It was not difficult to trace this abasement of the profession to its true cause. It had ceased to be a highly educated class."[74] From the very beginning the reform of medical education became the one absorbing topic of the AMA, and its hopes for reforming medical education were always intimately linked to its goal of restoring the social status of the profession. Through the establishment of entrance requirements, longer terms of instruction, and more rigorous requirements for graduation, the AMA hoped that the empirics and the sectarians could be squelched and that the prestige of the profession could be re-established. It was the cause of great unhappiness to the AMA that it could not effectuate changes at any of the medical schools. Educational reform, lamented one president of the organization in 1873, was something "our Association has been laboring for years, but in vain, to induce."[75]

At mid-century, therefore, a sense of frustration pervaded the medical profession. For those who wished careers in research and teaching, there were no opportunities. For the rest of the profession, the social and economic rewards of practicing medicine were relatively modest. Socially elite physicians did exist—the Warrens of Boston[76] were a particularly notable example—but this small minority enjoyed their status because of who, not what, they were. As members of upper crust, blue-blooded families, they were socially prominent *despite* being doctors, and their family backgrounds assured them of social prominence no matter what career they might have undertaken.

What united the frustrations of these various segments of the profession was the focus on medical education. The medical school of the 1860s served the interests of neither the medical scientist nor the general practitioner. And with the revolution in medical science building up steam abroad, it was no longer clear that having a ready-made supply of doctors served the interests of the public if such doctors were without adequate training. Exactly how and in what direction the medical school was to change was not yet clear, nor was it yet apparent who was to lead the changes or when they were to achieve their first successes. Nevertheless, at the close of the Civil War, the American medical school, like its academic sibling, the nascent American university, was ready to undergo far-reaching changes. And, like the university, it would ultimately become the focus of a multiplicity of groups with diverse and often conflicting interests, values, and goals.

2 Origins of Reform

WHILE MEDICAL EDUCATION in the United States was floundering in the mid-1800s, events that would ultimately lead to the revolution in medical training in America were already underway. Between 1850 and 1890, these events provided the infrastructure for the remarkable transformation of American medical education that became manifest in the early twentieth century. Improvements in medical education began at a few schools in the 1870s and 1880s, spread throughout the country in the 1890s and 1900s, and occurred in almost seismic fashion after 1910. But, like most revolutionary change in history, the emergence of modern medical education in America was rooted in important historical forces that slowly, quietly, and unpretentiously laid the foundation for the rapid and dramatic developments that followed.[1]

German Medical Science and the Emergence of an Academic Elite

The modern world has never been without a medical mecca. During the first half of the nineteenth century this mecca was France. For two generations, a cadre of brilliant French clinicians inspired physicians everywhere with their accomplishments: the development of modern pathology and physical diagnosis; the application of numerical (statistical) techniques to clinical research; and the establishment of the hospital as the center of medical teaching and research. Under the critical gaze of the astute French clinical observers, who believed only what their senses told them, medicine was shorn of the speculative, monistic theories that had encumbered it for centuries, and disease was found not to be the result of disordered humors but a localized phenomenon that could be anatomically detected in specific organs.[2] French medicine influenced physicians around the world, and throughout the first half of the century Americans who could afford the pilgrimage to Europe made Paris their first choice for postgraduate medical study. Pierre Louis, one of the pre-eminent clinical teachers of all time, probably had the greatest influence on American physicians. Between 1830 and 1840, Louis inspired a host of American students, who brought his teachings and ideals back home.[3] For the first three-quarters of the century the French influence remained the dominant one on American medicine.

For several decades French medicine stood pre-eminent, but by the 1840s that situation was rapidly changing. French medicine, for all its brilliance and originality, was beginning to appear limited in how far it could progress because of its neglect of the basic biological sciences and its disdain for experimental research. Ironically, astute observation—the great strength of the French clinical school—became the cause of its ultimate eclipse, insofar as it led French clinicians to distrust experimental laboratory investigation. French medical science did not investigate the causes of disease, and by the time of the European revolutions of 1848 it had lost its former ascendancy. As Erwin Ackerknecht has observed, *"French medicine had maneuvered itself into a dead end,* as all empiricisms had done so far in medical history."[4]

As the influence of French medicine was declining, German medical science became more prominent. Prior to 1840, German medical science had languished, encumbered by the same drag of *Naturphilosophie* (naturephilosophy) that had vitiated all work in German biology of the period. This inherently obscure, speculative, philosophical doctrine—an offshoot of the writings of Friedrich W. J. Schelling—had stressed the unity of nature and the fundamental identity of biological and physical phenomena. So influenced, German medical writers looked to the world at large for clues to human nature, drawing analogies, for instance, between the shape of the earth and that of human red blood corpuscles. Such an approach was scarcely conducive to the development of objective medical science.[5]

After 1840, however, German medicine, like the rest of German biology, threw off the shackles of *Naturphilosophie* and entered the modern era. The next three decades witnessed major medical discoveries by German workers: the cell theory of Schleiden and Schwann; the restructuring of modern physiology through the work of Müller, Ludwig, Helmholtz, Du Bois-Reymond, Brücke, and others; the cellular pathology theory of Virchow; and the emergence of experimental pathology through the pioneering studies of Cohnheim, Weigert, Recklinghausen, and Virchow. In the 1870s, the prominence of German medical science was further established by Koch's bacteriologic investigations, which culminated in the isolation of the bacillus of tuberculosis in 1882.[6]

The strength of the German approach lay in the use of experimental methods. Unlike the French, German workers relied on the laboratory as the way to unravel medicine's mysteries, and they recognized that the fundamental medical sciences (biochemistry, physiology, experimental pathology, pharmacology, bacteriology) were indispensable tools for understanding disease and therapeutics. With laboratory research, they investigated the ultimate causes of disease, hoping to explain disease processes in chemical and physical terms. As they pursued this approach, they brought medicine into the mainstream of nineteenth-century biology, which itself was changing from a primarily descriptive to a primarily experimental science—that is, one in which the study of function was superseding in importance the study of form and morphology.[7]

Even though the amount of new medical knowledge uncovered by the laboratory approach was still small and no major therapeutic innovations had yet been developed using experimental techniques, the successes of German medical science in the mid-nineteenth century created great excitement. For the first time the causes of disease were being explained. This allowed an epistemological shift of revolutionary proportions. It became clear to knowledgeable physicians that experimental methods could be applied to the study of disease and therapeutics as well as to the study of the healthy state. Scientific information no longer constituted curious knowledge, irrelevant and diverting to the ordinary practitioner, but now began to represent the core of what a modern doctor needed to know.

Experimental medicine, of course, was never in the sole possession of Germany. Modern physiology, for example, had been born in France, and the work of François Magendie and Claude Bernard was of the first magnitude, rivaling that of the German physiologists. And in bacteriology, no name is more famous than that of France's Louis Pasteur.[8] Nevertheless, medical research in Germany enjoyed a distinct advantage: its home was the German university, whose freedom, flexible organization, well-provided laboratories, and free-flowing spirit of inquiry allowed Germany to become the undisputed center of scientific medicine. Just as Germany had achieved international supremacy in other areas of higher education—the social sciences, philosophy, literary criticism, linguistics, and the natural sciences—so, too, did it replace France as the new mecca of the medical world.[9]

After 1850 the pattern of American medical migration to Europe began to change. Because commercialism and low standards continued in American medical schools, the impetus to do postgraduate study abroad remained the same. However, Germany began replacing France as the magnet attracting American students. The experience of Henry Pickering Bowditch, the first full-time professor of physiology in America, was typical. In 1868, Bowditch journeyed to France to study, just as his uncle Henry Ingersoll Bowditch had done in 1832. However, upon arriving, young Bowditch found the facilities and opportunities for research to be distressingly inadequate, even in the laboratory of the great Claude Bernard. In 1869 he expressed his frustrations in a letter to his former teacher, Jeffries Wyman. "Bernard's laboratory, where I work nearly every day, is dark, poorly provided with apparatus, and with no proper arrangements for pupils. . . . The Frenchmen acknowledge the great advantage that the Germans have over them in this respect."[10] Having learned in the mean time of the elaborate scientific opportunities in Germany, Bowditch departed Paris for Leipzig, where he spent two highly productive years in the laboratory of Carl Ludwig.[11]

During the 1850s and 1860s the number of American physicians who studied in Germany was relatively small, but after the Civil War the floodgates opened. Thomas Bonner, in his excellent study of American physicians in Germany, has estimated that between 1870 and 1914, 15,000 American doctors undertook some form of serious study in Germany or at German-speaking universities in Switzerland and Austria.[12] American physicians were joined by doctors from England, Italy, Greece, Turkey, Russia, Japan, and Latin America—testimony to the unchallenged superiority of nineteenth-century German medical science.[13] This intellectual migration peaked in the 1870s and 1880s; it was the generation of physicians educated after the Civil War that most concertedly responded to the lure of Germany for advanced clinical and scientific study. During the 1890s this migration lessened but remained strong. After 1900, when American medical schools began to provide opportunities once available only abroad, the flow markedly decreased. This era of migration lasted until 1914, when the outbreak of World War I destroyed German-American relations and impoverished and demoralized the German universities.[14]

Americans who studied in Germany shared certain common features. They tended to be young, male, from the East coast, and from the upper strata of society. The author of one widely used guide to German study for American students estimated in 1883 that the minimum cost of a year of study in

Germany for a person willing to live under Spartan conditions was between $700 and $800—a sum large enough to insure that most travellers possessed at least some means.[15] A few persons, usually of German birth or descent, undertook their undergraduate medical studies and obtained their medical degrees in Germany. This practice was widely frowned upon in the United States, however, and the vast majority of Americans who went to Germany did so with an American medical degree already in hand, seeking instead to obtain postgraduate instruction. Those who studied in Germany often became the leading physicians of their generation, as measured by the frequency with which they were listed in standard biographical guides of that period.[16]

The great majority of Americans who went abroad to study medicine were attracted by Germany's unusual strength in the clinical specialties. Students sought to perfect their clinical skills and become familiar with one or more of the new medical specialities—dermatology, ophthalmology, laryngology, obstetrics, gynecology, and surgery—that were taught so well in the German-speaking lands. Abundant clinical facilities were present, which allowed students to obtain extensive practical experience not available in America. The most popular places of study were Berlin and Vienna, where courses were short (frequently only several weeks in duration) and instruction was often provided in English. In Vienna, the city most frequented by American students, at least 10,000 Americans studied medicine between 1870 and 1914.[17] On their return to the United States, they usually pursued successful careers as consultants or specialists. Few of them aspired to academic or scientific careers, but they emerged from their German experience with an understanding of the true university spirit, an appreciation of the importance of research, and a recognition of how the scientific branches of medicine might contribute to clinical practice.

Some Americans who went to Germany, however, were lured by the country's exceptional opportunities to study the fundamental medical sciences. This group was small in number but disproportionately large in importance because its ranks included such notables as William Welch, Franklin Mall, Graham Lusk, Henry Bowditch, Charles Minot, Russell Chittenden, T. Mitchell Prudden, John Jacob Abel, Victor Vaughan, Warren Lombard, George Dock, and Frederick Novy. This group is especially important because of their immeasurable influence on the subsequent development of American medicine. These men came to form the faculties at Johns Hopkins, Harvard, Michigan, Cornell, and other medical schools that were the first to introduce modern teaching methods in the United States, and they were also responsible for establishing America's reputation in medical research.

Unlike the aspiring medical specialists, who flocked to the shorter, more practical courses in Berlin and Vienna, those interested in scientific study migrated to Germany's smaller universities—particularly those in Leipzig, Strassburg, and Breslau—where they would spend two or three years in quiet, patient, intensive study and research. Whether they studied anatomy, physiology, pathology, biochemistry, pharmacology, or bacteriology, they all pursued basic investigations and gained laboratory experience under the guidance of Germany's leading medical scientists. The most inspiring teacher was Carl Ludwig, the inventor of the kymograph and possibly the greatest teacher of physiology of all time. Ludwig became the mentor to an unusually large number of first-generation American medical scientists, and his influence on American students abroad rivaled that of Pierre Louis in Paris forty years earlier.[18]

Americans studying the scientific subjects in Germany luxuriated in the exciting atmosphere of the German laboratories, where student and master worked side by side, where every facility needed for advanced study or research was provided, where discipline and dedication to the ideals of scientific inquiry invariably prevailed, and where there was a sense of anticipation from being on the cutting edge of medical discovery. "We have nothing in America like these laboratory courses,"[19] an exuberant William Welch wrote to his sister from Germany in 1876. Those, Welch later recalled, "were memorable and inspiring days in which to have lived."[20] Some physicians, like Welch, returned for a second period of study. Welch's colleague at Johns Hopkins, the pharmacologist John Jacob Abel, stayed in Germany nearly seven years.

Two aspects of Americans' experience in the German laboratories were especially pertinent to the subsequent development of medical education in the United States. First, the Americans absorbed German attitudes toward medical knowledge. Like their German teachers, American students believed that medical phenomena were governed by chemical and physical laws. This position was clearly stated in an 1886 address by Welch. "Many departments of medicine now possess the interest and the attraction of a natural science," he told his audience. "Here will be found problems of absorbing interest, some of which call into requisition . . . a profound knowledge of physics, or of chemistry, or of mathematics."[21] Similarly, American students unhesitatingly accepted their mentors' conviction that the key to medical discovery lay in controlled experimentation, not in the passive observation of nature. Thus did Franklin Mall in 1894 express his disdain for the observational approach in medical and biological research: "It is useless to hope that the individuals educated only in descriptive sciences can contribute much to an experimental science for the methods of thinking and investigating are so different and the aims so widely separated."[22] In a popular work a generation later, the eminent physiologist Walter Cannon also described the advantages of the experimental over the observational approach. "Of the two ways of learning about nature," Cannon explained, "experiments have proved much more fruitful than simple observations—chiefly, I think, because experimentation is addressed more directly to the means of controlling natural forces."[23]

Those who made the German laboratories their temporary homes returned to America with a new world view. They were the first American physicians to understand the importance of experimental scientific methods to medical education and research. For this reason they were intellectually and temperamentally at odds with other physicians in the United States, including the elite, French-trained physicians of the older generation—many of whom had been their teachers in America and still occupied positions of influence and authority in the country's medical schools, hospitals, and professional societies.

Second, Americans who worked in Germany's medical laboratories became enamored of a new role model: the full-time teacher and investigator. Inspired by their German mentors, this small band of basic scientists wanted to pursue careers in scientific medicine rather than in medical practice. Writing from Vienna in 1877, Welch told his long-time friend Frederic Dennis, "You know that my ambition is less for acquiring a practice than it is for obtaining opportunities to follow up pathological investigations, and if I could support myself without practicing I should be willing to relinquish practice."[24] Franklin Paine Mall similarly wrote to his sister from Germany in the late 1880s:

> During the past year I have changed ideas materially as regards the objects of life. . . . My aim is to make scientific medicine a life work. If opportunities present I will. This has been my plan ever since I left America and not until late, since having received encouragement, have I expressed myself.[25]

Unlike earlier generations of American physicians, this group sought intellectual distinction rather than monetary rewards, and they defined their goals in terms of medical scholarship rather than medical practice. To them, the career of a professor of medicine was just as important and honorable as that of a traditional practitioner.

On returning to the United States these physicians were extremely frustrated, for nowhere in America at the close of the Civil War could a living be earned by engaging in full-time medical teaching and research. Even worse, there was little sympathy among fellow physicians, family, friends, or the American public for the type of work they wished to do. This was perhaps the greatest source of frustration for these aspiring medical scientists, who craved not only jobs but moral legitimacy and an emotional sense of belonging, of respect, and of not feeling alien in their own society. Such was the case with Welch, whose desire for an academic career cost him his long-time friendship with Dennis. Dennis was a physician himself, and his father had paid Welch's steamship passage to Europe. Yet he could not understand Welch's decision to accept the call to the pathology professorship at Johns Hopkins rather than to remain in New York as his partner in practice. An irate Dennis wrote to another friend: "If he [Welch] goes, he must sacrifice the friendships of a life and isolate himself in a provincial city among untried and inexperienced persons. . . . He *must not go* and I feel that it is worth any sacrifice of time to help him decide. . . . His ideas imbibed in Germany are impractical in our form of government."[26] Such attitudes stood in stark contrast to conditions in Germany, where professors enjoyed high social status and were treated with deference and respect.

Because of such difficulties, most Americans returning from the German laboratories in the 1870s and 1880s were thwarted in their desire to pursue academic careers. America lacked the institutional structure to support serious medical research; full-time medical teaching and investigation did not yet exist as a profession in the United States. Accordingly, most German-trained American physicians ultimately entered private practice and were lost forever to the scientific community they longed to join. In an address in 1888 William Welch explained the situation:

> A distinguished professor of physiology in a German university asked me not long ago: "What becomes of the young men from your country who work in our medical laboratories? While they are here they do good work and show an aptitude for scientific investigation, certainly not less than our native students. But after their return to America, we hear no more of them." I was obliged to explain to him, that the facilities and encouragement for carrying on scientific investigations in the medical institutions of this country are in general very meager, and that one great impetus to such work is almost wholly lacking here, namely, the assurance or even likelihood that good scientific work will pave the way to an academic career.[27]

Even those who gained recognition sometimes expressed dissatisfaction with their lot. At a fireside conversation one evening, William Halsted, the most eminent American surgeon of the late nineteenth century and the first professor of surgery at Johns Hopkins, astonished a young George Corner by relating "the story of his own youthful ambition to be a scientific investigator at a time when American medicine offered a young doctor no such opportunity. He

. . . said that if he were beginning again at my age and time he would unhesitatingly choose the laboratory career."[28] Halsted had apparently achieved success on everyone's scale except his own.

A few did succeed, however, transcending enormous obstacles in the process. In 1871 Henry P. Bowditch, aided by influential friends, received an appointment at Harvard Medical School and became the first full-time professor of physiology in the United States. Bowditch began his work at Harvard in a laboratory located in the attic of the medical school, stocked with equipment paid for in part by his father.[29] T. Mitchell Prudden, after Welch, the best known American pathologist of his generation, secured a position in 1878 at the College of Physicians and Surgeons in New York, where he worked successfully despite sometimes deplorable conditions. When college appropriations were insufficient, he would frequently pay for laboratory equipment out of his own pocket, and as late as 1897 he was pleading with the president of Columbia for, among other things, such essentials as enough electric light to keep the pathology laboratory operating.[30] Physiologist Warren Lombard, returning to the United States in 1885 after three years in Ludwig's laboratory, was dismayed to find no physiology laboratories in New York. He thought himself lucky when a friend at the College of Physicians and Surgeons secured for him a tiny room at the college that had been used as a carpenter's shop. It was there that Lombard did his first piece of research work in the United States.[31] And John Jacob Abel, appointed America's first professor of pharmacology at the University of Michigan in 1890, found that he had to begin his new position without a laboratory of any kind. Using whatever space he could find, he had to borrow even such simple laboratory equipment as test tubes, flasks, and beakers.[32]

In the 1870s and 1880s, in short, a handful of dedicated, pioneering medical scientists managed to secure and maintain academic positions by virtue of the great economic and personal sacrifices they were willing to make. The few jobs that could be found were seized by those who were willing to overlook meager salaries, arduous working conditions, and suboptimal facilities for the opportunity to devote themselves to teaching and research.

In post-Civil War America, the plight of aspiring academic physicians was shared by others hoping for careers in advanced teaching and research. Those in the natural and physical sciences encountered identical obstacles. Physicist Josiah Willard Gibbs and paleontologist Othniel C. Marsh worked for years at Yale without pay. Both were able to pursue research only because they were independently wealthy.[33] Other scientists struggled on miserly salaries, and many had to purchase laboratory equipment with their own money. Scholars in the humanities and social sciences also had to contend with the scarcity of jobs, low pay, and lack of cultural approval of their work. Speaking of the academic profession as a whole, Charles Eliot said at his inauguration as president of Harvard University in 1869: "It is very hard to find competent professors for the University. Very few Americans of eminent ability are attracted to this profession. The pay has been too low, and there has been no gradual rise out of drudgery, such as may reasonably be expected in other learned callings."[34] Medical scientists were far from alone.

Nevertheless, by the 1880s conditions in medicine, as in other fields, were beginning to improve. Universities were becoming more responsive to research,[35] and to many Americans it was starting to become clear that there was a payoff to medical research. Two generations earlier this had not been the case. Better diagnosis of disease—the great achievement of the Paris clinical school—had not brought with it progress in disease prevention or cure. To a practical-minded country, which could see little of immediate clinical utility coming from such efforts, there was no reason to support or encourage medical research.[36] After the Civil War, however, the situation began to change. The inquiries of German experimental medicine offered much more in the way of practical implications than did the earlier pathological studies by French clinicians—a point that could no longer be disputed by the 1880s, with the birth of modern bacteriology and its immediate implications for antiseptic surgery and public health. American physicians returning from the German medical laboratories brought back this new medical knowledge as well as an understanding of the methods by which such knowledge was obtained and a personal desire to uncover more basic medical truths. In the immediate post-Civil War years the opportunities to apply their skills were still few, but the leaders were assembling who would soon propel American medical education and research into a new era.

The Emergence of the American University

After the Civil War another underlying force for reform was taking shape: the American university. The modern university appeared in America between 1865 and 1890, and it quickly and aggressively began to exert its authority in all matters pertaining to higher education.[37] This development had an immeasurable effect on the training of doctors, as medical education moved into the university. By the turn of the century the university was medical education's greatest friend and protector—the provider of a secure institutional home, a source of financial support, and a reservoir of intellectual and emotional encouragement. The American university provided a prominent place for medicine in the country's system of higher education.

At first glance, the American college might have seemed an unlikely candidate to nurture medical education because the pre-Civil War college was ill equipped for the pursuit of any form of higher learning. In the rigid, constricting, stultifying atmosphere of the antebellum college, there was little room for creative intellectual activity. A narrow and archaic curriculum emphasized the classical languages, philosophy, theology, and mathematics. Knowledge was regarded as fixed and catechistic. Hence, colleges of that era sought to conserve and transmit knowledge, not to expand it through research. Teaching was authoritarian and paternalistic. Students took rigidly prescribed courses and learned their lessons by rote, with retention of the undigested corpus of information serving as the sole end of instruction. A college education of the period provided much "furniture for the mind," but its emphasis on memorization and mental discipline allowed for little critical analysis or independent thought.[38]

After the Civil War, the old-fashioned college evolved into the modern university. At the root of this transformation was the astounding growth of information that occurred in all scholarly fields. The successes of the natural sciences were especially prominent, and many people began to believe that scientific truth rather than religious authority was the most dependable form of knowledge. A similar growth of knowledge also occurred in the humanities, many of which began to emulate the methods of the natural sciences. Historians began writing "scientific history;" law schools began teaching "scientific law;" and new disciplines such as political science, economics, and sociology emerged. A vehicle was needed to harness this proliferation of knowledge, and the university, following the example of German universities, assumed this task. In doing so, the university expanded the scope of its concerns to include every branch of human knowledge and culture. It even assumed control of many educational functions once served by apprenticeship, such as the training of lawyers, dentists, pharmacists—and doctors.

On the surface it might seem like somewhat of an accident that universities included medical education within their new educational responsibilities. In many cases medical schools were already there. That is, many universities that began to grow after the Civil War, including Harvard, Yale, Dartmouth, Pennsylvania, New York University, and Michigan, found themselves already in possession of a medical school. Even though the associations between these universities and their respective medical schools were still very loose in the

1860s, it might have seemed that the universities had no choice but to proceed with the cultivation of medical education.

However, after the Civil War universities began to view medical education with much greater interest than would be expected if they had merely condoned the endeavor. Universities that had not previously been involved with medical education sought to acquire medical schools, and those that already had medical schools took charge of the schools and helped them develop. From Charles Eliot of Harvard and James Angell of Michigan in the 1870s to Charles Thwing of Western Reserve, Charles Dabney of Cincinnati, and Seth Low and Nicholas Murray Butler of Columbia at the turn of the century, leading university presidents assumed responsibility for their affiliated medical schools and vigorously promoted their welfare. Through financial support and strong administrative leadership, they provided genuine encouragement to their medical schools to grow and develop.

To understand why university officials worked so hard for medical education, one must appreciate more fully how the proliferation of information changed the institutions of higher learning in the United States. In response to the ever increasing growth of information, knowledge was no longer seen as a fixed body of dogma but as something that grows and evolves—a metaphor that was not lost upon observers in the wake of the theory of evolution. The center for redefining knowledge became the modern university, which distinguished itself from the pre-Civil War college by its concern for research as well as for teaching, for discovery as well as for transmission, for expanding and searching for knowledge rather than simply conserving. Whereas the skilled teacher before the Civil War was one who could defend established dogma, the skilled teacher in the postwar decades became one who could overturn a position and expose the fallacies of the past. With knowledge so rapidly evolving, the modern university became concerned with process, not just with subject. Educators were thinking not simply about knowledge per se but about how it grows, how it accumulates, and how it changes. Scholars and educators began to focus on how to understand, increase, and transmit knowledge, regardless of the particular discipline in question.

As the amount of medical knowledge proliferated, medicine, too, fitted directly into the purview of the modern university. Medical scientists, like scholars in all fields, were charged with the same new mission: to discover knowledge, not merely to conserve it. In medicine, as in other disciplines, authority was simply no longer to be trusted, especially when its dicta could not be verified by one's senses. "Experiment and observation of nature have taken [the] place, in the medical as well as in other sciences, of deductive reasoning and appeal to authority,"[39] William Welch told an audience in

1886. If the university were to maintain credibility in claiming research as its area of special expertise, then it had no choice but to make room for the most important profession, now that medicine had become a paradigm of experimental inquiry.

Medicine attracted the attention of university leaders for another, related reason. The teaching of medicine, like teaching in other fields undergoing rapid intellectual expansion, was now a much more difficult task than before. The wheat had to be separated from the chaff. Not all that was known could be fitted into the curriculum; someone had to decide what was to be taught, and in what order and what relation to other topics. In addition, since much of what was thought true one day might be disproved the next, greater attention had to be placed on the processes of education. Instructors had to teach much more by example than by fiat, exploring approaches to information gathering and assessment. Often it was necessary to place more emphasis on the correct approach than on the specific outcome.

The view thus emerged that not just anyone could teach medicine correctly—that only those who had mastered proper educational techniques were qualified. William Welch spoke of the necessity of elevating the standard "not only of those who study, but also of those who teach medicine. A few books and some oratorical gift no longer suffice to make a medical teacher."[40] The best teachers, Welch went on, were "the well-trained students and the fruitful investigators in their special departments, even if they do not possess the greatest facility of expression."[41] To be a medical educator began to take on a separate meaning from being a medical practitioner. By intellectual necessity, medical teaching was rapidly becoming a full-time profession. The casual, random approach to medical teaching no longer sufficed.

No one felt more strongly about the importance of employing proper educational techniques than the molders of the modern university. "The actual problem to be solved is not what to teach, but how to teach,"[42] Charles Eliot said at his inaugural as president of Harvard University in 1869. In the post-Civil War years, university leaders knew that standardization of the teaching process and a concern for curriculum planning were developing in all areas of education. Many professional educators shared a desire to command method and order; a teacher's expertise consisted in possessing knowledge of how to structure the educational environment to maximize learning. As teachers of medicine began to examine their methods more closely, their work began to attract the attention of university leaders, who were just as intent on establishing the university's authority in matters of advanced teaching as in research.

There were other reasons why universities in the late nineteenth century became interested in promoting medical education. One related to the university's role as a place for the integration of knowledge—a function implicit in the term "university." This integrative role was particularly important in the case of medicine, for medical knowledge was becoming increasingly dependent on the fundamental sciences, such as biology, chemistry, and physics, which were based in universities rather than in medical schools. As medical research developed, boundaries between fields blurred, and medical science became more and more unified with the other sciences. "In the relation, then, of medicine to certain of the natural and physical sciences is to be found one of the most important advantages of the association of a medical school with a university,"[43] Welch wrote.

The placement of professional schools in universities appealed to another important value of the modern university: the idea of liberal culture. Physicians, according to William DeWitt Hyde, the president of Bowdoin College, should be "men of broad training, rather than of mechanical memory."[44] Or as Angell put it:

> The university life with its manifold stimulations must greatly aid every professional student in avoiding the perils of entering upon his work in life with either an exaggerated view of its relative importance or a narrow view of it as a trade, a mere means of earning bread. It sends him forth with a broader, larger, more vigorous manhood than he would be likely to acquire in an isolated school.[45]

Universities provided the best opportunities for the free exchange of ideas and the cultivation of a broad outlook.

The modern university at its inception, as today, was a diverse place, fulfilling many functions and serving many constituencies. Amid fraternities and football, amid young women seeking husbands and the idle rich pursuing "gentlemen's C's," amid ideals of public service as exemplified by the "Wisconsin Idea" (the idea that universities should provide expert advice of all kinds), amid the pressure to provide vocational training for the masses, ideals of scholarship sometimes appeared to get lost in the shuffle. Nevertheless, no matter how great the pressure to provide different services, at the core of the modern university was always a commitment to advanced research and teaching. To university leaders, research and teaching in medicine carried a special imperative, for such work offered the hope of better diagnosis and treatment of disease. There was potential practical benefit in medical education, not just intellectual excitement. Therefore, universities became eager to promote it.

To many physicians in the decades following the Civil War the idea of moving medical education to the universities came as a shock. Physicians who controlled the country's medical schools had little desire to give up their profitable enterprises. Older doctors trained in France, who had not witnessed the example of university-based medical education, viewed this idea as strange and unworkable. However, to physicians returning from postgraduate study in Germany, the affiliation of medical schools with universities made great sense. Welch felt that the preeminence of German medical education resulted from "the fact that medicine in Germany is taught only as a department in a university. . . . There is a conviction that the highest interests of medical education and science are best subserved by this association."[46] This group believed that the university offered the best opportunity to implement the type of medical training they had observed in the German-speaking countries. And to those members of the group who desired full-time careers in research and teaching, the university also offered an identity—that of the professor. The new generation of academically oriented physicians was glad to join aspiring scholars in other fields by casting the lot of medical education in the United States with that of the university.

The Creation of the School System

In the immediate post-Civil War years medical education was hampered by another severe problem: a preponderance of poorly prepared students. Throughout the country's medical schools the most stringent entrance requirement was the ability to read and write, and many schools accepted less if the students could afford the fees. President Angell of Michigan wrote in 1873 that "the most we can at present easily do [in terms of entrance requirements] is ask for a substantial knowledge of the fundamental elements of an English education."[47]

The poor preparation of medical students made it very difficult to teach medicine effectively. No matter how capable and dedicated the faculty, efforts at inspired medical teaching were destined to failure when the majority of the class was barely literate. As medical schools started to teach the laboratory subjects in the 1870s, 1880s, and 1890s, the problem became even more acute. No student, however bright, could study these subjects effectively without a thorough preliminary education that included work in biology, chemistry, and physics. The internal logic of medicine dictated that students should enter medical school with certain basic skills already mastered and with certain fundamental training already completed. Otherwise, the quality of instruction would descend to a very low level, wasting the time of both students and instructors. "It is as unkind to the student as it is embarrassing to the school," Angell wrote, "to retain him in classes for two or three years, if it is clear at the outset that his ignorance of learning is so dense, that he cannot proceed with his course with profit to himself or with reasonable hope of graduating."[48]

In the 1870s, there were relatively few persons like Angell who worried about the easy entrance to medical school. Those who voiced concern could do very little to alter the situation. In an era when it was still not completely clear that a thorough education made a person a more effective doctor, many schools intentionally kept standards low so that they could attract more students. Angell observed that many prospective medical students who could not meet Michigan's easy entrance requirement, which consisted only of a basic English education, were readily granted admission to other medical schools.[49]

Much of the reason for the poor quality of medical students was related to the condition of the country's school system. The nation's educational system was just being created, and the number of students with the appropriate preliminary training to take advantage of scientific medical instruction was very small. Angell noted that the effort to elevate the standard of admission at the Michigan medical school could proceed only "as rapidly as the diffusion of education among the class which furnishes medical students . . . will warrant."[50] Without well-prepared students, entrance requirements could not be enforced.

In the 1870s, as the country's industrial and economic system began to expand, so did its school system. Education beyond the elementary grades, once a luxury largely for children of the well-to-do, became more and more important to the working and middle classes in their efforts to find employment and achieve social mobility in an emerging industrial society.[51] Public education was further fostered in the late nineteenth century by the enactment of compulsory attendance laws, the provision of free textbooks in the public schools, and the extension of the public library system. In 1870, there were only 1,026 public high schools with 72,158 enrolled students; by 1900 the number of schools had increased to 6,005 and the number of students to 519,251.[52] Fueled by the growth of the secondary schools, university enrollments also increased dramatically. In 1870, 563 colleges enrolled 52,000 students—1.7 percent of the nation's population between eighteen and twenty-one years of age. By 1900, there were 977 colleges with 238,000 students—4 percent of the eighteen to twenty-one year age group.[53] The increase in secondary school and college enrollments between 1870 and 1900 presaged an even more remarkable growth during the first two decades of the twentieth century.[54]

The growth of secondary and higher education proceeded in tandem with each other. In the early 1870s, colleges across the country began establishing "diploma relations" with high schools, wherein graduates of approved high schools who had passed all the subjects prescribed for college admission would be accepted into the freshman class without examination. From Bowdoin College to the University of Michigan, from Western Reserve to the University of Nebraska, universities and colleges worked to create a system of education that began with the elementary grades, continued with the high school grades, and finished with the college years.[55] The fluidity and multiplicity of paths that had characterized education in America before the Civil War began to disappear. Instead an educational ladder started to emerge that connected the lowest steps of the educational system with the highest. By the 1890s, the outline of America's educational system was in place.

Later, doubts would surface as to some of the educational and social problems of a rigidly structured system. Some would voice concern about the loss of flexibility inherent in such a system; others would contend that equality of educational opportunity remained more myth than reality. Nevertheless, to medical educators of the late nineteenth century it was clear that there was an overriding benefit from the development of the nation's school system: an increasing supply of students academically qualified to begin the study of scientific medicine. Sound medical instruction presupposed the existence of well-prepared students who could adapt to the rigors of modern medical training. As the supply of such students increased, medical faculties could impose more exacting entrance requirements and still be assured of having enough students for the school to operate. Moreover, the growth of the underlying educational system permitted greater economy of instruction. By the early 1900s, a subject such as general chemistry, once a standard medical course, could be moved from the medical schools to the colleges, where it became a medical school prerequisite. This left more time in the medical curriculum to teach advanced subjects.[56]

In the late nineteenth century, relatively few medical students were college graduates. In 1890, according to one survey, only 8 percent had undergraduate degrees.[57] Furthermore, even a college degree did not guarantee adequate preliminary preparation. Some institutions that called themselves colleges did not deserve the name, while some of the exceptional high schools and normal schools provided better instruction than did many colleges. Nevertheless, by the end of the century it was clear that the overall quality of students embarking on medical study was beginning to improve, and this change helped pave the way for the provision of more sophisticated medical instruction. In this manner all scientific disciplines benefited from the improvements in public education, not just medicine. Daniel Kevles has noted, for instance, that as the quality of high school physics courses improved in the late nineteenth century, a growing number of students took physics courses in college, thereby becoming aware of career possibilities in the field. This development contributed to the rise in stature of American physics.[58]

In the 1870s and 1880s, the consequences of the growth of the country's educational system were still scarcely felt in the nation's medical schools. The tangible improvements in medical education during those decades were few compared with the remarkable changes that occurred after 1890. Nevertheless, in the 1870s and 1880s the underlying developments that would later make possible the rapid and dramatic improvements in medical education of the Progressive Era were already underway. Medical knowledge was rapidly increasing, and mastery thereof was becoming more and more important to the practice of good medicine. A cadre of teachers was arising, intent on transmitting scientific medicine to their students. The university was developing, preparing to provide a home for modern medical education. And the supply of students educationally qualified to begin the rigorous study of medicine was becoming much larger. To this should be added the country's economic growth and expansion of wealth that later became crucial to financing scientific medical instruction. On this infrastructure was ultimately to be built modern medical education in the United States.

3 The Innovative Period

ON THE SURFACE, medical education in the 1870s and 1880s appeared scarcely different from what it had been before the Civil War. The proprietary schools continued to provide the same superficial course of lectures. The casual admission and graduation requirements of the antebellum period also continued essentially unchanged. Among better trained physicians, the influence of the French clinical school remained strong, fostering a continuing skepticism about the utility of scientific knowledge in clinical practice. However, during those same years, a stream of young laboratory-trained physicians was returning from Germany, and the modern American university was beginning to exert its hegemony in matters of higher education. Between 1871 and 1893, these forces were to come into conflict at four pivotal schools: Harvard, Pennsylvania, Michigan, and Johns Hopkins. The result would be the first genuine, lasting improvements in medical education in the United States.

Pioneers of Reform

In 1869, Harvard Medical School, like all American medical schools of the period, stood desperately in need of reform.[1] Admission was open to anyone who could pay the fees. Only 20 percent of the students held college degrees, and one faculty member estimated in 1870 that over half the students could not write.[2] As elsewhere, the curriculum consisted of two four-month terms of lectures, the second the same as the first. There was no gradation of studies, nor were there written examinations. To graduate, a student needed only to pass five of nine perfunctory five-minute oral quizzes at the end of the term. Instruction was almost wholly didactic. In the scientific courses, except for anatomy, students did not engage in laboratory work; in the clinical subjects, students did not participate in patient care. Only a nominal connection existed between the medical school and the university. The medical school operated on a separate calendar, managed its own financial affairs, and divided the profits among the faculty. For this reason the school joined in the race for large student enrollments and large receipts. One study of Harvard Medical School has described the school at that time as "a money-making institution, not much better than a diploma mill."[3] Such were the conditions at the school many considered the best in America.

In that same year, however, Charles W. Eliot became president of Harvard University—an event that heralded the metamorphosis of both the medical school and the university. Eliot understood the need to teach medicine in a more rigorous, scientific fashion. Born in 1834, Eliot, a member of a prominent Boston family, was a graduate of Harvard College and a chemist.[4] Since his introduction to chemistry as a college undergraduate working with Josiah Cooke, he had learned the subject by working in the laboratory rather than by simply attending lectures and reading textbooks. From 1863 to 1865, he had studied chemistry abroad and had observed the French and German systems of medical education. Upon his return to the United States, he was convinced of the importance of science to medicine and of the need to teach scientific principles with laboratories as well as with lectures. "The whole system of medical education in this country needs thorough reformation,"[5] he wrote in his first report as president in 1870. "The ignorance and general incompetency of the average graduate of American Medical Schools, at the time when he receives the degree which turns him loose upon the community, is something horrible to contemplate."[6] Following his election as Harvard's president, Eliot made reform of the medical school one of his immediate goals. He believed the medical school should become an integral part of the university, expand its offering of scientific subjects, and teach those subjects in a way consistent with modern pedagogic principles.

Eliot's proposals precipitated a bitter controversy at the medical school that threatened to split the faculty in two. His ideas were greeted favorably by several of the younger professors, particularly James Clarke White, David Cheever, and Calvin Ellis. In the 1860s, each of these men had studied in Germany and Austria, and this experience had convinced them that knowledge of the basic sciences was fundamental to the practice of good medicine.

"Skinny" White (so nicknamed because he was the nation's first dermatologist) was the president's strongest supporter. An outspoken person, White had already angered some of his older faculty colleagues by writing a series of editorials in which he severely criticized the conventional system of medical training in America.[7] In one editorial, he praised the virtues of scientific medicine that had made Berlin and Vienna the world's "great schools of medicine."[8] Parisian medicine, in contrast, by its neglect of the basic sciences, was in a state of "decadence," living "chiefly on the reputation of its past greatness."[9]

Eliot's plan, however, was opposed strenuously by several of the most influential professors, led by Henry Jacob Bigelow and Oliver Wendell Holmes, the senior and most powerful members of the faculty. Bigelow and Holmes objected to Eliot's proposals in part because they were reluctant to surrender the school's autonomy. More important, they were traditional physicians who resented what Eliot's ideas represented to them: the faddish glorification of German science and an offensive disdain for clinical acumen. As young men, Bigelow and Holmes had taken postgraduate training in Paris, where they had become skilled in the clinical, pathologic, and statistical methods of their mentors. Like their French teachers, however, they never appreciated the importance of the laboratory to medical research and practice. Throughout their lives, they remained unconvinced of the role of the basic sciences in medicine. To them, the purpose of a medical school such as Harvard was to train doctors, not scientists, and the two were seen as mutually incompatible goals.[10]

To take on the imposing Holmes and Bigelow was no enviable task. Holmes, the "autocrat of the breakfast table," wielded enormous influence as one of America's great literary as well as medical figures. Bigelow, professor of surgery at Harvard since 1849, was the leading New England surgeon of his generation and the most powerful person in Boston medicine. Dogmatic, intolerant, flamboyant, and strong willed, he opposed Eliot's reforms with fanatic fervor. Later, he opposed not only coeducation at the medical school but also vivisection.[11] But if anyone was prepared for the challenge it was Eliot. Born into one of Boston's "Brahmin" families, Eliot, like many other members of his caste, felt an obligation to seek personal achievement and play a constructive role in society. A diligent student, he pursued the study of chemistry with the zest that many of the undergraduates gave to extracurricular activities. Although he was tall, sturdy, and imposing, he suffered from a disfiguring birthmark that covered the right side of his face and extended to the lip, twisting it upward. Perhaps as a result of his sensitivity over the birthmark (he never allowed a photograph to show that side of his face), or the childhood taunts and fights it engendered, Eliot developed a characteristic aloofness and an indomitable resolve to accomplish socially useful tasks. His was a life of self-discipline and dedication to higher causes.[12]

In November 1869, Eliot took the unprecedented step of assuming the chair at a meeting of the medical faculty, a seat he did not relinquish for the next forty years.[13] No other event more dramatically symbolized the desire of the modern university to take charge of medical education. With the support of his faculty allies, Eliot tried to push through his ideas of reforming the medical school. For a year, as the two factions locked horns, the faculty was torn with strife. This was no conflict between elite and ordinary physicians but a civil war within the ranks of the elite. A deep chasm divided those with French from those with German views of medical science, providing a microcosm of the conflict besetting the elite medical community throughout America. Numerous strained, bitter meetings of the medical faculty ensued.[14] Holmes and Bigelow were furious, and their outrage threatened to abruptly end Eliot's career as president. By diplomacy, perseverance, conviction, and sheer determination to triumph, Eliot imposed his will on the medical faculty. Why, Bigelow asked at one meeting, introduce so many changes into a program that had been successful for eighty years? The reason, Eliot answered in an immortalized reply, was quite simple: "there is a new President."[15]

In 1871, Eliot succeeded in introducing a set of sweeping reforms at the medical school. The reforms encompassed three principal areas. First, a series of administrative changes were introduced that made the medical school an integral part of the university. The medical school began to adhere to the university calendar and surrendered management of its finances to the university administration. The professors no longer divided the fees among themselves but were placed on salary from the university. Second, major changes were made in the curriculum. The course of instruction was expanded to a three-year program with nine-month terms, and written examinations were introduced into each course. In addition, the subject matter for the first time was ordered in a logical sequence—the basic sciences preceding pathology and therapeutics, and the scientific courses preceding the clinical work. Third, and most important, the new curriculum emphasized the laboratory sciences. Previously the only scientific subject taught in a thorough way was anatomy, but now, along with instruction in anatomy being increased, courses were introduced in chemistry, physiology, microscopic anatomy, and pathology. Furthermore, in 1871, Henry Pickering Bowditch received a full-time, salaried appointment in physiology. Bowditch, just back in the United States from two years in Ludwig's laboratory in Germany, was the first medical professor at Harvard and in America to spend his entire time in teaching and research. For the first time at an American medical school, science was legitimized.

The most notable consequence of the 1871 reforms was the provision of much better instruction in the basic sciences. These subjects were given more time in the revised curriculum, but an even more important improvement occurred in the *way* that science was taught after 1871. The new program required that each student work in the laboratory. Previously, the only required laboratory work had been in anatomy, and the school contained only sixteen chemistry desks for three hundred students. In 1871, the number of chemistry desks was increased to one hundred; three spacious laboratories were built for physiologic and microscopic work; and upon completion of the construction, laboratory instruction became mandatory in anatomy, physiology, chemistry, and pathologic anatomy. Scientific principles were now to be learned not from lectures or demonstrations alone but from the student's own experimentation in the laboratory—as Eliot had learned chemistry as a college undergraduate with Cooke, and as the German medical schools were teaching the sciences to their students. This emphasis upon "learning by doing" was by far the most important innovation of the 1871 reforms. It constituted a qualitative change in teaching methods that dwarfed in significance the quantitative changes of a longer curriculum, new subjects, and more rigorous standards of admission and grading.

The emphasis on laboratory instruction was not by accident but by design. All who had previously experienced it—Eliot as a college undergraduate and his young faculty allies during their postgraduate work in Germany —recognized the superiority of this empirical method of teaching over conventional didactic techniques. Eliot emphasized this point in his inaugural address in 1869. Harvard University, he maintained, "would have science taught in a rational way, objects and instruments at hand—not from books merely, not through the memory chiefly, but by the seeing eye and the informing fingers."[16] Scientific studies, he argued, should cultivate "the powers of observation, the inductive faculty, the sober imagination, the sincere and proportionate judgment. A student in the elements gets no such training by studying even a good text-book, though he really master it, nor yet by sitting at the feet of the most admirable lecturer."[17] Scientific principles, Eliot contended, were more readily grasped by those who actually experienced them than by those who merely heard about them.

To Eliot and his faculty supporters, there was a further purpose to making the laboratory the primary vehicle of scientific instruction. The empiricism of laboratory training fostered a distrust of traditional explanations and speculative theories—a distrust that was increasingly felt to be justified as the pace of medical discovery grew during the mid-nineteenth century. As Bowditch explained, the laboratory method is "to be regarded as a reaction against the too exclusive use of the so-called didactic method of instruction, as a result of which students, getting their knowledge wholly from lectures and text-books, . . . were thus insensibly led to depend upon authority instead of upon the direct observation of nature."[18] Nothing less than a new philosophy of education emerged out of the 1871 reforms. The primary goal of medical education, in the eyes of the Harvard faculty, was not to provide students an encyclopedic knowledge of facts but to foster the student's ability to think critically, to solve problems, to acquire new information, to keep up with the changing times. This could best be done in the laboratory rather than in the lecture hall. "Contact with the phenomena themselves and not with descriptions of them trains the mind of the student for power by teaching him to observe carefully and reason correctly,"[19] Bowditch wrote.

It has commonly been thought that Eliot and his faculty supporters had the same reasons for seeking to improve the medical school. In fact, however, they viewed medical education from different perspectives. White, Cheever, and Ellis wanted to improve medical education, and they saw in Eliot's proposals a specific way to do so. Eliot shared their desire to improve medical education, but he was also concerned with the role of higher education in America and with the part that Harvard should play in shaping its development. Early in his administration, he also introduced reforms to upgrade the law, divinity, and scientific schools at Harvard, which also had suffered from very low standards. The reforms at the medical school were only part of his plan to improve all the university's professional schools and to create a cohesive university from what had been disparate, autonomous departments.

In his broad plan for the university, Eliot had good reason for seeking tighter control of the medical school. The emerging American university was aspiring toward objectivity and universality—properties implicit in the term "university" itself. "It cannot be said too loudly or too often," Eliot wrote in 1869, "that no subject of human inquiry can be out of place in the programme of a real university."[20] As medicine entered the scientific age, it was quickly becoming a paradigm of rationality and objectivity. It was absurd for a modern university not to include such a discipline within its offerings. Moreover, the modern university was developing expertise in all matters pertaining to education. Students of every academic subject were learning to question traditional authority and to value empirical observations more than textbook teachings. Eliot summarized this trend in his inaugural address:

> The very word "education" is a standing protest against dogmatic teaching. The notion that education consists in the authoritative inculcation of what the teacher deems true may be logical and appropriate in a convent, or a seminary for priests, but it is intolerable in universities and public schools, from primary to professional.[21]

This was why Eliot was so intent on reforming the medical school. He was not only concerned with the study of medicine but with how medicine was taught. To Eliot, medicine, and every other academic discipline, belonged within the province of the modern university. "It is only necessary that every subject should be taught at the university on a higher plane than elsewhere,"[22] he wrote. In this way Harvard, like other nascent American universities, could further advance its still tenuous claim to authority in educational affairs.

Other important changes were introduced during the Eliot administration. In 1880, the school added an optional fourth year to provide additional clinical teaching, and in 1892, the fourth year became mandatory. With the increasing rigor of both the scientific and clinical training, the faculty observed that performance in medical school correlated with the quality of preliminary training. Accordingly, in 1900, the faculty made the bachelor's degree a requirement for admission. However, since 1877 there had been the requirement that students without a degree must pass an entrance examination, and by 1900 approximately half the students were taking the bachelor's degree anyway.[23] Unlike the reforms of 1871, all subsequent changes occurred quietly, without a brouhaha. The faculty now took it for granted that it was desirable to upgrade the curriculum; they no longer needed to be convinced of that point. To their great joy, none of these improvements caused class size to fall. Enrollment did drop transiently for a year or two after the 1871 reforms, but thereafter enrollment increased despite the more rigorous program.

The next major reform occurred at the University of Pennsylvania Medical Department.[24] Founded in 1765 by John Morgan and William Shippen, Jr., the medical school, the oldest in the country, basked in a glorious tradition. However, in the nineteenth century the school fell victim to the same pressures besetting other proprietary medical schools. The faculty, dependent on student fees for income, was reluctant to make any improvements in the curriculum for fear that class size would drop. When the enrollment of the school was surpassed in 1859 by two other medical schools, the school thought it had embarked on a "downward course."[25] In 1866, the faculty voted to increase tuition but only if crosstown rival Jefferson Medical College would do the same, so that the school not be at a competitive disadvantage for students.[26] In the early 1870s, the school still offered only two five-month courses of lectures, required no laboratory work, and had virtually indiscernible standards of admission and graduation.[27]

In 1877, however, the school dramatically changed its medical teaching and administrative structure. The course of instruction was expanded to three five-month terms, and the scientific subjects were added. The subjects were arranged in a graded sequence, the scientific courses preceding the clinical courses, with admission to each successive course being granted only after successful examination in the preceding subjects. Unlike before, when the faculty personally collected fees from the students and paid the operating expenses themselves, tuition was now paid directly to the university, which placed the professors on salary and assumed administrative responsibility for operating the school.[28] These changes foreshadowed many further advances in subsequent years, such as the elongation of the term from five to six months in 1882, the establishment of a voluntary fourth year in 1883, and the requirement that the fourth year be mandatory in 1893.

The reorganization of the medical school was not accomplished easily. Faced with the need to attract enough students to guarantee solvency, and encumbered by traditional attitudes that held the laboratory sciences in disdain, the faculty for years had refused to consider any changes in the program. The one previous reform effort in 1847—prolonging the lecture term to six months—was met with such a drop in enrollment that it had to be discontinued six years later. As late as 1864, the faculty voted not to extend the course of instruction because any change "which would materially increase the expense or add to the labor of the students in completing his medical studies would tend to diminish the classes and be detrimental to the prosperity of the school."[29] Even in 1877 several conservative members of the faculty fiercely opposed the reorganization of the school. Robert Rogers, the professor of chemistry and dean of the school, resigned in protest and moved to the Jefferson Medical College.[30] The struggle was hard and the wounds were bitter. Recalling the events sixteen years later, William Pepper, Jr., spoke sadly of "the long and painful controversy" and of how "the end had been attained only at the cost of old friendships and of the allegiance of valued associates."[31]

By the early 1870s, however, the majority of the Pennsylvania faculty had come to believe that the time to expand the program and strengthen scientific teaching had arrived. In this view they were prodded by several new members of the faculty, most notably Pepper, later to become professor of medicine and provost of the university, and James Tyson, a young pathologist. Neither Pepper nor Tyson had undertaken formal training in European laboratories or clinics (in this sense the German influence was the least direct at Pennsylvania of any of the four pioneering medical schools); however, both had closely followed the progress of German medical science, and in doing so they had become convinced of the need to place medical education on a firmer scientific footing. Tyson, for instance, had traveled abroad in 1872 to study methods of teaching microscopy, an experience that convinced him that the only viable way was for each individual student to use the microscope.[32] Pepper had learned much about German methods from corresponding with friends, who would describe to him European systems of medical education.[33]

Reformers also gained a strong ally on Pennsylvania's Board of Trustees: S. Weir Mitchell. In 1876, Mitchell was elected to the governing board of the same institution that had denied him the professorship of physiology a decade before. Soon he became chairman of the board's medical committee, where, for the next thirty-five years, he championed improvements in the university's medical teaching.

The reforms of 1877 would have been introduced a few years earlier except for the school's fear that it would not be able to afford the costs. Anticipating a precipitous drop in enrollment, the faculty hesitated to enact any changes until an endowment could be raised to offset the expected decline in revenue.[34] But in 1876 the school was jolted by the success of Harvard's reforms and the statement of intentions of the new medical school at Johns Hopkins. The proud Pennsylvania faculty felt that it could no longer delay "unless we are content to see the University school take the second rank in a career in which it has always held the first place."[35] Accordingly, in 1877 the school implemented its new program, and the board of trustees secured $50,000 from anonymous friends to cover any deficits that might be incurred. This fund was never tapped, for although enrollment decreased for a year or two following the reorganization, soon it was rising again, and student fees proved sufficient to cover the costs of the new program.[36]

The basic thrust of the reforms at the University of Pennsylvania was the same as at Harvard. The scientific subjects for the first time received a prominent place in the school's curriculum. More important still, a major change occurred in the way in which the scientific subjects were taught. The emphasis shifted from didactic to practical instruction, as required laboratory work was introduced in anatomy, histology, general chemistry, materia medica, and pathology. During the first two years of the new curriculum, students spent fourteen hours a week in the laboratory compared to twenty hours in lectures.[37] In introducing practical work, the Pennsylvania faculty understood that it was helping to revolutionize medical education in America. The school explained:

> Exclusively didactic teaching has been universally abandoned in every branch of scientific and technical education, save the medical. . . . sooner or later, medical teaching in this country must conform to the system which has long been recognized as the only suitable one in the great medical centres of Europe.[38]

The reforms of 1877 also proceeded amid a more general restructuring of the University of Pennsylvania. Under the leadership of the provost, Charles Stillé, a coordinated university was being forged out of what had been autonomous units, and higher academic standards were being introduced into every department. In approving the reforms, the Board of Trustees was guided by the fact that "in all other departments of the University, the constant effort is to raise the standard of admission, of studies, and of graduation."[39] The process of strengthening the university's organization and of increasing its coordination with the medical school was completed under the next provost, William Pepper, Jr., medicine's gift to the university movement. Announcing his retirement in 1894 after thirteen years in office, Pepper explained that his most important work as provost was the "unification of the University and the establishment of broad lines of policy."[40] At Pennsylvania, as at Harvard, the introduction of modern medical education was closely allied with the transformation of the sponsoring institution into a modern university.

As Harvard and the University of Pennsylvania were strengthening their medical teaching in the 1870s, so was the University of Michigan. In 1877 it extended its annual session from six months to nine, the first of a series of reforms that placed the school in the vanguard of medical education. This was followed in 1880 by the introduction of a three-year graded course and in 1890 by the addition of a required fourth year. In the late 1870s the school also began to emphasize the scientific subjects and practical rather than didactic forms of instruction. Prior to 1877 instruction was primarily by lecture and demonstration—indeed, only two microscopes could be found in the entire school. By 1880, however, all students were receiving laboratory instruction in every scientific subject, with particularly extensive opportunities being provided in anatomy, chemistry, and physiology.[41] Conditions were crowded; in 1878 there were 175 chemistry desks for 297 students, and many had to double up.[42] Nevertheless, teaching had taken on a genuine scientific form. As at Harvard and Pennsylvania, these improvements were undertaken with trepidation, for the faculty worried that students might flock to schools with easier standards. Yet after each reform, enrollment held.[43]

The main instigators of the reforms were James B. Angell, the president of the University of Michigan, and Victor Vaughan, a biochemist and later the dean of the medical school. Angell, another of the great first-generation university presidents, involved himself in every phase of the university's activities and guided Michigan's development into a major university. The first twenty years of his leadership (1871–91) saw an increase in the number of courses in the undergraduate college from 57 to 378; the introduction of modern languages, science, engineering, and laboratories; the adaptation of the German seminar; the promotion of independent study and research; the introduction and expansion of the elective system; the substitution of voluntary for compulsory attendance at chapel prayer; and the establishment of increased requirements for admission.[44] During the same period Angell strove to invigorate all of the university's professional schools, which he felt should catch the "spirit" of university life.[45]

Angell's agent at the medical school was Vaughan—genial, relaxed, and soft-spoken, but tireless and indomitable in his mission to elevate standards of medical education. Another veteran of German laboratory study—he had spent a year with Koch learning the new science of bacteriology—Vaughan was determined to reshape the medical school into a center of advanced teaching and research. The task at Michigan was not easy, for the school was handicapped by geographic remoteness and the lack of even remotely adequate hospital facilities. In addition, the senior member of the medical faculty, Alonzo B. Palmer—a spokesman of what Vaughan later termed the "old" rather than the "new" medicine—bitterly opposed Vaughan's first nominee to the faculty, the German-trained physiologist Henry Sewall.[46] Nevertheless, Vaughan persisted, appointing not only Sewall but also a group of eminent medical scientists who had gained experience in Germany: Franklin Mall in anatomy; John J. Abel and Arthur Cushny in pharmacology; William Howell and Warren Lombard in physiology; Paul Freer in chemistry; and Frederick Novy in bacteriology. By the early 1890s, Michigan had become, in the opinion of many, the strongest scientific medical school in the country. Vaughan proudly reminded readers in his autobiography that of the original eight full professors of the Johns Hopkins Medical School in 1893, four had Michigan degrees and two were taken directly from the Michigan faculty.[47]

The reforms at Harvard, Pennsylvania, and Michigan presaged the most spectacular innovation in the history of American medical education: the opening of the Johns Hopkins Medical School in 1893. From the very start, Johns Hopkins was a radical departure in medical education. Students were carefully selected, with the bachelor's degree a prerequisite for admission. Classes were small and students frequently tested and evaluated. Two years of instruction were provided in the basic sciences, with extensive laboratory work mandatory for every student, and two years of rigorous training were also provided in the clinical subjects, with the students gaining experience at the hospital bedside. A true university spirit pervaded the school, for it viewed research as one of its primary missions, and it strove to train investigators and teachers of medicine as well as practitioners. It boasted the finest faculty in the country—each person selected solely for his accomplishments in teaching and research. With its new hospital and medical school buildings, huge endowment, and genuine university affiliation, Johns Hopkins was the envy of every forward-looking medical school in the country. As the Johns Hopkins University in 1876 had become the nation's first genuine graduate university, so the Johns Hopkins Medical School in 1893 became the country's first modern medical school.[48]

Although the medical school opened in October of 1893, the plan upon which it operated had been developed fifteen years before. Innovation had been encouraged by the university's founder, Johns Hopkins of Baltimore, a bachelor who had amassed a fortune as a merchant and banker and who became the largest stockholder in the Baltimore and Ohio Railroad. Upon his death in 1873, Hopkins left $7 million for the establishment of a university and a hospital, with a medical school to unite them. This represented the largest philanthropic donation in America up to that time. Where Hopkins's interest in educational philanthropy arose is still a matter of speculation, but in his will he clearly indicated that the medical school and hospital should be closely connected with each other and that the institutions bearing his name should be comparable in quality to the best anywhere in the world.[49]

Planning for the medical school and hospital fell on the shoulders of Daniel Coit Gilman, the president of the Johns Hopkins University, and John Shaw Billings, who was appointed special adviser on medical education and hospital organization. Gilman, Eliot's rival as the greatest of the first-generation university presidents, had become familiar with modern concepts of medical education while president of the University of California in the early 1870s.[50] On assuming the presidency of Johns Hopkins, he was eager that modern pedagogic principles be applied to medical teaching as well as to the rest of the university's teaching. Billings, probably the most versatile of all American physicians, was the real architect of the school, literally as well as figuratively, since he designed the Johns Hopkins Hospital in addition to enunciating the educational principles on which the medical school and hospital were based. Perhaps because Billings never practiced medicine (except in the military during the Civil War), or perhaps because he pursued such a diverse career, achieving eminence as a medical bibliographer, statistician, hygienist, hospital architect, civil servant, and medical educator, his name is not as celebrated as that of other figures associated with the early Johns Hopkins Medical School. For this reason A. McGehee Harvey has called him the "forgotten hero of American medicine."[51] Yet it was Billings who was primarily responsible for the revolution in medical education at Johns Hopkins. He articulated the school's educational philosophy and oversaw the selection of its faculty. William Welch called him "the wisest man I ever knew."[52]

Curiously, Billings was one of the few pioneering medical educators who had not undertaken formal postgraduate study in Germany. The son of an Indiana farmer, he received his education close to home at Miami College of

Oxford, Ohio, and at the Medical College of Ohio. Nevertheless, he still managed to become fully conversant with modern concepts of medical education. In part this resulted from his own medical training in the United States: he was one of the very few medical students of the 1860s who dissected in the anatomy laboratory and who worked in a hospital as a house pupil—experiences that did much to convince him of the importance of learning by doing.[53] In addition, his view of how to teach medicine matured during a long trip abroad in 1876 to study European systems of medical education. His extensive notes from this experience are still extant.[54] While in Europe, he recognized certain virtues in French and English medical education but concluded that the German system provided the best model for America. His admiration of German medical education was apparent in a series of essays in the mid-1870s in which he articulated the concepts of medical education that were later adopted at Johns Hopkins.[55] The German influence was also reflected in his subsequent efforts to find the new medical school a faculty. It was Billings who hired William Welch and approved the appointments of William Osler, Howard Kelly, William Halsted, Franklin Mall, William Howell, and John Abel—the eminent teachers and scientists of the original Johns Hopkins medical faculty, and a group that gave the school a predominantly German spirit during its formative years.

On the surface it would appear that Gilman, Billings, and Welch, who was appointed professor of pathology and dean of the medical school in 1884, faced an easier task than reformers at Harvard, Pennsylvania, and Michigan. The school was their creation. There were no established traditions to overcome, nor did they have to combat an entrenched faculty hostile to scientific innovations. Nevertheless, so radical was the experiment carried out at Johns Hopkins that its leaders initially feared for the school's success, and widespread doubts existed in the medical community that the school would ever realize its goals. In 1893, Welch forewarned Mall that the educational ideals of the new school "will not appeal to the mass of the public, not even to the medical public for a considerable time. What we shall consider success the mass of doctors will not consider success."[56] Most members of the faculty thought it would be at least ten years before the school could attract even twenty-five students per class.[57]

Adding to the insecurities of the new school were its financial misfortunes. Funds for the medical school were invested in Baltimore and Ohio Railroad stock, which in the 1880s fell upon hard times. After a period of shrinking dividends, from 1888 to 1891 the company eliminated its dividends altogether. This delayed the opening of the school and raised the possibility that the school might not open at all, unless it adopted lower standards so that it could be guaranteed a large student body. Here occurred one of the greatest ironies in the history of American medicine. Mary Garrett, the daughter of the president of the Baltimore and Ohio Railroad and an ardent feminist, came to the rescue. In December 1892, she gave the school more than $300,000 on the condition that the school adhere to its educational ideals and concede the admission of women.[58] A wave of optimism swept through supporters of women's medical education. Seventeen women's medical colleges were then in operation, all of them financially unstable. By 1903, fourteen had closed, due to the belief that women would be better served if they were trained at premier coeducational schools like Johns Hopkins. However, at Johns Hopkins and other schools in the decades that followed, coeducation occurred in token form only, not in the large numbers that Garrett had intended. Thus, the opportunities for women to make medicine a career were in fact less than before, since most of the medical colleges for women had shut down.[59]

When the Johns Hopkins Medical School opened in the fall of 1893, it was a modern school in every respect, a model upon which all other schools could gauge themselves.[60] Compared with the advances that had already occurred at Harvard, Pennsylvania, and Michigan, its greatest innovation was in the realm of clinical teaching. On the wards of the Johns Hopkins Hospital the clerkship became the vehicle of clinical instruction in internal medicine, surgery, obstetrics, and gynecology for every third and fourth year student. Under this system, which was introduced by Osler, the greatest American clinical teacher of all time, the hospital became the medical school, with the students continuously participating in the care of real patients. As clerks, students were assigned five or six beds and sometimes more. Under appropriate supervision, students took patients' histories, performed physical examinations, and carried out procedures such as examining the blood smear or urine, inserting catheters, and applying dressing changes. The students followed the daily progress of their patients until discharge, and they met three or four times a week with an attending physician, with whom they could discuss the cases, ask questions, and make suggestions regarding diagnosis and therapy. In the surgical clerkship they assisted at operations, and in many clerkships they helped perform the autopsy if their patients died. In this way students obtained a first-hand knowledge of disease and clinical methods. The clerkship thus represented a pedagogic revolution of the first magnitude. It allowed the principle of learning by doing to be applied in the clinical subjects, as laboratory instruction had done in the scientific work.

The origins of the clerkship were multiple. The Canadian-born Osler, familiar with the English system of clinical clerks and surgical dressers, a method of bedside clinical teaching, cited this system as his inspiration for introducing the clerkship at Johns Hopkins.[61] To this he added the German residency system for graduate physicians and the use of hospital laboratories for teaching and diagnostic purposes to create the most effective system of clinical instruction ever known in America. It should not be forgotten, however, that a similar plan was briefly used at the New Orleans School of Medicine prior to the Civil War. In addition, the principle of medical students performing clinical work under a teacher's supervision was central to the apprenticeship system, and even today the term "preceptor" is often used to designate the physician who teaches medical students on the wards. Finally, the house pupil system had also provided the same type of experience as the clerkship. Indeed, Billings had been a house pupil himself, and in his essays in the 1870s he pointed out that this type of opportunity should be provided for every student, thereby anticipating Osler's innovation at Johns Hopkins.

The programs at Harvard, Pennsylvania, Michigan, and Johns Hopkins represented a qualitatively new approach to medical education in the United States. They differed from other attempts at reform, which through the 1880s continued to reflect traditional viewpoints. For instance, after the Civil War the AMA was still concerned with the trappings of medical education: the preliminary education of students; requirements to be exacted for graduation; extension of the term of study; manners of testing; and the mode in which teachers should be appointed and paid. It did not yet address the fundamental pedagogic issues of what subjects should be taught or how they should be taught, the issues that had captivated the faculties of the pioneering medical schools. In addition, the AMA did not yet appreciate the importance of the laboratory sciences. To the AMA in 1872, this "ghastly complexion" of German science was something "no philanthropist can be impatient" to see supported in American medical schools.[62] Although the AMA and the pioneering medical schools both spoke of the need to "reform medical education," by those words they meant different things.

It may seem obvious that the reforms at the pioneering medical schools developed independently of the AMA's rhetoric on the subject, but to those who read only the AMA's published pronouncements on medical education it would not be so obvious. In its *Transactions,* the AMA claimed credit for the new programs at Harvard and Pennsylvania, a myth that has been perpetuated by some writers subsequently. "This revolution which is taking place in the minds of medical teachers [at Harvard and Pennsylvania] is, I am inclined to believe, almost entirely due to the public and professional opinion which has been originated by the frequent discussions before this body,"[63] the president of the AMA asserted in 1878. Yet, examination of archival records of all four schools reveals only one significant mention of the AMA: when the president of the association, explaining he had just learned of Harvard's recent reforms, wrote to the dean requesting a description of the new program.[64] In the twentieth century, the Council on Medical Education of the AMA was to become one of the most potent forces for reforming medical education, and its views of medical education were to be very sophisticated. However, in the 1870s and 1880s, the AMA had not yet entered the modern era and played no role in the innovations of that period.

Throughout the 1870s and 1880s, the fate of modern medical education in the United States remained highly uncertain. From the quiet skepticism of the American medical community toward the likelihood of success at Johns Hopkins to the bitter disputes that divided the faculties of Harvard and Pennsylvania, reforms at the pioneering schools were not greeted enthusiastically. Once the pioneering schools had implemented their new programs, they remained glittering islands of reform amid a sea of mediocrity. Throughout the country, medical education was still generally regarded as a business, and the number of medical schools continued to proliferate, growing to 100 in 1880, 133 in 1890, and 161 in 1900.[65] The loudest advocate of reform, the AMA, provided these schools little assistance, since it had a much different idea of what changes were needed. In 1876, twenty-two medical schools established the American Medical College Association, but six years later the organization disbanded following a dispute over the simple proposal that three terms instead of two be required for graduation.[66]

The pioneering schools were subjected to vicious attacks. They were accused, among other things, of fostering aristocratic, unegalitarian ideas. One of the most bitter denunciations came from Henry Jacob Bigelow. In 1871, he wrote:

> The schools and colleges graduate every year a horde of young men, born to education, who settle away into insignificance, while the whole land is full of heroes who have fought their way to usefulness and eminence, . . . by sheer force of will and determination.[67]

Overlooking his own advantages as a highly educated Boston Brahmin, Bigelow claimed that "most eminent men are in a large degree self-made."[68] The Horatio Alger spirit was widespread. Reformers of medical education, like all academic reformers, had to justify intellectual elitism in a practical country traditionally hostile to elites, where deeply rooted democratic values remained strong, and where the belief persisted that capable young men from impoverished circumstances could, if provided the opportunity, work their way up.

Nevertheless, by the opening of Johns Hopkins in 1893, the outline of reform was in place. Despite trying circumstances, each of the pioneering schools survived. The forces promoting modern medical education had become apparent: the rise of scientific medicine; the emergence of an academic elite seeking full-time careers in teaching and research; and the rise of the modern university, which saw that it could extend its influence by controlling medical education. The events at Harvard, Pennsylvania, Michigan, and Johns Hopkins were to provide the model for all subsequent reform efforts in the United States.

Progressive Medical Education

From the proprietary schools of the Civil War to the Johns Hopkins Medical School of 1893, the teaching of medicine had changed dramatically. For convenience, these changes can be delineated as proceeding along three lines. First, a more rigorous curriculum was introduced—entrance requirements were established, terms were lengthened to nine months, the medical course was expanded to four years, and compulsory oral and written examinations were adopted. Second, many new subjects had been added. In the 1860s, the only scientific subject taught in detail was anatomy. By the opening of Johns Hopkins the curriculum had expanded to include anatomy, physiology, physiological chemistry, pathology, pharmacology, and bacteriology. Similarly, the clinical teaching had increased in scope to include not only the traditional courses of medicine, surgery, and obstetrics but also new courses in gynecology, pediatrics, dermatology, genito-urinary diseases, laryngology, opthalmalogy, otology, psychiatry, and hygiene. In addition, the courses were now arranged logically, with the scientific subjects preceding the clinical branches.

The third, and most important, change occurred in the methods by which medicine was taught. A revolution occurred in pedagogic style: the role of the student changed from passive observer to active participant in the learning process. The expansion in scope of the scientific and clinical teaching was important, but more fundamental still was the replacement of the lecture and demonstration by the laboratory and clerkship. Lectures, wrote the sharp-tongued Mall, were a "slow and stupid method of instruction," an outright "absurdity." The student must learn instead through personal study so that "he is upon the stage, not in the audience."[69] Through the laboratory and the clerkship students could learn by doing, not by watching. When William Thayer, a successor of Osler as the professor of medicine at Johns Hopkins, summarized the meaning of modern medical education as exemplified by Johns Hopkins since its inception, he chose the words: "Self-Education Under Guidance."[70]

This new philosophy of medical education, with learning by doing the key to its successful execution, had been fully enunciated by the time the Johns Hopkins Medical School opened. The new attitude appeared in the writings of virtually all of the first-generation medical educators, but no one articulated it more clearly or persistently than Billings. At issue were not only the techniques of medical education but its purpose and function. As Billings told the trustees of the Johns Hopkins Hospital in 1876, the mission of an educational institution is not "to turn out perfect scholars, so much as it is to fit men to go on studying and investigating for the rest of their lives."[71] He wrote in 1880: "An important part of the higher education of modern times is the teaching how to increase knowledge; and the best way of teaching this, as of many other things, is by doing it, and by causing the pupils to do it."[72] To Billings, such ideas applied to education at all levels, not just to medical education. Thus he said of elementary education: "The object of a school is not only to give information as to facts but as to how to ascertain facts, to teach the child how to investigate, how to think, where he is to look for information, and thus arouse and direct the desire for knowledge."[73] He wrote similarly about learning at the college level.[74]

To this group of educators, medical schools were now charged with a new mission: that of teaching how to acquire and interpret information. Old truths were not to go unchallenged, and the knowledge gained by doing and experiencing was to be valued far more highly than that learned from the traditional authorities, the lectures and textbooks. It was now deemed more important for students to be able to understand biological phenomena and to formulate judgments than to recite facts. This view of medical education stood in bold contrast to the prevailing view that the goal of medical education was to enforce the memorization of established facts and dogma. Without calling it such, the medical educators were espousing the ideas of what later came to be termed "progressive education," and if the above quotations were not known to be from Billings, one might easily presume they had been written a generation later by John Dewey.

The origins of progressive medical education lay in part in the procedural nature of medical practice. Doctors had always performed procedures, and this had provided the primary justification for such traditional educational devices as the apprenticeship, the house pupil program, the extramural schools, the

English plan of clerks and dressers, and the French system of interns and externs. In the nineteenth century, however, physicians began to use their hands and their senses much more extensively in managing patients. Physical diagnosis developed into a sophisticated and complex art; a host of new medical instruments had to be mastered; and surgeons became much bolder in the operations they attempted. Like any practical skill—whether navigating ships, drawing portraits, or playing a musical instrument—experience was necessary. A lecturer or textbook could not satisfactorily describe the peculiar rumbling sound of the heart murmur of mitral stenosis or the characteristic nodular consistency of the cirrhotic liver—these were things that had to be experienced to be understood fully. After the Civil War, medical educators became far more vocal about the urgency of learning by doing. "The whole art of medicine is in observation," Osler wrote ". . . to educate the eye to see, the ear to hear and the finger to feel."[75]

Even more at the heart of the new philosophy of medical education was an insight of revolutionary proportions: the recognition that medical knowledge is not something fixed but something that grows and evolves. By the 1870s an enormous increase in medical information was radically transforming medical thought and practice. The amount of medical literature began to become overwhelming. Even in America, where throughout the nineteenth century contributions to the literature had lagged far behind Europe, the number of medical journals had grown from eight in 1828 to fifty-four in 1878, and this merely presaged even more dramatic increases in the ensuing decades.[76] In 1880, the University of Michigan adopted a policy, soon followed by many other medical schools, whereby the purchase of textbooks for the library was deemphasized and the effort made instead to subscribe to every major medical journal of the world.[77] So great and so rapid was the increase of knowledge that as early as the 1890s medical educators were already admitting that medical schools, even with four-year courses and nine-month terms, could not even begin to scratch the surface of existing medical information. Physicians were groping for ways, wrote William Porter of Harvard, to cope with "the mass of knowledge in every department of medicine" that has "grown so huge as to overwhelm both professor and student."[78] Medical education, Osler wrote, had to be "a life-long process."[79]

Accentuating this sense of drowning in information was the coexistent revolution in the technology of communications. Between 1870 and 1900, daily newspaper circulation increased by seven times, the number of new books by over three times, the sale of postage stamps by eight times, and the miles of telegraph wire by nine times. Between 1876 and 1900, the number of telephones increased from 3,000 to 1.3 million.[80] For the first time in human history events across the world could be made known almost instantaneously. Osler remarked in 1905 how "within a week or ten days a great discovery in any part of the world is known everywhere."[81]

To those trying to cope with the onslaught of information in the computer age of the 1980s, the communications technology of the late nineteenth century was primitive and the amount of new information still modest. But to medical educators of the late nineteenth century, less important than the amount of new knowledge—though that was certainly important to them— was the idea that knowledge is not fixed. This realization conjured up images of a barely tapped pool of ideas that might take decades or even centuries to understand and that invalidated the traditional catechistic view of knowledge. This represented a qualitative change in outlook of inestimable importance and helped explain the change occurring in medicine and other fields whereby academic stature no longer resulted from the ability to defend but from the ability to overturn a position.

Medical educators of the latter nineteenth century were the first physicians in history to feel the real shock of the information explosion. "The time has gone by when one mind can encompass all which has been ascertained in the medical sciences,"[82] Welch wrote in 1886. Even more disconcerting than the impossibility of knowing the whole of medicine, a medical student or physician could take little comfort in that which he thought he did know; old beliefs might easily be disproved in the onslaught of new information. So quickly will medical knowledge grow, Billings told a graduating class at the University of Pennsylvania Medical School, that "your new text books will be antiquated in five years."[83] A student or physician could no longer rely on precepts enunciated *ex cathedra*, even when proclaimed by the greatest of authorities. Proof had to be adduced—proof that could be verified with one's own senses. "The method of authority has given way to the method of observation and inquiry,"[84] Thayer noted. Or, as Mall stated more bluntly, "When anatomy is studied in this way [through dissection rather than through lectures], the student must indeed be stupid not to discover the many defects as well as errors in some of our favorite English text-books."[85]

To this group of pioneering medical educators, there was only one viable response to the challenge imposed by the proliferation of medical knowledge: to recast medical education so that it should have a procedural rather than a substantive emphasis. The aim of medical education had to be that of instilling proper techniques of acquiring and evaluating information rather than merely providing facts. "To cover the vast field of medicine in four years is an impossible task," Osler wrote. "We can only instill principles, put the students in the right path, give him methods, teach him how to study, and early to discern between essentials and non-essentials."[86] Medical students needed to be taught that knowledge obtained or verified with one's senses was much more reliable than that provided by books and lectures. "To really know about things it is necessary to come into direct contact with them and study them," Welch explained. The medical student learns that "only this knowledge is real and living, and not that which comes . . . from reading or being told about things, or, still less, merely thinking about them."[87] A physician could no longer depend on what he had learned in medical schools to last a professional lifetime, but by mastering the skill of acquiring information—what Welch called the "scientific habit of thought"—he might still manage to keep up-to-date. To provide such critical skills was perceived as the new purpose of medical education. The era of "mental discipline" had passed at the American medical school as well as at the American college.

In the late nineteenth century, medicine was not the only discipline undergoing a rapid proliferation of information. In many cases, as Morton White has shown, scholars in quite different fields responded to a growing state of knowledge in a similar way: by rejecting deductive logic, traditional authority, and dry, sterile textbook learning. Instead many intellectuals became cultists of experience, embracing empiricism and an evolutionary concept of knowledge. White has called this their "revolt against formalism," and in this way he related the efforts of such thinkers as Thorstein Veblen in economics, Oliver Wendell Holmes, Jr., in law, and Charles A. Beard in history.[88] As the new breed of medical educators rejected the lecture and textbook for the laboratory and the bedside, as they abandoned traditional medical concepts when contradicted by empirical discoveries, and as they recognized the growing and evolving nature of medical science and practice, they revolted against formalism in medical education in an analogous fashion to thinkers in other fields.

Among those who revolted against formalism was John Dewey. He, too, as White has pointed out, was one of the many at the turn of the century who was influenced by the recognition that knowledge grows and evolves.[89] There appears to have been no direct intellectual connection between the pioneering medical educators and Dewey. Many studies of Dewey's educational views have correctly emphasized the formative influence of Hegel, pragmatism, and experimental psychology.[90] Nevertheless, the medical educators and Dewey lived in analogous environments. Late nineteenth-century society was rapidly changing, not just the various academic fields. What was necessary for survival, for both the physician and citizen, was not merely the possession of certain facts but rather the ability to solve problems, to find out new information for oneself, to cast aside old habits and beliefs for the new. The logical relation of these developments to the philosophy of progressive education is clear, and Oscar Handlin has appropriately pointed out their significance as another formative influence on Dewey's thought.[91] It was no accident, therefore, that Dewey and the medical educators independently developed similar educational theories despite the great distance between their respective academic disciplines. Both were responding to general phenomena—the idea that knowledge and the environment are not fixed—that transcended their particular disciplinary spheres. Herein lay the connection between progressive education in the elementary school and progressive education in the medical school.

In the basic science teaching, the epitome of progressive education in the medical classroom was Mall's anatomy course at Johns Hopkins. Mall, one of the most biting spokesmen for the inductive approach to medical education, made clear his desire to train the "scientific physician" rather than the "shoemaker physician who will drift into ruts and never get out of them."[92] His concern was not so much to equip the student with facts as to instill in him the capacity to acquire facts as needed. "To establish the habit of observing and reflecting, while at work with the scalpel and microscope, is of far greater importance to the student than memorizing the subject matter for the sake of a quiz, an examination, or some subsequent clinical study."[93] Mall's method was to teach by not teaching. He would assign students to part of a cadaver, provide them a list of references and simple instructions on dissection and the use of the microscope, and leave them to their work. The anatomy laboratory was kept open from Monday morning until Saturday evening, and although Mall and his staff would be present daily to quiz students and discuss problems, Mall never lectured or provided any structured instruction of the spoon-feeding type. He told students that the human body was their textbook and that they should each be responsible for their own learning. To students not accustomed to taking their problems into their own hands and solving them, such seeming neglect caused many anxious moments of floundering and frustration. A favorite apocryphal story students enjoyed telling of Mall was that when he was asked by his wife how to bathe their first baby, he replied, "Just throw her in the water and let her work out her own technique."[94]

In the clinical teaching, the embodiment of progressive education was Osler's clerkship in internal medicine. As Mall had his students learn from cadavers, Osler's students learned from live patients, with lectures and textbooks regarded as adjuncts only. In "the natural method of teaching," as Osler called it, "the student begins with the patient, continues with the patient, and ends his studies with the patient, using books and lectures as tools, as means to an end."[95] Osler made the hospital a medical school, the students living and working in the hospital "as part of its machinery, as an essential part of the work of the wards."[96] Students were expected to take careful histories of their patients' illnesses, perform thorough physical examinations, conduct the routine laboratory tests, follow the moment-by-moment course of their patients' condition, and make suggestions regarding management. In this way they obtained a personal knowledge of disease and therapy, gleaning some sense of the infinite phases and variations that disease takes in real patients in contrast to its stereotyped behavior in textbooks. Students were not expected to learn everything that is known about internal medicine but to master "principles of practice," to gain some feeling for "when to act and when to refrain," thereby possibly escaping the " 'nickle-in-the-slot' attitude of mind" with which so many physicians treated patients.[97]

In introducing the laboratory and clerkship into the medical curriculum, the pioneering medical educators were aware that they had borrowed those teaching devices from Europe. The laboratory tradition was already strong in Germany, and bedside clinical teaching was equally well established in England, Scotland, and France. Clearly, the new ideas owed little of their origin to an indigenous American tradition. Rarely, however, do ideas undergo drastic changes of location and culture without undergoing modification. Such was the case in medical education. In England, the opportunities to work as clerks and dressers were limited, in part because positions were few, open only to winners of competitive examinations, and in part because they were costly, affordable only by the wealthier students. At eminent teaching institutions such as Guy's Hospital, clerks and dressers formed a student aristocracy, the majority of students having to be content with merely walking the wards.[98] Similarly, in France, residency in a hospital had become firmly established as the desirable way to learn medicine and surgery, but here, too, hospital residency was reserved for an elite selected by competitive examination.[99] In Germany, the opportunity to work in the laboratory was not provided for undergraduate medical students but was limited to advanced students doing research. The German system neglected the ordinary student as it rewarded the brilliant one. The typical undergraduate medical student had to be content with a diet of didactic lectures and mechanical, listless laboratory demonstrations, while he watched his postgraduate colleagues luxuriating in the magnificent environment of the German laboratory.[100]

In America, medical educators transformed as they borrowed. The unique feature to their ideas was the concept that ideal medical education should be provided for *every* student, not just for the few. A firm foundation, Osler pointed out, was necessary for the seven-eighths of the medical students hoping to become sensible practitioners, not just for the one-eighth who might be contemplating careers in teaching and research.[101] It was necessary, argued

Mall, that "good habits in working, observing, and thinking" through proper laboratory instruction be acquired by every student, regardless of "whether his future career is in medicine, in laryngology, or in embryology."[102] This, then, was the American achievement in medical education: making the best available training the standard for every student who entered the field. As the profession became more and more reserved for the educated elite, it became more democratic within. This provided one useful counter for educators trying to establish an aristocracy of intellect in a country whose fundamental values remained democratic and egalitarian.

Even in the 1890s, however, as progressive medical education was flourishing at Johns Hopkins and the other pioneering medical schools, notes of disquietude began to appear. A few began to worry whether the new approach could accomplish in practice what it promised in theory. It was easy to disparage the lecture or textbook, but no one, even Mall and Osler, could do without them. Mall would not lecture himself, but he assigned lectures in the anatomy course—admittedly few in number compared with traditional anatomy courses—to members of his staff.[103] Osler continued the tradition of the amphitheater clinics and urged students to read, particularly the classic descriptions of diseases by the great masters. In a period of burgeoning information, his interest in the history of medicine was exceeded by no one, and he wrote the most important medical textbook of the era.

"Self-education under guidance" had become the theme of the new breed of medical educators, but they failed to confront the issue of how much self-education was needed and how much guidance. Nowhere was that more apparent than in the classes of Mall, the most extreme advocate of the new educational ideas. Mall essentially left his students on their own, copying the model of liberty in education he had seen employed with the postgraduate research students in the German laboratories. The brilliant students loved him (at least twenty of his students became professors of anatomy).[104] But the average students often found his methods exasperating, and they deeply resented his apparent indifference toward anyone without the potential to be an independent researcher. Once Mall encountered a student in the dissecting room doing nothing and inquired what was wrong. When the student answered that he did not know what to do, Mall placed a janitor's broom in the student's hand and left, without saying a word.[105] Perhaps Mall had forgotten that the students he had known investigating medicine in the German laboratories represented only the unusually gifted.

In theory, progressive medical education emphasized a procedural rather than a substantive approach, but in practice it quickly became apparent that such an ideal was difficult to achieve. As the amount of medical knowledge increased, a growing body of information became indispensable for every competent physician. The curriculum became more and more crowded, and faculty concerns for developing their students' powers of reasoning were often forgotten in a frantic effort to make certain that the students had mastered —by memory—all the facts they needed to know. Under such stresses, even so brilliant a medical student as the neurosurgeon Harvey Cushing became clinically depressed during his second year at Harvard Medical School in 1893.[106] By the end of the first generation of Johns Hopkins, William Thayer was publicly acknowledging "the discouragement felt by some students owing to the extremely crowded and dull character of the curriculum."[107] From the beginning, the modern medical curriculum contained much more rote than enthusiasts sometimes cared to admit. The courses could be dry and unstimulating even at the very best schools.

Nevertheless, to knowledgeable observers in the 1890s, it was clear that a substantial and necessary change in emphasis had occurred. At the pioneering schools the students' role had been transformed from a passive one to a much more active one in the learning process. "Learning by doing" had become the hallmark of the new education. Few who understood the new methods doubted their superiority over the old, the many deficiencies and unresolved problems of the new methods notwithstanding. Such an attitude was demonstrated in 1899 by a committee of fifteen Harvard Medical School students that prepared, at the faculty's request, a long report ascertaining the attitude of the student body toward the methods of instruction employed at the medical school.[108] The report was detailed, candid, and at times caustic. The students agreed completely in principle with the philosophy of progressive medical education; their criticisms pertained to the imperfect realization of those principles in practice, particularly in the clinical subjects, where they felt much more extensive bedside experience was needed. The Harvard curriculum was clearly only an incomplete success. Nonetheless, it was apparent that the new educational principles had fully permeated the school. With students evaluating their own courses, there could be no better example of medical students taking responsibility for their own education. That was what progressive medical education was meant to accomplish. Even though it rarely achieved in practice what it promised to accomplish in theory, progressive medical education became the ideal to which medical educators have aspired from the pioneering period through the present.

4 The Spread of

Educational Reform

WHETHER the early reforms of medical education would succeed was anybody's guess. In the 1870s the cause of educational reform was perilous; in the 1880s, it was highly uncertain at best. Harvard, Michigan, and Pennsylvania were commonly regarded as well-intentioned anomalies. Their reforms were widely praised, but few initially dared follow in their path.

In the mid-1880s, American medical education entered a new era. The changes were already apparent by the opening of the Johns Hopkins Medical School in 1893, and in the seventeen years thereafter improvements occurred even more rapidly. During this period the ideas implemented at the pioneering medical schools spread to the rest of the medical schools and took firm hold. Schools expanded their programs—at first to three years, later to four; from terms of four, five, or six months to seven, eight, or nine. Entrance requirements were strengthened and new subjects introduced. Most important, the new methods of teaching were copied: following the innovations employed at the pioneering schools, the shift was from didactic to practical instruction, using the laboratory and clerkship whenever possible. By 1910, contrary to the popular myth engendered by the Flexner report, American medical education was at its most advanced condition ever.

Unlike the innovative period, the period between 1885 and 1910 witnessed no major contribution to the pedagogic discussion of how medicine should be taught. The importance of teaching the scientific subjects; the shift from didactic to practical training; the view that traditional teachings should be discarded when contradicted by empirical evidence; the ideal that students should learn to reason rather than be forced to memorize—these concepts had been unequivocally stated by the pioneering medical educators in the 1870s and 1880s. The developmental period instead was a time for the diffusion and implementation of the new educational principles. Medical schools across the land—the second, third, fourth, and fifth tier schools as well as the front-ranking schools—started to emulate the changes introduced by Harvard, Pennsylvania, Michigan, and Johns Hopkins. This process occurred slowly and hesitatingly at first, but after 1900 it accelerated into a powerful and unstoppable movement.

Although the developmental period represented another stage, one thing remained in common with the pioneering period: the impulse for reform came from the medical schools. Through the Civil War the medical schools had been the archenemies of reform but now the better schools were the primary forces working on behalf of modern educational ideals. In the pioneering stages of the 1870s and 1880s, as well as in the developmental stages of the 1890s and 1900s, educational reform did not need a strong American Medical Association, aggressive national foundations, or enlightened (some would say dictatorial) philanthropists, although these groups certainly supported and helped further the reforms at a later date. Nor did the cause of reform yet require a knowledgeable and demanding public as manifested by state licensing boards. State licensing laws, as the dean of the Drake College of Medicine remarked in 1905, "came too late to do more than punish the deliberate wrongdoers."[1] Rather, in the developmental period, as in the pioneering period before it, educational reform sprang from the schools—or, that is, from the German-influenced physicians who had gained control of them, and from the affiliated universities that encouraged them to remain true to pure academic ideals.

The Reform Movement Gains Strength

In the mid-1880s, a new attitude began to appear at American medical schools. Gradually, the successes of the pioneering schools inspired attempts at emulation. In 1885, the College of Medicine of the University of Southern California in Los Angeles was founded. At its first meeting the faculty unanimously declared its unwillingness "to have any hand in the organization of any school other than the *very best.*"[2] Joseph Widney, the dean, corresponded with officials at Harvard and Pennsylvania to learn the details of their new programs.[3] After studying these programs, the College of Medicine decided to follow a similar plan. When it opened, it offered a three-year graded course with six-month terms, with the first year devoted to the scientific subjects.

Across the country, an established school, the College of Physicians and Surgeons in New York, was evolving from an old-fashioned proprietary school into a modern medical school to be affiliated with Columbia University. In 1888, after studying the admission policies of Harvard and Pennsylvania, Physicians and Surgeons established an entrance examination for those who did not have a degree from a college or scientific school.[4] In 1893, after examining the details of the programs at Pennsylvania, Harvard, and Michigan, the faculty established its own four-year course so that it might keep "the College of Physicians in the front rank of the medical schools."[5]

In the early 1880s the reform movement was still weak. Yale had adopted in 1879 a three-year graded program that substituted laboratory and clinical work for instruction by lectures alone, but the school's enrollment fell precipitously and did not recover for a full decade.[6] In 1882, as noted earlier, the suggestion that members be required to provide a three-year graded course with six-month terms brought about the demise of the American Medical College Association. In the next decade, however, the reform movement gained much more strength. In 1890 the defunct Association successfully reorganized as the Association of American Medical Colleges, with the three-year rule now a requirement.[7] By 1893, over 90 percent of the medical colleges offered a three-year course,[8] and the leading schools were already introducing compulsory four-year programs. The purpose of the longer course was to introduce the scientific subjects, the clinical specialties, and more personalized methods of instruction. Enrollment at the University of Pennsylvania remained at a satisfactory level following the school's introduction in 1893 of a four-year rule. Provost William Pepper ebulliently exclaimed, "It was recognized at once that the battle for Higher Medical Education [at his school] was won."[9]

Reformers of the 1890s enjoyed certain advantages compared with reformers of the 1870s. One was the success of the pioneering schools. In medical education, as in other spheres of life, it was easier to follow than to establish an example. A second advantage was that of sheer numbers. When Harvard, Pennsylvania, and Michigan introduced laboratory instruction in the 1870s, few in America understood or valued what they had done. This was not the case in the 1890s. Year-by-year, older physicians ignorant of scientific medicine had retired, and their ranks had been partially refilled with graduates of Harvard, Pennsylvania, and Michigan. For instance, between 1879 and 1893, the University of Pennsylvania trained 1,834 doctors, and of these, 44 had already been elected to professorships in medical schools by 1893, while 29 held appointments as lecturers and 48 as assistants.[10]

After it opened, the Johns Hopkins Medical School became the single most potent influence ever for the dissemination of scientific medical education in America. Not only did it inspire by example, but many of its graduates and instructors subsequently joined medical schools all over the country. In this way the influence of Johns Hopkins eventually spread, as Richard Shryock has pointed out, "to Harvard, Yale, and Rochester in the Northeast; to Minnesota, Wisconsin, and Washington University in the Middle West; to Duke, Vanderbilt, and Virginia in the South; and to California and Stanford on the West Coast."[11] The first Johns Hopkins professor of surgery, William Halsted, saw eleven of his seventeen surgical residents become full professors at important medical schools.[12] William Welch could not hide his glee when he described to Franklin Mall the Johns Hopkins influence at the Harvard-run service of the Boston City Hospital in 1900. "They have only Hopkins men there, and want no others. . . . It really was a spectacle to see our men occupying all the places there."[13]

The ranks of scientific physicians in the 1890s were increased by those who had returned from postgraduate study in Germany or Austria. When Harvard introduced its new program in 1871, the number of American physicians who had undergone such training was still small, but two decades later the intellectual migration was in full force. Those who studied abroad returned to the United States with an understanding that scientific methods and knowledge were important to medical practice. While in Europe they acquired, as Thomas Bonner has pointed out, "an abiding respect for knowledge and research and an understanding of the spirit of a true university."[14] This group of returning emigrees played a crucial role in the acceptance of modern medical education in the United States. Many of them joined the faculties of medical schools, and as a group they represented a disproportionately large percentage of the leadership of the medical profession of their generation.[15] By the 1890s, therefore, there was much more fertile soil in which the new educational views could take root.

Most important, reformers in the 1890s had firmer evidence to support their conviction that scientific medicine worked. In the 1860s and 1870s it was still an article of faith that laboratory discoveries could be of clinical significance; in the 1890s that contention could no longer be legitimately doubted. There were many great discoveries in the latter nineteenth century. One thinks immediately of such fundamental advances as the theory of cellular pathology. However, no development carried more force than the germ theory of disease and the emergence of modern bacteriology. The germ theory was to medical thought of the nineteenth century what the theory of evolution was to biological thought—the overridingly important idea of the century, and one with very broad social implications. Compared with the theory of evolution, whose development, reception, and impact has received detailed and insightful attention among historians, the germ theory of disease, surprisingly, is a relatively unexplored historical topic.[16] Nevertheless, its impact was no less real, immediate, or dramatic, and it prepared the way for the acceptance of a laboratory-based medical education more than any other single scientific event. Explaining why laboratories in recent years had come to be regarded as so important to teaching and research, an official of the University of Minnesota in 1902 identified one predominant cause: "the theories now well advanced of the germ origin of disease."[17]

The germ theory in its modern form was articulated in the 1860s by Louis Pasteur, who disproved the notion of the "spontaneous generation" of life. In 1876, Robert Koch demonstrated that anthrax, a disease of cattle, was caused by a specific bacteriological organism, and he developed in 1882 the first solid culture media and the accompanying methods by which single species of microorganisms could be isolated and identified. Within the next several years a host of diseases had been proved to be of microbiological origin, including many of the greatest scourges of the human race (table 4.1). To William Welch, attending Koch's first public course in the new science of bacteriology at the Hygienic Institute in Berlin in 1884, the germ theory meant that "the glorious sun of the new day was well above the horizon."[18] So powerful was the sweep of the germ theory that it gave rise to hopes, which were not unreasonable in the context of the period, that perhaps all diseases might one day be found to have a microbial origin. Thus the dean of the medical school of Tufts predicted in 1901 that "other diseases still regarded now as of questionable origin, as cancer, rheumatic fever, chorea, and various other affections, will shortly be included in the ranks of the germ diseases."[19]

The germ theory of disease was not merely a useful intellectual construct; it brought with it indisputable practical benefits. Applied to the prevention of infection in the operating room, it ushered in the era of modern surgery. Applied to the public health, it provided scientific direction to the sometimes flagging and ineffectual efforts of old-fashioned hygienists and sanitationists. The boundary between medicine and public health in this period was never distinct. By enabling more accurate diagnosis and identifying how diseases were spread, medical knowledge contributed directly to the growing improvements in public health. For instance, in 1884, a specific microbial cause was found for the dreaded typhoid fever. This led to the discovery that typhoid

TABLE 4.1

Bacteriologic Origin of Certain Diseases

Disease	Microorganism	Year Relationship Established
Relapsing fever	Spirocheta recurrentis	1873
Anthrax (splenic fever)	Bacillus anthracis	1876
Gonorrhea	Micrococcus gonorrhoeae	1879
Malaria	Plasmodium malariae	1880
Glanders	Bacillus mallei	1882
Asiatic cholera	Spirillum cholerae	1883
Diphtheria	Bacillus diphtheriae	1884
Pneumonia	Diplococcus pneumoniae	1884
Tuberculosis	Bacillus tuberculosis	1884
Typhoid fever	Bacillus typhosus	1884
Malta fever (undulant fever, brucellosis)	Bacillus melitensis	1887
Cerebrospinal meningitis	Micrococcus meningitidis	1887
Tetanus (lockjaw)	Bacillus tetani	1889
Influenza	Bacillus influenzae	1892
Bubonic plague (black death)	Bacillus pestis	1894
Dysentery	Bacillus dysenteriae	1898
Syphilis	Treponema pallidum	1905

SOURCE: Adapted from N. P. Colwell, "Medical Education, 1915," in U.S. Department of the Interior, Bureau of Education, *Report of the Commissioner of Education* (Washington, D.C.: Government Printing Office, 1915), 191.

fever was usually transmitted through water that had been contaminated by sewage containing the bacterium, which in turn led to intensified efforts to purify the water supply that ultimately brought that deadly illness under control.[20] In the context of late-nineteenth-century society, where life expectancy had not yet reached fifty years and where suffering and premature death had been considered unalterable realities of the human condition, these developments were thrilling.

The germ theory of disease was accompanied by other major achievements in medical science and technology. The late nineteenth century witnessed the beginnings of immunology and endocrinology. The most important practical application was the use of thyroid extract to treat myxedema. Vaccines were developed against rabies, typhoid, and bubonic plague, and effective treatments with antitoxins were discovered for diptheria and tetanus. Diagnosis became more refined with the development of chemical, hematologic, serologic, and bacteriologic tests of blood, urine, and other body fluids and tissues. Suspicion of an infection could be readily confirmed by an elevated white cell count in the blood or by a positive culture of a specific organism; diabetes could easily be detected by testing the urine or blood for sugar. Diagnostic sophistication was heightened by other new technologies such as

X rays and electrocardiographs.[21] What was crucial in the minds of medical educators was that these were not chance empirical discoveries (X rays being the major exception) but the results of systematic laboratory investigations applying fundamental principles of chemistry and biology. No longer was scientific knowledge something esoteric; it was now essential for everyone who wished to be considered a modern practitioner.

In the 1890s and 1900s, definitive medical preventions or cures were still very few. Many recent writers have reminded us of the limited curative potential of medicine circa 1900 and have shown that most of the improvement in human life expectancy in the latter nineteenth and early twentieth centuries resulted from better sanitation and nutrition, not from the direct intervention of medical therapies.[22] Although this claim cannot be disputed, such a viewpoint is incomplete because it does not permit us to understand the enthusiasm for scientific medicine that was clearly pervading the medical profession and general public by that time.

Why such enthusiasm for scientific medicine, if definitive cures were so few? Part of the answer lies in the fact that equating the effectiveness of medicine with therapeutic cures represents a very narrow view of what doctors do and ignores the other important functions of medicine, such as alleviating suffering, prolonging life, and providing reliable diagnosis and prognosis. By such standards, medicine at the turn of the century had already made much progress. Victims of crippling bone fractures could enjoy a much better life because of modern orthopedic surgery, and sufferers of arthritis benefited enormously from the introduction of aspirin in 1899. Those with severe chest colds would be greatly relieved to be told by a doctor that they had not contracted pneumonia. Cure was not the only benefit of a visit to the doctor.

In addition, one must not overlook the excitement that was created as more and more came to be known about the causes and mechanisms of disease. The baffling and terrifying world of illness was finally becoming intelligible and comprehensible. For the first time a sense of intellectual order was being brought to these dreaded problems. As researchers learned what went wrong to cause disease, popular terror diminished, for people feared less that which they could understand. For this reason, confidence in experimental medicine increased, even though cures were not immediately in sight.

Finally, and perhaps most important, much enthusiasm resulted from physicians' confidence that they had captured the method by which future discoveries, including treatments, would be made. No physician of the period was content with the state of knowledge, and none are today. But a new conviction was arising among doctors that the technique for the future conquest of disease—experimental laboratory research—had come into their possession. In the 1870s, this view was very much an article of faith, largely confined to the nucleus of physicians who had studied in the basic science laboratories of Germany. By the 1890s, however, the power of the experimental approach had become a matter of demonstrated accomplishment through the germ theory of disease and other discoveries. It did not matter that practical clinical benefits of scientific medicine were still few; what counted was that the process of discovery had been normalized. Through experimental research, there was the promise of better things to come. The result was an outpouring of enthusiasm for scientific medicine far out of proportion to the tangible practical results that had been thus far produced.

This emphasis on scientific method, as social historians will recognize, was part of a larger faith in science held by many Americans during the Progressive Era. Fostered in a major way by the theory of evolution, this reverence of science was manifested by a number of related popular attitudes: the notion that scientific knowledge represented the most dependable form of knowledge; the mystique of the expert; and the erosion of the layman's confidence in his ability to handle problems by himself. These attitudes pervaded many areas of American life at the turn of the century, from business to government to social reform. Such attitudes underlay the rising prestige of the medical profession in the early twentieth century and, as we shall later see, helped persuade philanthropists and state legislatures to begin providing funds for medical education and research.

By the 1890s, then, American medical education had entered a new era. The imperative to place medical education on a scientific foundation with personalized instruction was unequivocal; any residual doubts could no longer be justified after the enunciation of the germ theory of disease. As Welch later observed, "The advancement and development of medicine in itself required an improvement in the methods of teaching medicine."[23] With the quality of American medical graduates beginning to improve, and with so many doctors returning from postgraduate study abroad, the number of physicians who understood that medical education needed to change had grown much larger. The circumstances had become propitious for reform.

The Diffusion of Educational Ideals

The events at Washington University in St. Louis between 1890 and 1910 were indicative of how medical education at the better schools improved during those two decades. Medical education at Washington University began in 1891 when the St. Louis Medical College, an independent institution, became the Washington University Medical Department.[24] In 1899, the Missouri Medical College merged with the school, and in 1906, the medical school became a full university department. Although until 1906 the school had been a proprietary school (owned and operated by the faculty, and dependent for income upon student fees), from the very beginning it had distinguished itself from the other thirty-odd schools that had come and gone during the first one hundred years of Missouri medicine.[25] By 1900 the school had lengthened its term to eight months, adopted a four-year curriculum, expanded its course offerings, increased its teaching staff, and constructed new laboratories for instruction in chemistry, anatomy, and physiology. All such changes were accomplished in spite of the faculty's fear that the innovations might result in a significant loss of class size and revenue. Enrollment, in fact, declined much less than expected and soon was rising again.

The pace of improvement accelerated after 1900. In 1902, the school obtained a new building for laboratory teaching in anatomy, pathology, histology, bacteriology, and organic chemistry. The various laboratories possessed the latest and most precise instruments and apparatus.[26] Early in the century, after the school remodeled the Washington University clinic and hospital, it expanded the amount of clinical teaching as well. The school began offering new clinical electives, mainly in the various specialties, and the clinical faculty grew substantially in size.[27]

In the 1900s Washington University also introduced important changes in its methods of teaching. More and more, the lecture, recitation, and textbook were supplanted by the student's active participation in learning. With laboratory experiments in the preclinical subjects and bedside case teaching in the clinical courses, students were expected to experience the actual conditions of medical practice rather than simply to hear about them. Emphasis was placed on problem solving rather than on the mere mastery of a large number of facts. Students were warned in the school's catalog that more mistakes "were made in the practice of medicine by failure to 'examine' and 'look' and 'search' than by lack of knowledge."[28]

Before 1910, such methods were most effectively employed in the preclinical subjects, where the necessary laboratory facilities were available. In gross anatomy, almost the entire course was taught by dissection; in physiology, students performed experiments in groups of two on the frog and in groups of four on mammals; in pathology, students prepared and studied histological sections and performed several autopsies; in bacteriology, students learned to cultivate bacteria, isolate organisms in pure culture, and identify the various species. The school was less successful in introducing such techniques into the clinical instruction, mainly because its hospital facilities were poor.

Even so, in surgery students performed practice operations upon cadavers, and in obstetrics they attended several deliveries. Instruction in physical diagnosis was extensive and thorough.[29] It was thought that "no student ought to be graduated . . . who has not had the opportunity to observe and study sick people in bed."[30] In the four years of the medical course, about half the hours were spent in laboratories, autopsy rooms, clinics, and wards, the other half being given to didactic teaching.[31] The new educational philosophy of "learning by doing" was not yet employed as fully or effectively as at Johns Hopkins, Harvard, or Pennsylvania, but the faculty had clearly adopted a similar approach.

The events at Washington University were not unusual. Between 1885 and 1910, similar changes occurred with monotonous regularity at medical schools across the country. From faculty and trustee minutes, catalogs, corresondence, special reports, and other surviving archival materials, the same story could be told about the medical schools of Bowdoin, Dartmouth, Tufts, and Yale in the Northeast; New York University, Columbia, Georgetown, and George Washington along the mid-Atlantic coast; Pittsburgh, Western Reserve, Cincinnati, Minnesota, St. Louis University, Nebraska, Kansas, and Drake in the Middle West; Tulane and the Atlanta College of Physicians and Surgeons in the South; and Denver and Gross, Colorado, Southern California, and California in the West. None of these schools became a modern medical school instantaneously. Rather, they developed gradually, year-by-year, improvement by improvement. The impulse in each case came from within the faculties. External organizations such as the Association of American Medical Colleges, the American Medical Association, and the state licensing boards were rarely mentioned in the records of any of these schools during this period. Unlike the reforms at Harvard, Michigan, and Pennsylvania, the improvements at these schools occurred quietly, almost without notice. The importance of expanding and strengthening the curriculum was now taken for granted. Some schools enjoyed more success than others. By 1910, Western Reserve and Minnesota had developed much further than Georgetown and George Washington. Nevertheless, all had unmistakably entered the modern era.

The pattern of gradual, quiet, unpretentious evolution was the common route by which modern medical education emerged at most schools. In some instances, however, modern medical education appeared in mature form precipitately with the birth of the schools. Examples of this pattern included Oklahoma (organized in 1898), West Virginia (1902), Wake Forest (1902), Indiana (1903), Mississippi (1903), Fordham (1905), Utah (1906), and Wisconsin (1907).[32]

The prototype of such schools was the Cornell University Medical College, an unusually strong medical school that was founded in 1898. This school opened with the good fortune not only of having an exceptional faculty but also of having received a $1,500,000 gift for the construction of a well-equipped laboratory building.[33] From the start, the faculty was committed to providing scientific instruction of the highest type. It required four years of instruction, and it had its students learn by doing. Teaching in the first two years was given "almost wholly in the laboratories and dissecting-room and by recitations," while instruction in the final two years was marked by "the almost complete abolition of didactic lectures in the practical branches of medicine and surgery, and the substitution therefore of daily bedside teaching in the [hospital] wards."[34] Immediately, Cornell joined Johns Hopkins, Harvard, Columbia, Pennsylvania, Western Reserve, and Michigan in the forefront of the country's medical schools.

The thrust of the reforms of this period, whether at new schools or old, was the same as in the pioneering years of the 1870s and 1880s. The medical course became much longer and more rigorous, and the basic sciences and clinical specialties were brought into the curriculum. More important, the new methods of teaching were adopted, making the student an active participant in the learning process. The most effective method of medical teaching, the president of Yale wrote in 1890, is "the method of personal instruction, which has taken the place of the method of instruction by lectures only."[35]

In addition, the new educational ideal of making students thinkers rather than memorizers spread widely among American medical schools. In practice that meant three things. One was the cultivation of critical skills—"a habit of mind," as a publication of the University of Maryland School of Medicine called it—that would enable students "to see and judge facts in their true relations, to know the true from the false, to discriminate and adjust."[36] A second skill was the ability to learn for oneself, enabling a doctor to stay up-to-date once his formal education had been completed. A third related skill was the ability to deal with the unknowns that regularly occur in medical practice. Every physician, George Dock told a group of clinical clerks at Michigan in 1907, "must be able to recognize from what he has learned before new things, e.g., recognize unknown diseases by working them out from the diseases he has known before."[37] This could be done only if students developed the capacity to generalize from facts and principles already known.

Although certain educational ideals gained wide acceptance during this period, the teaching of all subjects did not progress equally. In general, instruction improved more dramatically in the scientific than in the clinical subjects. As will be discussed in chapter 8 in detail, this was because medical schools at this time possessed much better facilities for laboratory than for clinical teaching. Among the basic sciences, as the excellent essays in an important volume edited by Ronald Numbers have indicated, progress also occurred unevenly.[38] Physiology tended to be the best taught of the basic sciences. By 1896, William Welch could say that "every properly equipped medical college has a physiology laboratory."[39] Pharmacology tended to be the weakest of the group, lagging behind the others despite the intense promotional efforts of John Jacob Abel at Johns Hopkins. Biochemistry and anatomy were in the middle and were inconsistent in quality from school to school, but with biochemistry rising in influence and anatomy falling, as measured by time and resources devoted to the subjects. Even in the subjects that were not as well taught, however, the difference in quality from medical education of the previous generation was immense. In all subjects the worst teaching of 1900 was usually better than the best of 1870.

Compared with the innovative period, a new group of physicians was taking charge of medical education. Many leaders of American medical education of the 1890s and 1900s had not taken postgraduate medical study abroad, though doctors with European training remained prominent. Nor were many medical educators native Germans who had emigrated to the United States after completing their studies. Although a few such persons achieved national reputations in teaching or research—for instance, Adolf Meyer, Abraham Jacobi, Samuel Meltzer, Jacques Loeb, and Christian Fenger—this group was not particularly large in numbers or in influence (unlike the small group of emigree physicists that in the 1940s was instrumental in the creation of molecular biology).[40]

Rather, in the 1890s, and even more in the 1900s, it was American medical graduates without any European educational experience who assumed the leadership of medical education. This occurred as the American pilgrimage to Germany began to decline and as American schools improved in quality. Such prominent early twentieth-century medical school deans as George Blumer of Yale, Henry Christian of Harvard, Thomas Arbuthnot of Pittsburgh, Christian Holmes of Cincinnati, and W. Jarvis Barlow of the University of Southern California were trained entirely in the United States. So were eminent medical scientists of the period such as Joseph Erlanger and Walter Cannon. These features were also apparent in the composition of medical school faculties. For instance, every member of the Tufts medical faculty in 1893 had been trained exclusively in America, as had thirteen of thirty members of the Washington University faculty of 1900, nine of eleven senior members of the Bowdoin faculty of 1905, and fifty-nine of eighty-seven members of the Minnesota faculty of 1910.[41]

Nevertheless, at the turn of the century, the German influence remained strong. Indeed, it provided the dominant ethos of American medicine. However, the German influence was becoming indirect. Nowhere was this transition illustrated more clearly than it was in Cannon, perhaps the greatest of all American experimental physiologists, who did not train abroad. Cannon was a student of the Harvard physiologist Henry Bowditch, who had worked closely with Carl Ludwig in Germany. Under Bowditch's expert tutelage, Cannon had mastered the German experimental approach as well as anyone. For this reason Cannon described himself as an "intellectual son" of Bowditch and an "intellectual grandson" of Ludwig.[42] Thus, a major step had occurred in the domestication of German academic ideals. An American no longer needed to go abroad to learn about scientific medicine and understand the need to place medical education upon a sound scientific footing.

As a result, less and less in the 1890s, and hardly at all in the 1900s, did medical schools introduce reforms with an eye toward the methods of teaching in Leipzig, Strassburg, Breslau, Berlin, or Vienna. More and more, they strengthened their programs with an eye toward one another instead. Improvements at one school often led to similar changes at other places. For instance, in 1898 the faculty of Cornell organized its pathology course after studying how the subject was taught at "the various leading medical colleges," including Columbia, Harvard, Pennsylvania, Johns Hopkins, Yale, and Bellevue.[43] In 1899, the Pennsylvania faculty reviewed the teaching of obstetrics and gynecology at Harvard, Johns Hopkins, and the Long Island Medical College.[44] Nebraska changed its curriculum in 1904 after studying the course of instruction at ten leading medical colleges, east and west.[45] In 1907, an official of Western Reserve looked to Johns Hopkins for guidance with the reorganization of his school's clinical teaching. The "perfect organization," he felt, would be the type of department "that Dr. Osler had at Johns Hopkins."[46] The next year Western Reserve established a college degree as an entrance requirement after noting that Harvard and Cornell had recently done the same thing.[47] Pittsburgh, in 1912, prepared a statement of educational policy after studying the organization of what it considered the ten foremost medical schools in America.[48] Such examples, of which these are only a few, illustrated an important path by which modern medical education was spreading and how self-conscious the schools were becoming about their stature in the eyes of their competitors.

As the schools improved, they developed enormous rivalries with each other. Fierce competition had always existed among medical schools in America, but in the mid-1880s, the schools began to compete for academic respectability rather than for large enrollments as before. In 1887, the Pennsylvania faculty worried that improvements at Harvard and Columbia would impair their school's ability to enroll "the higher class of medical students whom we desire to attract."[49] In 1901, Harvard tried to gain control of a medical journal that had previously been based at Johns Hopkins. One faculty member expressed concern that "if we do not do this we shall see this new journal go to strengthen the hands of some other school."[50] The president of Columbia University told the medical faculty in 1910 that the recent rebuilding of the medical schools of Harvard and Pennsylvania emphasized the need for Columbia to do the same. Columbia, he said, should have a plant "without equal, either in this country or abroad." That way Columbia could "lead the way for all Medical Schools in the United States."[51] A much weaker school, the University of Maryland Medical School, took little joy in being fifteenth in the country in the number of graduates in 1909. "Let us see to it," a school publication proclaimed, "that it [the school] shall rank amongst the best, not only numerically, but in results."[52]

In the 1890s and 1900s, in short, ambitious schools still wished to be considered "the best." What had changed was that being "the best" no longer meant producing large numbers of graduates; what mattered now was the quality of their graduates and the academic reputation of their school. The better medical schools had evolved into genuine educational enterprises. A generation before, medical schools had opposed any tampering with the curriculum, but now they had become the chief advocates of reform.

So great was the academic competition among schools that time and time again they did not hesitate to make decisions that were educationally sound but financially hazardous. For the sake of better teaching they began acting against their direct economic interests. For example, the decisions to lengthen the sessions and increase the number of academic terms were regularly made despite fears that enrollments would shrink. When the Minnesota faculty voted unanimously to extend its terms from six months to eight beginning in the fall of 1890, it knew that the "immediate effect will be probably to lessen somewhat the number of students."[53]

Similarly, decisions to introduce laboratory teaching were educationally wise but financially risky in view of the greatly added expenses that were incurred. Economically perilous as well was the introduction of entrance requirements. In 1902, the University of Pennsylvania took such a step, despite knowing it might face "an enormous decrease in its student-fees." It did so "because it is right to exact [higher] requirements for admission to the Medical Department." It could no longer consider "the financial or commercial side of any question in reference to medical education."[54] Similarly, in 1903, Columbia raised its entrance requirement, even though it anticipated the action would produce a major decrease in the size of its incoming class.[55]

Indeed, in the next five years enrollment dropped by more than 50 percent, and the school's yearly income fell from $150,000 to $60,000, even while the cost of maintaining the school was increasing.[56]

The ultimate financial sacrifice for educational ideals was the voluntary limitation of class size so that each student might receive practical instruction. Tufts, Minnesota, Michigan, Pittsburgh, Johns Hopkins, St. Louis University, and Cornell were among the schools that established limits on class size to permit more laboratory and clinical opportunities.[57] "This number of students [237 in four classes] is as large as the school can accomodate to the best advantage with its present plant," the dean of the St. Louis University Medical School wrote in 1909. "While we shall be glad to see the institution grow in attendance, it must be borne in mind that equipment and buildings must also be enlarged if good work is to be done."[58] In a similar vein, the dean of Cornell told his faculty in 1899, "We do not desire such huge numbers [of students], as we cannot handle more than about a hundred in a single class and give practical teaching, as we are doing at present."[59]

Medical schools faced the challenge of rising expenses and falling tuition revenues either by running at deficits or by the faculty members dipping into their own pockets. The financially stronger schools—those affiliated with important universities—would frequently operate at a deficit to provide better teaching, hoping the parent university would make up the difference. In 1890, for instance, Columbia had an income of $80,000 from tuition fees but incurred $120,000 in expenses; the next year the university paid the leftover bills.[60] In the 1900s, Western Reserve, with more modest resources, was contributing $10,000 a year to meet the deficit of its medical school.[61] Financially weaker schools—independent institutions, or those affiliated with poorly endowed universities—often promoted higher medical education by paying for part of it themselves. Since 1885, the medical professors of the University of Southern California had been assessing themselves $10 a month to keep the school running; in 1908 they increased their monthly contribution to $12.50.[62] Dartmouth, Tufts, Nebraska, Maryland, and Washington University were among the other schools where the faculties consistently made private donations to the schools.[63]

This phenomenon did not occur only at the more prestigious schools. The faculty of Georgetown took a $10,000 loan in 1893 to furnish and equip the college building "with laboratories, dissecting rooms and other appliances and buildings necessary and appropriate in well-equipped medical schools."[64] The Medical Department of Columbian College, the predecessor of the George Washington University School of Medicine, also had a tradition of taking loans for the good of the teaching program. In 1886, the faculty borrowed

$10,000, and in 1893, $15,000, to purchase a new building and scientific apparatus for the school.[65] The Miami Medical College, a forerunner of the College of Medicine of the University of Cincinnati, continually rechanneled its profits into the school's operations, and in 1899, the faculty voted to forego dividends altogether and "to immediately invest any surplus funds for the benefit of the College."[66] Even the faculty of the Kansas Medical College (the medical department of Washburn University), an undistinguished school that closed in 1913, established a fund for a dispensary clinic building. They could sincerely claim that they aimed at "quality and efficiency" rather than at "developing a huge institution by which they may personally profit."[67] That they did not achieve this was a matter of great frustration to them.

By the early 1900s, therefore, ideals of modern medical education had clearly pervaded the American medical community. Medical schools across the land, recognizing how dramatically experimental medicine was transforming medical thought and practice, had expanded to a four-year curriculum, introduced the scientific subjects, and made genuine efforts to have students learn by doing rather than by listening, reading, and watching. These developments were not confined to the best schools alone but involved many of the smaller and less prosperous schools as well. That some schools succeeded more than others during this period should not obscure this important point.

The Growth of a National Movement

It was thus in the 1890s that the reform of medical education became a national movement. This occurred partly because of a better trained professoriat and the emulation of one school by another. But other factors contributed as well. Medical journals, clubs, and societies all provided a forum for the discussion and dissemination of educational ideas. Among the most prominent of these were the *Boston Medical and Surgical Journal,* the Association of American Physicians, the American Surgical Society, and the Interurban Clinical Club. Much exchange of ideas resulted from personal contact, whether at meetings or through visits and correspondence. Medical educators from different schools were often friends or at least belonged to the same professional community, which facilitated the sharing of ideas and created a climate of encouragement and mutual support.[68]

The diffusion of educational ideals was also promoted by two important national organizations: the Association of American Medical Colleges (AAMC) and, after the establishment of its Council on Medical Education in 1904, the American Medical Association (AMA). As a sign of how much medical education in America had changed, both organizations now viewed medical education in the same way as the professors of the leading schools. Indeed, both the AAMC and the Council on Medical Education were comprised of medical educators. In this sense, they had become educational voices of the schools, providing a forum for debate and discussion and, through their publications, helping to bring the topic of medical education to the attention of the entire medical community. In 1907, when the council began rating the schools, a further prod to the reform movement—and a very sharp one indeed —was provided.

Neither organization before 1910 imposed any reforms on medical schools. Indeed, as late as 1910, only one-third of the nation's schools belonged to the AAMC, and its minimum standards for membership were much lower than many schools had introduced on their own.[69] Nevertheless, both organizations exerted a regularizing and coordinating influence on medical education. For instance, at meetings of the AAMC, policy decisions would be made that in theory would be binding on member schools, even schools that might have voted in the minority. Thus, in 1891, the representative of Western Reserve asked the AAMC to clarify the definition of a three-year medical course; in 1905, the Miami Medical College agreed to "abide by the decision of the convention" on an educational issue in dispute; in 1907, the University of Colorado reviewed its curriculum to make certain that the hours devoted to the various subjects conformed with the AAMC's requirements.[70] Because the AAMC was comprised only of medical schools, it represented their voice, not that of an external agency. Yet, because decisions were made and policies adopted, it had a regularizing and coordinating effect on constituent schools, even those that might have been unwilling to abide by the decisions. Nonmember schools also benefited from the clarification of educational issues.

One result of these various discussions, which by 1900 had become nationwide in scope, was a decided move toward greater uniformity in the curriculum. More and more schools began to look alike, with similar courses, similar hours, similar teaching approaches, and similar texts. Books such as Gray's *Anatomy, Descriptive and Surgical,* Howell's *American Text-Book of Physiology,* Ziegler's *General Pathology,* Abbott's *Principles of Bacteriology,* Wood's *Therapeutics: Its Principles and Practice,* Osler's *Principles and Practice of Medicine,* Holt's *Disease of Infancy and Children,* Keen's *American Text-Book of Surgery,* and Lusk's *Science and Art of Midwifery* were listed regularly in the catalogs of medical schools everywhere. The movement toward uniformity was fostered by the AMA and the AAMC, both of which began publishing model curricula suggested for medical school adaptation. A four-year curriculum proposed by the AAMC in 1905 is shown in table 4.2.[71] Later, the movement in state licensing provided even greater impetus toward standardization (see chapter 13).

In the early 1900s, however, medical education was far from regimented. A great diversity of opinions and practices existed, and wide differences in the curriculum could be found from school to school. One report in 1904 demonstrated how much variation there was in the amount of time devoted to the standard subjects. Anatomy ranged from a maximum of 1,248 hours to a minimum of 126 hours; pathology, from 646 to 48 hours; obstetrics, from 460 to 52 hours.[72] These variations suited many medical educators who felt that a uniform curriculum was "probably neither feasible nor desirable."[73]

Nevertheless, the move toward standardization was the overwhelming trend. Despite wide variation at the extremes, most schools clustered in a narrower range. Medical education could not remain immune from the processes that were so radically transforming the traditional way of living and working in America. The country had become much more closely integrated than at any previous time in history, and as a result of new technological breakthroughs in transportation and communication, Americans had become much more mobile as well. Medical education felt the effect of these changes. If a college student in Indiana wished to attend medical school in California, or if a medical student at Oklahoma, a two-year school, desired to do his clinical training at Minnesota, or if a graduate of the University of Michigan wanted to practice in the state of Wisconsin, a certain amount of uniformity in medical education was mandatory. Absolute equivalency was not necessary, only a high degree of similarity. However, this was the direction that medical education in the early 1900s was already taking. The innumerable discussions occurring among representatives of medical schools from all parts of the country served to reconcile differences and guarantee that courses and requirements would mean the same thing everywhere.

At all schools in the early 1900s, the road to a medical degree was much more difficult than before. With the change to a four-year course, the addition of the scientific subjects, and the requirement of practical work, medical education had become extremely demanding. Even at the weakest schools, the subjects were harder to master and the time spent in training much longer. So much was there to know that some schools for a while considered adding a fifth year of study.[74] Examinations had also become much more challenging. Table 4.3, listing some of the questions given to students in the internal medicine course at Western Reserve in 1903, illustrates the increasing care

TABLE 4.2

Proposed Standard of a 4,000-Hour, Four-Year Medical Course

Subject	Lecture Hours	Laboratory Hours	Clinical Hours	Total
First Year				
Histology	30	60	0	90
Embryology	30	60	0	90
Osteology	30	0	0	30
Anatomy	100	230	0	330
Chemistry	50	100	0	150
Physiology	90	60	0	150
Materia medica	40	20	0	60
TOTAL	370	530	0	900
Second Year				
Anatomy	90	60	0	150
Physiology	90	0	0	90
Chemistry	50	100	0	150
Bacteriology	40	100	0	140
Pathology	100	140	0	240
Pharmacology	40	20	0	60
Minor surgery	15	0	60	75
TOTAL	425	420	60	905
Third Year				
Postmortem medical zoology and clinical microscopy	30	60	0	90
Physical diagnosis	20	0	80	100
Practice of medicine	90	0	180	270
Surgery	90	0	105	195
Obstetrics	50	0	30	80
Pediatrics	20	0	30	50
Gynecology	25	0	55	80
Mental and nervous diseases	30	0	30	60
Therapeutics	90	0	0	90
Hygiene	30	0	0	30
Dietetics	30	0	0	30
TOTAL	505	60	510	1075
Fourth Year				
Practice of medicine	90	0	180	270
Surgery	90	0	180	270
Obstetrics	50	0	30	80
Gynecology	25	0	55	80
Mental and nervous diseases	30	0	30	60
Electrotherapeutics	20	0	40	60
Eye and ear	30	0	30	60
Nose and throat	30	0	30	60
Genito-urinary diseases	30	0	30	60
Pediatrics	20	0	30	50
Dermatology	20	0	20	40
Medical jurisprudence	30	0	0	30
TOTAL	465	0	655	1120

NOTE: "Report of the Committee on Uniformity of Curricula," in Minutes of the Fifteenth Annual Meeting of the Association of American Medical Colleges, 10 April 1905, p. 12, Association of American Medical Colleges Archives.

with which students were being tested. The four years of medical school had become difficult and strenuous. William Pepper stated bluntly: "The students are overtaxed."[75]

However, students did not seem to mind. Although many schools still offered much easier paths to the M.D. degree, more and more students expressed their preference for the more arduous programs. For example, in the early 1890s, when Georgetown still offered evening medical classes, many of the school's graduates would voluntarily take additional clinical training in Philadelphia or New York rather than go immediately into practice. This helped give the faculty at Georgetown the courage in 1895 to change from a night to a day school so that they could increase the amount of practical instruction.[76] In 1897, after Washington University increased the scientific content of its program, the students surprised the faculty with a petition of support.[77] Such behavior was not often seen in students of the previous generation, who customarily would take the easiest possible route.

In addition, as many educators attested, students entering medical school tended to be better prepared and more ambitious than before, even though few schools had yet enacted entrance requirements. The first to note this change was Charles Eliot at Harvard. In his 1879–80 report he wrote: "In this University, until the reformation of the School in 1870–71, the medical students were noticeably inferior in bearing, manners, and discipline to the students of other departments; they are now indistinguishable from other students."[78] The faculties of Pennsylvania, Western Reserve, and Michigan observed similar changes in their students.[79] Unlike a generation before, when

TABLE 4.3

Sample Examination Questions in Medicine

---

1. Diabetes Mellitus: Give brief account of the (a) early symptoms; (b) various pathological conditions present which have been suggested as possible causes; (c) classification of cases; (d) prognosis of each class; (e) complications likely to develop; (f) treatment.
2. Rheumatism, Acute Polyarticular: Give briefly your idea of (a) etiology; (b) clinical course; (c) complications; (d) treatment.
3. Ulcer of Stomach: (a) Classify cases. (b) Give various pathological conditions resulting from or developing out of gastric ulcer. (c) Give differential diagnosis. (d) Give treatment.
4. Tuberculosis: (a) Give development of tubercular infection. (b) What is meant by a "mixed infection"? (c) What are its symptoms? (d) Give your idea of the prognosis of early cases under favorable conditions. (e) Name those conditions and other treatment.
5. Jaundice: (a) Give definition. (b) What are its symptoms? (c) Distinction between obstructive and toxic jaundice? (d) What is grave jaundice? (e) Causes of obstructive jaundice? (f) Test for bile in the urine and blood?
6. Pneumo-pyo-thorax: (a) Give differential diagnosis. (b) Give causes. (c) Give treatment.

Source: Medical College of Western Reserve University, *Catalogue* (1903–04), 60–61.

the brightest college students eschewed careers in medicine, by the early 1900s medical schools were attracting the most capable undergraduates with the highest academic standing.[80]

As medical education became more demanding for the students, so it did for the professors as well. There was too much material to fit into the curriculum, so that difficult decisions had to be made about the medical course: which topics to include and which to leave out, the best logical relationship of one subject to another, the appropriate time to be given to each subject, the determination of suitable prerequisites of study, and the most effective methods of examination and grading. William Osler stated in 1899: "The phenomenal strides in every branch of scientific medicine have tended to overload it with detail. To winnow the wheat from the chaff and to prepare it in an easily digested shape for the tender stomachs of the first and second year students taxes the resources of the most capable teachers."[81] In addition, educational techniques had become more difficult to master. To have students learn by doing, to teach them how to acquire knowledge—these were challenging tasks for every instructor. According to Osler, the greatest problem facing medical teachers was "not so much what to teach, but how to teach it."[82] The teaching of medicine had become far more difficult than a generation before, when the professors needed to be concerned mainly about eloquence of lecture style.

Accordingly, in the 1890s medical educators became involved with the educational side of their responsibilities to a far greater extent than ever before. School after school (among them Georgetown, Nebraska, Minnesota, Tufts, and Western Reserve) established curriculum committees to examine the minutiae of the medical course and the methods of instruction.[83] At the national level, the most important organization bringing doctors together for such discussions was the Association of American Medical Colleges. At its meetings medical school officials pored over the details of the course of study and argued the fine points of medical pedagogy.[84] Medical teaching was beginning to emerge as a specialty of its own, and many physicians started to think of themselves as medical educators. "We represent . . . medical pedagogics,"[85] one Association president reminded the group in 1910.

Not only had teaching become conceptually more challenging, it had become more time consuming as well. With practical work, many more hours of faculty time were required so that the students could be properly supervised and assisted. This lesson was learned early by the Medical Department of the University of the City of New York, the forerunner of the New York University School of Medicine. In 1883 it discovered that a seemingly modest step, the introduction of section teaching in hospitals to groups of twenty-five students for one hour a day, increased its weekly teaching load by twenty hours.[86] Accordingly, during the 1890s and 1900s medical faculties began to grow in size. By 1910, even small schools had acquired teaching staffs of a few dozen, and the faculties of a few schools exceeded two hundred in number.

Even with more instructors, problems still remained, for it was becoming increasingly difficult for professors to discharge their educational duties while engaged in private practice. At Washington University, the use of part-time instructors led to considerable disorganization, especially in the clinical years. With no one clearly in charge, there was insufficient planning and coordination of effort. Some subjects would be covered by several instructors, while others, equally important, would not be treated at all.[87] The situation at the University of Southern California was even worse. There, absenteeism and tardiness among professors plagued the school's teaching. During the 1908–09 academic year, as much as 27 percent of the scheduled hours of instruction in some courses was lost because professors, unable to leave their practices, had failed to keep their teaching assignments.[88] W. Jarvis Barlow, the dean, complained bitterly: "Too many of us allow our private affairs to interfere with college hours. When we have set an hour for our instruction or an examination, that hour belongs to the students and when it is absolutely impossible for us to meet that hour we should arrange for someone to fill the time."[89] Absenteeism affected the teaching at Drake, Washburn, the Denver and Gross College of Medicine, and other schools as well.[90]

For these reasons, some medical schools in the 1890s and 1900s began hiring full-time instructors, who received salaries from the medical school and did not engage in private practice. Freed of the time- and emotion-devouring burdens of private practice, they could devote their entire energy to teaching, research, and managing the school's affairs. Initially hired to teach the scientific subjects, full-time teachers began to be employed during World War I at some schools in the clinical departments as well. More will be said of this subject later.

Medical Education in 1910

By the early 1900s, a new system of medical education had taken root in the United States. This system, with its emphasis on the scientific subjects, laboratory methods of teaching, and the hiring of full-time professors, was predominantly German in inspiration. English, Scottish, and French influences were also clearly apparent through the emergence of the clinical clerkship and other forms of hospital teaching.

European academic ideals were not simply exported to the United States; they were modified in their adaptation so that they could flourish in the American setting. The German system of *Privatdocenten*—young physicians of proper qualifications who offered private medical courses—was occasionally discussed in the United States but never implemented. As medical education in America became a university endeavor, universities were not about to permit private individuals such liberties. Also, the German custom of traveling from one school to another was rarely adopted in America, except for graduates of two-year schools who went elsewhere for their clinical training. William Welch admired the system as it worked in Germany but felt that in the much vaster United States students should wait until their internship before migrating to another institution.[91] The German system of "liberty in education," whereby students took courses in the order they wished and studied at their own rate, did not develop to the same degree in America, despite the appearance of the elective system. Higher education in Germany remained much more fluid than in the United States, where a rigid, tiered school system appeared that did not permit students to linger or readily pursue paths of their own choosing. Most important, as noted earlier, in the more egalitarian United States a good medical education became the standard for all, in contrast to Europe, where the best training was reserved for the elite.

By all indications the new system of medical education worked. As various states began to require licensing examinations in the 1890s, graduates of the leading schools performed noticeably better than graduates of the schools slower to reform. One early report noted that 25 percent of graduates of "the low grade colleges" failed their licensing examination, in contrast to 1.5 percent of students from "the higher grade colleges."[92] Physicians in practice, recognizing that something had been missing in their own training, began taking a variety of postgraduate courses that had become available. These short courses helped bring practitioners up-to-date with recent scientific developments and provided them practical laboratory and clinical work that most had not received as students.[93]

The public also recognized that an important change in medical education had occurred. In the 1890s, the longstanding archrival of medicine, homeopathy (a system of therapeutics in which patients are treated with minute doses of drugs capable of producing in healthy persons symptoms like those of the disease to be treated), began to lose popularity, and within twenty years it vanished as a significant competitor to "regular" medicine. Ironically, the decline of homeopathy occurred after organized medicine had called a truce with the homeopaths to end decades of vitriolic warfare. In the 1890s, other less prominent medical sects, if they still existed, were also rapidly falling into eclipse.[94] The 1890s was also the period when the states began to enact licensing laws, the very existence of which stood as testimony to the public's belief that there was certain knowledge that every physician should possess.[95] After 1900, the public began to view medicine as a much more glamorous profession, and physicians were rewarded with increasing social status and larger incomes.[96] Although the public had not yet become as enamored of doctors as they were to be by the 1930s, when opinion polls placed physicians at the very top of the occupations, the process was underway, and at its root was the public's conviction that it made a difference how a doctor was trained.

Progress in medical education had not occurred smoothly and evenly. Backward and lateral steps occurred along with the steps forward, and medical educators everywhere experienced disappointments, frustrations, and failures along the way. Even at the better schools much remained to be done. At Washington University, laboratory facilities and teaching were uneven in quality, and many courses were greatly overcrowded. In some years Robert Terry, the professor of anatomy, was not given the budget to hire assistants, and thus he would have to supervise by himself the laboratory work of as many as one hundred students.[97] The situation was similar at Yale, where insufficient space and equipment impaired the faculty's efforts to provide good laboratory teaching.[98] Pennsylvania, too, suffered from inadequate facilities for practical work as well as from the lack of an adequate library.[99] Simon Flexner, the noted virologist and brother of Abraham, felt that improvements at the school were occurring much too slowly. This, in 1902, was a major reason why he decided to leave Pennsylvania to become director of the Rockefeller Institute.[100] Problems of insufficient funds and inadequate laboratory and hospital facilities plagued even the very best of schools.

What was worse, the proprietary schools, aided by weak state licensing laws, continued to proliferate. Between 1870 and 1900, the number of medical schools in America more than doubled, even as the financial requirements of medical education were increasing. The peak year was 1906, when 162 schools were operating. This represented nearly one-half of all the medical schools in the world. In actuality, far more than 162 schools had been established, for many of them existed for only a short while. By 1910, 457 schools had operated at some time or another in the United States or Canada.[101] Most proprietary schools had undergone many improvements, but on the standards of the early 1900s, they were no longer adequate. Terms had been lengthened and the scientific subjects added, but laboratory and clinical facilities were very meager, and published standards of admission and graduation were commonly ignored. At the worst schools, anyone who could pay the fees was admitted, and graduation was a virtual certainty. Some of these schools resorted to fraud, for they advertised laboratory and clinical opportunities that did not exist and admission and graduation requirements they had no intention of enforcing. "We find in them a deplorable amount of dishonesty,"[102] one critic observed.

A closer look at American medical education in 1910, therefore, suggests that conditions were unusually varied. The overall caliber of medical education was at its highest point ever, but progress had not been uniform. A greater distance separated the best from the worst schools than at any time before or since. Table 4.4 illustrates the six major tiers that existed among American medical schools in 1910. The table is not intended to provoke debate over the rankings of the schools used as examples but to give a sense of the vast differences in quality that could be found among the schools.

At the top were schools such as Johns Hopkins, Harvard, Columbia, Michigan, and Minnesota that had already become modern medical schools. What distinguished Johns Hopkins from the rest, as chapter 8 will discuss in detail, was that Johns Hopkins already possessed a first-rate hospital for clinical teaching, whereas the others had not yet acquired comparable clinical facilities. In the scientific subjects, some of the others already rivaled the Baltimore school. All of these schools had become integral parts of major universities and important centers of medical research, and all have remained leaders of medical education.

Schools of the middle two tiers had achieved adequate if not spectacular success. Like the schools ranked both above and below, they provided better scientific than clinical teaching. However, unlike the top dozen schools, they had not yet become very productive in medical research. Many of these schools had developed true university relationships, and most survived the post-Flexnerian purge of medical education.

Schools in the bottom two categories were struggling. The Flexner report lumped these schools together, but archival records reveal important differences between the two groups. Schools ranked in Tier 5 were of higher quality than those in Tier 6, providing some semblance of real laboratory and clinical work rather than merely pretending to do so. More important, the faculties of Tier 5 schools were genuinely committed to educational reform, whereas those of Tier 6 regarded their schools strictly as businesses. Tier 6 schools adopted what few improvements they made because they had no choice; Tier 5 schools, because they wanted to. No Tier 6 school survived the post-Flexnerian period, whereas some of the Tier 5 institutions ultimately developed into good schools.

The enormous range in quality among medical schools of 1910 is often difficult for observers of the present to appreciate. Consider, for instance, the condition of laboratory teaching in the early 1900s. Michigan offered a superb

TABLE 44
Tiers of Medical Schools, 1910

Examples	Approximate Number	Quality of Scientific Instruction	Quality of Clinical Instruction	University Affiliation	Research	Survived Post-1910 Purge	Educational or Commercial Enterprises
Tier 1 Johns Hopkins	1	Excellent	Excellent	Yes	Yes	Yes	Educational
Tier 2 Columbia, Harvard, Michigan, Minnesota	10	Excellent	Good	Yes	Yes	Yes	Educational
Tier 3 Cincinnati, New York University, Washington University, Yale	20	Good	Acceptable	Yes	Some	Yes	Educational
Tier 4 Colorado, Drake, Nebraska, Tufts	30	Acceptable	Less Acceptable	Many	Little	Most	Educational
Tier 5 College of Physicians and Surgeons (Baltimore), Georgetown, Southwestern, Washburn	30	Less Acceptable	Weak	Some	None	Some	Educational
Tier 6 Atlantic Medical College, Bennett Medical College, National Medical University, Toledo Medical College	40	Unacceptable	Unacceptable	None	None	None	Commercial

physiology course in which each student, working with a partner, performed thirty-six experiments. Students would spend each afternoon from 1:00 to 4:30 P.M. in the laboratory, studying such phenomena as the extensibility and elasticity of frog muscle, the contractions of nonstriated muscle, the reaction time for sound, and the measurement of circulation, cardiac output, blood pressure, and respiration in mammals, usually rabbits or dogs.[103] Some of the proprietary schools, in contrast, provided no laboratory work in physiology at all. Harvard and Johns Hopkins offered courses designed to encourage student research (William Porter's course in experimental physiology at Harvard and Harvey Cushing's research course at the Hunterian Laboratory at Johns Hopkins). In contrast, an ambitious student at the Denver and Gross College of Medicine who wished to do independent laboratory work on his own time was denied the use of the facilities.[104] At Johns Hopkins and Harvard, incoming students were mature, serious, and well prepared; both schools (Johns Hopkins, 1893; Harvard, 1901) required bachelor's degrees for admission. At Georgetown, on the other hand, the requirement of a high school diploma for admission was frequently overlooked, and problems with cheating and classroom disorder were rampant.[105]

Even within the ranks of the proprietary schools, great diversity existed. At Georgetown, cited as an example where lax standards flourished, the faculty spent their personal funds to acquire laboratories and equipment and to institute many improvements in teaching. An examination of the school's records reveals that it was engaged in a persistent, difficult, frustrating battle to upgrade standards, one in which it was greatly hampered by the lack of an endowment and of a parent university that was able to provide much financial support. Similarly, the Flexner report spoke harshly of the College of Physicians and Surgeons (Baltimore), dismissing it as a crass school without merit.[106] True, the faculty voted itself modest dividends, and the quality of work was low relative to many other schools, but at the same time, led by German-trained William Royal Stokes, the faculty expanded to a four-year program, added courses in embryology and bacteriology, and borrowed $100,000 to construct a new laboratory building after inspecting medical centers in New York, Boston, and Philadelphia.[107] The faculty also organized a research club to publish reports of interesting hospital cases, and entrance requirements were not as easy as at some schools, as one student discovered when he could not gain admission after failing medical studies elsewhere.[108] Another Baltimore proprietary school, the Baltimore Medical College, earned the gratitude of the AAMC for hiring a private detective to expose a scheme of forgery of medical college credentials.[109]

Proprietary schools such as Georgetown, the College of Physicians and

Surgeons, and the Baltimore Medical College differed markedly from proprietary schools whose only thought was commercial profit. As other schools were making financial sacrifices to improve medical education, these low-grade schools were not. A representative of the Atlanta School of Medicine told Abraham Flexner that the weakest feature of his school was "the total lack of proper bedside facilities." Yet he denied this problem could be corrected because "we cannot . . . go into our [own] pockets."[110] At the University of Tennessee Department of Medicine, professorships were bought and sold. A retiring member of the faculty would sell his chair to his successor, the average price being about $1,500.[111] Such schools deserved Flexner's wrath.

Evaluating the schools as a whole, it was clear that by 1910 the conceptual revolution in medical education was complete. Schools everywhere were familiar with the new educational ideas, even those in the bottom tier. It became impossible to tell the difference between the best and worst schools from catalogs alone, for all advertised the same courses, methods, and opportunities. "What a dove-like confidence you have in catalogues of medical schools!" William Welch chided Franklin Mall in 1900. "Some of the two-penny schools have almost as beautiful announcements as Rush or Johns Hopkins."[112] The fact that the weakest schools now spoke the same educational language as the best was just one more indication of how widely the new ideals of medical education had spread.

Within the top five tiers, schools differed from one another in their success at implementing the new educational goals, but not in their desire to do so. Some of these schools enjoyed much more abundant resources than others, but all shared the same ambitions. Tier 6 schools differed from the others in terms of values. These schools still regarded medical education as a business, and they stood apart from the majority of schools, since they did not see their mission as educational and did very little to upgrade conditions.

By 1910, notwithstanding all the problems that remained to be solved and the great variations from school to school, enormous strides had clearly been taken in medical education. The overall quality of medical training had reached its highest point ever in America, and the leading dozen schools were already beginning to rival the best schools abroad. William Osler in 1905 proudly noted "the rapidity with which the scientific instruction in our medical schools has been brought to a high level . . . [over] the past twenty years."[113] To another prominent medical educator in 1909, the changes in medical education of the preceding twenty-five years amounted "to little less than a revolution."[114] There were many indications that a new era had started. After 1900, American students were being advised by their teachers that there was no longer a need to study abroad, if they attended one of the dozen leading schools in America.[115] These schools provided an education equal if not superior to that afforded in Europe. The migration of American physicians to Europe for postgraduate study fell substantially from levels of previous decades, and Germans began coming to the United States instead.[116] Science, once anathema in medical education, had won a secure place. In 1910, Weir Mitchell received an honorary degree from Jefferson Medical College, the school that had twice denied him a professorship as a young man because he had been interested in research.[117] It has long been assumed that the modern era of medical education had to await the publication of the Flexner report in 1910, but if the growing sense of satisfaction and accomplishment among medical educators before 1910 is any indication, that era had already begun.

There comes a point in any successful movement when it is certain that the movement will achieve its goals. In medical education that point was reached around 1905. The final steps after 1910 would have occurred without the Flexner report, though probably not so dramatically or suddenly or in a form that placed so much emphasis on research.

One indication that modern medical education was here to stay was the degree of progress that had been made before the Flexner report was published. In 1910, by Flexner's own admission, there were "thirty-odd schools now supplying the distinctly better quality of medical training,"[118] and another fifty schools were rapidly approaching the same level of quality. Paralleling the distribution of the population and the growth of the country's educational system, medical schools were strongest in the Northeast, Atlantic coast, Midwest, and Great Lakes regions. However, improvements were occurring everywhere. In an address in 1894, the prominent surgeon and educator William Keen noted with approval that after 1898 all physicians admitted to practice in the state of Oregon must have taken four years of medical study. He told his Boston audience, "We must look to it that in the East we are not outdone by the West."[119] Whether Keen really thought that medical education on the West Coast in the 1890s would soon surpass that on the East was highly doubtful, but his point that the movement had become a nationwide phenomenon was accurate.

A second indication was that students were flocking to the better, and more difficult, medical schools at a time when they still had the option of choosing an easier route. Since the late 1880s schools that instituted higher standards were quickly rewarded with larger numbers of students. The experience at Pennsylvania was typical. "With each [curricular] advance there is a temporary falling off in the number of students; after each ebb there is the surging in of a larger tide."[120] The dean of Western Reserve noted in 1904 that "in the past twenty-five years every school which has adopted increased standards of training, either preliminary or medical, has ultimately been the gainer, not only in reputation but in attendance of students."[121] The modern medical school had become a success measured by the old-fashioned standard: numbers of students. So large did enrollments become that many schools, as noted before, began restricting the size of their entering classes to ensure a high level of personalized instruction for every student.

Conversely, before 1910 proprietary schools were already struggling. Contrary to popular opinion, such schools had always been precarious ventures, as the high fatality rate among them indicated. Financially, the vast majority were shoe-string operations, making much less money for their professors than commonly perceived. At the Denver and Gross College of Medicine, faculty dividends in 1902 ranged from $50 to $250; at Georgetown in 1902, from $25 to $500; at the College of Physicians and Surgeons (Baltimore) in 1902, dividends were $1,000; at the Medical Department of Columbian College in 1903, $1,000.[122] Even if they wanted to, few medical professors were getting rich from the proprietary schools. After 1900, as the overall caliber of medical education in the country became much higher, proprietary schools found it much more difficult than before to attract students. Between 1906 and 1910, the number of medical schools fell from 162 to 131, with the attrition occurring primarily in the ranks of the proprietary schools.[123] The public, which provided the nation's supply of doctors, had already accepted the more demanding path of training as a necessity. Before the Flexner report, commercialism had already ceased to pay.

A third sign came from the medical faculties themselves. Nowhere—Tier 6 schools excepted (see table 4.4)—were medical professors content with what they had accomplished. They continually kept in focus how much remained to be done to achieve the highest level of medical education. In 1901, the faculty of Washington University took no solace in being the best school in St. Louis. In a special report they wrote: "This, however, only shows that we are doing better work than the other local schools and by no means implies that we are doing as well as we ought. We are still far from the ideal for which we have always striven and which we hope to reach."[124] In 1906 the dean of Yale Medical School, frustrated that the school did not have as much money for laboratory equipment as some schools, conceded that as a result "this School is now relatively less attractive than it was a few years ago."[125] The medical faculties felt that their schools should be judged by what could be accomplished in medical education rather than by how far they had progressed. As a result they became their own harshest critics. This represented the most certain sign of all that further improvements were on the way.

5 The Shaping of the
Modern Medical School

THE PERIOD BETWEEN 1890 and 1910 was crucial not only to medical education but to medical schools. In this period medical research began to find a place in America's medical schools. The American system would ultimately exclude "practical," that is, nonresearch-oriented, schools from its province. In addition, in the United States, as in Germany, medical education entered the university. Independent medical schools, as had existed before, or hospital-based schools, as in England and France, were not to be the mature American style. Finally, toward the end of the period, entrance requirements were established, and medical schools started to articulate with the country's educational system. Movement in these directions had already begun before the 1890s, and the institutionalization process was completed only during World War I. But it was in the two decades between 1890 and 1910 that the particular form the mature American medical school would take became unmistakably clear and its development, irreversible.

Teaching and Research

Medical educators of the 1890s and 1900s had a dual mission. They sought to teach medicine in a more scientific way, and they also wanted to do research and put an end to America's scientific subservience to Europe. As Victor Vaughan explained, "In [medical] science we are still young but the time has come when we must cease to be mere followers of Germany and France."[1] In seeking to advance their disciplines, they were partaking in a struggle similar to that of scholars in such disparate fields as philosophy,[2] the social sciences,[3] and physics[4]—all of whom were striving at this time to achieve independence in their respective academic areas.

Through the mid-1890s the status of research in the country's medical schools remained precarious. Its pursuit was not easy, for salaries, equipment, and facilities, to say nothing of encouragement and moral support, had to be provided in quantities far beyond that required for teaching alone. In the 1870s and 1880s some research was being done at Harvard, Michigan, Pennsylvania, and a few other leading schools, but at that time the predominant focus even at those places remained on the development of their teaching programs. At most schools there was very little interest in research. A few members of the Tufts medical faculty thought of starting a research journal in 1900, but as there was not enough general interest among the faculty to indicate a journal could be sustained, the idea was dropped.[5] The country's first journal devoted exclusively to medical research, the *Journal of Experimental Medicine,* was established only in 1896. At the time of its creation, many feared that scientific productivity in the United States was so low that the journal would not receive enough good material to keep to its intended publication schedule.[6]

In the mid-1890s, attitudes toward research rapidly began to change. Dire predictions to the contrary, the *Journal of Experimental Medicine* succeeded, and soon a variety of other research journals appeared. Clearly a core of medical investigators had already found opportunities to work, however barren and ill-provided some of the earliest positions might have been. The opening of Johns Hopkins in 1893 provided an enormous impetus to medical research, stimulating other schools to begin supporting that activity as well.[7] By 1906, about thirty medical schools had at least one or two faculty members engaged in research; by 1911 that number had grown to sixty.[8] Not only the quantity but also the quality of American medical research was improving. American medical research was to develop much more fully during World War I and afterwards, but by 1910 the framework was already in place. Medical schools by that time were acquiring as much recognition for their contributions to research as for their leadership in educational affairs, and experimental medicine in America was starting to stand on its own feet vis-à-vis Europe.[9] To Welch in 1910, "The recognition that has been won for American [medical] science on the other side of the water has been one of the most important developments of the last century."[10]

The development of medical education and the development of medical research proceeded hand-in-hand with each other. The two could not always be distinguished from one another. It was in this period, for instance, that new scientific societies devoted to the advancement of specific medical disciplines were founded: the American Society of Physiology (1887); the American Association of Anatomists (1888); the American Association of Pathologists and Bacteriologists (1900); the American Society of Biological Chemists (1905); the American Society for Pharmacology and Experimental Therapeutics (1908); and the American Society for Clinical Investigation (1908). The membership rosters of these organizations were replete with names prominent in the reform of medical education. At Johns Hopkins, persons such as Franklin Mall in anatomy, William Welch in pathology, William Howell in physiology, John Jacob Abel in pharmacology, and William Halsted in surgery left their imprint firmly both on medical education and on the academic development of their disciplines.

This process was illustrated by the appointment of Otto Folin to the first chair of biological chemistry at Harvard Medical School in 1909. To members of the Harvard medical faculty, the establishment of a department of biological chemistry had become a matter of great urgency, especially since other schools had already begun developing that subject at their institutions. Walter Cannon warned Charles Eliot that Harvard at present had "no one to compare with Chittenden and Mendel at Yale, Gies of Columbia, Abel and Jones of Johns Hopkins, or Vaughan of Ann Arbor." This situation had to be corrected quickly because "there is no doubt that the most promising field for the future development of medical science is the field of chemical physiology."[11] Exactly who should fill the chair was a controversial matter, as Robert Kohler has discussed,[12] but the influential Henry Bowditch wanted Folin. Bowditch urged action "which will prevent a physiological chemist of the first rank, now in our neighborhood, from slipping through our fingers. I refer to Folin."[13] After the smoke had cleared following Folin's appointment, there was no question that having a person like Folin, the country's foremost analytical biochemist, head a new department of biochemistry was good for Harvard Medical School, and there was also no doubt that a secure position for Folin at a first-rate school like Harvard was good for the development of biochemistry in the United States.

That research should gravitate to the medical schools was not a necessary occurrence, for alternative locations existed, most notably the research institutes. Indeed, in the European system so admired by Americans, some of the most important investigations were done at research institutes, such as the Koch Institute, the Pasteur Institute, and the Institute of Physiology. In the

United States, the most prominent research institute of the period was the Rockefeller Institute for Medical Research, founded in 1901. Not only did the Rockefeller Institute contribute enormously to medical knowledge but it became a fertile training ground for medical scientists, many of whom later assumed professorships at medical schools across the country and world.[14]

In the United States, however, medical schools became the most important site for medical investigation. Most medical scientists in America perceived teaching and research to be closely related activities. They believed that the investigator isolated from students was deprived of an important source of excitement and stimulation. This viewpoint took hold even at the Rockefeller Institute, which all along was engaged in advanced teaching, and which half a century later officially acknowledged the importance of teaching by changing its name to the Rockefeller University.[15] Other sites of medical research were always to be important—witness the National Institutes of Health after World War II—but the center of medical investigation was destined to remain at the university medical schools.

The idea that medical schools should promote research arose in part from the German university tradition of the mid-nineteenth century. However, the impulse for research was also fostered by the ideas of progressive education that were sweeping American medical schools. According to this viewpoint, everyone was a student, teacher and beginning learner alike, differing from each other only in maturity and sophistication. All true students had a love for inquiry, whether they be beginners discovering things already known to others, or teachers discovering things new to everyone. In either case the process was the same. William Osler described "the pupil and teacher working together on the same lines, only one a little ahead of the other."[16] The professor, according to Osler, "is a senior student anxious to help his juniors. When a simple, earnest spirit animates a college, there is no appreciable interval between the teacher and the taught—both are in the same class, the one a little more advanced than the others."[17]

So thoroughly did progressive education pervade the medical schools that it gave rise to an infatuation with the teacher-investigator. Many believed that teachers had to be imbued with an investigative spirit so that they could transmit it to their students. "The spirit of enquiry is only to be communicated by those who habitually enquire themselves," Franklin Mall wrote.[18] A unity of good teaching with good scholarship was projected; research was held to be essential for the most effective teaching. It was never expected that every medical teacher would be a researcher, but, as Welch stated bluntly, "The best medical teachers are investigators."[19]

Not everyone was as convinced as the investigators that only investigators could teach. Even Lewellys Barker, an enthusiast for research, later conceded that some investigators were "handicapped" as teachers.[20] Nevertheless, critics remained on the defensive. It was never proved that researchers made better teachers, only assumed. Yet many made that assumption with ease because it fitted in neatly with the social and emotional conditions of the early twentieth century. The notion that the best teachers were researchers represented one more manifestation of a medicine increasingly scientific and of a social context increasingly enamored of the mystique of science. The argument also proved useful to academic physicians trying to gain a foothold for research in the country's medical schools. In the teacher-investigator, medicine had its analogue to the "expert" in Progressive Era business, government, and social reform.

By the early 1900s, medical research had won a secure place in America's medical schools. N. P. Colwell, the secretary of the American Medical Association's Council on Medical Education, observed in 1913: "No medical school can keep up-to-date either in medical knowledge or in methods of teaching, unless it is itself seeking to discover new truths in medicine. . . . Medical research is the very soul of medical education."[21] The faculty at the University of Pittsburgh felt similarly. In 1910, they wrote that a "medical school does most for its students, for its teachers and for the state, which fosters within its walls, a research laboratory, wherein every member of its staff may find space and equipment equal to his needs."[22] Though it was not felt that teaching and investigative abilities always had to be combined in the same person, it was thought that teachers at the very least needed close contact with those who were advancing knowledge.

Nevertheless, as American medical research came of age, it quickly became apparent that the congruity between teaching and research was not always as smooth as advocates maintained. The two frequently came into conflict. Nowhere was this better seen than at the University of Pennsylvania, which was a pioneer in medical research as well as in educational reform. Between 1890 and 1900, the faculty expanded to a four-year curriculum and increased still further the amount of practical instruction. To the faculty's consternation, the improved teaching caused "a decided falling off in the experimental productions," for there was "little time and energy left" for research. Better instruction had come "at the expense of scientific production."[23] Good teaching and good research both devoured a professor's time; one could often be pursued only at the expense of the other. For this reason, smaller classes were as much in the interest of the faculty as the students, since with fewer students, professors would have more time left for investigation.

Research also placed a financial burden on medical schools. It was expensive enough to acquire laboratories and hospitals for modern medical teaching. To provide for research was more costly still, in view of the additional space, equipment, and staff that would be required. Thus, in 1902 a number of surgical faculty members at Harvard were extremely frustrated not because they lacked good teaching facilities, but because they did not have the space and equipment for original work in surgical pathology.[24] Research added greatly to the already rapidly growing expense of medical education.

By the first decade of the twentieth century science occupied a peculiar position in the country's medical schools, and the ambiguity resulted from the tension between teaching and research. Insofar as the discussion focused on teaching, the position of science was secure. There was no longer any doubt that the scientific subjects and the laboratory belonged in the medical curriculum. Endless discussion occurred over particular issues, such as how much science was enough, how best to correlate the scientific with the clinical teaching, and whether future practitioners needed the same type and amount of scientific work as future researchers. However, few disagreed with the general principle that a good scientific education was necessary for all medical students, regardless of their future ambitions. "The discussion which has gone on as between theoretical and practical doctors has no significance," Henry Pritchett of the Carnegie Foundation wrote. "The same things which make for good theory make for good practice."[25] Even at Johns Hopkins, the most rigorous scientific school in the country, 80 percent of the graduates during the school's first decade entered practice.[26] It was felt that good schools produced scientific practitioners, not scientists or practitioners alone.

However, insofar as the discussion focused on research, great confusion arose. In the quest to establish modern medical schools, larger questions concerning the direction and purpose of the schools went unresolved. What was the proper function of a medical school: teaching? research? the provision of medical services to the community? No one denied the importance of medical research, or that it belonged at a medical school. Most observers recognized that under the right circumstances, research would invigorate a faculty's teaching, as it did at Johns Hopkins. However, disagreement arose over particulars: Did research belong at all schools or just some? Was it the duty of every faculty member or just a select few? How important was research relative to teaching and the provision of health care? How could medical schools reconcile the needs of professors, who demanded time for research, with those of students, who benefited the most when the instructors taught? Did public-supported medical schools have the same obligation to advance medical knowledge as private schools? Who should make such decisions, and to whom had the medical schools become accountable? In short, it was not clear where or how to draw the line between teaching and research. Much the same conflict still exists in today's medical school.

One suggestion frequently made in the first decade of the century was to divide the labor of teaching and research between "practical" and "scientific" schools. A "practical" school was one that provided good teaching without trying to foster research. The president of Bowdoin argued, for instance, that quality teaching alone justified the existence of schools such as his own. Research could be left to the better endowed schools.[27] Such a proposal did not seem unreasonable in 1910, when most schools still operated on a financial shoestring. It therefore made sense to leave research to those schools with the facilities, staff, and budgets to pursue it properly. The division of labor, a popular approach to problem solving among Progressive Era reformers and efficiency experts, appealed to many medical educators as well.

Others, however, rejected the idea of having practical and scientific schools. To Franklin Mall, research was a school's highest duty, one that was much more important than the routine teaching of medical students.[28] Echoing this view was the dean of Yale, who wrote that "no medical school can ever reach the first class unless it is steeped, so to speak, in the spirit of research."[29] Academically inclined physicians at poorly endowed schools felt the same way, desiring to have the same opportunity for research as their counterparts at the richer schools. Thus, the junior faculty at the University of Illinois resented their onerous teaching load and wrote to Victor Vaughan for advice on how to obtain more time for research.[30] In summary, by 1910, research could no longer be kept out of American medical schools. However, the exact form that research would take—whether it would be for some schools or for all; for some faculty members or for everyone who desired a permanent position; whether it would be subservient, equal, or supreme to the teaching function—still remained to be determined.

Medicine Enters the University

In the 1890s and 1900s another important event occurred: medical education moved into the universities. Universities had been eyeing medical education since the 1870s, but in the 1890s they started to assume real control of the medical schools. A reform coalition emerged whose most prominent members consisted not only of medical school professors and deans but university presidents as well. This development was crucial for further progress in medical education, for the universities infused money and intellectual vigor into the medical schools and helped ensure that the schools would adhere to high academic ideals.

Considering the direction that medical education had been moving, its absorption by the universities was a natural occurrence. Medical educators, like educators in other fields, were increasingly concerned with how their subject was taught. The president of the Association of American Medical Colleges in 1901 outlined some of the educational issues confronting medical teachers:

> . . . the length of time to be devoted to laboratory teaching? How much to didactic lectures? To quizzes? To clinical lectures? To dispensaries? How frequently should written tests be exacted? How many subjects should be taught at one time? How should they be grouped together so as to economize the student's time to the best advantage? Should clinical teaching be restricted to the last two years?[31]

Process was seen to matter in medical education, and educational process was the special province of the universities. In addition, the case for a university environment grew stronger as medical faculties started to pursue research. This activity more than any other guaranteed that medical schools would be broad professional schools with university aims rather than narrow technical schools.

Despite these points of affinity, the unions between medical schools and universities initially proceeded with difficulty. This was the lesson at Harvard, where Charles Eliot's will had to be imposed upon a resentful medical faculty in 1871. Up until the end of the nineteenth century, the great majority of medical schools were privately owned and operated, and the professors had no intention of turning their businesses over to anyone. Most medical faculties were highly content operating independently or with university affiliations that were purely nominal. Thus, when William DeWitt Hyde, the president of Bowdoin College, tried to assume responsibility for his college's affiliated medical school in 1885, he encountered the resistance of every member of the faculty.[32] Similarly, in 1889, after attending a meeting of the medical faculty without an invitation, the president of Western Reserve University was curtly told to stay away from future meetings.[33] As late as 1898, when the University of Vermont attempted to end the proprietary era of its medical college by taking charge of the school, the move was described by opponents as "nothing short of revolutionary."[34]

However, the movement was too formidable to be stopped by recalcitrant medical faculties. A generation of aggressive university presidents with extraordinary talents of executive leadership had made it part of their mission to assume responsibility for their affiliated medical schools. As Eliot had attended faculty meetings regularly at Harvard Medical School and James Angell occasionally at the University of Michigan, so did Seth Low and Nicholas Murray Butler at Columbia, Charles Dabney at Cincinnati, and Charles Thwing at Western Reserve.[35] Names like those above as well as Daniel Coit Gilman of Johns Hopkins, Arthur Hadley of Yale, Samuel McCormick of Pittsburgh, George Vincent of Minnesota, Charles Van Hise of Wisconsin, William Rainey Harper of Chicago, and Benjamin Wheeler of California were important not only to the development of their universities but to the development of their medical schools. In the 1890s and 1900s, these and other "personal university presidents" involved themselves in all the details of running their medical schools: hiring faculty members, establishing salaries, determining educational policies, and allocating resources. They sought control of their medical schools as they did their law, divinity, engineering, and education schools, with the understanding that as more occupations required university training, the more the university would gain in importance as a social institution. Medicine was rapidly replacing divinity as the most prestigious profession, which made them especially eager to take charge of medical education. Perhaps this is why Charles Eliot once said that his effort on behalf of the medical school "has been, I think on the whole, the most constructive part of my work."[36]

In addition, as the German influence pervaded American medicine, many medical faculties had grown more receptive to the idea of establishing stronger ties with universities. Any residual doubts about doing so were greatly diminished after Johns Hopkins proved to be a success. Thus, whereas many early university affiliations were thrust upon medical faculties, by the 1890s many medical schools had become eager for such arrangements. For instance, Western Reserve was at first as hostile to surrendering its independence as any medical school, but the faculty soon grew to like the new arrangement. In 1896 the professors even sought a "more intimate" relationship with the university so that the trustees could help raise funds for the medical school and provide advice on educational matters.[37]

Once medicine had gained a foothold in the universities, the process became self-sustaining. Universities and medical schools had become dedicated to the same academic ideals, and through their new relationship, they invigorated each other. The movement also was facilitated because additional advantages to both parties resulted. Medical schools gained badly needed financial assistance and the promise of more stable financial support in the future. In turn, universities with strong medical schools gained in educational stature. In addition, by controlling medical education, universities could discharge some of their utilitarian duties—training physicians to serve society's medical needs; promoting research to combat disease. Finally, from their medical schools, universities gained a large body of influential and well-to-do alumni—invaluable for the support of a university's further growth. When over 700 medical graduates of the University of Minnesota gathered at a banquet in 1927, it then represented the largest assembly of Minnesota alumni ever.[38] Practical benefits as well as ideological compatibility brought medical schools and universities together.

Unions between medical schools and universities occurred frequently between 1890 and 1910, and time and time again the transformation of a school to a true university department was accompanied by the introduction of more thorough teaching. Columbia, which forged a genuine alliance between medical school and university in 1891, was one of the earlier examples where this occurred. Seth Low, the president of the university, wrote to James McLane, the dean of the medical school, in 1890:

> It seems to us that the primary question for the College of Physicians and Surgeons to decide is whether it is better for medical education in the large view that it should be carried on in a proprietary school which is a medical school and nothing else, or whether education is likely to be more scientific and more thorough in a medical school which is a vital part of a great university.[39]

After arrangements were completed, the university offered financial help to the medical school, contributing $284,756.60 between 1891 and 1902. These funds made possible the enormous strides taken at the school during those years.[40] At the University of Pittsburgh progress was much slower, but in 1908 the medical school was reorganized to become an integral part of the university. Following its change of status, the school improved very quickly, undergoing what Henry Pritchett called a "magnificent transformation."[41]

The unions between medical schools and universities usually assumed a different form from what many had anticipated. Some had envisioned medical schools and universities in close physical proximity to each other, with the faculties interacting regularly in a congenial way and with the medical students benefiting from the culture and ambience of the university environment. Nicholas Murray Butler, the president of Columbia University, described to the medical faculty his view of the proper relationship:

> I cannot refrain from pointing out what I believe to be the immense educational advantage of bringing about a physical unity between the Medical

School and the rest of the University. The consequent close association with other University teachers and students on the part both of members of the teaching staff and members of the student body at the Medical School cannot fail to be in every way advantageous. A closer alliance will be formed between the work of men engaged in research under the Faculty of Pure Science and those engaged in research under the Faculty of Medicine. The Medical students will be able to enjoy, what they have not heretofore had, namely, the pleasure and profit of academic residence and of close academic association.[42]

However, this seldom happened. Medical schools and parent universities usually occupied separate campuses, and contact between the faculties was seldom close. Strong rivalries often developed; emotional as well as physical distance frequently separated the campuses.

Nevertheless, a true university spirit entered more and more medical schools. This occurred as an increasing number of medical professors became concerned with the issues of medical pedagogy and as they developed the desire to do research. As Theodore Janeway, a successor of Osler, wrote, "Uniformity of environment is not the distinctive feature of the university, but unity of purpose."[43] Although medical schools often remained isolated from the rest of the university, they adopted university values.

Before 1910, only about fifty medical schools had become genuine university departments. Of these, few received as much financial support as Columbia. Nevertheless, the university schools had become the undisputed leaders in medical education. Independent schools of high quality—the most important being Jefferson Medical College—decreased in number, and in 1969, even Jefferson officially became a university. To provide the best training possible, a group of medical educators pointed out in 1908, medical schools had but one choice: to become "connected with Universities."[44]

The emergence of the university medical school was clearly perceived by medical educators of the period to be the driving force underlying the recent development of medical education. Mall noted in 1911 how "the improvement in medical education during the past twenty-five years is in large measure due to the absorption of medical schools by universities."[45] The president of the University of Minnesota observed in 1910:

A number of powerful agencies are contributive to this movement [in medical education]. Notable among them are the Educational Council of the American Medical Association, the state boards of medical examiners in Minnesota and other states, and the Carnegie Foundation for the Advancement of Teaching. *The great universities of the country are the chief factors, however, in this progress;* for so rapid has been the rise and so great has been the development of medorn [sic] scientific medicine, within the past quarter of a century, that medical education can no longer be fitly conducted save under the fostering care and with the ample opportunities afforded by state-supported or highly endowed schools.[46] [Emphasis added]

Insofar as the modern university in America was secure by 1910, so was the future of medical education. Here we find still another reason why before the Flexner report the development of medical education had acquired an irreversible momentum: the universities had already gained control.

If the university medical school marked the emergence of a new age, it also marked the passing of the old. The medical school had become the sole arbiter and dispenser of medical education. Gone were the multiplicity of paths to the practice of medicine that had been so prominent in the 1860s. The apprenticeship, the house pupil system, the private summer schools—all were eliminated by the university medical school, which was to permit no challenger to its educational hegemony. Events at Harvard Medical School illustrated this change as clearly as anywhere. In 1871, with the introduction of the new curriculum, the school dropped the apprenticeship as a formal requirement for the degree, and the Tremont Street Medical School, an extramural summer school operated by members of the Harvard faculty, was closed. In 1873, the Massachusetts General Hospital began restricting its appointments of house pupils to Harvard medical graduates who had completed the three-year course, instead of to Harvard medical students after the first year of study. In the first decade of the twentieth century, of all the alternative routes of training, only foreign study remained, and even this path was rapidly fading in importance. Medical education, like the rest of higher education in the United States, had become the province of the university.

Entrance Requirements

As the twentieth century opened, one aspect of educational reform lagged behind all others: entrance requirements. In 1900, only Johns Hopkins required a college degree for admission, and in 1901, Harvard became the second school to institute such a requirement. Of the others, only Western Reserve, with a three-year college requirement introduced in 1901, insisted on any college work at all. As of 1900, only 15 or 20 percent of the schools even required a high school diploma for admission. At most schools, students could gain admission with a high school equivalency certificate of uncertain educational value or by passing an easy qualifying examination. Students unable to meet these requirements were routinely accepted "on condition." Less education was required to gain admission to most medical schools than to a good four-year high school. In 1896, the president of the University of Minnesota called low entrance standards "the greatest hindrance to medical education in this country."[47]

Medical schools in the early 1900s were attracting some of the finest young minds in the country, but they were also continuing to enroll many with dubious academic credentials. A multiplicity of paths to medical school still existed. For example, at the University of Pennsylvania in two representative years, 1898–99 and 1899–1900, members of the first-year classes ranged from college graduates to individuals with less than a high school education who "passed" an entrance examination (table 5.1). Students of all levels of ability and preparation started the same medical course together.

By the early 1900s, however, medical educators started to become more insistent about establishing entrance requirements. They were finding that without any standards for admission, educational chaos was occurring. Advanced and beginning students were being mixed in the same classes, to the boredom of the former and the frustration of the latter. Elementary scientific subjects were still commonly taught in medical schools, leaving less time for the medical courses. "It ought not to be necessary to teach elementary chemistry or elementary biology in the medical school any more than it ought to be necessary to teach elementary English in the law school,"[48] one observer

TABLE 5.1

Educational Background of First-Year Students, University of Pennsylvania

	1898–99	1899–1900
Passed entrance examinations	4	23
Took part of entrance examinations; remainder of requirements covered by diplomas from high schools or normal schools	4	—
College graduates	28	22
Graduates of approved high schools and academies	40	93
Graduates of approved normal schools	3	12
Members of a senior class in college	1	3
Members of a junior class in college	3	6
Members of a sophomore class in college	11	24
Members of a freshman class in college	13	19
Dropped from preceding first-year medical class and repeating	34	25

Source: "Report of the Dean of the Department of Medicine," in *Annual Report of Provost and Treasurer of the University of Pennsylvania* (1900), 113, University of Pennsylvania Archives.

wrote. Most important, as medical studies became scientifically rigorous, inadequately prepared students were frequently forced to repeat work or drop out of school. It was recognized that even superior teachers "cannot turn out a good product if inferior material is admitted."[49] For these reasons, the provost of the University of Pennsylvania wrote in 1907, "Increased entrance requirements have become absolutely necessary in all Schools of the first rank."[50]

Entrance requirements had been frequently discussed long before 1900. However, the context of those earlier discussions was much different. Most nineteenth-century "reformers," such as the American Medical Association and the American Academy of Medicine, wanted the requirement for admission to be a college degree because the popular stereotypes of "coarse and common doctors" could be readily combated if only cultivated persons were permitted to become physicians. Medical educators in the early 1900s viewed "entrance requirements" differently. To them the term signified science—a minimum of one year each of college-level biology, chemistry, and physics—rather than the college degree per se. They also wanted to require German and French, so that students could keep up with the current scientific literature. Although medical educators of the early 1900s admired culture for its own sake and encouraged students to take a college degree whenever possible, they deemed college-level science, not general education, the essential ingredient of a premedical program.[51] Once again in the history of medical education, the same term—in this case, "entrance requirements"—meant different things to different people.

The desire to institute entrance requirements was not enough to bring them about. In the late nineteenth century efforts to raise admission standards were thwarted by the lack of qualified students. In 1899, the faculty of Cornell Medical College wanted to require a college degree for admission, but because they thought this was too ideal a standard and doubted whether they could attract twelve to fifteen students per class, they reluctantly made the requirement only a high school diploma.[52] Similarly, in 1896, the University of Minnesota decided to require a high school education after 1899. "This is not all that could be desired," the president of the university wrote, "but it is a decided advance on the past."[53] The framework of a system of medical education was in place before there were many students who could take full advantage of it.

By the early 1900s, however, the nation's educational system had become much stronger. First the elementary schools had expanded, later the high schools, and ultimately the colleges and universities. With the growth in size was a concomitant growth in the quality of high school and college teaching.

The natural sciences, formerly a neglected area, received increasing attention in both secondary schools and colleges. As education advanced along preliminary lines, medical schools reaped a major benefit: a much larger supply of well-prepared students.

As a result, medical schools at the turn of the century were finally able to impose more exacting entrance requirements. At first they did so hesitantly and cautiously, requiring high school degrees only; but success bred confidence, and academic rivalry perpetuated the process, and soon the better schools were rushing to require one, two, or more years of college preparation.[54] Schools that were slower to strengthen their admission requirements were exceptions that illustrated the rule that a strong underlying educational system was necessary. Thus, the medical schools of Arkansas and Vermont, both located in states with weak high school systems, continued to admit poorly prepared students even after the national trend toward higher entrance standards had begun.[55] Admission requirements were lowest in the South, where the public school system was the weakest in the country.[56]

The thrust of the movement to establish entrance requirements was to make college-level science a prerequisite for admission. By 1908, fifty-seven medical schools had announced their intention to require at least one year of college study, to take effect no later than 1910.[57] And by 1915, of the ninety-five medical schools in existence, fifty required one year of college and forty, two or more years.[58] Some schools also began requiring the bachelor's degree for admission, but only if the college work included the mandatory courses in biology, chemistry, and physics. To the Association of American Medical Colleges, "The holder of a baccalaureate degree cannot receive credit for his degree only. It must represent a definite amount of work in certain prescribed subjects."[59]

In introducing entrance requirements, the medical schools for a time forged ahead of the high schools and colleges. Not enough qualified students were immediately available, and many schools experienced marked drops in enrollments—far greater than that caused by any other reform. For instance, at Columbia between 1902 and 1908, the school increased admission standards to a point where it required college-level science. As a result, enrollment fell during this period from 815 to 304.[60]

Nevertheless, medical school officials—at least those with strong universities to back them up financially—rejoiced when classes shrank because of higher admission requirements. In response to the school's new entrance requirement of a high school education, enrollment in Pennsylvania's first-year class fell substantially in 1897 from the year before. Charles Harrison, the provost of the university, declared that any loss of students from this rule "is by no means to be regretted, the present requirements for admission to the department being so moderate that no student unable to meet them is fit to be a candidate for the degree of Doctor of Medicine."[61] In 1902, the dean of Columbia found the decline in attendance to be "a source of gratification" because the incoming students as a group were noticeably better than before.[62] To medical educators, entrance requirements were as academically necessary as proper laboratory and clinical facilities, and if smaller enrollments were the price, it was a price they were gladly willing to pay.

Soon the educational system caught up with the medical schools. Attendance at high schools and colleges was growing rapidly, and the quality of teaching was improving every year. In 1913, Tufts did not experience the expected decline in enrollment after raising admission requirements because "there has been a more wide spread disposition to provide the necessary instruction in our secondary schools to meet this elevation of medical entrance requirements than it was feared might be the case."[63] In 1909, Cornell did not hesitate to tell prospective students that biology, chemistry, and physics were required for admission, "as these courses are now given in practically all colleges."[64] Attending college, by implication, had become a matter of course. By the end of World War I, the educational system had grown so that medical school classes had again become full, but now with students who had attended or completed college. Indeed, at many schools the problem once again became the limitation of class size—a harder problem than before, now that there were more than enough qualified applicants.

Medical schools not only benefited from a developing school system; through their entrance requirements they helped shape that system. Medical schools, along with other professional schools, played an important role in structuring from above a new four-tiered system that began with the elementary schools and proceeded through the high schools and colleges to end with the professional and graduate schools. As medical schools established entrance requirements, colleges made certain that they provided the necessary premedical courses. In addition, by accepting college work only if preceded by a complete four-year high school course, medical schools helped create a system with single portals of entry to and exit from each level.

Medical schools helped shape the school system both individually and collectively. Schools that were part of university systems often helped establish premedical programs at the undergraduate campuses. One important goal of such programs was to avoid the overlap or duplication of courses. The natural sciences would be taught strictly in the colleges; the medical subjects only in the medical schools; and the whole system would thereby be made more efficient.[65] Medical schools also helped disseminate information about entrance requirements by sending high school and college officials announcements of the latest standards. The Council on Medical Education worked especially hard in this area, and, in 1915, it published a pamphlet, "Making the Right Start," for prospective medical students. Copies were sent to all liberal arts colleges, all state superintendents of public instruction, and the principals of one-fifth of the high schools in the United States.[66] The general experience of most medical educators after 1905 was that the colleges were eager to gear their programs to meet medical school requirements. One group of medical educators observed in 1908: "Colleges need and are seeking the advice of the better medical schools as to what premedical and medical subjects they should teach and how they should be presented. Experience has shown that they are ready and eager to make their courses more effective as a preparation for medical study."[67]

As many myths exist about the establishment of entrance requirements as about any single topic in the history of medical education. It has been fashionable in recent scholarship, for instance, to attribute the requirements to the profession's desire to uplift its image and social status. Yet one cannot legitimately read such motives into the work of the medical educators who introduced the requirements. These men acted out of educational conviction, not out of concern for how much income or prestige the average practitioner in the community enjoyed. If they had personal reasons, it was so that they would not have to waste their time with ill-prepared students. Franklin Mall wrote, "When the schools are filled with a high class of students it will be found that less teaching is required than at present, leaving more time for instructors to devote to scientific work."[68]

Confusion on this issue has arisen from the common error of viewing the medical profession as a monolith. To clarify the matter, it is necessary to distinguish the concerns of academic physicians from those of ordinary practitioners. There is little doubt that the establishment of entrance requirements helped elevate the image and position of physicians, which was why so many doctors heartily welcomed their arrival. However, entrance requirements were introduced not by the profession as a whole but by medical educators, whose interests lay with the development of academic medicine as a career rather than with how much money the average doctor in practice made. Recognition of these internal distinctions within the medical profession is crucial if the misconceptions of the past are to be corrected.

In addition, it has been widely assumed that entrance requirements created a new sociological mix within medicine, changing it from a profession open to anyone to a profession limited to the middle and upper classes. Although entrance requirements undoubtedly reinforced that trend, they were not the main cause, for such changes were already underway before entrance requirements had become common. In the 1890s and 1900s, there was considerable attrition among medical school classes, and this took its greatest toll on the disadvantaged students who entered medical school with the least preliminary preparation. Abraham Flexner noted in his 1910 report that the higher the standard of admission to a medical school, the lower the rate of attrition.[69] Thus, even before entrance requirements were introduced, the sociological composition of the profession was already shifting toward the well-to-do segments of the population.

Academic attrition occurred at medical schools of all levels of quality. In the early 1900s, Cornell's policy was "to weed out students in the first year and if possible to graduate our entire class in the fourth year." From 1900 to 1907, between 27 percent and 42 percent of the first-year students were dropped each year for poor scholarship.[70] At New York University, Minnesota, and Tufts, approximately one-half of the entering students were gone by the third year, and further attrition occurred thereafter.[71] "It is not an occasion for gratitude that such defective scholarship should exist," the dean of the University of Minnesota wrote in 1896, "but it is an occasion for gratitude that students showing defective scholarship are not permitted to take their degrees."[72]

The same phenomenon also occurred at lesser schools. Even those schools with the most lax admission requirements often proved to be much stricter about promotion and graduation. The Denver and Gross College of Medicine, for instance, acted unethically by soliciting students to apply.[73] It routinely admitted students if they would enroll by November 15, even though the school session began around September 1. In this way the school complied with the form if not the spirit of a rule of the Association of American Medical Colleges that a student's attendance be at least 70 percent.[74] Yet, the school was much tougher in its grading. Its records are replete with letters informing students that they had been placed on academic probation, and the school had no hesitation about flunking students who could not improve their performance. Responding to one irate father, a physician, whose son had been dropped from school, a representative of the faculty wrote, "I wish to impress upon you the fact that the Denver and Gross College of Medicine is no kindergarten."[75] The student was not readmitted. Of the forty students who enrolled as first-year students in 1901, only sixteen graduated four years later.[76]

Not all schools had tough standards of grading and promotion, but poor students who might make it through such schools were often weeded out by state licensing boards. Such was the case at Georgetown, where the faculty acknowledged that "the increasing percentage of failures of our graduates before State Boards strongly points to the fact that our final examinations are not sufficiently rigid."[77] In St. Louis, graduates of Washington University and St. Louis University, two good medical schools, had a far lower rate of failure on the state licensing examination (14.9 and 13.4 percent, respectively) than graduates of the city's four very weak schools, whose failure rates ranged from 34 to 60 percent.[78] Nationwide, one report in 1906 showed that among graduates of thirty-eight medical schools, the failure rate on licensing examinations exceeded 20 percent.[79]

From the 1880s to World War I, the sociological composition of the medical profession underwent a dramatic change. Once open to anyone who cared to practice, the profession increasingly came to be recruited from the well-to-do segments of society, to the exclusion of the working classes, immigrants, ethnic minorities, and blacks. This was primarily the result of a changing system of medical education that had become so academically rigorous that the poorly prepared could no longer compete. The working classes suffered the most from this change because they had the least access to higher education. For instance, as late as the decade between 1915 and 1925, the children of fathers with less than eight years of formal education had one-sixth the chance of entering college as those whose fathers had attended college.[80] Thus, academic attrition took its greatest toll on the underprivileged. Entrance requirements were not needed for those groups to be excluded from the profession.

What entrance requirements did bring about was the denial of opportunity to the disadvantaged student who wanted to attempt to make the grade. Before, poorly educated but capable and motivated youths had the chance of becoming physicians, even if more and more of them by the early 1900s were failing. Now, if they could not meet the official prerequisites, they were denied the opportunity to try. The profession had in fact already become relatively inaccessible to the poor, but with entrance requirements that process became formalized. A once flexible system had become rigid and uncompromising. Academic standards were the victor; equality of social opportunity, the loser.

In the early 1900s, no one was arguing that a physician should enter the practice of medicine ill prepared. Even a struggling proprietary school like the Medical Department of the University of Maryland declared: "A poor boy has no right to go into the practice of medicine with any lower qualification than the rich boy. No man has a right to go into it unless he will fit himself fairly for the work."[81] However, many medical educators began to question the proper role of medical schools. To what degree should schools be selective in their admission policies and to what degree inclusive? In other words, should they serve educational or egalitarian purposes? In a country whose ideals, if not ever the reality, remained democratic, the idea of a selective medical school was cause for discomfort. The president of Tufts argued, "It would unquestionably be a misfortune to impose conditions that would exclude all but the sons of wealthy families from securing a medical education."[82]

This underlying tension between educational and egalitarian purposes has never abated. Nevertheless, from the early 1900s through the present, advocates of educational elitism have scored all the major victories, while proponents of egalitarianism have suffered all the corresponding defeats. (The most recent defeat of egalitarianism in medical education was the widely publicized Bakke case in California, in which the principle of affirmative action was deemed less important than admitting to medical school only the most qualified applicants.) If necessary, consciences could be assuaged by pointing to a growing system of public education that was enhancing social mobility, if not creating the true equality of opportunity as apologists of the school system were claiming it did. In an era of scientific medicine, the need to train all doctors thoroughly came to be regarded as medical education's greatest imperative. A further division of labor began to characterize the school system. The lower levels assumed the task of providing educational opportunity for all; the professional schools assumed a purely educational function for those who survived. Because time was so precious in medical school, medical educators felt that they were serving society better by producing well-prepared doctors than by trying to increase the number of underprivileged youths who became physicians. Through the establishment of entrance requirements, medical schools declared their primary function to be educational, not egalitarian.

On the surface entrance requirements accomplished their desired goal. Schools like Harvard, Yale, and Johns Hopkins took pride in being able to predict students' performances in medical school on the basis of their preliminary preparation. They found that students with the desired college background performed much better than those without.[83] As medical school classes began to fill with well-prepared students, attrition rates markedly dropped.

Lurking beneath the surface, however, was a persistent uneasiness about the requirements for admission. Personal qualities, not intelligence alone, were indispensable to future success in medical practice or research, but medical school officials, like all educators, found these characteristics much more difficult to judge. College grades could predict a student's ability to learn a subject in medical school, but they could not indicate whether a student possessed the compassion, understanding, and dedication desirable for the practice of medicine. Nor could they indicate which students had the creativity, ingenuity, and originality of thought necessary for a successful career in medical research. The medical faculty at Pittsburgh recognized this problem. "It is obvious that no description or formula can be written to describe the personality which is best adapted for the practice of medicine and so it is that today many who pass from medical schools, diploma in hand, never measure up to those standards which all would hope to see."[84]

Medical educators, in short, found themselves able to select good medical students, but they operated on faith that they were selecting good future doctors. They knew that they needed to evaluate an applicant's personal characteristics, but they were frustrated at their inability to do so. Medical educators today are still trying to determine the best way to choose students for medical school, for no relation has yet been shown between either college grades or medical college admission test scores and the quality of future performance as a physician,[85] and the evaluation of an applicant's personal attributes remains as elusive as ever. To medical educators, who prided themselves on their special expertise in matters of pedagogy, this realization was—and is—humbling.

6 The Birth of

Academic Medicine

BEFORE THE CIVIL WAR there had been two types of persons within the medical profession: students and practitioner-teachers. A separate class of teachers did not exist, for all instruction was provided by private practitioners. With the rapid growth of medical knowledge, that situation irrevocably changed. Practitioners continued their chief work of taking care of patients, but a new group of doctors arose to stand between the student and the practitioner: the full-time professor. It was these new doctors who increasingly became responsible for the production, assessment, and transmission of new information. And it was this new class of physicians that from the 1870s onward assumed leadership of the movement to reform medical education in the United States—a leadership it never relinquished. All along many physicians had talked about medical education, but at the vanguard of the reform movement were its chief instigators, the academic physicians. The development of medical education and the rise of academic medicine as a profession proceeded hand-in-hand with each other.

As medical knowledge proliferated, academic medicine became necessary. The medical scholar became indispensable to the continued discovery of new medical findings and to the dissemination of recent medical advances. Nevertheless, the medical professor was initially perceived by many physicians as a threat, and the birth of academic medicine was one of the most difficult and painful events ever to occur in the history of American medicine. Far from being embraced by other doctors, academic physicians were greeted with skepticism at best, overt hostility at worst. The animosity that many practitioners held for medical professors was matched only by the arrogance with which many professors viewed the ordinary practitioner. "Town-gown" tensions between private practitioners and university doctors spread through the medical profession, threatening to rip it apart.

Ultimately, however, an accommodation was reached and tensions abated, as both sides begrudgingly came to realize that they could not survive without the other. Boundaries between professors and practitioners were never entirely distinct, but the former increasingly took responsibility for teaching and research while the latter became the provider of the fruits of experimental medicine to the population, but now with the enhanced prestige and status that had so long eluded them. Once a homogeneous profession, where almost everyone had engaged in general practice, medicine underwent differentiation into a heterogeneous profession. A host of medical careers were now available —academic medicine and private practice were both broad areas encompassing many specialities—but the most important demarcation lay between medical scholarship and medical practice. As medical education developed, the profession evolved into its present sociological form.

Professors and Practitioners

As discussed in chapter 2, academic medicine in the United States had its beginnings with the migration of American physicians to German universities for the study of the experimental medical sciences. The Bowditches, the Vaughans, the Abels, the Malls, and the Welches returned to the United States from their studies abroad with the thought that medicine should be taught in a scientifically rigorous way in which each student worked in the laboratory and hospital. This group also sought for itself full-time positions in medical teaching and research, careers that were modeled after those of their German professors. They wanted to change not only the methods but the institutional framework of medical teaching in the United States. For them it was a trying and frustrating struggle, for academic opportunities were exceedingly scarce in America at that time.

In the 1870s and 1880s, a few full-time teaching and research positions began to appear, particularly at pioneering medical schools like Harvard and Michigan. Nevertheless, the existence of academic medicine remained highly precarious. There were few positions, salaries were inadequate, and facilities and working conditions were substandard. The Pennsylvania faculty in 1893 admitted that its salary of $1,500 for its assistant professor of physiology was "lower than is paid to certain Assistant Professors in our High Schools, and insufficient to guarantee the retention of thoroughly competent men."[1] Even more discouraging, the work of the professor of medicine was still widely unappreciated in a pragmatic country that continued to ask why such persons were not out in practice like other doctors. Medical scholars sought, after all, not only an economically secure career but respect and the assurance that their work was appreciated and valued. However, in the late nineteenth century the full-time professor was still widely regarded as eccentric at best, as unproductive and useless at worst. In such an unfriendly climate, most who sought academic careers did not succeed.

In the 1880s, as experimental medicine increasingly proved itself to be relevant to clinical practice, the situation began to brighten. The same factors that facilitated the improvements of medical teaching also helped give birth to academic medicine as a career in the United States. By the early 1890s, a number of medical schools had already hired full-time faculty members in one, two, or three of their basic science departments. In 1883, Harvard Medical School had even appointed Henry Bowditch to be dean, the first medical scientist to occupy such a position at an American medical school. The greatest breakthrough came from Johns Hopkins, which opened in 1893 with every laboratory science department placed on a "full-time" or "university" basis. By 1910, 613 full-time, salaried instructors could be found in the 131 medical schools then existing. Because 47 of the 131 schools employed no salaried instructors at all, those that did averaged between seven and eight full-time instructors each.[2] In ensuing years the opportunities to pursue careers in medical teaching and research increased even more rapidly, so that by 1915 the General Education Board was remarking that "nowadays no reputable medical school uses practitioners to teach these [laboratory] branches."[3] Before 1910, the full-time salaried instructors were found primarily in the laboratory departments, but during World War I and afterwards this movement spread to the clinical departments as well.

In the two decades before 1910, jobs in academic medicine were often poorly paid. The dean of Yale Medical School complained in 1900 that his school was unable to offer more than $2,000 to anyone devoting his whole time to medical teaching.[4] In 1909, the highest salary received by a full-time professor at the University of Nebraska College of Medicine was $2,100, with most earning $1,500 or $1,600.[5] Those still in training for academic careers endured even greater hardships. As late as World War I, George Dock complained that "many good men [in training] are lost now to scientific medicine because schools will not give them from $250 and living [expenses] up."[6] A successful doctor in private practice, in contrast, might have earned $25,000 or $30,000, although most private practitioners earned only one-tenth that amount.

Nevertheless, conditions had clearly begun to turn for the better, as more and more good positions were established. As early as 1895, Columbia paid its full professors $7,500.[7] In 1907–08, as indicated in table 6.1, the full professors at Harvard Medical School all received respectable salaries. Professors in the clinical departments could supplement their incomes with consulting practices; instructors and assistant professors in the basic sciences earned between $800 and $1,600.[8] A few lucky academic physicians even found themselves in the novel position of being wooed. The dean of Columbia complained at one faculty meeting in 1899 that another school had tried to lure away an eminent medical professor for twice the salary he was receiving in New York.[9] A particularly celebrated case was that of the neurosurgeon Harvey Cushing. While at Johns Hopkins from 1901 to 1909, Cushing declined seven invitations to accept the chair of surgery at good medical schools, until finally accepting a position at Harvard.[10]

The emergence of an academic elite, along with the rise of the modern

TABLE 6.1.

Salaries of Full Professors, Harvard Medical School, 1907–08

Name	Department	Salary	Age
Blake, Clarence	Otology	$1,000	62
Bowen, John	Dermatology	1,500	48
Bradford, Edward	Orthopedic Surgery	500	57
Burrell, Herbert	Surgery	2,500	49
Cannon, Walter	Physiology	4,000	38
Councilman, William	Pathological Anatomy	5,000	51
Dwight, Thomas	Anatomy	5,000	61
Ernst, Harold	Bacteriology	4,000	50
Fitz, Reginald	Theory and Practice of Physic	2,500	62
Green, Charles	Obstetrics; Secretary of the Faculty of Medicine	500	—
Harrington, Charles	Hygiene	1,500	49
Minot, Charles	Comparative Anatomy	5,000	52
Pfaff, Franz	Pharmacology and Therapeutics	2,000	45
Porter, William	Comparative Physiology	4,000	40
Putnam, James	Diseases of the Nervous System	1,000	58
Richardson, Maurice	Surgery	2,500	53
Rotch, Thomas	Pediatrics	1,250	56
Shattuck, Frederick	Clinical Medicine	2,500	57
Smith, Theobald	Comparative Pathology	5,000	46

SOURCE: File, "Harvard University 1904–1917," Carnegie Foundation Archives.

university and the growth of the school system, was the critical event in the progress of medical education before 1910. At school after school, academic physicians gained control, whereupon they immediately improved the curriculum as far as available finances would permit. Their ranks were actually larger than the number of full-time salaried instructors would suggest, for a more accurate estimate of their numbers would include all those dedicated to a genuine academic life, regardless of how they were paid. Thus, preclinical faculty members of less prosperous schools who were committed to careers of teaching and research should be considered members of this group, even if their schools could afford to pay them only partial salaries. Research-oriented clinicians whose main work was at the medical school should also be regarded as medical professors, even though they might have supplemented their incomes with private consultations. In this period the clinical departments of Johns Hopkins were not strictly "full-time," but a clinical professor like William Halsted, the chief of surgery and a member of the National Academy of Sciences, was no less an academician than his colleagues in the basic science departments. In this book the term "medical educator" has referred to all such persons. The introduction of modern methods of teaching medicine, the rise of American medical research, and the emergence of academic medicine as a profession in America were all related events, for as academically trained individuals gained footholds in medical schools, medical education and medical research prospered.

Members of the academic community did not wait silently for opportunities to present themselves. They worked hard and aggressively to create those opportunities. Many leaders of this group were not just teachers and investigators but entrepreneurs and institution-builders who worked arduously to create the institutional and financial conditions that would make the pursuit of medical scholarship possible. With truly missionary zeal they carried their message to university presidents, philanthropists, political officials, legislators, fellow physicians, and all else who would listen, working desperately to acquire the financial, institutional, and popular support necessary for academic medicine to survive. Whether medical teaching and research would exist as a career in the United States hinged on the results of their efforts. This had been the overriding goal of scientifically-oriented physicians since the beginning of the German migration, and it became a matter of professional life or death to them. The nature of medical knowledge had created the need for a separate class of medical professors, but the medical scientists had to engineer a sociological and economic revolution so that they could have a place that was permanent and secure.

Many academic physicians contributed to the institution-building of the period. Most operated within their own communities, working with local philanthropists, school officials, physicians, and politicians to generate support for full-time positions. Some possessed the academic prestige and administrative and diplomatic skills to become effective spokesmen for the cause regionally or nationally. Others used job offers elsewhere as leverage to gain more support. Thus, when Joseph Erlanger, later to receive the Nobel Prize for his work in neurophysiology, was solicited to leave the University of Wisconsin by the University of Pittsburgh in 1909, he provided the dean of Pittsburgh his view of how an ideal department of physiology should operate. "I could not think of casting my lot with a new venture that would not agree in the main in writing to the conditions specified above,"[11] he explained. A few years later his conditions were met by Washington University and he accepted a position there.

No one was more important in developing academic medicine as a profession than William Welch, the professor of pathology and dean of the Johns Hopkins Medical School and the most influential spokesman for academic medicine ever in this country.[12] In the 1870s, Welch had studied with Julius Cohnheim in Germany and decided to spend his professional career in teaching and research rather than in practice. Subsequently, he performed creditable investigations in pathology and bacteriology, but his real importance lay in his astute judgment and in his mastery of the political and economic processes by which support for academic medicine could be obtained. Throughout the country, his advice was sought on academic appointments. Such was his influence, as Donald Fleming has observed, that he had the "power to transform men's lives almost by a flick of the wrist."[13] He advised presidents of universities as well as presidents of the United States on medical policy. He established the country's first journal devoted to experimental medical research; he helped organize the Rockefeller Institute for Medical Research; he founded the country's first school of public health; he helped establish the first "full-time" plan for clinical faculty; and he was a superb medical fund raiser. A lifelong bachelor, medicine had become his mistress, and he approached these difficult tasks with a sober judgment, a shrewdly calculated strategy, and an unswerving conviction that were sometimes belied by his rather absent-minded and disorganized behavior. "Popsy," as the students and staff at Johns Hopkins referred to him, lived in such a cluttered fashion that he could not entertain at home, and he remained oblivious of his personal finances. Friends frequently observed him at baseball games poring over galley sheets of the journal he edited. Throughout all his disparate activities, however, one activity gave him joy above all others: training young medical scientists and finding for them opportunities to work. As a young man, Welch had been no stranger to the anxieties endured by those of his generation who wished to pursue an academic career in America. Later in life, he told his sister that of everything he had done, he had derived "the most satisfaction" from his success at increasing the opportunities for scientific work in America.[14]

The line between professor and practitioner was never entirely distinct. Both arose from a common source—a scientific training in medical school. Differentiation occurred only as they pursued different paths after graduation. Particularly in the clinical departments, those with academic orientations usually continued to see patients, while many full-time practitioners continued to teach at medical schools and make contributions to the medical literature. Especially during the early years, a number of practitioners belonged to the Interurban Clinical Club, a prominent organization of academic internists from the East Coast.[15] Conversely, many who had once worked at the Rockefeller Institute Hospital later left academic medicine to enter private practice.[16] Neither academic medicine nor private practice were ever exclusive categories.

Nevertheless, by the early 1900s academic medicine had clearly differentiated itself from medical practice as a separate career alternative. Academicians and practitioners each had their own professional organizations, and they had different goals, values, and attitudes. Professors saw their chief role as the production and dissemination of ideas, not the provision of medical care. For the opportunity to do so, they were willing to accept far lower incomes than they could earn in private practice. In return, they hoped to receive widespread academic recognition. As Franklin Mall frequently put it, they sought glory, not gold.[17] They measured success not by whether they had enough of their own money to live in luxury but by whether they had received enough of someone else's money to acquire a large laboratory with many assistants. Although considerable overlap existed, academic physicians were much more closely identified with the Association of American Medical Colleges and the various medical research societies, in contrast to practitioners, whose interests were represented more directly by the American Medical Association and the various clinical specialty organizations. Academicians tended to be much more tolerant of homeopathy than the rest of the profession, but the medical professors had a cause célèbre of their own: the antivivisection movement. No other issue spurred a greater cohesiveness among the academic elite, forcing them to justify and explain their work to a skeptical public.[18] This list of contrasts could be expanded, but the point has been made. Despite certain bonds that never disappeared, sharp differences existed between professors and practitioners. As Welch said of practitioners in 1914, "Theirs is a different career."[19]

Although medical professors pursued a different career from practitioners, their career was not very different from that of professors in other academic disciplines. All shared the same commitment to advanced teaching and research; all were involved in the same struggle to "professionalize" their respective disciplines, that is, to establish standards of teaching and scholarship and to acquire the means by which academic careers in their fields could be properly supported. The dean of Yale Medical School pointed out in 1901 that "the demands on the instructors of anatomy, physiology, chemistry, and pathology are practically the same as those made on the instructors in similar branches in other departments of the University."[20] In the late nineteenth century, as Robert Wiebe has discussed, a new middle class was arising that consisted of various professional groups identifiable by their skills.[21] Professors formed one such group. Scholars in every field, William Thayer of Johns Hopkins explained, possessed identical attributes, regardless of whether their interests happened to be in medicine or in history or in philology. "The seeds of scholarship lie mainly, not in what a man is taught, but in what a man is."[22] Herein lay one of the strongest links between medical education and the universities.

By the turn of the century, academic physicians had become necessary. If medical knowledge were to continue growing at a rapid rate, their existence was demanded by the nature of that knowledge. However, the birth of academic medicine did not occur easily or without trauma, and much of the practicing profession viewed this new class of doctors with fear, suspicion, and resentment. One midwestern practitioner belittled the "flunkeyism and truckling" to the eastern academic "magnates" who were gaining control of the Association of American Medical Colleges. Medical teaching in America must not, he asserted, be controlled by that "large coterie of gentlemen who part their hair and names in the middle."[23] As the professors strove to establish themselves, a civil war within the profession erupted.

Part of the friction resulted from the different views toward experimental science held by practitioners and professors. The French influence remained strong, and many practitioners continued to question the utility of laboratory studies for clinical practice, even as the scientific subjects were developing. Not even the germ theory of disease eliminated all such skepticism, and many practitioners accepted the germ theory only very slowly, if at all.[24] To medical scientists, such conservatism was indefensible. In 1882, Alfred Loomis, a distinguished clinician of the "old" school, publicly mocked the germ theory. "That's too bad," William Welch responded. "Loomis is such a nice man."[25] Franklin Mall viewed ordinary clinicians with even greater scorn. In 1904 he snorted, "Were the ranks of the medical profession filled with men who had done some scientific work in their student days, we would not have witnessed the opposition to the tubercle bacillus as the cause of tuberculosis or to the treatment of diphtheria with anti-toxin."[26] A schism arose, with practitioners viewing the researchers as impractical, and the laboratory workers disdainfully considering ordinary clinicians as unscientific.

Another, and more serious, friction arose between practitioners and professors. They were engaged not only in a battle of ideology but in a struggle for power over who was to control medical education. Traditionally this responsibility had belonged to private practitioners, but in the late nineteenth century, medical professors began claiming this responsibility as their own. This was clearly seen at the opening of Johns Hopkins. The new school had recruited its faculty from all over the United States, and to the dismay of the local practitioners, not a single Baltimore physician had received an appointment of consequence. Abraham Flexner, academic medicine's most ardent supporter, stated the academician's viewpoint in 1909: "The teaching of medicine cannot nowadays be wholly or mainly left to the general practitioner. . . . they are not teachers, and teachers alone can create a modern school of medicine."[27]

As professors and practitioners fought, few medical scientists, even the most rigid in their views, argued that private practitioners should be excluded from medical teaching. The very large numbers of instructors that were needed made that impractical. What academicians did contend was that they should be in charge. Practitioners would still be permitted to teach, provided that they acquiesced to the authority of the full-time staff. A sociological revolution within the profession was occurring, for the emerging academic elite was usurping control of medical education from those who had traditionally held that power. As the academic profession gained strength, practitioners started to lose much of their traditional power, responsibility, and status. In their opposition to the professors was all the fury, terror, animosity, and outrage of a displaced group.

Accommodation

The 1890s and 1900s represented a turning point in the development of the medical profession, just as in many other areas of American life. It was a time when conflicting traditions mingled and competed. For instance, in 1893 the Johns Hopkins Medical School opened, a completely modern medical school. Yet in the early 1890s, many physicians in the United States had never even laid eyes on a microscope.[28] As scientific medicine and the academic physicians who represented it came to the forefront, their presence caused numerous conflicts with practitioners. But at the same time processes were at work that were to help win the acceptance of scientific medicine among the profession at large and foster a rapprochement between practitioners and professors. The result would be a sociologically transformed medical profession—an event crucial for the development of academic medicine as a career as well as for the rise in image, income, and prestige that the profession as a whole enjoyed after 1900.

Throughout most of the latter nineteenth century, a tremendous gulf continued to separate the laboratory scientists from the practicing clinicians. Although occasional laboratory findings carried implications for clinical practice, the bulk of the knowledge was esoteric and without any immediate practical benefit. Medical investigators like Bowditch or Mall did not take care of patients and, to many of their practicing colleagues, seemed indistinguishable from natural scientists without medical training. So great was the gap between scientific and clinical medicine that some physicians even stood among the ranks of the antivivisectionists.[29]

Nevertheless, no amount of persistent skepticism about experimental medicine could halt the proliferation of medical knowledge, and more and more of the new knowledge was found to have clinical utility. The physician of 1900 had available the diphtheria antitoxin, and the physician of 1910 could treat syphilis with salvarsan. As laboratory workers expanded the scope of their investigations, new eras were starting in endocrinology, immunology, and other areas. Medical cures were still few, but the acceptance of antiseptic techniques had facilitated the birth of modern surgery and safer childbirth, and the germ theory of disease had invigorated the public health movement. Even where specific treatments did not exist, much had been learned in the way of the etiology and pathophysiology of disease, making possible far better diagnosis, prognosis, and supportive care. Vast amounts remained to be learned, but order was being brought to the understanding and management of disease. More important, through scientific research, it was felt that many more of medicine's pressing problems would be solved in the future. Thus Walter Cannon spoke to Charles Eliot "of the importance of understanding the nature of a disease, even if the cure of the disease is not yet compassed."[30] In Cannon's words, the faith of the era lay bare. If diseases were understood in terms of their fundamental mechanisms, cures would inevitably follow.

The ultimate accommodation of experimental medicine to medical practice began in the early 1900s with the emergence of clinical science, which provided a bridge between the care of patients and the fundamental medical sciences. Clinical science sprang from the growth of experimental medicine, but the field developed an identity of its own as experimental methods were increasingly applied to the study of disease and therapeutics—not just the healthy state. The clinical scientist eventually became what A. McGehee Harvey has called the "middle man in the medical world."[31] Trained in the methods of both laboratory science and practical medicine, clinical scientists were equally at home in the laboratory and at the bedside, and they could converse with fundamental scientists and clinicians alike. Like their scientific colleagues, clinical scientists were experimentalists rather than observationalists, and they employed the same tools of chemistry and biology. However, clinical scientists were more directly interested in problems of disease and therapeutics and hence they saw their natural environment as departments of medicine, surgery, pediatrics, or obstetrics rather than anatomy, physiology, biochemistry, or pathology. Like the basic scientists, many of them aspired toward full-time academic careers, but they wanted to pursue investigations more closely related to the actual practice of medicine. Their credo, as Harvey has pointed out, was that "the diagnosis and treatment of disease should go hand in hand with their study in the laboratory."[32]

On an individual level, the emergence of the clinical scientist was illustrated by the contrast between William Osler and Lewellys Barker, who succeeded Osler as professor of medicine at Johns Hopkins in 1905. Osler, the quintessential clinician, reflected the French and British traditions of astute bedside observation and the correlation of clinical with pathological findings. Although he introduced laboratories to the Johns Hopkins Hospital, he used them as a diagnostic aid only. Barker, in contrast, had a much more scientific view of medicine, and he used the laboratory not only to assist in clinical diagnosis but to study disease. He saw that chemistry and biology could help answer clinical questions and felt that faculty members of clinical departments should be provided time to pursue research.[33]

On an organizational level, the same contrast was seen in the differences between the Association of American Physicians, a society of traditional clinical teachers organized in 1886, and the American Society for Clinical Investigation, an organization established in 1908 that consisted of younger, laboratory-oriented physicians.[34] Clinical scientists, unlike basic scientists, usually continued to see patients, and ultimately they found academic positions in the clinical departments of medical schools everywhere in the country. As they combined the teaching and practice of medicine with experimental medical research, they formed the strongest link yet between clinical medicine and the basic sciences.

By the early 1900s, a new attitude toward experimental medicine had come to characterize practicing physicians in America. Even the most skeptical could no longer credibly deny that medical research worked—that it produced discoveries of clinical utility—even if large amounts of the new information remained esoteric and seemingly distant from the immediate problems of patient care. Physicians of the previous generation, doubting the value of experimental science to medical practice, had charged it with the most severe criticism of all: that it was not relevant. By 1900 that contention was no longer tenable. For all its art, medical practice had come to rest upon a scientific foundation.

The change in physicians' attitude toward laboratory science was analogous to the fundamental change in meaning of the word "liberalism" that was occurring in late nineteenth-century America. As Sidney Fine has discussed in his classic study, "liberalism" had always had as its goal the promotion of individual freedom. In a nontechnological age, liberal goals were equated with a governmental policy of laissez-faire; in a more complex society, those goals increasingly came to be identified with a policy of governmental intervention in the affairs of its citizens.[35] In medicine, a comparable shift in viewpoint occurred. To the older generation of physicians, experimental science was impersonal, pursued out of intellectual interest only, and unrelated to medicine's traditional concern for alleviating human suffering. By the early 1900s, as laboratory research was leading to better understanding and treatment of illness, it was recognized that earlier attitudes toward experimental science had to be modified. Clinicians came to realize that the laboratory had a role in their affairs, as society at large had come to understand that there was a role for the judicious use of government. This change was reflected in literature, as the image of the medical scientist changed from demonic to heroic, from Nathaniel Hawthorne's Rappaccini to Sinclair Lewis's Arrowsmith.[36] As this fundamental shift in viewpoint occurred, practitioners began to accept the medical scientist.

In the 1890s and 1900s, the rank and file of the medical profession acquired more and more appreciation of scientific medicine. Year-by-year, older physicians who distrusted science retired, to be replaced by young physicians indoctrinated in scientific methods at the country's improving medical schools. To an increasing number of medical graduates, academic physicians were not the enemy but their teachers. Many doctors acquired an understanding of scientific medicine through the postgraduate medical courses that some medical schools had begun to sponsor and through postgraduate study abroad. Numerous clinical journals and societies were established to help educate practitioners about recent developments in their field. Through all these vehicles, practitioners came to realize that their work rested upon a scientific foundation and that this foundation was rapidly growing. As this occurred, they became more tolerant of the academic physicians who represented scientific medicine.

No person or organization exerted a greater healing effect on the profession than William Osler.[37] As professor of medicine at Johns Hopkins, Osler symbolized the new scientific medicine to the profession, and he frequently voiced his admiration of German accomplishments in medical teaching and research. He was one of the first to use the clinical laboratory routinely as an aid to diagnosis, and he helped establish the Interurban Clinical Club, an important society devoted to fostering clinical research. However, unlike other of his Hopkins colleagues, such as Welch, Abel, and Mall, Osler was a clinical man always, studying the natural history of disease in hospitalized patients. His own medical training had been limited to pathological description and bedside observation; he never made any contributions to experimental medicine. He was always at his best as a teacher and diagnostician. In these respects he resembled the French and British clinicians of the early nineteenth century and the leading American clinicians of the previous generation much more than the modern clinical investigator. As Osler embraced scientific medicine, in short, he maintained the clinical acumen and spiritual and methodological values of an earlier era of great clinicians. He exemplified the modern medical scholar who had arisen from a simpler time when science had not yet intruded on the study or practice of medicine. He was not unlike Henry Ford, Thomas Edison, Alexander Graham Bell, Luther Burbank, and other popular heroes of the early twentieth century who represented "old-fashioned" rural values even as they forged a technological society.[38] Older practitioners could relate to Osler, even if they might not understand Welch or Mall.

Osler was not the only product of the earlier clinical tradition who embraced scientific medicine. In this regard L. Emmett Holt was to pediatrics and William W. Keen to surgery what Osler was to internal medicine. What made Osler unique, however, was the singular force of his personality. His charm, his wit, his energy, his dedication to the highest ideals of the profession, his extraordinary ability to remember names—all contributed to making him the most revered and beloved member of the medical profession that America has ever seen. "There was no one else like him,"[39] William Thayer recalled.

Osler used his unusual personal strengths as a force for harmony within the profession. No other physician had such a vast acquaintance with the profession at large, and he participated actively in medical societies in Baltimore and throughout the United States. He would not hear ill of any physician, and it was said that "every physician felt himself safe in Dr. Osler's hands."[40] Unlike many of his academic colleagues, who made no secret of their scorn for general practitioners and country doctors, Osler felt drawn to practitioners and treated them with respect as well as kindness. "I have an enduring faith in the men who do the routine work of our profession,"[41] he once said. To Osler, worthiness as a physician was not a matter of "satisfactory collegiate or sartorial credits" but devotion to the "highest interest" of the profession—something that is "widely diffused, sometimes apparent only when you get beneath the crust of a rough exterior."[42] At a time when medical knowledge and practice were beginning to change almost from day to day, Osler manifested his reverence for the profession by his fascination with the history of medicine, and he would caution doctors about how much remained to be learned—a useful check to the ebullient overconfidence of some of the medical scientists. Such a person could not be a threat to practitioners, even if he happened to be a professor at Johns Hopkins. If Welch may be considered medicine's symbolic secretary of state for his success at generating support for scientific medicine among governmental bodies and influential laymen, then Osler must be deemed the secretary of the interior for having allayed much of the suspicion of scientific medicine within the profession. No other person did more to help forge a reconciliation between the values of scientific medicine and those of traditional medical practice. This, it may be argued, was Osler's greatest contribution to American medicine.

Numerous signs of a new order within the medical profession had appeared by 1910. A program of continuing education had begun, with its focus in the postgraduate courses offered by the medical schools. The very fact that practitioners attended such courses implicitly showed that they acknowledged, however grudgingly, academicians' claims to authority in educational matters. Vigorous alumni organizations had sprouted up at medical schools everywhere. Through these organizations, the alumni offered their schools valuable financial, political, and spiritual aid. Further signs of an emerging rapprochement emerged as practitioners, often uneasily and rarely as leaders, joined hands with the academicians in combating experimental medicine's greatest threat, the antivivisection movement. Finally, in the early 1900s a reorganized American Medical Association brought practitioners and professors more closely together than at any time before or since, and on no other issue in the two decades that followed did they stand more united than on the development of the country's medical schools.

By 1910 the medical profession had undergone a sociological transformation into its present-day form. The profession now made room for both professors and practitioners. Academicians had achieved the opportunity to spend their professional lives in full-time teaching and research. To do so, they had relinquished the opportunity to earn unusually high incomes. They were rewarded in turn with power and prestige. Their power arose from the control they had gained over the training of physicians and the determination of "standard medical practice"; their prestige resulted from the recognition they might receive for their researches. Prominence within the profession, once a matter of family background, now rested on academic achievement. The great medical families of Boston, New York, Philadelphia, and other cities were losing influence within the medical community; in their place leadership was being provided by successful medical scholars whose allegiance was to the profession at large rather than to particular localities. In relation to the rest of American society, the medical profession was rapidly becoming elitist as higher and higher entrance standards were introduced, but internally it was becoming more democratic since academic success could not be bought or inherited.

As the academic physicians came to power, practitioners surrendered much of their traditional control over the internal affairs of the profession. The selection and training of future physicians and the determination of standards of practice had been usurped by the medical educators. In turn, however, practitioners started to acquire the social status and economic power that had eluded them for a full century. They had lost authority in strictly professional matters, but their enhanced social prestige enabled them to arbitrate more effectively with government and the public the external affairs of medicine. The American Medical Association, a disorganized and ineffective organization for over half a century, at last achieved the influence envisioned by its founders, and decade by decade, as it strove to protect the economic interests of practitioners, its power grew.

The reorganized medical profession demanded cooperation between professors and practitioners because they had become dependent on one another. Professors needed practitioners, for practicing physicians provided a lifetime market for the professors' services. Medical educators trained physicians once in medical school and then retrained them again and again in their medical practice through publications and continuing education courses. In addition, professors soon learned that they could raise funds for medical education much more easily if the practicing profession in their community supported them. In 1920, the efforts of the University of Oklahoma to obtain a new building for the medical school received a great boost when the state medical society voted unanimously to urge the state legislature to appropriate the money.[43] On the other hand, in the early 1920s the University of Arkansas School of Medicine was handicapped in its efforts to become a high grade institution because of the lack of support from the doctors of the state.[44]

Conversely, practitioners needed professors just as much. Practitioners benefited immeasurably from the knowledge that academicians were always there backing them up. Their growing social position and political power arose from the public's belief that they were always up-to-date and that being up-to-date mattered. Modern medical practice would not have been effective if the researchers had not been there to generate new discoveries, and the practitioners would not have been able to remain current without the help of the medical educators, who were continually investigating disease and informing the rest of the profession of the results.

As the professor of medicine gained acceptance in America, traditional tensions with practitioners never vanished. Many medical educators continued to look upon practitioners with an air of professional superiority, while practitioners did not necessarily stop viewing the professors as impractical and lacking in clinical skills. Arguments continued to flare. Still ahead was the enormous uproar during World War I over full-time positions as they applied to clinical departments. In the 1920s there was lingering doubt even among some clinicians at Johns Hopkins that laboratory work was compatible with clinical acumen.[45] "Town-gown" disputes have continued to mar the medical scene through the present. Nevertheless, by 1910 the point had been reached in which the two groups recognized each other's legitimacy. Both groups had come to understand that they were essential for each other's success and that there was room in the medical profession for both. Despite persistent tensions, the bonds between them had grown stronger than the forces driving them apart.

7 Financial Woes

MEDICAL EDUCATORS of the late nineteenth century quickly came to a painful realization: that they were engaged in an expensive enterprise. Ideals had to be translated into reality through the acquisition of laboratories, equipment, teaching hospitals, and an expanded corps of teachers. In 1891, the total endowments to medical schools in the United States amounted to only $500,000, in contrast to $18,000,000 for theological schools.[1] William Keen of Philadelphia declared in 1894: "You all know the great need, the crying need, of our medical schools at the present day is larger and more thorough laboratory facilities; and that means immense sums of money."[2]

If the cost of medical education was large, the cost of medical research was even greater. Huge expenses were involved. Salaries were required for full-time professors as well as for their assistants and technicians; stipends had to be provided for young investigators in training; and vast funds had to be found to construct, equip, and maintain laboratories that would be used solely for purposes of research. By 1910, over half the medical schools were offering respectable if not ideal medical teaching, but only twenty-five or thirty were contributing regularly to medical science. Because of financial constraints, more had been accomplished in improving the quality of instruction than in developing academic medicine as a career.

Although resources available for medical education began to grow in the mid-1880s, the infusion of funds over the next generation was not sufficient to support medical education and research properly. Medical educators for many years echoed the complaints of Keen that more funds were needed. The president of the Association of American Medical Colleges wrote in 1908: "The greatest single difficulty in the way of progress in medical education is undoubtedly poverty. Beside it all other difficulties appear trivial."[3] For this reason, medical education at the time of the Flexner report in 1910 was beset with problems. Notwithstanding the profound improvements of the previous generation, even the very best schools struggled with overcrowded laboratories and clinics, inadequate equipment and facilities, and a less than desirable level of personalized supervision of work. Conditions at the mediocre schools were even less acceptable. Medical education in 1910 had far to go, and many of Flexner's criticisms were deserved. Contrary to popular opinion, however, the schools had not failed at the level of intent. Their difficulties resulted from their lack of success in raising enough funds to do what they wanted to. The limiting factor in medical education was no longer conceptual but financial.

The Rising Costs of Medical Education

In the 1870s, medical teaching was an inexpensive task: the number of instructors required was small; the space, modest; and the equipment and apparatus, practically none. A school might incur yearly operating expenses of only a few hundred to a few thousand dollars. With fees typically $100 per year, an enrollment of even one hundred students guaranteed that there would be money left over for dividends at the end of the term.

The introduction of personalized methods of instruction placed new financial demands on medical schools. Major outlays were required for land, buildings, laboratories, clinics, and equipment. Modern methods also demanded a far higher ratio of teachers to students. Previously an instructor might have spent an hour delivering a lecture to an entire class. Now, an instructor might have to devote a full hour to a single student. It was necessary, Charles Eliot wrote, "that every individual medical student must be personally instructed by a skillful person in the use of his eyes, ears, and fingers in a great variety of operations which require much knowledge and highly trained senses. It is obvious that such instruction must be very costly."[4]

From the earliest years of the reform movement, the rising costs of medical teaching had caused the ambitious medical schools many moments of anxiety. The University of Pennsylvania had realized for two years prior to 1877 that a new program was necessary, and it delayed the reforms out of fear it would not be able to pay for them.[5] In 1888, the College of Physicians and Surgeons (New York) changed to a three-year program with required laboratory work, but with great fear that its operating expenses would markedly increase.[6] Its concern proved well founded, for by 1890 the school had already accumulated a debt of over $81,000.[7]

The expenses of the 1870s and 1880s were modest relative to those of the generation that followed. Year by year the costs of providing medical education surged uncontrollably. By 1910, according to Abraham Flexner's calculations, the minimum annual operating cost of a four-year school that provided "ideal" training to 250 students had grown to between $100,000 and $150,000.[8] Moreover, by 1910 the cost, independent of operating expenses, of acquiring the land and constructing laboratory and clinical facilities could easily run to several million dollars. To medical schools of the period, such sums were staggering.

Flexner's calculations applied to a particular type of medical school—the university medical school, where full-time faculty members vigorously pursued research. However, other alternatives were available. In theory, good teaching could be provided by "practical schools," which left the task of research to others. One advantage of a "practical" school was that its expenses could easily be halved, for far fewer salaries and laboratories would be required. Even so, that left a financial requirement of between $50,000 and $75,000 a year—a still far greater sum than medical schools had been accustomed to spending. In addition, some up-to-date laboratory facilities would have to be acquired. As Henry Pritchett put it, there was "a minimum of equipment and resources" below which no medical school should operate.[9] Even schools that focused exclusively on the training of practitioners faced imposing financial requirements. The cultivation of research merely increased those requirements further.

Whereas the costs of providing medical education were soaring, tuition fees, the traditional source of income for medical schools, were not keeping pace. The majority of schools were no longer striving for large classes. In 1910, only three schools—Jefferson (591 students), Pennsylvania (546 students), and Northwestern (522 students)—kept enrollments high to help offset operating expenses, and their enrollments were twice that of the next largest school in the country. Much more typically, schools chose to limit the number of students so that some semblance of personalized instruction could be provided. For instance, the University of Michigan, which was as worried about its financial plight as any other medical school, excluded the possibility of admitting more students as a way of increasing revenues. "The number of students is about as large as we can accommodate," James Angell wrote in 1896. "As a very large part of the instruction is now given by laboratory methods, there is a limit to the number [of students] we can properly receive."[10]

To add to the dilemma, the price of tuition had risen only modestly from the preceding generation. By 1910, a typical year's tuition was $150 (compared with $100 in 1880), and some state-supported schools charged only one-half that amount. In Flexner's hypothetical example, tuition fees would yield only $40,000. Gifts or endowment income were needed for the rest.[11] The cost of a proper medical education had grown to more than three times that which could be assured by fees alone, and each year the expenses were continuing to rise. "It is impossible for any school to keep up with the reasonable demands of the time on such fees as students can pay,"[12] one medical faculty complained.

In the years after 1880, the financial condition of most medical schools improved, as many faculties acquired the funds to construct new facilities and increase their operating budget. This was accomplished through some increases in tuition, through the elimination of the profit motive, through gifts and bequests made by faculty members, through loans, through private donations, through the assistance of state legislatures, and through the infusion of money to schools lucky enough to have a strong university behind it. These funds made possible the substantial improvements of the period detailed in chapter 4.

Nevertheless, the resources available to medical schools in the early twentieth century were far from sufficient. Very few schools had managed to keep pace with the burgeoning costs. In 1910, fifty-six schools still operated with yearly budgets of less than $10,000, and seventy-two had budgets between $10,000 and $50,000. Only twenty schools had budgets that exceeded $50,000, the minimum considered necessary for good teaching, and only nine of these had budgets over $100,000, the smallest amount thought adequate to conduct a university school.[13] The ten most prosperous schools are listed in table 7.1. Not surprisingly, these were all schools that had become leaders of the movement to improve medical education. However, even these schools did not have enough money to accomplish everything they hoped to achieve, and the great majority of less fortunate schools lagged much further behind.

The paucity of funds frustrated medical educators immensely. "Many plans for the advance of the Medical School, as of the whole University, are held in abeyance by lack of money,"[14] the dean of the St. Louis University Medical School wrote in 1909. Committed schools went as far as they could with what little they had. "Our problem is to do the best we can with the means at our disposal,"[15] the faculty of Western Reserve University lamented. At school after school, desired improvements were unrealized because there was no money to pay for them.

Not every school worried equally about costs. As pointed out in chapter 4, enormous variation in quality characterized the medical schools of the early 1900s. At least one-quarter of the schools simply did not care about providing

TABLE 7.1

The Ten Largest Medical School Budgets, 1910

Harvard	$251,389
Columbia	239,072
Cornell	209,888
Michigan[a]	153,000
Pennsylvania	104,612
Jefferson[b]	102,995
Texas (Galveston)[a]	102,953
Johns Hopkins	102,429
Tulane	101,781
Northwestern	88,861

SOURCE: Abraham Flexner, *Medical Education in the United States and Canada* (New York: Carnegie Foundation for the Advancement of Teaching, 1910), 185–319, appendix.
[a]Budgetary figures include outlay for the school's university hospital.
[b]Estimated from tuition revenues.

a decent education. They were crassly commercial and sought to keep costs low so that profits would be higher. For the remaining schools of the period, however, the lack of adequate funds for construction, salaries, and endowment represented the greatest source of anxiety. The higher a school aspired, the more its anxiety, for schools with the largest objectives needed money for research as well as teaching. "The aspect of this whole subject [medical education] which gives me most concern is the financial one,"[16] an official of the University of Pennsylvania wrote in 1902. From virtually every school in the first five tiers (see table 4.4, p. 97) came a continual litany of concern and frustration.

In the early 1900s, insufficient funds plagued even the strongest and best financed schools in the country. Schools such as Michigan, Minnesota, Pennsylvania, and Western Reserve complained repeatedly about the lack of funds to improve their facilities.[17] Pennsylvania took little solace in its $100,000 budget, since it came mainly from student fees, a situation that had led to severe overcrowding. In 1908, the faculty noted that "no medical department could exist for any length of time upon the fees of its students."[18] It appointed a committee to seek an endowment of $750,000 to produce an income that would offset the school's deficit and allow for many badly needed improvements.[19] Similarly, Western Reserve had sought an endowment ever since its reorganization into a modern school in 1893.[20] In 1910, the president of the university insisted upon an endowment of at least $1,000,000. "Without further and large endowments it is certain that further progress cannot be made. . . . We have arrived at a stage in our history where there is but too much reason to fear that if large additional funds cannot now be obtained, the School must soon begin to retrograde relatively to others more adequately supported."[21]

Of the elite medical schools, Columbia complained the loudest of its financial difficulties. The school had the second largest budget of any in the country, but the lack of money for new construction and equipment frustrated it in its ambition "to lead the way for all medical schools in the United States."[22] For many years the faculty had aspired to make the school "a real university school," but it quickly discovered that "it would be easier to formulate policies than to put them into effect, for the reason that immense sums of money are required to do what it is plain should, and could, be done."[23] In 1903, school officials enumerated in detail the improvements it considered necessary. The changes included more rigorous standards of admission (two years of college with a year each of physics, chemistry, and biology), the construction of new laboratories, obtaining control of a teaching hospital, appointing "full-time" professors in every department, increasing the salaries of the junior faculty, and promoting research throughout the medical school. The minimum sum projected as necessary to effect these changes was $4,000,000.[24] Five years later, the new entrance requirements had been introduced, but little progress had been made toward the other goals. The president of the university noted: "So far as funds have been available, steady progress has been made toward carrying out this comprehensive program. . . . So far as the remaining elements of the program have not been accomplished, it is only because funds have not been at hand for the purposes."[25]

Financial problems troubled the schools of Tier 3 as well. From the time that Yale first adopted personalized methods of medical teaching, it worried about the increased costs that would be incurred.[26] In the early 1900s, the dean complained year after year of the lack of funds, enumerating the many changes the school would provide if it had the resources. Especially needed were new laboratories for anatomy and pathology and full-time professors who would have the time to devote to research.[27] "The School is worthy of an equipment adequate to maintain its ideals,"[28] he pleaded. Similarly, in 1901 Washington University wanted to construct new laboratories, acquire control of a teaching hospital, build a better library, increase the salaries of its paid instructors, and expand its facilities for research. The faculty noted that whether it would be able to do so "resolves itself into a question of money."[29] Complaints about the inability to finance desired improvements also came from such respectable medical schools as the University of Pittsburgh, the University of Cincinnati, and the University of Virginia.[30]

Inadequate funds for upgrading the standards also hampered the efforts of the Tier 4 and 5 schools. These schools usually had more modest goals than the more prestigious ones, but they experienced equal consternation over their inability to pay for desired improvements. From the mid-1890s onward, the president of Tufts appealed regularly for an endowment of the school, which he called "the real need of the College."[31] In 1913, the Council on Medical Education was still stating "the chief weakness of this school is the lack of ample financial support."[32] In 1903, the dean of the College of Medicine of the University of Nebraska complained of the "radical defects in our present system" that arose from the lack of space, equipment, and sufficient instructors. These problems could be solved, he pointed out, if more money were made available to the school.[33] Similar frustration over the inability to acquire funds was expressed by officials of the medical schools of Bowdoin, Dartmouth, Fordham, the University of Maryland, St. Louis University, Drake, the University of Tennessee, the University of Mississippi, the University of Utah, and the University of Southern California.[34] In 1910, the trustees of Washburn University (the Kansas Medical College), one of the country's very weak schools, confessed that they were "painfully conscious of the inadequacy of the equipment of the medical college" and declared their intention to acquire a new laboratory building and an endowment of not less than $100,000.[35]

The financial plight was the most severe at the country's black medical colleges. For instance, Howard University Medical College's ideals of medical education were no different from those of the country's predominantly white medical schools. However, its efforts to provide quality instruction were severely hampered by the extremely poor condition of its property and laboratories. The school existed on fees alone. In 1910, the dean declared the procurement of an endowment of $500,000 to be "beyond question the most pressing need of the hour."[36] However, little progress was made in the next several years, even though the era of large-scale medical philanthropy in America was entering full bloom. Black schools were easily passed over by philanthropists, despite having needs that were far greater than those of most white schools. By 1919 officials of Howard had reached the point where they were almost ready to give up. The new dean confided, "Most of us have reached a point of almost complete discouragement and some of us are questioning whether it would not be well for us to discontinue our efforts completely before degeneration sets in."[37] The situation at black schools was made all the more poignant because of the odious presence of Jim Crow. By World War I most medical schools in the North were accepting blacks as medical students, but Northern hospitals were frequently refusing to appoint them as interns. At least black medical schools could offer their students and graduates something in the way of hospital opportunities.[38]

By the early 1900s, therefore, many problems remained to be solved in medical education, and much of the difficulty revolved around too little money. The financial requirements of modern medical education were real and painful, and the schools were caught in a never-ending spiral of rising costs. A mood of profound dissatisfaction pervaded many of the faculties. In 1899, the provost of the University of Pennsylvania acknowledged his medical school's achievements, but he was not satisfied because the school "has not fully realized the ideal it has set up for itself."[39] The better schools were severely critical of themselves, and in 1910 Abraham Flexner would tell them little they did not already know.

Early Fund Raising

In the generation before 1910, medical schools did not sit back idly as the costs of medical education surged. Medical educators understood, as the faculty of the Bellevue Hospital Medical College (New York University) noted, that operating a school required a "combination of sagacious business and educational knowledge."[40] From the beginning of the reform movement, many schools worked very hard to increase their resources, and a few enjoyed some impressive successes. Although money remained scarce, by 1910 a modest beginning toward placing medical education on a firm financial footing had been made. Equally important, an American style of medical philanthropy had started to take form.

The schools that pioneered the reforms of medical teaching also pioneered medical fund raising in America. In 1874, Harvard Medical School launched a campaign to raise $200,000 for the construction of better laboratory facilities. The faculty aimed its appeal at the local professional and business classes of Boston, who provided the sum through a large number of small gifts. The campaign owed its success to the faculty's leaders, the physiologist Henry P. Bowditch and the surgeon John Collins Warren, and to the new prestige the school was enjoying now that it had become a true university department.[41]

Similarly, Pennsylvania's reforms of 1877 prompted that school to try to raise endowment funds to support its new program. The physiologist Weir Mitchell, now a member of the university's board of trustees, persuaded one donor in 1877 to contribute $50,000 to endow a chair of surgery.[42] After becoming provost in 1881, William Pepper became the school's most effective fund raiser. In 1889, with Mitchell's help, he convinced the wealthy publisher and philanthropist Henry Lea to donate $50,000 for a bacteriological laboratory. Two years later, Pepper organized a successful drive to raise an endowment of $250,000, contributing the first $50,000 himself. This sum permitted the school to adopt the more rigorous four-year curriculum in 1893.[43]

In the 1880s and 1890s a few other schools began to enjoy some alleviation of their financial troubles. By the mid-1880s, the College of Physicians and Surgeons (New York), with over 500 students, had become severely overcrowded. In 1884 James W. McLane, the dean and obstetrician to the Vanderbilts, persuaded the railroad magnate William K. Vanderbilt to donate $500,000 for the purchase of land and the construction of a new medical school plant. Other large gifts from the Vanderbilt family for buildings and clinics soon followed.[44] In 1891, John L. Woods, a wealthy Cleveland businessman and philanthropist, bequeathed $125,000 to the Western Reserve University School of Medicine to support teaching in histology, anatomy, physiology, chemistry, pathology, and bacteriology. This gift by Woods, a long-time friend of the medical school, made possible a major reorganization of the school in 1893, which the trustees and faculty had long been wishing to make.[45]

Another early recipient of financial support was the Bellevue Hospital Medical College. In 1885, Andrew Carnegie, influenced by his personal physician Frederic Dennis, donated $50,000 to the school for a research laboratory. The unusual gift from Carnegie, who in later years rarely made contributions to hospitals or medical schools, was prompted in part by the solicitations of Dennis and in part by the impression that the new science of bacteriology had made upon him. Indeed, according to the school, "It was with the view of fostering original research in this line of inquiry [bacteriology] and of disseminating a practical knowledge of what has already been developed that Mr. Carnegie made his munificent gift to the College."[46] That spring, in a commencement address to the school, Carnegie praised the virtues of medicine —now that it had become scientific—in contrast to the less charitable remarks he made about the professions of law and divinity.[47] Carnegie's gift was a prelude to other large gifts that the Bellevue Hospital Medical College soon received. For instance, Alfred Loomis, a prominent member of the faculty, aroused philanthropist Oliver Hazard Payne's interest in the school. Payne donated $100,000 in 1886 for the Loomis Medical Laboratory and $150,000 in 1892 for the Medical College Laboratory.[48]

The most spectacular fund-raising successes of the era were achieved by

Cornell and Harvard. For several years the trustees of Cornell University had contemplated starting a medical school. In 1898, Oliver Hazard Payne made that undertaking possible with a gift of $1,500,000. In addition, Payne—whose one condition was that the Cornell Medical College should be "second to none in the world"—followed that gift with yearly contributions of $140,000 to help offset operating expenses.[49]

By the mid-1890s, Harvard Medical School had already outgrown its physical plant and desperately needed new facilities. In 1901, the faculty, again led by Bowditch and Warren, undertook another fund-raising drive. In the next twelve months, they raised $3,000,000 for the medical school, enough to build the physical plant the school still occupies today. In contrast to the earlier campaign, which relied on small gifts from large numbers of local citizens, this campaign obtained nearly 80 percent of the money from just three persons: J. P. Morgan ($1,135,000); John D. Rockefeller ($1,000,000); and Mrs. Arabella Huntington, the widow of the railroad magnate C. P. Huntington, ($250,000). None of the three were Bostonians, and none approached the school. Each was solicited by Bowditch and Warren. Even Rockefeller, later the most energetic medical philanthropist of all, had to be aggressively pursued and almost avoided capture. All three, however, professed their admiration of recent breakthroughs in medical research, and they were favorably influenced by Harvard's image as a scientific medical school.[50]

Fund-raising successes, like the larger and better known ones that occurred after 1910, depended very much upon the entrepreneurial skill of medical school officials, who approached the task of institution-building with zeal and flair. Although their main targets were the major philanthropists, who could rescue a medical school with a single gift, small contributions from private citizens remained important, and in the aggregate such gifts could result in sizable sums. However, the large amounts of money necessary mandated that the primary benefactors be those of extraordinary wealth. As in the later period, the philanthropists responded to the solicitations for a variety of reasons—some humanitarian, some self-serving. Most entertained a genuine desire to aid medicine, but they also profited from the good publicity that attended their gifts. Such acts helped justify their wealth, status, and power to a suspicious public that intensely disliked them and viewed them as "robber barons." They considered medicine an appropriate object of their benefactions because it was now giving signs that it worked. Thus, gifts to medicine represented philanthropy rather than charity—a crucial distinction to these "scientific philanthropists."[51]

Early medical philanthropy did not occur in a systematic fashion. Philanthropists had not yet developed the habit of contributing to medical education; donations in the hundreds of thousands or millions of dollars were distinctly unusual. Such events required an exceptionally strong medical school, skillful entrepreneurship, and sympathetic friends. Permanent sources of continued support, as exemplified later by the private foundations and the National Institutes of Health, had not yet been created. Instead, medical schools of this period had to determine their needs and search for donors. In this sense medical fund raising of the period was similar to fund raising in the natural sciences. Nineteenth-century scientists had to act as their own agents, taking advantage of any opportunity for aid as it arose. They could not yet rely on spontaneous support for research; they had to arouse interest among the wealthy and direct the contributions into areas they considered necessary.[52] In medicine and science both, it was thus an age of innocence. With support so sporadic, no one yet worried that those who provided the funds might try to control the direction or purpose of research.

In the generation before 1910, medical schools found another important source of funds besides direct gifts. Those fortunate enough to enjoy a genuine university affiliation often learned that such arrangements resulted in financial assistance. Endowments for universities were already rising markedly, even though endowments for medical schools were still small. For instance, between 1901 and 1911, Columbia University received $16,551,568.74 in gifts.[53] Although much of that money was for designated purposes, the university still had enough unrestricted funds to help the medical school offset its huge operating costs. To lesser degrees other universities, both private and public, underwrote the expenses of their medical schools. In the early 1900s, Western Reserve University was allocating $10,000 a year for its medical school, while the University of Michigan in 1905 spent $48,487.70 from its general fund on medical school salaries.[54] In 1912, the University of Minnesota built two new medical laboratories at a cost of $636,000.[55] By 1910 at least thirty medical schools were routinely operating at deficits, that is, their expenses exceeded their income from tuition fees. All of these were schools that had become affiliated with universities that were helping to pay the costs of medical education.[56]

However, a university affiliation did not represent an automatic solution to the financial problems of medical education. By 1910, medical education had already become the most costly form of technical education in which a university could engage, and a university had to provide for all its departments, not just the medical school. The president of the University of Utah in 1910 wanted to do more for his university's medical school but realized that "under our present condition, to expend much more for this department would impoverish other departments."[57] Henry Pritchett of the Carnegie Foundation warned the president of Stanford that "the Medical School would squeeze the life out of the University at Palo Alto."[58] Yearly expenditures from university treasuries were not the answer; large endowments specifically for medical schools were needed.

Nevertheless, by 1910 the medical schools that had become genuine university schools enjoyed distinct financial advantages over the rest. In part, their good fortune related to the appropriations a university could make from its general funds; in part, to the credibility a university medical school commanded when appealing to the public for funds. Pritchett observed how Harvard Medical School had been greatly aided in its fund-raising efforts by virtue of the fact that "the medical school forms an integral part of the university system."[59] The public was not so readily inclined to endow nonuniversity medical schools, no matter how dedicated to modern educational ideals their faculties might have become.

By the early 1900s, the large costs had made it impossible for independent schools to compete with university schools. It was no longer possible to provide adequate instruction on tuition fees alone, and only university schools could hope to acquire the necessary endowments. For these reasons, the dean of the Drake University College of Medicine observed in 1903, "Only universities with endowments can now conduct a medical school worthy of the name." Nonuniversity schools "must soon seek such an alliance or become extinct."[60] This, above all other reasons, was why proprietary schools were already struggling and why university medical schools had already assumed the leadership of the reform movement.

Finally, prior to 1910 medical schools could find one other source of financial encouragement: the burgeoning interest in sanitation and public health. To some public and private agencies, these had already become attractive avenues of support—witness John D. Rockefeller's financing of the campaign to eradicate hookworm disease in 1909.[61] Such programs indicated that the public had already developed a large interest in health-related matters, even if relatively few dollars had yet made their way to medical schools directly. To many doctors, the support of medical education seemed like a logical extension of a tradition of philanthropy already underway.

It must be remembered, though, that before 1910 inadequate funds remained a critical problem, even at the strong university medical schools. Far more typical than the fund-raising successes of Harvard and Cornell were the failures of Washington University and Yale. In 1908, Robert Brookings, the president of Washington University, enlisted Charles Eliot's help to try to persuade Andrew Carnegie to make a major contribution to the medical school, but the effort failed.[62] The next year, Brookings described his ambitious hopes for the medical school, but he could see "no way of putting the larger scheme into operation at this time, unless some man like Mr. Carnegie or Mr. Rockefeller could be interested in a large way in the institution here."[63] Similarly, in the early 1900s, Yale Medical School struggled desperately to raise money, but it could secure few gifts larger than $2,000.[64] In 1909, the dean was privately saying that $10,000,000 was necessary to institute all the changes the school desired. In public, however, the school only dared ask that its endowment be increased from $100,000 to $300,000.[65] Even most university schools did not know where the necessary funds would come from, and a mood of despair prevailed.

It must also be kept in mind that the nature of early medical funding was such that medical research was handicapped more than medical teaching. Medical schools had experienced much more success in acquiring funds for buildings and teaching laboratories than for salaries, endowments, and research laboratories. At Western Reserve, which was teaching medicine as well as any school in the country with the exception of Johns Hopkins, research had not yet prospered. According to the dean, this was because the school lacked an "endowment sufficient with which to pay men for their time, so that their energies might be devoted to investigation and teaching, instead of to making a livelihood."[66] Similarly, Yale's inability to obtain a large endowment retarded research at the school much more than it retarded teaching. Faculty members managed to discharge their educational duties, but they labored under conditions of "long hours . . . meager salaries, limited equipment and few or no assistants." Under these conditions, the dean explained, "The work of the School . . . has been limited largely to teaching students, with but small opportunity for research."[67] Because of financial constraints, the future of academic medicine was still in jeopardy even as medical teaching was rapidly improving.

Nevertheless, by 1910 all the elements were developing that would permit the outpouring of medical philanthropy that was soon to occur. Charles Eliot had once said that "the first step toward getting an endowment was to deserve one."[68] It was clear that medical education had become deserving. The overall quality of instruction had improved enormously over the preceding generation; medical education had progressed far toward becoming a university endeavor; the elite medical schools pursuing research had begun to receive worldwide recognition for their results; and the public had started to appreciate that there was a payoff to medical investigation. In addition, the preceding generation had witnessed the accumulation of unprecedented wealth in America, the emergence of a class of philanthropists whose giving was unmatched in history, the strengthening of the nation's universities, the development of a broad interest in public health, and the appearance of a group of dedicated and persuasive medical entrepreneurs. The circumstances had become ripe; only a catalyst was needed.

8 The Plight of

Clinical Teaching

MEDICAL EDUCATION IN 1910 was hampered by another severe problem: the poor condition of clinical teaching. Very few medical students could be found caring for patients, which contrasted sharply with the scientific teaching and its use of laboratory instruction.

The problems in clinical teaching arose from the extraordinary difficulties medical schools were encountering in acquiring control of large, well-equipped hospitals. Without true teaching hospitals at their disposal, medical schools could not introduce the clinical clerkship, nor could they effectively pursue clinical research. In the same way that the lack of money had become the bottleneck in the reform of the basic science instruction, the lack of hospital facilities had become the major factor in limiting how far clinical education could proceed. Until different relationships between medical schools and hospitals could be established, further improvements in clinical teaching could not be made.

The Clinical Clerkship Struggles

In the generation before 1910, medical education in America had not developed evenly. Clearly, by 1910 the strength of the country's medical schools had come to lie in the basic science instruction of the first two years. Equivalent progress in the clinical subjects had not occurred. Although the clinical courses provided students the latest knowledge, instruction remained predominantly didactic, with limited opportunities for practical training.

Medical educators at even the strongest schools complained of this problem. For instance, Graham Lusk, an eminent physiologist at Cornell, felt that the necessary improvements in his school's clinical departments were "as far off as ever."[1] The president of Western Reserve University also lamented the discrepancy between his school's excellent scientific instruction and its problem-laden clinical teaching.[2] So did the faculty of the University of Minnesota, which called the development of their school "extremely one-sided." Progress in clinical teaching, they remarked, has been "wholly arrested, with the result that, while fully equipped for teaching and research in all fundamental branches, we are unable to meet even measurably our clinical obligations."[3]

These observations should not obscure the significant progress in clinical teaching since the Civil War.[4] The teaching corps had increased in numbers, the length of time devoted to the clinical subjects had grown to two years, and the curriculum had been revised to include all the new medical specialties. More important, the lecture had been supplemented by the section method of teaching, which allowed for more personalized instruction. In this form of teaching, groups of students, as small as eight or ten at the better schools, would spend an hour or two a day, three to five days a week, examining patients in the hospital and following the progress of selected cases. With section teaching, students were closer to patients than ever before.

However, the section method contained an inherent flaw. It did not incorporate the principle of "learning by doing," as did laboratory instruction in the scientific courses. Bedside section teaching was much more effective than the didactic methods of earlier years, but it was still demonstrative. In that regard it was no different than the lecture and demonstration in the scientific subjects. This fact did not escape the uncanny eye of William Welch, who likened section teaching to "the attempt to teach a subject like bacteriology by demonstrations of methods, cultures and microscopic slides instead of having the student make his own media, plant and cultivate the bacteria by his own hands, and follow and study from day to day with his own eyes the characters of the growing organisms."[5] In section teaching, patients were cared for in the presence of students, but not by students. Students were passive observers, witnessing rather than participating in the medical work. Although frequently perceived as practical bedside instruction, section teaching in reality was little more than an illustrated lecture.

This pedagogic weakness was rectified only by the clerkship. Under this system, students not only received instruction in the hospital but became an active part of the hospital machinery. Rather than visiting the wards for an hour a day, students would be assigned four or six patients of their own and spend much of their day carrying out duties related to their patients' care.[6] This allowed students to experience rather than observe the conditions of medical practice. William Osler noted that all other forms of clinical instruction—the systematic lecture, the amphitheater clinic, the ward and dispensary classes—were but "bastard substitutes" for the clerkship.[7]

The overriding weakness of American clinical education at the time of the Flexner report in 1910 was that the clerkship was struggling for survival. The clerkship was alive and healthy at Johns Hopkins, where it had been introduced by Osler in 1893, and it was functioning with moderate success at the University of Pennsylvania, the University of Michigan, Western Reserve University, and Jefferson Medical College. Elsewhere it was languishing, so that educationally meaningful contact between students and patients remained very uncommon.

After 1900 there emerged some glimmer of hope, as a number of schools began providing their students opportunities to work as clinical clerks. However, much remained to be done even at these schools, since only a small number of students could be accommodated. For instance, in 1902 Georgetown offered clinical positions at its university hospital, but the appointments were reserved for the two highest scorers on a competitive examination.[8] In 1906, Cornell was able to provide each fourth-year student clerkships in internal medicine and surgery, but only for fifty hours in each subject.[9] Columbia, in 1910, offered senior students two-month clerkships in internal medicine and surgery, but places were available for just one-third of the class.[10] At all these schools, the future of the clerkship was insecure, for continuation from year to year depended on the good will of an affiliated hospital. The Massachusetts General Hospital, for example, agreed in 1905 to permit a few Harvard medical students into its wards as clinical clerks, but within a year or two the hospital discontinued that practice.[11]

In the early 1900s, some medical schools were able to provide extensive practical training in their outpatient clinics.[12] Columbia made excellent use of its outpatient facility, the Vanderbilt Clinic. In 1906, the school discontinued section teaching in the clinic and adopted the clerkship, which allowed each student, under an instructor's tutelage, to evaluate and treat his or her own patients.[13]

However, dispensary teaching was merely a stopgap solution. Such instruction was frequently subject to overcrowding, poor organization, and inadequate supervision. At Western Reserve, the advisor to the third-year class spoke to the faculty "on the question of overcrowding in the third year dispensary service and of conversations with students in that class indicating dissatisfaction."[14] Even when conditions were good, as at Columbia, the outpatient clinic still had limitations as an educational tool. Students usually saw relatively healthy patients and often for just one visit. They did not observe acutely ill persons, nor could they follow the daily course of disease and therapy.[15] Medical students themselves were conscious of these drawbacks.[16]

Thus, the many improvements in clinical teaching since the Civil War could not mask the unsatisfactory condition that remained. For further progress, it was necessary for students to participate directly in patient management, not just in a dispensary, but in a hospital ward. This type of clinical experience had to be made available to every student, not just the lucky few who won a clerkship after scoring well in a competitive examination. Welch lamented that teaching on the clinical side "has not, in my judgment, developed to the same extent as the laboratory side."[17] Abraham Flexner agreed. In his report for the Carnegie Foundation, Flexner wrote that the outlook for clinical education in the United States was far "less reassuring" than that for the basic science instruction.[18] It is often forgotten that his report indicted clinical education much more severely than the rest of medical education in America.

The Rift between Medical Schools and Hospitals

The clerkship was struggling for one overriding reason: few medical schools had acquired control of teaching hospitals. Although most schools had access to clinical facilities, they were severely restricted in how they could use those facilities. Accordingly, instruction in the clinical departments was greatly hampered. Medical schools had no responsibility for deciding whether students could work as clinical clerks, since permission of hospital boards was always required but seldom granted. Clinical professors were also handicapped in their own research, since they were often denied access to patients for purposes of clinical investigation. In addition, medical schools did not have the authority to appoint doctors to the staffs of their affiliated hospitals, which forced them to choose clinical faculty members from those who already had received a local hospital appointment—they did not have the liberty to select the best person who might be available anywhere. Harvard lost the opportunity to obtain the services of William Osler, and Yale those of its loyal college alumnus, the eminent neurosurgeon Harvey Cushing, because neither medical school could guarantee these renowned physicians hospital opportunities.[19] The few medical schools that did control teaching hospitals—the most notable example being Johns Hopkins—were exceptions that proved the rule, for it was only at these places that the clerkship was showing any signs of life.

By the early 1900s, it had become unmistakably clear that the problem of securing good teaching hospitals was the main obstacle to providing better clinical training. In the view of Samuel Lambert, the dean of Columbia Medical School, if clinical teaching were to improve to the level of scientific teaching, "it is necessary that the hospitals appreciate their possibilities in the domain of medical education."[20] William Welch considered the teaching hospital to be "the most urgent need of medical education today."[21] The strongest asset of Johns Hopkins, he often pointed out, was possession of its own hospital.[22] This situation did not escape the attention of Abraham Flexner. In Flexner's judgment, only the Johns Hopkins Medical School and Hospital enjoyed a totally satisfactory relationship, and in his 1910 report he made "one more plea for an understanding between existing hospitals and deserving medical schools."[23]

Ironically, this difficulty arose in spite of a long tradition of the use of the hospital for medical instruction. As early as the 1500s, Italian medical schools began to use hospitals for teaching, and a century later that practice had spread to Holland. By the nineteenth century, voluntary hospitals throughout Europe were commonly used for teaching.[24] The first great American general hospitals (the Pennsylvania Hospital, the New York Hospital, the Massachusetts General Hospital) were also involved with medical education from their beginnings.

Nevertheless, by the 1890s it had become clear that the traditional use of the hospital for teaching in America did not satisfy the needs of modern medical education. From 1763, when the Pennsylvania Hospital decided to charge its students $5.00 for the privilege of entering the hospital for ward walks, it was apparent that hospital trustees considered medical teaching to be merely a peripheral function of hospitals.[25] Throughout the nineteenth century that situation did not change. Hospitals tolerated teaching, reluctantly, as long as it was carefully regulated and did not interfere with their other functions. Trustees often professed their desire to participate in medical education, but what they had in mind was instruction of a very restricted sort: amphitheater lectures, ward walks, outpatient clinics, and section teaching— but not the clerkship. Students in the early 1900s could receive good training in physical diagnosis and the use of certain medical instruments, but they were rarely permitted responsible contact with patients. Indeed, students endured repeated indignities. Throughout the nineteenth century, if they were permitted to enter hospitals at all, they were frequently required to use separate entrances—a practice the trustees of the Peter Bent Brigham Hospital, soon to become a great teaching hospital, seriously considered implementing as late as 1907.[26] Only in the obstetrics teaching were students commonly given responsibility in patient management. This was because most deliveries were still performed in homes; hospitals were not necessary for students to gain obstetrical experience.[27]

To understand how this situation arose, it is necessary to appreciate the early history of medical schools and hospitals in the United States.[28] In America, as in the rest of the world except London, the two institutions developed apart from one another. Accordingly, until the latter nineteenth century, responsibility for medical education was seen as belonging to the schools, not the hospitals. Hospitals were considered benevolent for even the casual teaching they did allow. In an era when medical instruction was superficial and didactic, this arrangement was satisfactory to all. Medical professors expected nothing more from hospitals than the little they received, and for that they were grateful. Hospital trustees regarded a limited amount of instruction as good for public relations, and they did not worry that teaching would disrupt their day-to-day operations. If students were felt to be bothering patients, they could easily be barred from the wards and frequently were.

After the Civil War, however, this equilibrium began to break down. Medical professors started to recognize that advances in medical knowledge and practice created a different set of requirements for clinical instruction. Students had to be actively involved in patient care, not merely observers as before. The hospital could no longer serve as an adjunct to medical education; it had to *be* the medical school for the clinical years. Yet hospital officials felt threatened by such ideas. They dreaded the mere thought of students in the wards, and they staunchly opposed any changes that would interfere with the existing hospital routine. To them, arrangements such as the medical faculties were proposing were out of the question.

In the late nineteenth century, many medical schools tried very hard to secure better clinical facilities. One approach was for a school to build a hospital of its own. This strategy offered an obvious advantage to a school, because then the faculty could make staff appointments and organize its clinical teaching without the threat of outside interference. Such a plan worked exceedingly well at Johns Hopkins and with some success at the University of Michigan (1869), the University of Pennsylvania (1874), and the Jefferson Medical College (1907).

Before World War I, however, not many university hospitals were successful. The expense involved was nearly prohibitive, and medical schools were severely strapped for funds. As a result, most "university hospitals" of the period were too small and poorly equipped to be adequate. The Johns Hopkins Hospital was the only one that was totally satisfactory in these regards. The University of Pennsylvania Hospital was second, but its position was weakened by a smaller endowment and an uncertain supply of state funds. Like many private schools in the state, the University of Pennsylvania had been receiving financial assistance from the legislature, but political vicissitudes made that an insecure source of support.[29] The Jefferson Hospital was of the first rank from the beginning, but it did not open until 1907. It was a great stroke of luck for the Johns Hopkins Medical School that the city of Baltimore in the 1870s had no important hospital, as Johns Hopkins might not have left the school the money for a hospital of its own, assuming that it could rely upon an existing institution.

Other university hospitals of the period were severely deficient. Some that were large enough, such as the hospitals of the University of Maryland School of Medicine and the College of Physicians and Surgeons (Baltimore), did not have the money for proper equipment or maintenance.[30] Others, such as the hospitals of the University of Illinois, the University of Iowa, the University of Kansas, and the University of Minnesota, were too small to offer students enough clinical experience.[31] At Minnesota, with fewer than 900 medical and surgical admissions in 1912–13, the faculty acknowledged that "the insufficiency of our own clinical facilities has now become an actual source of danger."[32] The claim of Stanford University that it had a teaching hospital was "hardly sustained by the facts," according to Flexner, since the hospital required vast sums for upgrading and was poorly organized for teaching. The faculty controlled only forty to sixty beds.[33]

The situation at the University of Michigan Hospital was the most paradoxical in the country. There clinical teaching was extremely well organized, especially in internal medicine, in which the clerkship had been in use since 1899.[34] However, the small size of the Michigan hospital (average census seventy to eighty-five patients in 1899), the geographic remoteness of Ann Arbor, and the lack of operating funds all conspired to limit the scope and variety of patients that were seen in the hospital.[35] One faculty member in 1899 estimated that a minimum of $100,000 must be invested in the hospital, or the school will "fall behind a large number of medical schools in different parts of the country."[36] The lack of funds even forced the hospital to close one summer, and the scarcity of patients often resulted in each case being shared by several students.[37] As late as 1916, Victor Vaughan was still lamenting the school's "slow progress" in clinical teaching: "We are only a small farm and we must till it to the utmost."[38]

Because of expense, many schools chose not to build a hospital at all. In

1903, Washington University contemplated building a hospital until it discovered that the project would cost $1,000,000. Lacking the money, the medical school had no choice but to remodel its existing clinical facility for the much lower cost of $25,000.[39] Columbia in the early 1900s was also very eager to construct a teaching hospital, but it could not meet the projected price of $2,000,000.[40] Yale considered building a university-owned teaching hospital in New Haven in 1910, but it was thwarted by the estimated cost of $3,000,000.[41] In the early 1890s, even so wealthy a university as Harvard, under the presidency of one as sympathetic to medical education as Charles Eliot, refused to embark on such a venture because of the overwhelming expense.[42] The financial problems that impeded progress in the scientific teaching did so in the clinical instruction as well.

Owing to these difficulties, many schools adopted another approach: to try to establish educationally meaningful affiliations with existing community hospitals. This approach offered schools the advantage of not having to build and operate a hospital themselves. However, hospital officials, hostile to the newer teaching methods, were unwilling to offer their facilities to medical schools on terms the schools desired. Before 1910, only two community hospitals in America, Lakeside Hospital in Cleveland and Mary Hitchcock Hospital in Hanover, New Hampshire, could be persuaded to do so, which explained why the medical schools of Western Reserve University and Dartmouth College were able to implement the clerkship.[43] Elsewhere, hospital officials would allow medical schools privileges for demonstrative teaching only. Many hospitals had clinical resources that rivaled those of Johns Hopkins, but, as Osler pointed out, those institutions remained unsympathetic to modern methods of clinical instruction.[44] Without the right to appoint the hospital staffs and teach freely on the wards, medical faculties derived little reward from their close proximity to such clinical riches.

Undaunted, some of the best medical schools attempted to persuade their affiliated hospitals to see otherwise. However, their efforts were unsuccessful. In 1906, the medical faculty of Columbia petitioned Bellevue Hospital for permission to introduce the clerkship, as did the faculty of Cornell in 1908.[45] Both requests were denied. Several times in the early 1900s, the medical staff of the New York Hospital asked the Board of Governors to permit students to be assigned cases in the wards, but each time the board refused.[46] In the early 1890s, Harvard Medical School attempted to obtain a closer union with the Massachusetts General Hospital, but after four years of negotiations the hospital rejected the school's proposal.[47] In 1906, an editorial in the *Boston Medical and Surgical Journal* proclaimed a teaching hospital still to be "the greatest need of the Harvard Medical School."[48] During the first two decades of the century, the medical faculties of Yale, the University of Pittsburgh, the

University of Minnesota, the University of Colorado, and the University of Southern California were also unable to convince their respective affiliated hospitals to become true teaching institutions.[49]

Tulane Medical School encountered similar obstacles in New Orleans, where the faculty's desire to introduce the clerkship was thwarted by its lack of responsibility in the administration of Charity Hospital. At Charity, the city's public hospital, teaching was unequivocally regarded as secondary in importance to care of the sick, creating conditions for clinical instruction that in the words of Tulane's professor of medicine were "absolutely rotten."[50] Tulane, which in the era of Erasmus Fenner had been the jewel of the South in clinical teaching, had descended to the same level of mediocrity as schools elsewhere in the United States.

Thus, despite the vigorous attempts of many medical schools to obtain hospital facilities, there had been discouragingly little success before 1910. The problem was clearly not any lack of interest on the part of the schools. President Nicholas Murray Butler of Columbia University could not have been more explicit in issuing this demand in 1910:

> The haphazard relationship between medical school and hospital which has been quite common in the United States must give way, and at once, to a relationship that is precise, definite, and so secured and administered as to give to the medical school complete and permanent control of the hospital staff and of the facilities for clinical teaching which the hospital affords.[51]

The obstructing factor was the hospitals, which refused to assume the role in medical education that the medical schools were demanding of them. Hospitals had undergone enormous physical growth since the Civil War, and they had long ceased to be almshouses. However, they had not yet modified their ideals and organization in such a way that would benefit medical education. Hospitals simply did not consider teaching or research to be among their responsibilities, and medical schools pleaded to deaf ears.

Conflict in New York

Nowhere was there more tension between a medical school and hospital than in New York City between 1905 and 1910. At odds were the College of Physicians and Surgeons (Columbia Medical School), a prototypical example of a medical school that succeeded, and Roosevelt Hospital, the classic example of a hospital that had the opportunity to become a national medical center and failed. No other episode better illustrates the difficulties that medical schools were encountering in acquiring teaching hospitals.

By the early 1900s, Columbia was already one of the country's strongest medical schools.[52] However, like most schools, it had achieved much more success in developing its scientific than its clinical teaching. When Samuel Lambert became dean in 1904, he recognized that the school's greatest deficiency was the lack in the last year of the program of practical clinical work. He also saw that this situation had resulted from not having a large teaching hospital where every senior student could serve as a clinical clerk. In his first report, Lambert wrote, "The most urgent need of the College to-day is the control of a general hospital, large enough to give every student in the last year of his course an opportunity for bedside practice and a resulting personal contact with individual cases of disease."[53]

Roosevelt Hospital seemed the likely candidate to serve this need.[54] Made possible by a gift of $1,250,000 from James Henry Roosevelt in 1863, it opened in 1871 and proved to be everything that was good about the nineteenth-century general hospital. By the 1900s, it had grown enormously and offered its clientele the best medical services. In 1908, it handled 5,176 ambulance calls, treated a total of 34,351 patients, and had an average daily inpatient census of 188.[55] From the beginning the hospital had established an affiliation with Physicians and Surgeons, and soon it became the school's major clinical resource. Its amphitheaters and clinics were regularly used by the school for teaching, and it was a popular choice among Columbia students for fourth-year electives and postgraduate internships and residencies. The hospital also boasted a distinguished medical staff, most of whom had studied in Germany or Austria, and some of whom held faculty appointments at Physicians and Surgeons. With its impressive plant located across the street from the medical school, Roosevelt was ideally situated and endowed to become a genuine teaching hospital.

Recognizing this fact, Columbia, led by Lambert, in 1905 made the first of three formal overtures to the hospital proposing a new relationship that would allow the school to introduce the clerkship.[56] The school outlined its needs to teach and do research in the wards and promised that the hospital's patients would receive better care from such an arrangement. The school also offered to help raise $1,000,000 to enlarge the hospital so that it would have more room for educational activities. However, the hospital's board of trustees demurred, and the union was not effected.

161

Undaunted, the medical school continued the negotiations. In 1908, it petitioned Roosevelt a second time in behalf of a closer affiliation. The arguments were the same, but the school was now more insistent. Lambert, a former house pupil, recognized clearly that there could be no compromising about the clerkship.[57] "Any plan to regulate and improve clinical methods must include this modern development," he told a group of Roosevelt trustees.[58] The president of Columbia University, Nicholas Murray Butler, supported Lambert. The teaching hospital, Butler wrote, "remains to-day, as it has been for some time past, the Medical School's chief need."[59] To help secure the alliance, Lambert had even applied to John D. Rockefeller, Sr., for a $1,000,000 grant, the income of which would be used to pay the costs of accommodating clinical clerks. However, the Roosevelt trustees once again rejected the proposal. The hospital's only concession was in consenting to accept a few clinical clerks on a trial basis.

Still, the Roosevelt trustees actually had no intention of permitting clinical clerks to work in the hospital, and no steps had been taken nearly two years later to facilitate their entry. A vexed Lambert told the Roosevelt board that "the present relations however satisfactory they may seem to the hospital trustees are, quite the reverse to the College and to the teachers of the College who are members of the hospital medical board."[60] The medical school then approached the hospital a third time with the same proposal. By now representatives of the school were becoming very pessimistic that Roosevelt would ever agree to such an arrangement. The committee responsible for negotiating with the hospital claimed to be "fully persuaded that Roosevelt Hospital will not consent to any form of affiliation worthy of the name."[61] Nevertheless, as one concerned party phrased it, the school chose "to make a final kick . . . before deciding to go elsewhere."[62] To make the school's offer more enticing, Lambert had procured an agreement from Edward Harkness, heir to part of the Standard Oil fortune and a trustee of Roosevelt Hospital, to build the hospital a 150-bed surgical pavilion and provide an endowment of $1,300,000 if Roosevelt would consent to the union.

This time Roosevelt gave the issue especially close consideration. The hospital's Medical Advisory Board, which all along had supported the proposal, once again enthusiastically endorsed it, but the board of trustees was divided. After much discussion, the board defeated the proposal by one vote. The most influential person on the board, and the caster of the deciding ballot, was its president, James Wood McLane, who had voted against the proposal on the earlier two occasions as well.

This action had different consequences for the medical school and the hospital. The college became more determined than ever to acquire a teaching hospital, even if it had to move to another location to do so. Lambert told the Roosevelt Board of Trustees to be aware "that the College not only desires a permanent hospital connection but that it must get it; and that if it cannot get such a relation with Roosevelt Hospital that the College will secure it elsewhere."[63] Soon, in an episode that will merit attention later, the school was to obtain such a hospital, Presbyterian Hospital, and ultimately it took its place as one of the foremost centers of medical education and research in the world.

Roosevelt, on the other hand, went into eclipse. By the next year, teaching at the hospital, formerly the school's major clinical resource, was found by one observer "not . . . to be in active operation."[64] Two years later, McLane raised several hundred thousand dollars for the hospital, but Lambert was unimpressed. "I cannot feel over-enthusiastic about Dr. McLane's action in collecting some hundreds of thousands of dollars for needed improvements in the hospital when he has so recently helped to refuse millions and an opportunity to make Roosevelt one of the greatest hospitals in the world."[65] In 1914, after McLane had resigned, the hospital decided to admit clinical clerks in small numbers. By that time, however, the medical school had established its affiliation with Presbyterian Hospital. Consequently, Roosevelt became an ancillary hospital, used for some teaching, but never again the central hospital of Columbia or any other medical school. Roosevelt continued to provide, as always, first-rate patient services, but it never acquired the international prominence as a center of education and research that the affiliation with Columbia would have provided. Roosevelt was to the nation's hospitals what Clark was to the universities of the era—both were institutions that threw away their chance for greatness.

Why did the Roosevelt trustees object to the union with Columbia? There seems to have been nothing unusual about the membership of the board compared with that of other large New York general hospitals, particularly Presbyterian Hospital and the New York Hospital, which were soon to cast their lot with medical education. All these boards were comprised largely of bankers, financiers, businessmen, and physicians. Although the boards did not differ very much in their sociological composition, they did differ in their ideologies. Roosevelt Hospital, unlike the others, remained immersed in the traditional outlook of the nineteenth-century hospital. As it expanded its plant and patient services, it did not experience a corresponding awakening of interest in research or education. The trustees never demonstrated any real sympathy toward clinical investigation or to the idea of students working as clinical clerks.[66] In their letter rejecting Columbia's final proposal, they claimed to "have no power to divert the funds under their care from charitable to educational purposes."[67] The trustees, in short, were ensnarled in the traditional nineteenth-century view of the hospital as a charitable institution. They could not accept the idea that a hospital's functions might also include teaching and research.

Roosevelt's medical board could not persuade the trustees otherwise. At a time when the medical boards of many hospitals were becoming increasingly influential within their institutions, the medical board of Roosevelt Hospital was not. The chief surgeon at the hospital complained bitterly in 1909 of the trustees' tendency "to ignore the Medical Board in regard to matters of medical administration."[68] He felt that his efforts in behalf of the hospital had been "not only refused but misinterpreted" by the trustees.[69] The trustees' behavior regarding a new affiliation with Columbia Medical School indicated that he was right. Refusal to listen to its medical board certainly lessened the chance that Roosevelt would develop into a teaching hospital.

It is an irony that McLane, the leader of the reactionary forces at Roosevelt Hospital, was an eminent physician and Lambert's predecessor as dean of Columbia Medical School. In that office, McLane had performed many outstanding services for the school: he had secured the gift that had allowed the construction of the Vanderbilt Clinic; he had helped bring about the affiliation with Columbia University; and he had helped introduce the four-year curriculum. He also made personal financial gifts to the school's meager endowment in the 1870s and 1880s.[70] Had the Roosevelt imbroglio not occurred, McLane would be remembered as the person of his generation who more than any other furthered the cause of medical education in New York City, not as the anachronistic hospital trustee fighting a vain, rear-guard action against the clerkship.

It has been claimed that McLane's opposition to the affiliation with Columbia resulted from a personal feud with Lambert.[71] Although this may in part be true, it is unlikely to account for more than a portion of the explanation. A more likely interpretation may be found in McLane's professional background. Born in 1839, a graduate of the College of Physicians and Surgeons in 1864, he entered practice immediately after medical school, without ever having worked as a house pupil in a hospital or having taken postgraduate instruction abroad. Although he became one of his generation's outstanding clinicians and clinical teachers, he never acquired any experience in research. In opposing the clerkship, he was thus not so much a villain as a person immersed in the world view of his generation. A product of a medical training not yet scientific, he could partly but not completely accommodate his deeply ingrained ideas on hospitals and medical education to the needs of the new scientific medicine. He was at once a symbol of the best of the old order but also of its inadequacy for the future.

The Plight of Clinical Teaching

Thus, the quality of clinical instruction in America in the early 1900s lagged considerably behind that of the basic science teaching. The main reason for this, as the episode at Columbia so clearly demonstrated, was the difficulty that medical schools were having in acquiring control of large, well-equipped hospitals with which to introduce the clerkship. Virtually every forward-looking medical school in the country was trying to establish a close educational alliance with a hospital, but hospital trustees were not interested. As a result, clinical education suffered greatly.

9 The Flexner Report

BY 1910, American medical education had progressed greatly, but further improvements were needed to elevate the average school to a minimum standard of excellence as well as to institute additional improvements at the stronger schools. It was unclear whether further development would continue along the same gradual, evolutionary path or whether more radical, dramatic changes were in the offing. The difficulties that even the best schools encountered in obtaining financial support and control of teaching hospitals suggested that many hopes might not be realized until far in the future.

Nor was it clear what form the institutional structure of American medical education would ultimately assume. Should there be one uniform standard of excellence for all schools, or would it be acceptable to have different "tiers" of medical schools, each with its own mission and standards? Should research be conducted at all schools, or should there be a group of "practical" schools that concentrated on good teaching rather than investigation? Should research be an integral or peripheral function of the faculty, and how could a faculty's responsibilities to teaching and research be reconciled? Must all professors assume full-time status, or was there still a role in the modern medical school for private practitioners? Must all schools be university-affiliated, or could a school of independent status still function effectively? How selective should medical schools be in their admission policies? Each of these views had its advocates among responsible medical educators and members of the profession. There were a variety of fiercely competing models of how best to conduct medical schools.

166

The Flexner Report

This was the setting for Abraham Flexner's famous report, a classic of muckraking journalism, *Medical Education in the United States and Canada*, issued in June 1910 as Bulletin Number Four of the Carnegie Foundation for the Advancement of Teaching. The report emphasized the work remaining to be done in medical education rather than the progress that had already been made. With devastating candor, the report directed its fiercest attack on the proprietary schools, exposing the scandalous conditions and outright fraud that existed in the bottom quarter of the country's medical schools. To Flexner, only one type of medical school was acceptable: university schools, with large full-time faculties and a vigorous commitment to research. Although the report was not original—everything in it had been said by academically-inclined medical educators since the 1870s—it had a galvanizing effect on public sentiment, making the achievement of the ideal much more attainable. In addition, it made a choice among the competing models of medical education, supporting the most uncompromisingly academic model. The report thus not only influenced the speed at which medical education in the United States developed thereafter but the form it ultimately assumed.

As the report was a journalistic tour de force, so was it also a classic monograph in educational literature. Modern medical teaching, as discussed earlier, involved the same educational concepts as those developed by John Dewey and associated with the progressive education movement. Spokesmen for both the medical and elementary school emphasized the importance of carefully constructing the educational environment so students could learn from their sensory experiences in an individualized fashion. There is no evidence of a direct connection between Dewey and the medical educators, who developed their ideas independently of and before the great philosopher. However, Flexner, himself a professional educator, recognized that the medical educators and Dewey were advocating the same ideas about how learning might best proceed. The Flexner report, which should be considered a classic document in the literature of progressive education, symbolized the unity between the educational ideas of the academic physicians and those of John Dewey. As Flexner described modern principles of medical learning, he cited Dewey as his ultimate authority. Progressive education has traditionally been considered a movement of the elementary and secondary schools and to a lesser degree the college. However, conventional wisdom must be revised. As the Flexner report clearly demonstrated, the ideas of progressive education had permeated professional education as well. Ultimately, through Flexner, medicine would leave its own mark on progressive education in the United States.

Prelude to the Report

By 1910 a consensus had emerged among medical educators regarding the proper approach to teaching medicine. It was felt that the fundamental sciences could no longer be ignored and that students should be active learners through the laboratory and clerkship. Although many schools, particularly the commercial ones, advertised scientific and clinical opportunities that did not exist, such actions merely served to acknowledge the legitimacy of the higher standards.

The profession at large had also come to support the more rigorous methods of teaching. Previous generations of practitioners had little use for medical science, but by 1910 most doctors appreciated that scientific knowledge and methods were applicable to the practice of medicine—however much they might have resented the efforts of academic physicians to oust them from teaching. Practitioners wanted to improve medical education for reasons of both professional conviction and self-interest, for well-educated physicians found it easier to build a large practice. This message was not lost upon medical students. At Michigan, for example, George Dock, the professor of medicine, spoke to students of the advantages of taking additional hospital training rather than going into practice at the earliest moment. Hard study would later be rewarded because "usually the man in the hospital will have more practice and keep on getting a better one in the end."[1] Even medical students were indoctrinated with the idea that thorough training was good for doctors as well as patients.

Indeed, after 1900 a broad consensus began to appear in the medical profession regarding the desirability of improving medical education. Practitioners joined professors in calling for educational reform; leaders of the reform movement now found themselves with an expanding base of support among the profession at large. The reform movement provided an umbrella for all who supported higher educational standards. Educational purists, who saw that the public benefited from having well-trained doctors, argued incessantly for higher educational standards. So did academic physicians, who realized that educational reform would serve their personal ambitions by creating more full-time positions. Practitioners, who since the 1840s had been complaining of overcrowding of the profession and of medicine's low public image, found educational reform a convenient device for alleviating these problems. Higher educational standards meant less competition and improved social and economic standing for the average physician.[2] Different groups could, and did, desire the same educational improvements for different reasons. In the reform movement practitioners were generally the followers, academic physicians the leaders, but the widespread support that developed among practitioners became a valuable political asset to the medical educators.

Although by 1910 a standard approach to medical teaching had emerged, a standard medical school had not. The nation's 148 undergraduate and postgraduate schools represented nearly half the world's total, and their ranks included some of the finest and some of the most atrocious schools in existence. Some students entered medical school as mature, sophisticated students with undergraduate degrees earned at the country's best colleges, while other students were barely literate. At the North Carolina Medical College in Charlotte, Flexner was told that "it is idle to talk of real laboratory work for students so ignorant and clumsy. Many of them, gotten through advertising, would make better farmers."[3] Greater variation in quality characterized America's medical schools than at any time before or since.

Which schools should be permitted to survive and which forced into extinction? This perplexing question troubled medical educators. Representatives of many of the weaker schools felt that the line needed to be drawn only between the frankly commercial schools and those with genuine educational aims. An official of the perilously weak Kansas Medical College in Topeka wrote: "It is a rather puzzling problem to know precisely where to draw the line between schools that should exist and schools that should not. I presume that one clear line will be practically drawn between schools that are run for the benefit of the professors and those which are on a perfectly general educational basis."[4] Other medical educators felt that much higher standards must be maintained, but that there was room for "practical," nonuniversity schools that concentrated on teaching rather than research. Thus, the president of Bowdoin College argued in defense of schools "which, while adequately equipped to avail themselves of all practical results of medical research, yet make it their chief aim to train men to use those results in the actual practice of medicine."[5] Still other medical educators believed that all schools should follow the university model. This was the view of officials of ten elite schools that established an informal organization, the Federation of University Medical Schools, in 1908. Impatient with the lower standards of the Association of American Medical Colleges, which focused on what it thought *could* be done in medical education, the Federation concerned itself with what it felt *should* be done. In its view, every school should be a university school, with higher entrance and graduation standards and an unambiguous commitment to research.[6]

Among those who promoted the purest academic model was the Council on Medical Education of the AMA. Since its formation in 1904, the council had been one of the prime forces in organizing sentiment within the medical profession on behalf of educational reform. Although the AMA, after its reorganization in 1901, remained primarily the voice of medical practitioners, academic physicians had gained control of the council. The council's five permanent members—Victor Vaughan, dean of the University of Michigan Medical School; William Councilman, professor of pathology at Harvard Medical School; Charles Frazier, professor of surgery at the University of Pennsylvania; J. A. Witherspoon, professor of medicine at Vanderbilt University; and Arthur Dean Bevan, professor of surgery at Rush Medical College —were all stalwarts of the academic establishment, and they used their position on the council to advocate the highest educational standards. As a result, the AMA's official position on medical education after 1904 became the one that had been long advocated by the academic elite. Indeed, long after the reform period had ended, the council continued to be dominated by university medical teachers whose activities remained insulated from the AMA's practitioner-controlled House of Delegates.[7]

It was the council that had the idea to conduct an independent survey of the country's medical schools. In 1906, it had conducted an inspection of its own, in which its representatives had visited each of the 162 medical schools in the country. This report, distributed to the medical schools but never published, drew essentially the same conclusions as Abraham Flexner in 1910. Its standard for measuring schools was the most rigorous university model, and from this perspective most of the country's medical schools came out sorely lacking. Since it seemed politically imprudent for a medical organization to be so publicly critical of medical schools, the council invited the Carnegie Foundation for the Advancement of Teaching to conduct a similar study, and Henry Pritchett, the president of the Carnegie Foundation, readily accepted the invitation.[8] Records of both the council and the Carnegie Foundation indicate how closely the two cooperated in performing the survey. As another political stratagem, however, it was decided not to make public the council's role in organizing the study, and only in the preface does the report make even passing reference to the help the council provided the Foundation.[9] Thus, the report could be publicly perceived as the independent judgment of an outside agency.

The council found a natural ally in the Carnegie Foundation, whose activities reflected the indelible impress of its president. One paramount goal guided Pritchett throughout his career: the elevation of the position of scholarship in the United States.[10] In 1894–95 he had studied astronomy in Munich, where he witnessed the high standards of German scientific work and the spirit of freedom and inquiry of the German university. On his return to the United

States, he was dismayed at the lack of scientific opportunities. Instead of pursuing advanced teaching and research, he had to teach the freshman course in astronomy at Washington University—an experience not dissimilar to that of many medical scientists who, on their return from study in Germany, found so few opportunities for medical research in America. Later, first as president of the Massachusetts Institute of Technology and then as president of the Carnegie Foundation, he became one of the country's strongest spokesmen for the research university. His interest in the Carnegie Foundation, he explained, arose from the hope that the foundation might provide "an opportunity to better the conditions which make for scholarship."[11]

The Carnegie Foundation, established in 1905, strongly reflected the orientation of its president, who had proposed the idea for the foundation to Andrew Carnegie.[12] Its first work was the creation of a system of old-age pensions for certain college teachers, the forerunner of today's Teachers Insurance and Annuity Association. By removing the financial uncertainties of retirement, the foundation placed scholarship in the United States on a much firmer economic footing, thereby doing as much to foster its development as any other single event. Pritchett's interest in research was generalized, and thus it was no surprise that he was enthusiastic about medical research. Like the leading medical educators, he felt American medical schools should provide not only better teaching but more full-time positions, so that academic medicine might become a secure career.

Pritchett was delighted for the foundation to have the opportunity to study medical education. He understood the pedagogic issues involved, as he did those of other types of professional education. Thus, as Ellen Lagemann has related, he saw the survey as a way of further fostering the importance of professional educators as "the arbiters of all training matters," including those that concerned professional training.[13] He was fond of saying, "Medical education is, after all, not medicine but education."[14] Later, the foundation sponsored similar studies of legal and engineering education. With its interest in pedagogic matters, the pursuit of research, and the establishment of scholarship as a career, the concerns of the Carnegie Foundation encompassed many of the main themes that had been shaping the development of medical education.

The person selected by Pritchett to conduct the inspection of medical schools was Abraham Flexner.[15] Born in 1866 in Louisville to impoverished Jewish immigrants, Flexner overcame humble origins and economic deprivation to become one of the most informed critics ever of the American educational system. He received the A.B. degree from Johns Hopkins in 1886 after studying classics, and thereupon he returned to Louisville to organize a private high school. In 1905, he closed his school to pursue graduate work at Harvard, where he studied philosophy and psychology for their possible bearings on educational problems. In 1907 he traveled in Europe, where he closely observed the various educational systems. On returning to the United States, he served as a staff member of the Carnegie Foundation (1908–12) and as assistant secretary and then secretary of the General Education Board (1913–28). In his "retirement," he organized the Institute for Advanced Study at Princeton, served as its first director, and brought Albert Einstein to the United States. In personal affairs he was a loyal and affectionate man, but in his work he could be caustic, arrogant, and uncompromising. However, as Daniel Fox has shown, he was a master of organizational politics and capable of much more flexibility in his views and diplomacy in his words and actions than is commonly appreciated.[16]

How Flexner, at the time an obscure educator, came to Pritchett's attention is not known. In his autobiography, Flexner thought that perhaps Pritchett had learned of him through his first book, *The American College,* which appeared in 1908 and was a criticism of the lecture and elective system. It is possible that Flexner's brother, Simon, the director of the Rockefeller Institute for Medical Research and a former student of William Welch, played a role. In any event, the choice proved to be fortunate. Aggressive, articulate, and outspoken, Flexner became a forceful spokesman for modern methods of medical teaching and the most loyal friend that academic medicine ever had.

It is well known how little Flexner knew about medicine as he began the project in December of 1908. Indeed, in his autobiography, Flexner recalled that at first he had thought that Pritchett had confused him with his brother, Simon.[17] After accepting the assignment, Flexner immediately undertook a crash course on medical education: he read voraciously on the subject; he conferred regularly with the Council on Medical Education, which made all its records available to him; and he made many trips to Johns Hopkins. His greatest debt was to Welch, Mall, and the other faculty members who had created the country's premier medical school. He later recalled, "The rest of my study of medical education was little more than an amplification of what I had learned during my initial visit to Baltimore."[18]

Yet in recounting his work with the Carnegie Foundation, Flexner portrayed himself as an "unfettered lay mind," and it would be a serious mistake to regard him as a mere tool of the council or the Johns Hopkins medical faculty.[19] A sophisticated and unimpressionable educator, Flexner had already developed a coherent philosophy of education prior to embarking on the study of medical education. Though at first he knew little about the specifics of medical training, he understood the medical educators when they talked about the experiential nature of learning and the imperative of developing inductive reasoning and the power to generalize. The principal source of these ideas for

Flexner, as Lawrence Cremin has pointed out, lay in the teaching experience he had acquired as a young man in his private school in Louisville.[20] This experience later inspired Flexner to write an important essay, "A Modern School," in which he advocated that these educational principles be applied in elementary school teaching. In the essay he wrote: "The child's concrete experience cannot be abridged without serious damage to his unfolding powers. His intellectual and aesthetic capacities ought to develop on the basis of a first-hand experience, not a second-hand or bookish training."[21] Flexner's conceptual framework, in short, had already been developed. Welch and the others merely provided the details as they pertained to medicine.

Similarly, Flexner did not need the medical educators to persuade him of the importance of original research at a medical school. Rather, it was Daniel Gilman, the first president of Johns Hopkins, who had imparted to Flexner an appreciation of the importance of original investigation in all scholarly fields. This value Flexner internalized during his undergraduate study. Later in life, he remained committed to promoting original research in all his various activities at the Carnegie Foundation, the General Education Board, and the Institute for Advanced Study. "Those who know something of my work," he later recalled, ". . . will recognize Gilman's influence in all I have done or tried to do."[22] As the Johns Hopkins faculty described the different types of medical schools to him, Flexner needed no convincing to endorse the university model. This was the only model that satisfied his high standards of academic excellence.

With his preparation complete, Flexner began a busy year of travel to each of the 155 medical schools in the United States and Canada. Although he had been coached by the Johns Hopkins faculty and the Council on Medical Education, and council members accompanied him on each of his visits, the report was his and his alone, for it reflected the educational philosophy and academic ideals he had brought with him into the study. Perhaps no other lay person could have written such a document, and it immediately became a classic.

Medical Education in the United States and Canada

The Flexner report was written in two sections. The first consisted of a long essay on the principles of modern medical education. This theoretical section began with a chapter on the history of medical education, proceeded through several chapters that compared "ideal" with existing conditions of medical education in North America, and concluded with chapters on special topics such as the financial requirements of medical education, medical education for blacks and women, medical licensing, and sectarian and postgraduate medical education. The second section provided a description of each American and Canadian medical school. Schools were evaluated on the basis of five specific criteria: entrance requirements; size and training of faculty; financial resources; laboratories; and clinical facilities. The result was a brilliant exposé.

The starting point in Flexner's analysis was the observation that medicine had entered the scientific era. A tone of medical positivism pervaded the book; medicine was regarded as an experimental discipline governed by the laws of general biology. "Medicine is part and parcel of modern science," he wrote. "The human body belongs to the animal world. It is put together of tissues and organs, in their structure, origin and development not essentially unlike what the biologist is otherwise familiar with; it grows, reproduces itself, decays, according to general laws."[23]

To Flexner, "scientific medicine" encompassed two concepts. One was the recognition that physics, chemistry, and biology provided the intellectual foundation of modern medicine. He did not minimize the huge depth of the "unbridged gap" between the physical and medical sciences, but he felt that the mechanical standpoint had already "richly justified itself" from the medical point of view.[24] Physical laws, not metaphysical principles, explained the normal and abnormal workings of the human organism. Medical students must be "trained to regard the body as an infinitely complex machine."[25]

The second concept—and more important to Flexner—was the recognition that scientific method applied to practice as well as research. By scientific method, he meant the testing of ideas by well-planned experiments in which accurate facts were carefully obtained. The scientific character of an activity, he explained, "depends not on where or by what means facts are procured, but altogether on the degree of caution and thoroughness with which observations are made, inferences drawn, and results heeded."[26] Thus, research and practice, when properly conducted, both employed the same mental processes. In an important passage he wrote:

> And just as it makes no difference to science whether usable data be obtained from a slide beneath a microscope or from a sick man stretched out on a cot, so the precise nature of the act or experiment is immaterial: it matters not in the slightest, from the standpoint of scientific logic, whether the step take the form of administering a dose of calomel, operating for appendicitis, or stimulating a particular convolution of a frog's brain with an electric current. The logical position is in all three cases identical. In each a supposition,—whether expressed

or implied, whether called theory or diagnosis,—based on supposedly adequate observation, submits itself to the test of an experiment. If proper weight has been given to correct and sufficient facts, the experiment wins; otherwise not, and a second effort, profiting by previous failure, is demanded. The practising physician and the 'theoretical' scientist are thus engaged in doing the same sort of thing, even while one is seeking to correct Mr. Smith's digestive aberration and the other to localize the cerebral functions of the frog.[27]

Flexner abhorred the "rule-of-thumb" practitioner—the simple empiric who practiced medicine by protocol. Rather, he admired the "scientific" practitioner—the one who evaluated patients carefully, who performed tests only when they were dictated by a patient's particular circumstances, who modified his preliminary impressions on the basis of test results or the response to therapy, who realized the limits of his knowledge, and who had the capacity to keep up with changing medical practices. Flexner knew that the average family doctor would never engage in research, but he understood that the scientific method was indispensable to the everyday work of good patient care.

To Flexner, the scientific nature of modern medicine imposed new requirements on those who would teach it. "On the pedagogic side," he wrote, "modern medicine, like all scientific teaching, is characterized by activity. The student no longer merely watches, listens, memorizes; he *does.* "[28] This meant that students should learn through their experiences in laboratories and hospital wards. Descriptive teaching through lectures or textbooks could provide "no substitute for tactile and visual experience."[29] "A modern medical education involves both learning and learning how; the student cannot effectively know, unless he knows how."[30]

Flexner's scorn for didactic instruction pervaded the report. Teaching by lectures alone, he wrote, was "utterly worthless"—a "hopelessly antequated [*sic*]" form of instruction that belonged to "an age of accepted dogma or supposedly complete information, when the professor 'knew' and the students 'learned.' "[31] Didactic information left a student's sense of reality "pale and ineffective"; first-hand experience, in contrast, rendered the sense of reality "vivid."[32] At best the lecture had a supplementary role—summarizing, amplifying, and systematizing knowledge obtained in the laboratory and clinic—but it had "no right to forestall experience."[33] Flexner derided the anatomy quiz-masters, "who drill hundreds of students in memorizing minute details which they would be unable to recognize if the objects were before them."[34] He pitied the didactically taught students—and their patients—for their "slow and costly initiation into the art of medicine."[35] Quoting from an article of the period, he pointed out that learning medicine was much like learning anything else. "If one had one hundred hours in which to learn to ride a horse or to speak in public, one might profitably spend an hour (in divided doses) in being told how to do it, four hours in watching a teacher do it, and the remaining ninety-five hours in practice."[36]

Learning by doing fulfilled a dual purpose to Flexner. It represented the best way of mastering scientific knowledge, and it taught the student the scientific method. This latter point was crucial to Flexner because a medical student had to understand scientific concepts, not merely memorize facts by rote. The student must be a "thinker," not a "parrot."[37] This could be realized only if the student had mastered the scientific method—that is, the ability to handle experience critically. Flexner sympathized with the dismay and futility commonly felt over the vast amount of medical knowledge to be acquired, but he felt there was no cause for despair. The student who had mastered the scientific method "will still be ignorant of many things, but at any rate he will respect facts: he will have learned how to obtain them and what to do with them when he has them."[38]

Conceptually, Flexner's discussion of proper medical teaching contained no new ideas. However, he did what no medical educator had done before: he related the discussion of medical education to the discussion of public education. Flexner, who had studied philosophy and psychology for their relevance to educational matters, had become familiar with the work of John Dewey. He recognized that Dewey was advocating the same approach to elementary teaching as the medical educators were to medical teaching. In emphasizing that the essence of science was its method of inquiry, Flexner invoked the authority of Dewey. "Science," Flexner quoted from one of Dewey's papers, "has been taught too much as an accumulation of ready-made material, with which students are to be made familiar, not enough as a method of thinking, an attitude of mind, after the pattern of which mental habits are to be transformed."[39] Two years later Flexner cited Dewey again to explain why modern medical education involved practical rather than didactic work. In education, Flexner quoted Dewey as having remarked, "the initiative lies with the learner,"[40] which could be fostered only if students were required to learn by doing. Flexner thus symbolized the unity in educational viewpoints of the academic physicians and John Dewey. He realized that progressive education involved concepts that were generalizable to training at all educational levels.

In addition, through Flexner, medical education affected the course of the progressive education movement. Flexner's essay of 1916, "A Modern School," inspired the creation the following year of the Lincoln School, a private experimental school associated with Teachers College of Columbia University.[41] This school, which Flexner viewed as a laboratory for the promotion of a scientific spirit in education, epitomized more than any other institution the private progressive school of the period. Lawrence Cremin has written, "No single progressive school exerted greater or more lasting influence on the subsequent history of American education."[42] In proposing this model school, Flexner was influenced by what had happened in medical education. As he had advanced the Johns Hopkins Medical School as the model for medical schools, so he proposed "the modern school" as the model for elementary schools. In his autobiography he explained, "Mindful of the tremendous influence on medical education exerted by one modest but sound institution, the Johns Hopkins Medical School, I had long cherished the notion that a model school, quite modern in curriculum and discipline, might play a similar role in general education."[43] The strategy that had worked so well in medical education he used effectively in his later work in elementary education.

To learn by doing, to develop habits of inquiry and critical thinking, as Flexner so strenuously advocated in the report, said nothing of the type of medical school in which students were to be taught. Here, too, Flexner held a strong opinion. His discussion focused not only on subject matter and teaching methods, but on such issues as admission requirements, faculty qualifications, laboratory and clinical facilities, hospital relations, university affiliations, and medical research. He endorsed not only certain methods of medical teaching but a certain type of medical school. It was here that he was to have his greatest impact on the subsequent development of medical education in the United States.

The ideal medical school, to Flexner, had three major characteristics. First, it was properly equipped. Modern, spacious, well-stocked laboratories had to be available in each subject. Medical schools also needed control of teaching hospitals, where the faculty could teach on the wards by right, not by privilege. Finally, medical schools needed funds to purchase land, erect and maintain buildings, and pay salaries. Laboratories, teaching hospitals, and endowments each received detailed and impassioned discussion in the report. To Flexner, a school could be first-rate only if it were richly provided for.

Second, Flexner's ideal medical school admitted only academically qualified students. Because each of the medical sciences "hark back to a previous scientific discipline" and thus are sciences "at the second, not the primary, stage," this meant at the very minimum two years of college training featuring physics, chemistry, and biology.[44] A medical school, Flexner wrote, "cannot provide laboratory and bedside instruction on the one hand, and admit crude, untrained boys on the other."[45] For this reason, "The privileges of the medical school can no longer be open to casual strollers from the highways. It is necessary to install a doorkeeper who will, by critical scrutiny, ascertain the fitness of the applicant."[46]

To enforce entrance requirements, the medical school had to be properly articulated with the rest of the educational system. Entrance requirements, Flexner wrote, must "be formulated in terms that establish a distinct relation, pedagogical and chronological, between the medical school and other educational agencies."[47] He realized that this could be done only if the medical school and the other components of the school system developed in conjunction with each other. "The strength of an educational system is wholly a question of the competent performance of differentiated function by each of its organic parts."[48]

Third, original investigation was a core activity at Flexner's model medical school. "Research, untrammeled by near reference to practical ends, will go on in every properly organized medical school; its critical method will dominate all teaching whatsoever."[49] To Flexner, research was required of faculty members so that its critical method might animate their teaching. Modern practitioners must be "alert, systematic, thorough, critically open-minded."[50] They will receive no such training from "perfunctory teachers" but only from "men of active, progressive temper" who are engaged in research.[51] "Research is required of the medical faculty because only research will keep the teachers in condition. A non-productive school, conceivably up to date to-day, would be out of date to-morrow; its dead atmosphere would soon breed a careless and unenlightened dogmatism."[52] Flexner did not feel that every medical instructor had to be productive at research, but, as a general rule, he did believe that researchers made the best teachers. Thus, his ideal medical school required a large staff of full-time professors, in the clinical as well as scientific departments, and the school had to be part of a vigorous university.

How should a proper system of medical schools be achieved? Flexner recommended a drastic reduction of the number of schools in the United States and Canada to thirty-one. Only a few should be retained; the vast majority should be eliminated, either through extermination or consolidation into stronger units. All surviving schools would be of one type: university schools committed to medical research and academic excellence. With fewer schools, the task of raising money for laboratories, hospitals, and salaries would be made much easier. There need be no concern over the ability of the schools to meet the demands for medical manpower. The country already had a surfeit of poorly trained doctors—one physician for every 568 persons, in contrast to one doctor for every 2,000 persons in Germany.[53] The country needed "fewer and better doctors."[54] Moreover, since the remaining thirty-one schools would have the capacity to double enrollment, the supply of doctors would keep pace with future increases in the population. The instruments of reform would be the state boards, which had the legal power to destroy the unworthy schools.

Throughout his life, Flexner demonstrated a remarkable consistency in his educational views. Thus, it is no surprise that the Louisville school teacher and author of "A Modern School" advocated a method of medical instruction that required a student to learn by doing. It is also no surprise that the admirer of Daniel Gilman and creator of the Institute for Advanced Study should have supported an academic model of the medical school that made research a central activity. Insofar as Flexner discussed teaching methods, he endorsed a viewpoint that almost all medical educators had come to share. Insofar as he discussed the ideal medical school, he proposed a model favored by only some—the research-oriented physicians who comprised the nation's academic medical elite. To Flexner, uncompromising academic excellence was the only acceptable hallmark of a medical school. That meant good students, good teachers, and modern facilities. Because research as well as teaching was central, more full-time professors were needed. Small wonder that the medical scientists, who had been striving for decades to promote the acceptance of academic medicine in the United States, loved the report.

As Flexner surveyed the nation's medical scene, he recognized the great heterogeneity that existed. The country boasted some of the best physicians in the world; it also suffered some of the very worst. The medical schools also ranged in quality from world class to abominable. Now that it mattered how a doctor was trained, it was unconscionable to allow inferior schools to exist. The challenge to the nation's system of medical education, as Flexner perceived it, was to provide the best possible training to every physician—to bridge the great gap between what was known and what the average physician knew. This was Flexner's attitude, and it was an attitude that was shared by the overwhelming majority of his generation. Scientific knowledge and methods simply had to be made available to every doctor; there was no other issue so important or so immediately pressing. This could be done only if every school achieved a minimum standard of excellence, which meant that lesser schools could no longer be tolerated.

Accordingly, Flexner took dead aim at the weakest schools, saving his fiercest attack for the commercial schools that have made such a "discreditable showing."[55] The result was a classic piece of muckraking journalism that deserves to rank with the other great muckraking treatises of the era. Like other muckrakers, Flexner wrote caustically and minced no words. He provided a wealth of details, named names, and devastated the bad schools with humiliating public exposure. At Temple University, the Philadelphia College of Osteopathy, the Halifax Medical School, and others, the dissecting rooms "defy description. The smell is intolerable; the cadavers now putrid."[56] At the Kansas Medical College, the dissecting room "did duty incidentally as a chicken yard: corn was scattered over the floor—along with other things—and poultry fed placidly in the long intervals before instruction in anatomy began."[57] Many schools—indicated to the reader by name, of course—were

> . . . without redeeming features of any kind. Their general squalor consorts well with their clinical poverty: the class-rooms are bare, save for chairs, a desk, and an occasional blackboard; the windows streaked with dust and soot. In wretched amphitheaters students wait in vain for 'professors,' tardy or absent, amusing the interval with ribald jest and song. The teaching is an uninstructive rehearsal of text-book or quiz-compend: one encounters surgery taught without patient, instrument, model, or drawing; recitations in obstetrics without a manikin in sight, —often without one in the building. Third and fourth year men are frequently huddled together in the same classes. At the Memphis Hospital Medical College the students of all four years attend the same classes in many of the subjects taught.[58]

The nation had reason to be shocked.

What made the commercial schools so despicable to Flexner was that they placed their owners' interest above those of the public. Medical schools, he maintained, were public service corporations to be run for the benefit of society, not private businesses to be operated for the profit of their stockholders. Medicine has "no analogy with business. Like the army, the police, or the social worker, the medical profession is supported for a benign, not a selfish, for a protective, not an exploiting, purpose."[59] In medical education the interest of the public is "paramount."[60] Society should "crush out" the proprietary schools because they are "mercenary concerns that trade on ignorance and disease."[61] It was Flexner's sense of social purpose—his indignation, moral outrage, and concern with the public well-being—as well as his sensational journalistic style that made the report such an elegant example of muckraking literature. Flexner categorized the owners of the proprietary schools as archenemies of the public, as deserving of popular contempt as such other despised betrayers of public confidence as the operators of the beef trust, the railroad trust, and the Standard Oil trust.

The report accomplished its purpose. The public joined the medical educators in expressing disgust with the proprietary schools. No one became more convinced of the worthlessness of proprietary schools than Andrew Carnegie. In one of the great ironies in the development of American medicine, the report persuaded Carnegie, who had established the Carnegie Foundation and whose munificence in other areas was so well known, not to make medical education the object of future benefactions. He told Flexner: "You have proved that medical education is a business. I will not endow any other man's business."[62] Until Carnegie's death in 1919, the Carnegie Corporation, the steel-maker's grant-making corporation, eschewed the field of medical education. Only after the founder died, when the corporation was no longer run as Carnegie's personal agency, did it enter that field of philanthrophy.[63]

Although the Flexner report succeeded brilliantly in expediting the death of the proprietary schools, it blinded most observers, past and present, to the true state of medical education in 1910. As a stratagem, Flexner emphasized the distance to be traveled before achieving an ideal system in which all schools were university schools, not the progress that had already been made in that direction. He focused on what remained to be done in improving medical education rather than on the many accomplishments in that area since the 1870s. As a result, most observers did not appreciate that medical education in the United States at the time was in its best condition ever. A myth arose—one that Flexner never vigorously denied—that the report represented the demarcation between the "pre-modern" and "modern" periods of medical education and that Flexner in one swoop pulled antiquated medical schools, kicking and screaming in resistance, into the twentieth century. Not everyone was fooled. The Council on Medical Education went on record at one of its meetings "to correct a wrong impression conveyed by the latter [Flexner] report—that conditions in this country were at their worst, when in fact they had never been better."[64] Victor Vaughan told Pritchett, "I think that Mr. Flexner's report makes it quite evident that in the best schools in this country the undergraduate in medicine gets as good instruction, possibly better, than he finds in any other country in the world."[65] Historians for a generation have been pointing out that the Flexner report represented a point along a continuum of development and that the report had been preceded for years by considerable strengthening of the schools.[66] Nevertheless, the myth has persisted. Recent books on medical education have continued to popularize the fiction that little had transpired in medical education until Flexner in one stunning blow modernized an anachronistic system.[67] A recent, widely publicized report by the president of Harvard University called Flexner the "father" of modern medical education.[68] This myth, which violates all known principles of historical causation and human psychology, deserves once and for all to be destroyed.

The Flexner report represented a legitimate response to the pressing problem of the day: ensuring that everyone who practiced medicine be thoroughly trained. It transformed the reform of medical education into a broad social movement similar to other reform movements of Progressive Era America, and even today people still enjoy reading the pungent descriptions of the proprietary schools contained in the report. Conceptually, it said noth-

ing new about how physicians should be trained. However, it brilliantly succeeded in explaining modern medical education to the public, and it showed
that the principles of progressive education applied to medical teaching just
as they did to teaching at other levels. In terms of the competing models of
medical schools, the report made a choice—advocating the most rigorous
academic model. It decried a heterogeneous system of medical education; it
insisted on a homogeneous system in which all schools were university schools.
It was Flexner's impact on determining the form that the medical school
ultimately assumed that represented his greatest influence on the subsequent
course of medical education in the country.

The Flexner report has frequently been misunderstood. Because of its
strong emphasis on scientific medicine, it has often been accused of ignoring
the doctor-patient relationship, denigrating the importance of preventive
medicine, and fostering a crowded, inflexible curriculum. Exactly the opposite
was the case. Science, Flexner wrote, is "inadequate" to provide the basis of
professional practice. The practitioner also needs "insight and sympathy," and
here specific preparation is "much more difficult."[69] Practitioners must also
not forget that "directly or indirectly, disease has been found to depend largely
on unpropitious environment." These conditions—"a bad water-supply, defective drainage, impure food, unfavorable occupational surroundings"—are
matters for "social regulation," and doctors have the duty "to promote social
conditions that conduce to physical well-being."[70] Indeed, "The physician's
function is fast becoming social and preventive, rather than individual and
curative."[71] In discussing the curriculum, Flexner decried the "absurd overcrowding"[72] produced by 4,000 hours of prescribed work. He warned medical
educators against too much rigidity; medical schools must be trusted "with a
certain amount of discretion."[73] He believed that "the endeavor to improve
medical education through iron-clad prescription of curriculum or hours is a
wholly mistaken effort."[74] In later years, Flexner felt that the medical course
remained too structured, rigid, and overweighted with the scientific to the
exclusion of the humanistic aspect of medicine; and he undoubtedly felt
frustrated that such a system of medical education had come to be identified
with his name. He wrote in 1925, "Scientific medicine in America—young,
vigorous and positivistic— is today sadly deficient in cultural and philosophic
background."[75]

Another, more substantive charge commonly hurled against the report
was that it impeded the entry of disadvantaged youths into the profession.
Insofar as Flexner reiterated the need for high entrance requirements, and
insofar as such requirements made it more difficult for students of lower-class
backgrounds to gain admission, the criticism has merit. Yet that was not
Flexner's own animus. Neither was he prejudiced nor in the least concerned

with increasing the private practitioner's image and income.[76] Rather, he was motivated by his unswerving advocacy of high academic standards. "It is right to sympathize with those who lack opportunity; still better to assist them in surmounting obstacles; but not at the price of certain injury to the common weal."[77] Education, he wrote on another occasion, must "be provided for the mediocre, but not at the expense of the able."[78] To Flexner, the crux of the issue was the tension between democratic values and the elitism inherent in academic excellence. The "danger of democracy," he wrote, was that "it will fail to appreciate excellence." Such a tendency must be combated because "in very truth an aristocracy of excellence is the truest form of democracy."[79] Throughout his life, Flexner acted as the champion of excellence and the archenemy of mediocrity. His credo appeared in his autobiography: "We have to defend the country against mediocrity, mediocrity of soul, mediocrity of ideas, mediocrity of action. We must also fight it in ourselves."[80]

Flexner was influenced in this outlook by his personal experiences. After all, he had overcome severe deprivations as a child. Anyone else, if sufficiently capable and motivated, should be able to do the same. Indeed, Flexner offered his own life as an example of what could be done in America "as long as we cling to the ideas of self-reliance, ambition, toleration, and loyalty to . . . ideals."[81] Flexner, like so many others, had faith in the uplifting, democratizing effects of public education and of the accessibility of a good education to all. The "earnest poor boy," Flexner believed, would succeed regardless of obstacles. "He need only take thought in good season, lay his plans, be prudent, and stick to his purpose. Without these qualities, medicine is no calling for him; with them, poverty will rarely block his way."[82]

Flexner's viewpoint was not uncommon among those who grew to maturity in the latter nineteenth century. As Thomas Haskell has discussed, this attitude reflected the individualistic, self-reliant world view of the era—the idea that individuals were autonomous, the creators of society, the masters of their own fate.[83] One best-selling book in 1894 maintained that the primary determinant of success was the will to succeed; this book went through 250 printings.[84] Insofar as this world view encouraged individuals not to be content with their circumstances in life, it was a liberating attitude. Poverty could be seen not as a reflection of God's will but as a condition that could be overcome by education, hard work, and personal initiative. This outlook, however, obscured the fact that the parts of society had become mutually dependent. It failed to recognize that modern America had become indescribably complex and that environmental factors beyond a person's direct control might change someone's life for good or for harm. Hard work and self-sacrifice could not save the family farm if an economic depression had destroyed the market for crops. Only in the next generation, as Haskell has shown, did the recognition become widespread that to improve the republic, society, not just persons, had to be changed for the better. Flexner, and other medical educators, were blind to the full power of external forces on individual potential, but it was a blindness they shared with the rest of their generation.

The Flexner report was not envisioned by its author as a final document. "This solution," he wrote, "deals only with the present and the near future, —a generation, at most. In the course of the next thirty years needs will develop of which we here take no account. As we cannot foretell them, we shall not endeavor to meet them."[85] The report thus contained much more flexibility than commonly supposed. It recognized that academic medical centers would need to change as the demands upon them changed. Flexner's specific proposals were designed only to meet the problems immediately at hand.

Flexner could not have foreseen the degree to which specialization was to proceed after World War II, nor could he have predicted the strained relations that would develop between some academic medical centers and their local communities. He did not address these issues because they were not issues that his generation had to face. Thus, contrary to the opinion of some, there is no reason to suspect he would have disapproved of current efforts to combat these problems through the training of primary care physicians and the provision of community health services by university medical centers. He would have disapproved only if academic standards were compromised in the process. For instance, he probably would have objected to current proposals to shorten training or to deemphasize research in the name of community service on the grounds that such proposals were anti-intellectual and unscientific. Flexner would have feared that a medical center that sacrificed its academic values would rapidly descend to mediocrity. There is every reason to believe he would have been pleased with the sense of social responsibility shown by many of today's medical schools—as long as the commitment to academic excellence is not abandoned.

Aftermath of the Report

Immediately on publication, the Flexner report created a sensation. Fifteen thousand copies went into print, a very large number for a technical study. The report made instant headlines, and newspapers accepted its conclusions as gospel. Representatives of many of the schools chafed with anger and embarrassment. Several schools threatened Flexner with lawsuits, and he received at least one anonymous threat on his life.[86]

In retrospect, it is remarkable how closely the report hit the mark. Visits had been conducted hastily—often Flexner would spend only a few hours at a school. Flexner was not always impartial in reporting what he had observed. As seen from his correspondence, he was sometimes more lenient with schools that he felt had a future than with those he felt did not.[87] Indeed, even a staunch supporter like Hans Zinsser of the Rockefeller Institute admitted that Flexner "did, on occasion, hit below the belt."[88] Nevertheless, the report contained remarkably few errors. Henry Pritchett recognized that a work of such magnitude could not avoid "some mistakes in detail," but he correctly observed that "the essential facts are here."[89]

Contrary to popular impression, most medical educators endorsed the report. Although representatives of the commercial schools found much in it to condemn, representatives of schools that had been striving to improve usually accepted the report's conclusions, even if critical of their own institution. There is found a striking correlation between a school's ultimate success and its response to the Flexner report. Among Flexner's papers are replies to Flexner or Pritchett from twenty-six schools that succeeded—that is, that are still alive today. Twenty-two of these schools responded favorably, with only Indiana, Maryland, Northwestern, and Tufts taking umbrage. Conversely, eleven replies were from schools that are now extinct, and of these, ten were hostile, with only Fordham expressing approval.

The strongest support for the report came from the best schools. The dean of the University of Wisconsin Medical School congratulated Flexner on his "splendid report"; the dean of the University of Texas Medical Department called the statement "eminently fair and just"; the dean of the medical school of New York University called the book "an accurate report of the condition of the school at the time of the inspection"; the president of the University of Oklahoma claimed he did "not think that the statement you [Flexner] have made needs amending in any way."[90] Flexner's survey contained no criticisms that these schools had not for years been making of themselves, and the problems would have been corrected long before if not for the lack of funds and congenial relations with hospitals. The president of Columbia University noted:

> The criticisms of our own Medical School contained in this report seem to us entirely just and made with kindly and helpful purpose. They are precisely the criticisms which we have been in the habit of passing upon our own work and from which relief has long been sought in vain because the funds needed to remove these grounds of criticism were not available.[91]

Conversely, the most strident objections usually came from the schools that did not manage to survive. The president of the College of Physicians and Surgeons (Boston) called the report "libelous"; the president of the College of Physicians and Surgeons (Baltimore) described it as "absolutely inaccurate"; the president of the University of Denver said "there is scarcely a line of truth in Mr. Flexner's exhibit"; and the dean of the Lincoln (Nebraska) Medical College condemned Flexner's efforts "to discredit and falsify conditions."[92]

Some of the better schools, including some schools that survived, were also offended by the report, but usually for different reasons. Some chafed because in his muckraking Flexner had chosen to focus on the work remaining to be done rather than on the improvements already made. President William DeWitt Hyde of Bowdoin told Pritchett, "Having seen so much progress, I suppose I am inclined to judge the School by the direction it is taking rather than by the particular point at which it happens to have arrived."[93] Similarly, president A. W. Harris of Northwestern told Pritchett he considered the report "unfair" because "the general tone impresses me as that of one inclined to make the worst of things."[94] Other good schools worried that Flexner's critical style would impair their efforts for further development. Charles Dabney, the president of the University of Cincinnati, agreed completely with Flexner's evaluation of his school, but he objected to the tone, calling it "injurious" to his work to improve conditions there. He told Flexner: "I am glad to get the report at this time, as it supports me in all I am trying to do, but I think in fairness you should modify it in these [indicated] places. . . . In the case of an institution like ours, which is making such a hard, honest effort to get itself into shape, I believe you will [need] to be a little more optimistic."[95]

In some instances, the reaction from a school was mixed. The irate chancellor of Syracuse University sent Pritchett several angry letters, calling the work of the Carnegie Foundation "superficial, incorrect and unjust." He felt that the report did Syracuse an "extreme unjustice," and he accused the Foundation of "impertinent meddling with the work of the lawfully constituted educational departments of the States."[96] On the other hand, the dean of the College of Medicine, who knew conditions at the school much better than the chancellor, agreed with Flexner. He told Pritchett, "I have read enough [of the Flexner report] to assure myself that the Foundation has done a great service to medical education in this country." With respect to conditions at Syracuse, he considered the report "as nearly accurate as a report can be."[97]

There was no doubt in anyone's mind—supporter or critic—what

Flexner had done. He had espoused a model system of medical education in which all schools were to be of the same kind: university-based, research-oriented schools patterned after Johns Hopkins. Flexner decried pluralism; there was no room in his system for "practical," nonresearch schools, even if they happened to provide respectable teaching. This caused much consternation among many sincere medical educators, who argued after the report, as they had done before, that there was a role for more modest schools that emphasized teaching rather than research. As a faculty member of the University of Pittsburgh complained: "What is happening at the present time is, that Mr. Flexner and other investigators have taken what we conceive to be the highest type of medical school as a model, and have started the crusade . . . of forcing all medical schools to come up to what they have chosen as a standard type."[98]

Such protests, however, were to no avail. As one consequence of the Flexner report, even more pressure came to be exerted on proprietary schools to close. In his autobiography Flexner noted, "Schools collapsed to the right and left, usually without a murmur."[99] As observed in earlier chapters, as well as by many other writers, proprietary schools were already under siege before 1910, and for several years they had been closing at a faster rate than they were opening. Nevertheless, the report caused even greater pressure to be exerted on them. The faculties of many weak schools acknowledged openly thereafter that they had no choice but to approximate Flexner's ideal standards or become extinct.

Equally important, the report greatly stimulated the further development of the strong schools. Flexner made the public aware of what the profession already knew: that modern medicine worked, that the proper training of a physician mattered, and that experimental research offered the hope of even greater achievements in the future. Based on these premises, the report provided a blueprint of what the good schools needed to complete their development into "ideal" schools: high entrance standards; abundant laboratory space and equipment; teaching hospitals; a large corps of full-time professors in all departments; and a vigorous research program. All these items were expensive, which was why Flexner devoted so much attention in the report to the financial requirements of medical education. As seen in chapter 7, medical philanthropy was already on the verge of becoming a national preoccupation, but Flexner became the catalyst. His report—and later Flexner himself— helped persuade the public that it was in its own interest to support medical schools generously.

The report also catapulted Flexner and Pritchett to prominence as arbiters of the reconstruction of medical education. Few schools in the years immediately following the report made important faculty appointments or launched major developmental programs without first consulting one of them. Pritchett found himself "confronted almost every day with requests for advice from various universities engaged in medical education."[100] Flexner became even more active in such matters. To some, he became the "dictator of American Medical Practice."[101] Chancellor J. H. Kirkland of Vanderbilt University—no small figure himself in the emergence of the modern American medical school—congratulated the Carnegie Foundation on its "commanding position in the field of medical education" and noted that no institution "would now enter into this field of labor without securing from your office suggestions and advice."[102] As World War I began, the Carnegie Foundation became involved with other areas of professional and general education, and Pritchett gradually withdrew from the arena of medical education. However, Flexner continued his work with medical education in his new position at the General Education Board, where he became the country's most influential manager of foundational philanthropy.

Medical scientists were thrilled with the Flexner report. Flexner had accepted their version of the ideal system of medical education; all schools had to hire full-time faculty members and engage in research. The tension at medical schools between teaching and research was now well on its way toward being resolved in favor of research. As the "expert" was coming to dominate so many aspects of business, government, and community life in the Progressive Era, so, too, was the "expert" taking over medical education in the form of the full-time professor.

Pritchett was also pleased with the Flexner report. Underlying his interest in medical education was his concern for the professional educator in America. The Flexner report complemented his larger strategy at the Carnegie Foundation of upgrading the status of that group. Flexner had given no credence to the view that medical schools should be judged on the basis of how their students performed on state licensing examinations. Almost anyone could parrot enough to pass a written examination, he had argued, without really understanding the subject matter or having the slightest idea of what to do with a real patient.[103] Flexner had held the critical factors instead to be admission requirements, course content and methods, laboratory and clinical facilities, and faculty qualifications. The report had thus in essence maintained that in the training of physicians, educational process matters. It represented the culmination of the educator's efforts to impose himself on medical education that had begun in 1871 when Charles Eliot forced a new system of instruction on the faculty of Harvard Medical School. "I believe that the soundest view of medical education," Pritchett wrote, "is that which considers it as an integral part of the educational problem."[104] The Flexner report vindicated Pritchett's belief in the importance and uniqueness of the professional educator.

The practicing profession looked upon the Flexner report with mixed emotions. Insofar as Flexner convinced the public that medicine rested on a solid scientific basis and that proper medical training made a difference to the patient, the report elevated their status and prestige. Insofar as the report advocated high entrance requirements, it also reinforced the trend toward medicine as an exclusive rather than an inclusive profession, with further beneficial consequences for their income and social position. However, the report contended that there was no role in America for "practical" schools run by practitioners and that the university schools should be controlled by full-time professors. Thus practitioners, who had taught medicine in America since colonial days, saw their traditional authority and responsibility within the profession being challenged. For a full generation academic physicians had been trying to wrest control of medical education from them, and now Flexner cast his authority on the side of the professors. Practitioners of medicine lost influence and responsibility within the profession as they were gaining power and status without.

Ironically, the ideals of progressive education advanced by Flexner never came to be fully realized. Medical educators from Flexner's day until the present have regularly complained that the emphasis needs to be placed more on the process of thinking, less on the retention of facts. Medical students for generations have recognized that memorizing details of anatomy and performing dry, sterile "cookbook" experiments are not invigorating exercises in scientific thinking. Medical education to them often seems more like rites of passage than an experience in developing critical competence. Even today, students are often forced to cram but seldom are given time to reflect and contemplate. That was why David E. Rogers, the president of the Robert Wood Johnson Foundation, spoke harshly in 1982 of a system of instruction that spews "enormous boluses of facts" at students and makes them feel they are "being lectured to death."[105]

Nevertheless, in medical schools, progressive education has persisted as the ideal, however difficult the realization of that ideal remains in practice. Even the most severe critics of the medical curriculum would not suggest abandoning the laboratory and the clerkship and returning to the days when all teaching was by amphitheater lecture. To Rogers, for instance, the proper goal of medical education is still "to inculcate personal habits of learning" so that the student will be "a continuous learner throughout his or her lifetime." The medical student must not be forced to cram but must learn "to understand facts" and "think deductively." Indeed, "As knowledge outdates more and more rapidly, self-generated learning becomes yet more important each day."[106] Critics like Rogers have chastised medical education for not achieving its ideal, but they have not challenged the ideal itself. To most medical educators of the present, the original ideals are as valid as ever.

Progressive education has thus experienced a happier fate in the medical school than in the public school, where by the 1950s it was totally discredited. In the elementary and high schools, progressive education underwent various distortions and perversions, culminating in the notorious life-adjustment movement, which has been viewed as the prototype of anti-intellectualism within professional education.[107] When the Progressive Education Association died in 1955, there were, as Lawrence Cremin has observed, few mourners at its funeral.[108] In one of the greatest ironies in the history of education, progressive education, traditionally regarded as a manifestation of the democratic impulse in education, found its most lasting expression in an elitist rather than a mass movement.

Why should this doctrine have survived as an educational ideal within medical education but not elsewhere? This question deserves further study, but an answer may be suggested. Progressive education is a demanding theory of education. To be effective, it requires superior students and teachers. Only unusually bright students, at any level, are able to learn from their sensory experiences, think as well as memorize, distrust authority with confidence, and become self-learners for life. Similarly, outstanding teachers are required to inculcate such habits of critical thinking. Thus, the very nature of progressive education makes it less applicable to mass education, where everyone has to be taught, than to graduate or professional education, where students are selected for intellectual ability and instructors are generally more thoroughly trained. Progressive education did work well for three decades at the Lincoln School, but this was an exception that illustrated the rule. The Lincoln School was a private, well-supported experimental school with exceptionally gifted students and teachers, not the typical public school. Progressive education, by the requirements it made of students and instructors, was doomed to failure in mass public education, yet it remains a viable ideal in the medical school. This is the lesson of medical education for the general history of education.

10 The Era of Medical

Philanthropy

THE Flexner report made it clear that if medical education in the United States was to be properly conducted, assistance from outside the profession was necessary. The financial requirements of modern medical training had become awesome; medical schools everywhere were straining under the weight. The report stung the consciences of public and private benefactors. Almost immediately, individuals, foundations, and state legislatures began to find medical education a worthy object of support, and money started to pour into the schools. By 1930, American medical education was finally on a firm financial footing, and many long-desired improvements could at last be implemented.

National Foundations

In the early twentieth century, the means to provide for medical education were already present. The country had been experiencing unprecedented economic growth and expansion. In 1860, national wealth had stood at $16 billion; by 1890, that figure had risen to $65 billion, and by 1921, to over $300 billion.[1] In 1914, there were 4,500 millionaires in the United States; in 1926,

11,000.[2] Moreover, a habit of large-scale philanthropy had already started among the very rich.[3] That activities other than medicine had become the object of large benefactions only whetted the appetites of medical educators, who saw their task as directing some of these funds their way.

The Flexner report provided the catalyst. The public was shocked into realizing that medical schools had become deserving of support. Medical schools everywhere, weak and strong, capitalized on this opportunity by launching fund raising campaigns on a much larger scale than ever before. For example, the Corporation of Yale, expressing pride that Flexner had deemed its medical school worthy of survival, in June 1910 began a $2 million fund raising drive.[4] Aided by its designation as a deserving institution, the school quickly met its goal. In the next ten years its endowment increased from $220,000 to nearly $3 million and its yearly budget from $43,000 to $225,000.[5]

Yale's success was shared by dozens of medical schools in the period following the Flexner report. The public response that developed exceeded all expectations. Medicine, once the neglected stepchild of philanthropy, became the most vigorously supported of any cultural, scientific, or humanitarian activity. Support for medical education came from a multiplicity of sources. Between 1902 and 1934, nine major foundations poured $154 million into medical education and research—nearly one-half of the total they contributed to all areas.[6] Gifts from private individuals were also significant. Exact figures are difficult to determine, but in the aggregate this represented an even greater source of funds than the foundations. In addition, state legislatures contributed enormous sums to public medical schools. Between 1900 and 1923, the states increased their expenditures for medical education by a factor of fifteen,[7] and in subsequent years public appropriations continued to grow. So fueled, medical schools began to change with what one prominent educator called "revolutionary rapidity."[8]

It was during this period that medical philanthropy began to be conducted on a national scale. The large foundations (the General Education Board, the Carnegie Corporation, the Rockefeller Foundation, and others) participated in the philanthropic enterprise on a heretofore unimagined scale. Their vast resources became available to select schools across the country, and in examining the records of such organizations one gets a sense of a national system of medical education being rationally and purposefully created. In addition, the major foundations usually gave their gifts on the condition that equal or greater amounts be raised from other sources. In this way, the foundations stimulated much local philanthropy as well.

By far the most dominant single influence in medical philanthropy was the General Education Board. Founded in 1902 by John D. Rockefeller, Sr., the board entered the field of medical education in 1913 and immediately became the strongest and most pervasive force in the field. By 1928, the General Education Board had appropriated $61 million to medical schools across the country, and indirectly it generated even more support for medical education as a result of its policy of conditional giving.[9] The largest appropriations were made to Johns Hopkins University, Washington University, Yale University, the University of Chicago, Cornell University, the State University of Iowa, the University of Rochester, Vanderbilt University, Harvard University, Western Reserve University, Columbia University, the University of Virginia, Tulane University, the University of Colorado, and the University of Oregon.[10] Board policy clearly favored the strong institutions.

At the General Education Board, standard administrative procedures were followed. All grant requests originated from the schools—a strategy that was to the board's political advantage in defending itself against critics—although records show that the board would sometimes solicit applications from favored schools.[11] Early grants required schools to make full-time appointments in their clinical departments; later the board's policy was liberalized so that the full-time condition was eliminated.[12] The board would customarily provide only a portion of the amount necessary to reach a school's target; thus, the remainder would have to be raised from other sources.[13]

The General Education Board represented the institutional epitome of the principles of "scientific philanthropy." Grants were made only after exhaustive study of a school's application. To receive assistance, a school could not be operating at a deficit, and it had to have prospects for other financial support in the future. "No attempt will be made to resuscitate moribund schools,"[14] the board told the nation's press. In addition, a school had to be academically first rate; only scholastically "deserving" schools were considered worthy of support. The board's strategy was to assist schools in different regions of the country that met these criteria. In this way, Raymond Fosdick has written, "The influence of a Chicago or a Johns Hopkins would in the end reach every campus and every medical school in the United States."[15]

A typical illustration of how the General Education Board approached medical philanthropy was the case of Vanderbilt Medical School, which in 1919 received $4 million from the board, the largest grant made by the board to that time. Through World War I, Vanderbilt, like so many medical schools, had been crippled by insufficient funds. The enterprising chancellor, James H. Kirkland, solicited $1 million for the school from Andrew Carnegie in 1913

—apparently the only major grant made by the Carnegie Corporation for medical education prior to Carnegie's death.[16] But it was not enough to meet the school's needs, so Kirkland appealed to the General Education Board, telling the board that the school was in a "critical condition" and will "close in disaster unless a new chapter can now be begun."[17] After thorough study, the board concluded Vanderbilt deserved support. The board admired the faculty's ideals, the school's progress on modest funds, and Kirkland's strong leadership. Board officers were also impressed by the school's success at enticing $1 million from Carnegie, and they felt that the prospect of future support from the Nashville community was excellent. Furthermore, the Vanderbilt application provided the board the opportunity to fulfill its long-standing desire of developing a strong medical school in the South. Abraham Flexner, now secretary of the General Education Board, wrote that a modern school at Vanderbilt "will set up higher ideals and from which better trained men will percolate into medical practice and medical training throughout the section."[18] Vanderbilt had thus proved itself a deserving school, and its support fitted in with the General Education Board's southern strategy.

The General Education Board's interest in medical education was one manifestation of its broad interest in educational matters—a fact implicit in the term "general." Major areas of foundation activity, in addition to medical education, included the support of elementary and high schools in the South, the promotion of all levels of black education, and the development of higher education in the United States through contributions to the endowment funds of dozens of colleges and universities. The board viewed the country's educational system as an organic whole. This was made clear by the writings of Frederick T. Gates, the worldly Baptist minister who suggested the idea of the General Educational Board to Rockefeller and served for ten years (1907–17) as chairman of the Board of Trustees. In a memorandum outlining the General Education Board's methods of procedure, Gates declared: "The system of education is a unit. It is a living, articulated thing, every part dependent on some other part, and no single member or organ can be eliminated without the atrophy of some or all of the other parts."[19] This meant that every part of the educational system (the elementary school, high school, normal school, academy, college, graduate schools, and professional schools) had a specified sphere of influence and that each component had to be properly articulated with the others. The purpose of the General Education Board, Gates explained, was to promote a comprehensive system of education in the United States, with the emphasis on the word "system." The foundation must work "toward reducing our higher education to something like an orderly and comprehensive *system*, to discourage unnecessary duplication and waste, and to encourage economy and efficiency."[20] This view plainly reflected the efficiency-mindedness and Social Darwinistic attitudes that were so prominent in early twentieth-century American thought.

Although the foundations accomplished much good, their motives were never beyond suspicion. In the early years, doubts about their social utility were pervasive among a wary public that feared bigness and deeply distrusted the robber barons. The Rockefeller and Carnegie organizations came under the most attack. Could Rockefeller really have benevolent intentions in mind for his foundations, many people wondered, when the same man personally directed armed troops to carry out the notorious Ludlow massacre in 1914 and then publicly lied about his role?[21] Congress was also distrustful, when in 1910 it considered a bill to grant the Rockefeller Foundation a charter. Strong protest was evoked by the bill, and President William Howard Taft condemned it as an effort "to incorporate Mr. John D. Rockefeller."[22] Opponents won out, and the foundation had to apply to the state of New York for its charter. Records of the foundations show that they were extremely sensitive about public criticism. The Carnegie Corporation, for example, recognized that "doubts as to the basic social utility of these organizations have long existed in the minds of men and women regarding whose sincerity there can be no question."[23] Amid such a climate, the foundations frequently had to bend to public pressure. For instance, when the Carnegie Corporation in 1918 proposed establishing a pension of $25,000 for ex-presidents and their unmarried widows, public indignation forced the corporation to abandon the plan.[24]

To avert criticism, officers of the foundations insisted that they did not impose their wishes on recipient institutions. For example, the stated policy of the General Education Board was not to intervene in a school's internal affairs. Board officials claimed that they would make specific appropriations for promising undertakings in which "interesting work, already started, halts for lack of money."[25] In this mythical view of the General Education Board, which has been popularized by "in-house" histories of the organization, the foundation served the needs of recipient schools.[26] There could be no suspicion of external control because all applications arose from outside the board and grantees received money only for projects of their own choosing.

Nevertheless, records of the foundations indicate that at times they acted more dictatorially than their apologists would have one believe. For instance, the General Education Board sometimes did interfere with the operations of the schools it supported. On one occasion, Abraham Flexner involved himself with the details of the new clinical services of Columbia University, such as how many surgical beds it should have at Presbyterian Hospital. This prompted a gentle scolding from Henry Pritchett:

I doubt whether these philanthropic agencies ought to go too far in prescrib-
ing technical programmes for the medical schools it undertakes to assist. . . . The
best one can do is to be sure that the fundamental aim is sound and that a good
group of men have set themselves earnestly to work out its accomplishment. To
go much beyond this and lay down a definite regimen goes rather far in controlling rather than assisting medical development. . . . I think we ought to help it
[Columbia Medical School] without attempting to prescribe too closely the
technical details of administration and organization. With your clearly formed
notions on such matters I think your tendency is to go a little too far in laying
down the rules.[27]

Pritchett also criticized his friends at the General Education Board for the
rigid conditions laid down by the foundation in its contracts with Johns
Hopkins and the University of Chicago.

These contracts lay down a stated policy for conducting a medical school
which the Board approves and then in a formal contract the universities bind
themselves to carry out these policies, and agree not to change them except by
permission of the General Education Board, and in case they do change without
such permission the universities agree to return the money. Such a contract
binding a university to a fixed policy laid down by the giver of money seems to
me a dangerous thing. If these contracts were made public I am sure it would
bring down on all educational foundations no less than on the universities themselves severe criticism.[28]

In addition, the foundations, contrary to their public declarations, often
tried to influence broad educational policy. For instance, the General Education Board worked extremely hard to win support for its particular version of
the full-time system of clinical departments. One board trustee, referring to
the full-time controversy, admitted that the organization "has indeed assumed
a responsibility in using its influence to promote ideas which are still much
in debate."[29] More often, control was implicit rather than explicit simply by
virtue of the huge sums the foundations were dispensing. Thus, the University
of Kansas School of Medicine offered the General Education Board a "decisive
voice in shaping the School's future" in exchange for substantial financial
aid.[30]

Although some have accused the foundations of malevolent intent, there
is little evidence for this contention, and episodes of overt interference were
very few. Relations between the foundations and recipient schools were generally cordial. Schools that received foundation support invariably used the
money for programs they had genuinely desired. Nevertheless, the advent of
the foundations raised the specter of the external control of medical education.
Even if explicit control was seldom exerted, implicit control could never be

eliminated. This problem never disappeared, but grew even larger after World War II when a still more powerful agency—the federal government—entered the arena of medical funding.

With the rise of the foundations, American philanthropy entered a new era. Once a highly personal act, philanthropy became systematized and bureaucratized. This change was clearly evident at the Rockefeller foundations. By the 1890s, John D. Rockefeller, Sr., had become inundated with appeals, and under this burden his health began to deteriorate. In the words of Frederick Gates, he was "hounded almost like a wild animal."[31] To protect himself, Rockefeller appointed Gates in 1891 and his son, John D. Rockefeller, Jr., in 1897 to manage his investments and philanthropies, thereby removing himself from the innumerable details. But this was not enough; Rockefeller could receive hundreds of charitable requests in a day, and thousands in a year.[32] A formal organization was needed to handle his philanthropy—hence the General Education Board, the Rockefeller Foundation, and others. In creating these organizations, Rockefeller gave control of his philanthropies to a set of managers—the officers of the foundations and their staffs. Although the managers were highly conscious of the corporate interests of the foundation and the general concerns of the founder, on a day-to-day basis they acted independently. At least through 1923, the Board of Trustees of the General Education Board had never turned down a recommendation of the officers.[33] At the foundation level, medical philanthropy had thus become a business. Philanthropy had changed from a personalized to a managed mode. To Gates, the administrative efficiency of the General Education Board could be illustrated only "by the Standard Oil Company as it is, when compared with what easily might be imagined to be the condition in the oil industry, if, in its stead, the universal competitive system of say 1870 had been continued."[34] Salaried managers now ran the philanthropic foundations, as they did most modern corporations. The "visible hand of management" that Alfred Chandler has described in big business took over medical philanthropy as well.[35]

Local Support

The high visibility of the foundations should not obscure the fact that an even larger source of funds for medical education came from private citizens and benevolent state legislatures. Indeed, one can obtain two different pictures of how the schools raised money, depending on the sources consulted. Foundation records, particularly those of the General Education Board, convey a sense of a national system of medical education being systematically and purposefully created. Medical school records, however, show enormous initiative and activity at the local level, sometimes in conjunction with foundation assistance, but more often independent of foundation participation.

As the foundations supported medical education nationally, so did many wealthy patrons rush to the support of their local medical school. In many cases, these patrons made huge contributions that allowed the course of their favored school to be turned around almost overnight. Important benefactors included Robert Brookings, Adolphus Busch, W. K. Bixby, and Edward Mallinckrodt (Washington University); Samuel Mather, Oliver H. Payne, John Lund Woods, and Howard Hanna (Western Reserve University); Julius Rosenwald and Otho Sprague (University of Chicago); Mary M. Emery and William Cooper Procter (University of Cincinnati); Edward Harkness (Columbia University); Payne Whitney, George Baker, and J. P. Morgan (Cornell University); George Eastman (University of Rochester); James Buchanan Duke (Duke University); William Henry Eustis (University of Minnesota); and Earle Perry Charlton (Tufts University). Most philanthropists were businessmen or industrialists, but a few were physicians. Thus Christian Holmes, the dean of the University of Cincinnati College of Medicine, left the school $100,000 on his death in 1920. In 1917, Frank Billings, the dean of Rush Medical College, gave the school $100,000, and relatives raised the total contribution from the Billings family to $1 million.[36]

Although it certainly helped to receive million-dollar gifts, smaller donations could also make a difference. The most striking example was that of the University of Pittsburgh, which in 1926 needed $6 million to effect an alliance with Presbyterian Hospital and rebuild the hospital's physical plant. The school was denied funds from the Rockefeller and Carnegie foundations, and it lacked local benefactors of the sort described above. Yet, in an appeal to the citizens of the Pittsburgh area, school officials raised the sum. Literally thousands of persons contributed.[37]

State legislatures became another source of revenue, as almost all states with public medical schools began to take the enterprise much more seriously than they had earlier. Between 1910 and 1912, the state of California raised the annual budget for its medical school from $33,000 to over $100,000.[38] Between 1910 and 1916, the University of Minnesota's budget for medical education increased from $71,000 to $150,000 per year.[39] States such as California, Minnesota, Michigan, and Wisconsin began to support their medical schools munificently, and these institutions became the rival of any private school in the land. Less prosperous states could not afford the same level of expenditures, yet their spending for medical education also increased substantially. Thus, from 1917 to 1922, assets of the University of Oklahoma School of Medicine grew from nothing to $578,000—all from public funds.[40] Similarly, in 1913 the University of Arkansas had only five full-time faculty positions, with the highest salary $1,800. By 1927, annual state appropriations had grown from nothing to $66,000, the number of full-time faculty positions had risen to more than thirty, and the highest salary had increased to $4,500.[41]

Once medical schools began to receive local support, community pride perpetuated the process. Cities, states, and regions competed with each other in medical education as they did in commerce, industry, and the support of cultural activities. To the chancellor of Washington University, there was no undertaking other than the reorganization of the medical school that "would add more to the reputation of the University along educational lines, or to the reputation of the city of St. Louis along higher lines."[42] Residents of Cincinnati felt similarly. Christian Holmes wrote, "In Cincinnati's present forward movement there is no step of greater moment than this creation of a new Medical School and a new Hospital."[43]

As local sources joined the foundations in supporting medical schools, funding became a complex process. Few institutions received assistance from just one source; multiple channels of aid became available to every school. The University of Rochester was the classic example of cooperation between a foundation and a local philanthropist. The school was created in 1920, the result of $5 million grant from the General Education Board and a $5 million gift from the photography magnate George Eastman. Henry Pritchett facetiously told a General Education Board officer that he could not determine whether "you got $5,000,000 out of Eastman" or "Eastman got $5,000,000 out of you."[44]

Fund raising was even more complex at the University of Colorado. In 1922, the medical school applied for aid to the General Education Board. After a careful evaluation, the school was awarded $700,000, on the condition that it raise $800,000 on its own. University officials then procured a $600,000 appropriation from the state legislature. That left $200,000 to be raised, and the school turned to private sources in Denver. A local philanthropist, Mrs. Verner Z. Reed, responded with a gift of $120,000. From there the remaining $80,000 was easily raised through many small donations.[45] The Colorado fund-raising drive thus called upon all the major sources of money: a national foundation; the state legislature; and private donors, large and small. Even before the federal government entered the picture after World War II, support for medical education had already become broad-based.

Benefactors and Recipients

Although few concerns have such an enduring claim on the public as
health, medical philanthropy was a complex act that could be inspired by
anything from the personal to the altruistic. It is well known, for instance, how
the death of John D. Rockefeller's first grandchild from scarlet fever persuaded
him to proceed with the plan he had long been contemplating for an institute
of medical research.[46] Others might have been motivated by the recognition
of their own frailty and mortality. Some philanthropists, lacking heirs, could
use their gifts as an alternative way to dispose of their fortunes. Robert
Brookings and George Eastman, for instance, had no children. To some
benefactors, the support of medical education and research took on a quasi-
religious significance. John Ettling has recently described the religious
evangelical roots of the philanthropic attitudes of important aides to John D.
Rockefeller.[47]

Yet philanthropists were not wholly altruistic, and it would be naive to
believe that they did not personally benefit from their donations. Such gifts
offered fame and recognition. A building or laboratory could be a permanent
monument to the donor, a means of immortalization. Large gifts also conveyed a sense of power. Even the occasional donors who chose to remain
publicly anonymous could still derive a feeling of influence from their contributions, and their acts were known to a select few whose opinions mattered
to them. Medical philanthropy also helped legitimize the wealth and status
of the very rich. Donations for the civic good served as a useful ploy to
counteract their unsavory image as "robber barons." It is possible that medical
philanthropy also served the needs of the corporate class in a more general way.
E. Richard Brown and Howard Berliner have argued that such acts helped
dissipate potential social unrest by focusing public attention on health rather
than the underlying inequities of a capitalistic society.[48]

Support of medical education and research was also encouraged by the
growing tendency of considering the economic consequences of illness. Disease was harmful to the financial well-being of the worker, the corporation,
and the country. In proposing the idea of an institute for medical research to
John D. Rockefeller, Frederick Gates noted that "Pasteur's inquiries on anthrax and on the diseases of fermentation had saved the French nation a sum
in excess of the entire cost of the Franco-German war."[49] One medical
entrepreneur justified the support of medical research on the grounds that "if
[the] saving of human life can be reckoned in dollars, the researches in biology

relating to disease, prevention and cure, are each year of almost incalculable value to the world."[50]

To those who had formalized their approach to philanthropy, there was still another reason to support medical education and research. Such acts fitted in neatly with the principles of "scientific philanthropy" that guided so many large donors during the period.[51] The roots of scientific philanthropy were complex, but they had much to do with the faith that human beings could intervene in the world around them. In this sense, scientific philanthropy represented an outgrowth of the previously discussed ideas of nineteenth-century individualism. Scientific philanthropy emphasized preventive rather than ameliorative undertakings; it sought to alter the causes of problems rather than merely to alleviate surface conditions. As Frederick Gates explained: "Scientific philanthropy is not attained with superficial remedies, palliative, artificial reliefs. It seeks, insofar as it is wise, to find out the underlying causes and remove them, and will be content with nothing else."[52] Far better, a scientific philanthropist would say, to attack poverty by increasing remunerative employment than by dispensing charity for poor relief.[53] Herein lay a major appeal of medicine to philanthropists. Through the germ theory, medicine had explained not only the superficial manifestations of many diseases but their ultimate causes. As medicine became an experimental science, it offered the promise of being able to control nature by intervening in the untreated course of illness. Support for medicine therefore could easily be justified in terms of the era's prevailing philanthropic principles.

Although many factors contributed to medical philanthropy, two underlying themes were especially prominent. One was the widespread perception that scientific medicine worked. Widely touted were the germ theory of disease, the development of certain vaccines and antitoxins, the many advances in surgery, the conquest of certain nutritional and endocrine diseases, and the marked improvement in the public health. Indeed, by 1930 it was recognized that the traditional scourges—the infectious diseases—had been largely subjugated. For all that the philanthropists stood to gain from their gifts, they would not have made such contributions without the belief that there was genuine technical efficacy to scientific medicine.[54] Nor would the state legislatures have supported medical education so munificently had they not shared the same conviction.

Ironically, John D. Rockefeller, the most important medical philanthropist of all, never relinquished his skepticism toward modern medicine; he continued to consult a homeopath for his personal medical care even as he was donating millions to scientific medicine. Nevertheless, any doubts about modern medicine at the Rockefeller organizations were counterbalanced by Frederick Gates, the greatest lay supporter of scientific medicine of all time. In 1911, Gates sent Rockefeller five essays in which he derided homeopathic doctrines and praised the merits of scientific medicine.[55] Homeopathy, he told Rockefeller in an accompanying letter, was "fading away" because it was "wrong"; modern medicine, in contrast, was "a great new science."[56] If Gates was confident of scientific medicine in 1911, his conviction became even stronger in 1923, after he and his wife, both long-standing sufferers from diabetes mellitus, were among the first persons to receive the newly discovered insulin treatment at the Rockefeller Institute Hospital. To John D. Rockefeller, Jr., Gates described the immediate effect of the first dose of insulin as "simply magical." He continued:

> We [Gates and his wife] are both made over new, and each day are securing manifest accessions of new strength, life and cheer. For 14 years I have been afflicted with this distressing over secretion of sugar. I have not at any time so fully realized the damaging effects on my mind and outlook on life as I do now by contrast. For 14 years the landscape of human life and society, as seen through my eyes, has been that of the dead of winter, with hardly one relieving feature. Today, my outlook on life is filled with the glorious autumnal colors.[57]

Gates knew first-hand that scientific medicine worked. Fortunately for medical education, it was he who set the dominant tone at the Rockefeller foundations.

From the vantage of the present, the successes of scientific medicine were then relatively few. Gates himself acknowledged in 1911 that specific pharmacological cures numbered less than ten.[58] Yet from the perspective of the period, the achievements of experimental medicine were impressive. The nineteenth-century legacy was one of havoc from illness, suffering, and premature death. Epidemics continued to ravage the land; average life expectancy in 1900 was still less than fifty years. A certain fatalism toward disease characterized the attitude of virtually every American. "While other occurrences of daily life are accepted as operations of law," one informed observer wrote in 1901, "the matter of health is dealt with as though it were largely outside of such control."[59] In this context, the early achievements of scientific medicine were stunning. Disease and suffering for the first time were seen not to be inevitable features of the human condition; they could be alleviated, relieved, prevented. By World War I, American attitudes toward the conquest of disease had turned decidedly optimistic. Even the horror of the influenza pandemic of 1918–19 could not dampen that optimism.

To supporters of scientific medicine, even more important than its achievements were its promises for the future. Through experimental inquiry they felt that many more discoveries would be forthcoming. The General Education Board declared: "Though relatively few human ills have been subjugated, the method and the techniques by means of which successive diseases may and perhaps will be ultimately conquered have been definitely established."[60] In the late nineteenth century, the medical profession had awakened to the promise of what scientific method held for the control of disease; now the public did so as well. The imaginations of some began to run wild. By revolutionizing communications and transportation, science had conquered space and time. Why, then, should it not conquer death? Scientific medicine, wrote Henry Pritchett, "has possession of methods which ultimately will lead to the solution of most if not all of our [medical] problems."[61] "In fifty years," a prominent medical scientist told a lay audience in 1911, "science will have practically eliminated all forms of disease."[62]

This reverence of scientific method was not unique to the medical arena. Rather, it was a manifestation of the "scientism" of the period that pervaded so many of the era's intellectual and social movements. The most extreme form of scientism was found in Gates, who saw in science something mystical, something that promised to solve social as well as technical problems. Though Gates never lost sight of worldly concerns, he so exalted science that it assumed the guise of a secular religion to him. Thus he described the Rockefeller Institute for Medical Research as "a sort of Theological Seminary." Medical research, he wrote, "will find out and promulgate, as an unforeseen byproduct of its work, new moral laws and new social laws—new definitions of what is right and wrong in our relations with each other. Medical research will educate the human conscience in new directions and point out new duties."[63] In this context, it should be no surprise to find that Gates supported the eugenics movement. In medicine and eugenics alike, he looked to biological science for the key to human salvation.

The second theme that underlay medical fund raising was the fervid entrepreneurial efforts of the medical educators. Medical school officials did not sit quietly on the sidelines hoping for money to find its way into their coffers. They were institution-builders who aggressively solicited the funds to make their educational dreams a reality. The medical lobby consisted primarily of university presidents, medical school deans, and prominent medical faculty members. All had strong personal reasons to raise money for medical education, for they realized that the procurement of adequate funds was central to their long-standing goals—for university officials, that of expanding the authority of the university by building strong professional schools; for medical educators, that of establishing academic medicine as a secure career. They approached medical fund raising as if it were a life-or-death mission.

The entrepreneurial activities of the medical educators proceeded on many fronts. At the local level, there was frenetic activity as community philanthropists and state legislatures became the targets of well-orchestrated appeals for funds. At the national level, select medical statesmen enjoyed great influence at the large foundations, such as William Welch at the General Education Board. Furthermore, the campaign for funds was indirect as well as direct. Influential physicians wrote numerous articles and books for the lay public with titles such as "The Service of Medicine to Civilization," "Medical Research and Human Welfare," and "The Benefits of the Endowment of Medical Research." An era of mass communications and modern journalism had come just in time for the medical educators, who made effective use of public relations to generate support for their cause.

Medical educators who led the drive for funds, like institution-builders in other scientific fields, were highly suited for the task. They were blessed with remarkable administrative talents, and their executive abilities would have enabled them to be persons of affairs in any field. Not only were they raising money but at the same time they were establishing and managing academic departments, scientific societies, and professional journals. The biographer of one prominent medical entrepreneur portrayed his subject as a man who, had he chosen, could easily have been a leading financier or captain of industry.[64] Some were aided by their family credentials. Such leading fund raisers as Harvey Cushing, Henry Bowditch, John Collins Warren, L. Emmett Holt, and Christian Herter were as prominent socially as they were scientifically, and thus they had an easier time in gaining the ear of the very rich. Medical educators were not always successful in their appeals. Victor Vaughan, for instance, dreamed of persuading the nearby Henry Ford to take an interest in the University of Michigan—a dream that never materialized.[65] Nevertheless, they persisted even in the event of failure. Their effective entrepreneurship paid off.

The greatest fund raiser of all was Abraham Flexner. Not a physician himself, he was nonetheless academic medicine's most loyal friend. In his 1910 report, he had directed attention to the urgent financial needs of medical education. After 1913, as assistant secretary (later secretary) of the General Education Board, he shaped the foundation's policies that resulted in so much money being directed into the field. In addition, his abilities as a fund raiser were legendary, and he personally persuaded a number of important patrons into making medical education the object of their philanthropies. One was George Eastman, whose $5 million gift in 1920 to start the University of Rochester School of Medicine came as a result of Flexner's solicitation. A year later, Eastman expressed his dismay at the prospect of meeting Flexner again:

> He himself [Flexner] is the worst highwayman that ever flitted into and out
> of Rochester. He put up a job on me and cleaned me out of a thundering lot of
> my hard-earned savings. I have just heard that he is coming up here June 2nd
> to speak at the graduating exercises of the allied hospitals. I have been asked to
> sit on the stage with him, but instead of that I shall probably flee the town for
> fear he will hypnotize me again.[66]

Flexner's success at raising funds for medical education represented his second
most important contribution to that cause, surpassed only by his role in
imposing a single definition of medical education on the country.[67]

As the medical educators approached those with .money, a complex
interplay resulted. Unquestionably, the medical educators enjoyed enormous
influence with the lawmakers, philanthropists, and foundations. Medical
educators now spoke with great "cultural authority," to use Paul Starr's
term.[68] Philanthropists were dependent on them for ideas; funds were used
to support projects and activities desired by academic physicians for over a
generation. At the General Education Board, foundation officers continually
described their dependence on others for ideas for projects.[69] "What would
you do if you had a million dollars with which to make a start in the work of
reorganizing medical education?" Frederick Gates asked Abraham Flexner. "I
should give it to Dr. Welch," Flexner replied.[70] Herein was the immediate
origin of the full-time system in clinical departments and the classic example
of medical philanthropy seeking a cause.

On the other hand, philanthropists kept control, even as they acquiesced
in the demands of the medical educators. Medical philanthropy, as noted
already, was not wholly altruistic; it served philanthropists' own aims as well
as those of the medical educators. Bombarded with ideas as to how to spend
their money, benefactors of medicine picked and chose selectively, funding
some schools and projects and not others. The most famous choice was made
by the General Education Board when it opted to support Johns Hopkins's
version of full-time clinical departments over all other versions. Despite their
frequent disclaimers to the contrary, medical philanthropists had their own
thoughts on the subject. "When you go out to get $40,000,000 from a man,"
president William P. Few of Duke University observed, "you will find that
he has some ideas of his own."[71] Thus, what emerged from the discussions
between medical entrepreneurs and medical philanthropists was a complex
dialectic—a push and pull, each group interested in medical education for its
own reasons, each group making its influence felt on the form that medical
education in the United States ultimately took.

In seeking support, medical schools competed vigorously with each other.
Ample funding had become indispensable for survival; medical schools either

had to acquire enough money or retire from the field. Most schools encountered failures along the way. Albany, Baylor, St. Louis University, George Washington University, Arkansas, Georgia, Maryland, and Illinois were among the schools that applied unsuccessfully to the General Education Board.[72] Even very strong schools could be refused, as Harvard Medical School discovered when the General Education Board rejected its version of clinical full time and denied the school a $1.5 million grant.[73] In general, however, strength engendered strength. Schools with a good academic reputation and a solid financial base attracted more and more funds; schools without such advantages found it increasingly difficult to acquire new money, however honorable their intentions might have been. University schools held the greatest edge; proprietary schools were reeling. Much more money had become available for medical education, but almost all of it went to the university schools. Welch observed in 1914, "The only type of school which can expect to receive support from the public must be a university medical school."[74] Proprietary schools had long been on the defensive, but now their situation became terminal. For economic reasons the universities succeeded in capturing control of medical education.

The fund-raising successes ushered in a new era of medical education. Comparing the twenty years of medical education after 1910 with the twenty years before, there was little change in terms of ideals. However, change was immense in terms of results: the means had finally been acquired to organize modern medical schools across the land. More important still, through the state legislatures and philanthropic foundations, the support of medical education and research had become institutionalized. The supply of funds was now continuous and self-sustaining rather than left solely to chance and circumstance as before. Medical schools were to experience their lean and abundant years in the decades that followed, but no longer did the public doubt that medical education was deserving of ongoing support. Medical education had found a permanent, secure place.

11 The Maturation of

Academic Medicine

IN THE YEARS between 1910 and 1930, as in all subsequent periods including the present, much of the money raised by medical schools went into research rather than teaching. Thus, the funding of medical education served a dual purpose. It not only allowed for a high level of medical teaching; it greatly facilitated the pursuit of experimental medicine, and it made possible the creation of many new positions in academic medicine. The dreams aspiring medical scientists had held since the mid-nineteenth century at long last came true. In the United States an interested physician could now entertain a realistic hope of finding a well-supported position in full-time teaching and research. The effort to establish and legitimize academic medicine finally came to fruition.

The Full-Time System

As the public began to support medical education more liberally, medical research as well as medical teaching finally prospered. Pressing financial needs had been inhibiting to the former as well as to the latter. Fortunately for the medical scientists, the money that poured into medical schools was earmarked for both purposes, and much of the money was designated for academic pursuits alone. When George Crocker gave Columbia Medical School $1 million in 1910, he did so to promote cancer research, not to support teaching.[1] Similarly, the General Education Board entered the arena of medical education in 1913 to provide salaries for full-time professors, not to assist medical instruction directly. In the two decades between 1910 and 1930, academic medicine finally received the financial support needed to become a secure profession. As a result, American medical research as well as American medical education rose to international leadership.

Considering the growing pains that academic medicine experienced before 1910, its maturation in the basic science departments occurred quietly and easily. In the 1890s, almost all medical schools were using practicing physicians to teach the fundamental laboratory branches, but by 1910 no reputable school used practitioners to teach those subjects. As medicine developed an experimental basis, private practitioners found it increasingly difficult to teach the basic sciences. Knowledge was simply increasing too rapidly; it was impossible to practice medicine and maintain a reputation as an anatomist or physiologist. In the years between 1910 and 1930, when full-time professors were hired to teach those subjects at every medical school, no practitioner objected. These fields had become too specialized; it was taken for granted that they were best taught by persons able to devote their full time to them.

The rise in academic stature of the clinical departments was a more dramatic and less anticipated development. The clinical subjects had begun the post-1910 era at a scientific disadvantage to the preclinical (basic science) disciplines, which were further developed in America. None of the initial research grants made by the Rockefeller Institute in 1901 and 1902 went to clinicians—the result not of predetermined policy but of the relative infancy of the clinical laboratories at that time.[2] Moreover, practicing physicians did not routinely do biochemistry or microbiology, but they did take care of patients, which was the primary goal of clinical teaching. Why, then, should they not continue to teach in the clinical departments of modern medical schools? The need for full-time instructors in the clinical departments was not so immediately clear as in the basic science departments.

In the early 1900s, however, clinical science was undergoing a remarkable scientific revolution. A generation before, it had been recognized that experimental methods applied to the preclinical disciplines; now it became evident that experimental methods applied to the study of disease and therapeutics as well. No longer was the best research in internal medicine, pediatrics, surgery, or gynecology a matter of simply describing the manifestations of disease. Rather, research in these fields, like research in the basic sciences, had become laboratory-based. When the premier journal of clinical science, the *Journal of Clinical Investigation,* was established in 1924, it was unlike any previous clinical journal in America. It published not traditional case reports and clinical observations but original studies in physiology, pharmacology, bacteriology, and biochemistry.[3] The most important clinical discovery of the era, the discovery of insulin in 1922, was an example of painstaking work in applied physiology and biochemistry, not in bedside observation. A "transfer of problems" was occurring, as Hans Zinsser of the Rockefeller Institute explained in 1921, in which the clinical laboratories, usually physically located in hospitals rather than in medical school buildings, were "taking over the type of research that was formerly done in the pre-clinical laboratories of medical schools."[4] The observational tradition never vanished from the clinical disciplines, just as it never disappeared from general biology. However, by 1920 the laboratory had replaced the case report as the primary method of clinical research.[5]

The development of clinical science placed new demands on those who would be faculty members of clinical departments. A conventional medical education did not prepare a physician to do clinical research. Additional scientific training in physiology, biochemistry, immunology, or a similar discipline was required. Without such preparation, a general practitioner or specialist, an internist or surgeon, was ill equipped to embark in clinical research, even if the physician were willing to spend his full time in the endeavor. An investigative career in the clinical disciplines had become a matter of training, not just of temperament. That was why George Blumer, who had led Yale Medical School into the modern era, voluntarily resigned the deanship of the school and the professorship of internal medicine in 1920. An 1891 graduate of the Cooper Medical College in San Francisco, Blumer called his scientific preparation a "farce." He felt that the progress of clinical science mandated that clinical departments be run by persons properly trained in laboratory research.[6]

Accordingly, the rise of clinical science attracted a different type of physician into the clinical departments of medical schools. In addition to having taken standard medical training, these "new clinical men,"[7] as Abraham Flexner called them, had acquired the scientific background to investigate the fundamental mechanisms of disease. Six charter members of the Interurban Clinical Club, for instance, had worked in Russell Chittenden's biochemistry laboratory at Yale.[8] Clinical scientists like Kenneth Blackfan, Alfred Cohn, George Dock, James Gamble, John Howland, and George Minot were trained laboratory investigators, not medical consultants of the traditional type. A generation before, such persons would have joined the basic science departments of medical schools, but by World War I they were entering the clinical departments instead.

Clinical scientists shared the same academic values as their colleagues in the basic science departments, for both groups aspired to careers in teaching and research rather than in private practice. Although almost all clinical scientists saw patients, their primary goal was to study disease in the laboratory, and some made no secret of the fact that they regarded patient care as a chore because it took time away from research. Clinical scientists in America were envious of clinical professors in Germany, who had already acquired full-time academic opportunities. With the growth of clinical science, university values pervaded the clinical departments of medical schools, as they had done earlier in the laboratory departments.

The development of clinical science mandated that the clinical disciplines be pursued as genuine university subjects. This proposal was first formally made in 1902 by Lewellys Barker, then of the University of Chicago;[9] in the decade thereafter the idea provoked much discussion and debate. The first full-time plan was implemented in 1913 at Johns Hopkins. Assisted by a $1.5 million grant from the General Education Board, the school placed its departments of medicine, surgery, and pediatrics on a full-time basis. Faculty members in those departments were provided salaries from the medical school and permitted to see patients in the Johns Hopkins Hospital only. Their patient responsibilities were limited so that they would have ample time for teaching and research. In the years that followed, other schools adopted similar programs, and by 1954, full-time instructors had been appointed to the clinical departments of all but fifteen schools.[10] Today, full-time clinical instructors are used by all schools.

The full-time system in clinical departments arose because clinical science had become a true scientific activity, not because anyone had arbitrarily decreed that such a system should exist. However, the details of how best to introduce full-time clinical positions remained controversial, even among those who were firmly committed to the idea in principle. Should such positions be for department heads and senior faculty only or for junior faculty and assistants as well? Should full-time professors be paid solely by salary (strict full time; the plan advocated by the General Education Board and adopted at Johns Hopkins), or may they keep patient fees from consultations performed in the university hospital (geographical full time)? Would the program work only if medical schools were to use one primary teaching hospital, as most did, or could full-time services succeed if a school used several hospitals, as Harvard used the Massachusetts General Hospital, Peter Bent Brigham Hospital, and Boston City Hospital?

An especially controversial detail was the issue of how much medical practice a clinical scientist needed to maintain his clinical skills at a high level. After all, clinical scientists, unlike basic scientists, had responsibility for patient care and clinical teaching, and it was difficult to teach that which one did not do. Contrary to a popular misconception of the present, it had not been suggested that full-time professors not see patients. Rather, the idea, according to the "strict" plan, was that they see patients in university hospitals only and that the fees collected for their services go into a departmental fund for salaries rather than directly to the professors themselves. But questions remained as to how much patient contact was enough, and how diversified a hospital-based clinical experience could be. This was William Osler's concern. In 1913 he warned that full-time clinicians might become "clinical prigs." A strict full-time system, he told Welch, might be "a very good thing for science, but a very bad thing for the profession."[11] Osler and others worried that such a plan might remove physicians too far from medical practice to remain effective clinical teachers.

Within academic medicine, a bitter debate over full-time appointments ensued. The details of the system were argued incessantly. The greatest proponent of a strict full-time system was the General Education Board, which arrogantly defended its rigid position on the question. When Harvard Medical School refused in 1913 to comply with the board's definition of full-time, the board denied Harvard's application for a grant. Jerome Greene, a board officer, and former secretary to the Harvard Corporation, expressed his "mortification" that Harvard, without the board's version of a full-time department, would be unable to remain a first-class medical school.[12] Harvard was not alone, however, in advocating some modification of the strict full-time system. Most members of the Interurban Clinical Club, leading clinical scientists all, violently opposed the strict form of the plan as adopted at Johns Hopkins.[13] Objection to the strict full-time system may have had to do with financial incentives.[14] Full-time salaries for senior clinical faculty were around $10,000 —twice as much as full professors in the basic science departments were making, but considerably less than the $25,000 or $30,000 the top consultants in practice were earning. A geographical system, by allowing professors to retain consulting fees, offered the possibility of higher incomes. In addition, opposition to the strict full-time plan was heightened by its identification with the General Education Board; many feared the controlling hand of the Rockefeller philanthropies on medical education. This was one reason the Council on Medical Education objected so strenuously to that version of the full-time system. Arthur Dean Bevan, the chairman of the council, warned that the board had become a "disturbing influence by dictating the scheme of organization of our medical schools."[15]

Yet the furious controversy that surrounded the details of implementation should not obscure the fact that most academic physicians believed that the principle of clinical full time was sound. Most medical educators opposed the Johns Hopkins version of the plan, but almost all agreed that some type of a full-time plan was needed. The essence of the full-time concept was that a clinical professor's chief obligations should be to his university duties of teaching and research. How a full-time professor was paid was irrelevant to the central principle. Opponents and advocates of a strict full-time plan stood united in their acceptance of the general principle. Jerome Greene, so critical of Harvard's preference for geographical full time, nonetheless admitted that the school's clinical chiefs were already full-time men "in spirit."[16] Arthur Dean Bevan, a harsh critic of salaried clinical departments, felt that "the clinical teacher must devote much of his time to teaching and research and that his college work must have first call on his time."[17] On the other hand, Victor Vaughan, who favored the strict full-time system, saw no problem with a clinical professor carrying on some consultation practice so long as he "should give the bulk of his time to university work."[18] William Welch summarized the situation when he called the method of payment a "minor detail" of any full-time scheme.[19] Though payment was a detail that evoked intense emotion, Welch and many others recognized that the principle of the concept lay in establishing clinical departments on a university basis in which an instructor's first duties were to teaching and research. This was why the terms "full-time plan" and "university plan" were used interchangeably. William Thayer, a successor of Osler, called the term "full-time" a "hateful word." He much preferred the term "university plan" because it was shorn of emotion and more accurately reflected the origins of the concept.[20]

Ultimately, great diversity came to characterize the clinical departments of medical schools. Very few schools adopted the strict version of full time; most adopted some version of geographical full time instead. A. McGehee Harvey has described the introduction of full-time programs in clinical departments at a number of leading medical schools, almost all of which modified the strict full-time concept in some way to meet the needs of their particular circumstances. The issue of full-time, as Harvey pointed out, was a matter of "motivation," not of "how the books were kept."[21] In the 1920s, even the General Education Board gave up its insistence on strict full time and began supporting more flexible geographical versions instead.[22]

Nevertheless, by the late 1920s a change of great magnitude had occurred in the clinical departments of medical schools. The differentiation of the professor from the practitioner of medicine that had begun in the latter nineteenth century in the preclinical sciences had extended into the clinical disciplines as well. Professors in clinical departments were now on a par with professors in laboratory departments, with teaching and research the explicit object of both. William Welch told Flexner after the fury surrounding the full-time system had subsided: "If the full-time scheme were utterly abandoned, clinical teaching in America could never go back to the condition in which it was before the inauguration of full-time teaching in Baltimore."[23] The clinical departments had been irreversibly transformed: medical scholarship had become a distinctive professional activity in the clinical as well as the preclinical branches. The main purpose of the full-time reform had been accomplished.

The Subordination of the Private Practitioner

If the full-time system provoked controversy among medical educators, among practitioners it produced great alarm. For a generation, practitioners had reluctantly been adjusting to the idea that they had lost control of the preclinical departments to the full-time professors. Nevertheless, through World War I they had remained active in clinical teaching, and to most practitioners, it seemed logical that they should continue to do so. The advent of the full-time system, however, threatened practitioners with the loss of responsibility in clinical teaching. Worse still, it raised the possibility that practitioners might not be permitted to use the university hospitals when their patients required hospitalization—a catastrophic event, were it to occur, now that the hospital was becoming more and more central to medical practice. In a system of full-time departments, private practitioners stood in jeopardy of being eliminated from medical school faculties.

Private practitioners had reason to be worried, for the clinical scientists were intent on taking control of the clinical departments themselves. This had been apparent from the moment that the idea of clinical full time had first been proposed. Barker, in his 1902 address, had spoken of the "harmful" influence of the noninvestigating teacher. "There may be a place for the non-investigating teacher in a college or seminary, but he is certainly out of his sphere as the leader of a department in a university."[24] Others took up the cudgel. Victor Vaughan wrote, "Medicine is a live, growing science and no one is entitled to hold a chair in a state medical school who is not a contributor to the growth and development of his specialty."[25] To the medical educators, clinical teaching had become just as much a professional academic activity as preclinical teaching. Amateurs—those without the proper scientific background—had to be given lesser roles, if they were to be retained in the faculty ranks at all. Historians of science will recognize in this effort to subordinate the private practitioner a familiar animus. It was the same as that shown by professional scientists in the 1850s in excluding the amateur scientists from the American Association for the Advancement of Science and by professional social scientists a generation later in dissociating themselves from the amateurs in the American Social Science Association.[26] Academic medicine, like so many other fields, was undergoing a drive toward professionalization.

The position of the practitioner of medicine in the modern medical school was not altogether bleak. In an era of personalized instruction, the required number of clinical teachers had become unprecedentedly large. There was simply too much to do; even the most vigorous advocate of the strict full-time plan did not envision that practitioners would be excluded from clinical teaching. By 1961, only one of four clinical faculty members in America held a full-time appointment.[27]

The primary issue, however, was not whether private practitioners had a role but who should *control* clinical education. Medical educators maintained that practitioners could teach as long as full-time instructors were in charge. No one stated this more bluntly than Abraham Flexner. "The dominating group in control of policy and facilities should be the full-time group and the part-time group should be used for teaching, for hospital work and otherwise, in distinct subordination as far as position and authority go."[28] "Routine" teaching—essential but humdrum tasks like supervising dispensary work or providing instruction in elementary physical diagnosis—could be done by private practitioners, thereby allowing the full-time faculty more time for the activities they really wanted to do. Medical schools needed practitioners for subordinate tasks. With clinical full time, the sociological revolution within medicine that had begun when Henry Bowditch of Harvard became the country's first full-time medical professor in 1871 was now complete. Professors had usurped for themselves practitioners' traditional control and power over medical education.

As full-time professors were appointed to run clinical departments, brutal displacements occurred. Many private practitioners who for years or decades had given their time and their hearts to clinical teaching—customarily without compensation—were summarily dismissed from the faculty or demoted in rank. In 1913, President George Vincent of the University of Minnesota fired the entire faculty of 184 and appointed a reorganized faculty of 70—"Vincent's massacre," as it was called at the university. Many professors from other institutions were called in to hold important posts; former leaders of the school were usually reduced in rank, if they were retained at all.[29] At the University of Pittsburgh, one former associate professor of gynecology plaintively told the dean of his dismay at being made an assistant professor in the "new" medical faculty, especially since some of his former underlings had received academic positions higher than his.[30] At George Washington University, one victim was the former dean, who spoke bitterly of the "humiliating manner" in which he had been ousted.[31] The tradition of private practitioners in medical teaching had been long, honorable, and proud. As more and more full-time faculty were brought in, practitioners felt left out and unimportant, despondent and angry. "Town-gown" tensions, which had been abating before World War I, were rekindled with greater intensity than ever before. The medical profession was again beset with civil war as professors and practitioners fought head-to-head.

"Town-gown" tensions were aggravated by the fact that most full-time clinical instructors were imported from distant institutions. With the rise in academic stature of clinical science, careers in clinical teaching and research became national. A peripatetic professorship arose in the clinical branches as it already had done in the preclinical fields. Clinical scholars would move from one school to another as better academic opportunities presented themselves. Accordingly, full-time instructors generally interacted much more closely with their academic peers around the country than with the private practitioners of the local community. Readers of the historian Robert Wiebe will recognize in this phenomenon proof that academic medicine had emerged as another constituent of the new middle class that was distinguishable along occupational lines—that is, medical scholars were identifiable by the work they did rather than by where they lived.[32] The consequence, however, was even greater "town-gown" hostility, as private practitioners began to complain about the arrogance of the new clinical faculty who would seldom mix with them professionally or socially. At Washington University, members of the new executive faculty (preclinical as well as clinical chairs) were facetiously called "The Wise Men from the East."[33] At Vanderbilt, even greater tensions resulted. The local medical community deeply resented the aloofness of the school's imported new medical faculty, who participated only infrequently in the professional and social activities of the Nashville medical society.[34]

Nowhere did a more bitter "town-gown" dispute erupt than in New Haven. After years of unsuccessful struggling, Yale Medical School had finally gained control of the New Haven Hospital, and the full-time system was instituted. However, the enterprise was threatened by the open antagonism of the local practitioners, who boycotted the hospital in protest. One prominent New Haven physician cut the hospital out of his will because of his intense dissatisfaction with the growing influence of the medical school in the hospital's affairs.[35] Yet it would be a mistake to think that practitioners were acting out of mere spite. Consider the lament of an anonymous New Haven practitioner, who complained of the medical school's indifference to the local professional fraternity. Under the new plan, private practitioners could not take care of their own patients in the New Haven Hospital. If a practitioner should inquire about his patient's condition, he would be treated with "scant courtesy—sometimes even as an interloper," and patients would then wonder why their family physicians knew so little about their condition. Patients often mistakenly assumed that their doctors were unconcerned and inattentive. The physician continued:

> My confreres and I are not all darn fools. Neither are we all afflicted with swelled heads and petty jealousies. We appreciate the difficulties which beset the attending staff, and we know that they have definite methods, and they are treating the patient according to their ideas (frequently better than we would) and we are liable to "butt in". . . . But we are human, very human, and we do like a little professional courtesy and attention.[36]

Small wonder that many practitioners disliked the professors.

The ill feelings aroused by the "town-gown" disputes never disappeared. Indeed, they remain distressingly prevalent at every academic medical center today. Nevertheless, by 1930 the worst hostilities had abated. Professors and practitioners, always wary of each other, once again achieved a rapprochement in which they realized that their mutual interests outweighed their differences. Medical school officials of broad vision realized that they could not afford to treat practitioners' unhappiness cavalierly. They knew that university hospitals depended on private practitioners for the referral of patients and that medical schools could raise funds much more easily when they enjoyed the support of area physicians. So inspired, many deans and department heads worked vigorously to heal the wounds and make practitioners feel more welcome within the teaching centers. To practitioners, acceptance of the full-time system came more readily once they saw that their worst fears would not be realized. Practitioners continued to teach at medical schools, and they were allowed to take care of their own patients in most university hospitals. Time, as usual, was also a great healer. By 1930, seventeen classes of medical students had been graduated since the first full-time plan was implemented, and many older practitioners had retired. To the younger members of the profession, clinical scientists were their teachers, not their rivals. Most important of all, clinical science worked—with much of practical clinical value resulting from the research effort. The public recognized the achievements of clinical science by the increased income and status it was willing to confer upon the medical profession. What private practitioners lost in terms of control over medical education, they gained in terms of increased stature and influence in society at large. The same healing forces that had been operating before the full-time controversy continued afterwards as well.

The Enthronement of Research

Were medical educators correct in insisting that clinical scholarship be made a full-time activity? One reason they gave was that full-time professors made better teachers. This contention, however, was a sham. It was a convenient device, understandable in the context of an era that worshipped expertise, but without evidence in its behalf. Admittedly, teaching had become more complicated and challenging, but there was no proof that good teaching could not be done by practitioners who made the effort to stay abreast of their field. Indeed, private practitioners have made outstanding contributions to teaching at every medical school from World War I through the present.

Insofar as the goal of clinical scholarship was research, however, the argument for a full-time system had merit. Both professors and practitioners understood that clinical research was an arduous task that could not be pursued on a whim. If one were to conduct important clinical investigations, a full-time position was necessary. Always, of course, there were exceptions. Physicians like Joseph Capps, a president of the American Society for Clinical Investigation and the Association of American Physicians, made important contributions to clinical science while in private practice.[37] Nevertheless, individuals such as Capps were very rare. Few doctors, however brilliant, could run a biochemistry or immunology laboratory without a full-time position. That is why the ranks of great clinical teachers have continued to include numerous private practitioners, whereas the ranks of great clinical investigators have not. Clinical full time, in other words, arose from the requirements of research, not from those of teaching.

By the 1920s, research had pervaded the American medical school. In practice, some schools emphasized research more than others. For instance, private schools were usually freer to pursue research than public schools, which customarily operated under a greater mandate to produce good practitioners. Even so, state schools like Michigan, Minnesota, Wisconsin, and California were just as imbued with the desire to advance medical knowledge as the leading private schools. As a result, medical schools became more and more alike. Differences in quality among the schools never vanished, but no longer was there the extreme heterogeneity of goals and standards that existed at the time of the Flexner report.

As research became enthroned, academic medicine enjoyed its first bull market. Full-time positions in both preclinical and clinical departments became available in unprecedented numbers. By the 1920s, the demand for qualified faculty members exceeded the supply. "It would seem almost impossible to go any further in multiplying the number of medical schools until there are more available men," Simon Flexner observed in 1923. "Lack of qualified personnel is at present the chief difficulty confronting this country in the further development of medicine."[38] Competition among schools for good teachers and investigators also drove up academic salaries. C. Canby Robinson, the dean of the Vanderbilt Medical School, told the chancellor of his problems in recruitment: "When younger men can be found who give sufficient promise and who can be obtained at smaller salaries, no one will be more pleased than I. I have been hunting for them constantly, but so have a number of others."[39] A generation before, the limiting factor in academic medicine had been material —positions, facilities, money—but now the limiting factor was the availability of qualified manpower. Academic medicine, like the economy, was to undergo its cycles, with occasional periods of retrenchment punctuating a general trend toward growth. However, the position of the professor of medicine would never again be insecure. The issue in the future would always be how many medical professors were needed and how amply they should be supported, not whether they should exist.

With the maturation of academic medicine, the long-standing dream of medical scientists had become a reality—those who desired could now find careers in medical teaching and research. American medical research also prospered, for by the 1930s the historic gap in quality between European and American medical research had been closed. On the other hand, it appeared that teaching at American medical schools had taken a back seat to research. Research, as a special faculty committee of the University of Pittsburgh School of Medicine explained, was the "duty" of a medical school. Teaching and research were both essential, but of the two, research was "the more important."[40] The nagging tension between teaching and research had at last been resolved—in favor of research. More by implicit action than by explicit decision, the question of the direction of the medical school had finally been decided. The road taken was toward that of pure university values. Many have subsequently cheered the triumph of research; others have deplored it. Nevertheless, the emphasis on research has continued to dominate the course and direction of American medical schools ever since.

12 The Rise of the Teaching Hospital

DURING the two decades that followed 1910, not only did medical schools acquire adequate funding, but the problems specific to clinical teaching were also corrected. This was made possible by the rise of the teaching hospital. Nineteenth-century hospitals had strenuously objected to all but the most restricted forms of clinical teaching and research, but in the twentieth century many leading hospitals became patrons of those activities. In some cases, teaching hospitals were built at taxpayers' expense, usually for publicly supported medical schools, but more often, medical schools acquired teaching hospitals by establishing new relationships with nearby voluntary hospitals. In either case, with the appearance of the teaching hospital, the needs of modern clinical training could finally be met.

A New Era Begins

In the nineteenth century, few hospitals in America were cordial to teaching and research. Yet by the early 1900s, a number of events had improved the prospects that hospitals would reconsider their responsibilities in those areas. For one, the Johns Hopkins Hospital had been a success and had gained an international reputation for combining educational and scientific pursuits with traditional humanitarian purposes. Hospitals had changed. By the turn of the century they had abandoned their earlier paternalistic and moralistic focus to become centers of advanced technology, specialized medicine, and the most up-to-date scientific procedures.[1] As hospitals became temples of modern science, they began to take more interest in establishing closer connections with the high priests of medical science—the academic physicians. Medical schools, too, had changed. Now that they had become much stronger than before, they had much more to offer hospitals in the way of scientific associations.

Other factors were important as well. One was the entrepreneurship of medical educators, who campaigned as hard to persuade hospital trustees of their educational responsibilities as they did to obtain funds from philanthropists and state legislatures. Medical schools, one dean observed, must "educate the trustees of existing hospitals to an appreciation of the value to their institutions of the use of patients as clinical material."[2] In addition, the cause was aided by the fact that more and more people were consulting physicians, rather than other types of healers, for medical advice. Now that the public had a larger stake in how its doctors were trained, the demands of medical educators carried much greater authority than before.

These sentiments erupted in full force in 1910. In that year there were three seminal unions between medical schools and hospitals: the College of Physicians and Surgeons (Columbia) with Presbyterian Hospital in New York; Harvard Medical School with the Peter Bent Brigham Hospital in Boston; and Washington University Medical School with Barnes Hospital and St. Louis Children's Hospital in St. Louis.[3] The Brigham and Barnes Hospitals were new institutions, still in the planning stages, endowed by the wills of Peter Bent Brigham and Robert Barnes, respectively. Children's Hospital was a growing pediatrics hospital that had opened in 1879. Presbyterian was a prominent general hospital that had recently been energized by a munificent gift from the philanthropist Edward Harkness to pay the costs of the affiliation with Columbia. For each union, Johns Hopkins served as the model. The universities were granted the right to appoint the medical staff of their affiliated hospitals and to use the facilities for teaching and research. These alliances marked the first major breakthroughs since the opening of Johns Hopkins in the efforts to upgrade clinical instruction.

The consummation of two of these alliances in the same year as the Flexner report was a coincidence, although the Flexner report certainly stimulated the teaching hospital movement nationwide. In Boston and New York, the negotiations were already nearly completed, and these unions would have occurred even if the Flexner report had not appeared. Only in St. Louis did the report help facilitate the arrangements, largely through the influence of Flexner on Robert Brookings, the Washington University president. Inspired by Flexner, Brookings became the prime mover in forging a relationship between the university and the two hospitals, as well as in building a nationally important medical school at Washington University. Details of Brookings's role have been provided elsewhere.[4]

Planning for the three mergers proceeded in conjunction with one another. This was not surprising since the drive to establish teaching hospitals, like the other efforts to improve medical education, was a national movement. The trustees of Children's Hospital were influenced by the recent agreement of the Harriet Lane Home to become the pediatric hospital of the Johns Hopkins School of Medicine, while the trustees of Barnes Hospital carefully followed developments at Presbyterian and Peter Bent Brigham.[5] Officials at Columbia kept close track of the negotiations in St. Louis and Boston.[6] For officials involved with all three mergers, the Johns Hopkins Hospital served as the primary example of how, through teaching and research, a hospital could achieve higher service.

In two instances, the affiliations were facilitated by overlapping boards of trustees. In Boston at least six members of the governing board of the Peter Bent Brigham Hospital were graduates of either Harvard College or Harvard Medical School.[7] In St. Louis, the association was even stronger. Brookings was well connected at both Children's and Barnes Hospitals, and Grace McKittrick Jones, the president of the board of managers of Children's Hospital, was married to Robert Jones, a good friend of Brookings and a member of Washington University's committee on the reorganization of the medical school.[8] Samuel Cupples, one of the three trustees of Barnes Hospital, was Brookings's business partner and closest friend.[9] Even though not a member of the board himself, Brookings became extremely involved with the planning of Barnes Hospital. He frequently attended the meetings of the hospital board, and he personally worked with the hospital architects nearly every day.[10]

No one lobbied more persuasively in behalf of these mergers than John Shaw Billings—the same Billings who had helped make the Johns Hopkins Hospital the nation's first genuine teaching hospital. In 1905, after visiting the Johns Hopkins Hospital, the trustees of the Peter Bent Brigham Hospital appointed Billings to be their "expert medical advisor." In that capacity, Billings told the Brigham trustees that the hospital should "be a teaching hospital, and of the best class, because . . . this will greatly extend the benefit of the institution by contributing to the education of medical men."[11] The Brigham trustees followed Billings's advice. Billings also influenced the course of events at Presbyterian Hospital, where he had been a member of the board of managers since 1896 and secretary of the hospital's building committee since 1908. His advice was "constantly consulted with regard to hospital questions,"[12] and he continually reminded his fellow board members of the hospital's educational mission. The ubiquitous Billings, who had seemingly left medical education to pursue a variety of other interests, was in fact spending the twilight of his career promoting the same ideas about medical teaching as he had proposed for Johns Hopkins in the 1870s.

The aggressiveness of medical school representatives only partly accounted for the three affiliations that occurred. The hospital trustees were tough negotiators, loyal to the interests of the institutions they served. The novel affiliations with medical schools were not steps they undertook lightly. As late as 1908, after more than six years of discussions, it was not certain that the Peter Brent Brigham Hospital would consent to the type of relation with Harvard that the medical school desired.[13] Barnes Hospital, before agreeing to the affiliation with Washington University, had turned down similar overtures from three other medical schools.[14] Presbyterian officials insisted that any alliance with Columbia University must allow "the maintenance of the independent corporate existence and individuality of The Presbyterian Hospital."[15]

Rather, the hospital trustees agreed to the unions because they believed that their own institutions stood to benefit from the associations. As officials at Presbyterian explained, an alliance with a leading medical school was "important and indeed essential to the future progress and development of the Hospital."[16] Authorities at each of these institutions had come to believe "that the best hospitals of today and those which accomplished the highest service are intimately connected with great medical schools."[17] This attitude stood in marked contrast to the prevailing viewpoint of only a few years before, when hospitals across the country routinely refused to have more than a token role in medical teaching and research.

Representatives of the four hospitals saw many advantages in a medical school alliance. One was the provision of better patient care. In a teaching hospital "it is obvious that the routine care of patients will reach its highest efficiency,"[18] a representative of Children's Hospital declared. Whether a teaching hospital would actually provide the best care was never proved, only assumed, but it was an assumption that hospital and medical school officials made with ease.

Part of their trust in the capacity of the teaching hospital to deliver the finest care arose from the constant scrutiny that a teaching hospital, with its organized teams of attending physicians, house officers, and students, could provide. With a large staff, doctors were always present. Acutely ill or unstable patients were able to be continuously observed, and someone was always there to handle an emergency. With students watching and asking questions, teachers were more assiduous in their work, and the presence of so many observers allowed the most accurate information to be obtained about a patient's condition.[19]

In addition, the hospital trustees believed that teaching hospitals had the finest medical staffs. In their eyes, the most skillful and knowledgeable clinicians were the academic physicians who devoted their entire time to the study of disease, not the local practitioners who formerly had constituted the clinical faculties of medical schools. Thus, the Presbyterian board of managers was moved by the consideration that an alliance with Columbia would allow the hospital "to secure the best medical and surgical talent."[20] Events of the time seemed to be illustrating this point. Because it provided few opportunities for productive teaching and research, Roosevelt Hospital lost the services of the surgeon Joseph A. Blake to Presbyterian Hospital, and for the same reason, the Massachusetts General Hospital lost those of the surgeon Fred T. Murphy to Barnes Hospital.[21] Conversely, as a benefit of its affiliation with Harvard Medical School, the Peter Bent Brigham Hospital received the consulting services of three of Harvard's renowned basic medical scientists: Walter Cannon, William Councilman, and Otto Folin. Even though the three would rarely make rounds on the wards, they were available when needed.[22]

Hospital officials' respect for the academic doctor arose from the advances in clinical science of the late nineteenth and early twentieth centuries. As discoveries in chemistry, physiology, immunology, and bacteriology made their impact upon medicine, a greater knowledge of the basic sciences became essential even to the full-time practitioner. As numerous technologies and laboratory tests found their way into standard clinical practice, the practice as well as the theory of medicine also began to change very rapidly. To insure the most up-to-date care, hospital officials wanted to secure the services of the doctors whose work was so dramatically affecting clinical practice. Indeed, the pathologist of Barnes Hospital argued, the more scientific reports issued by a hospital, the better the quality of care available there.[23]

Officials of the four hospitals saw a second advantage to the idea of affiliating with medical schools: such arrangements would enhance their ability to contribute to medical research. The trustees of these institutions were again inspired by the development of clinical science, which required a hospital for its execution. Charles P. Curtis, the president of the board of trustees of the Peter Bent Brigham Hospital, explained that his board "is in entire sympathy" with the research work of the hospital and "appreciates its value."[24] This motivation was not entirely selfless, for the trustees recognized that clinical investigation would allow their institutions to be of worldwide as well as local importance. Indeed, the physician-in-chief of the Peter Bent Brigham Hospital had promised that the hospital's scientific work would bring the Brigham "to the attention of the world at large and make the institution stand in the first rank of the world's hospitals."[25]

With this viewpoint, hospital trustees felt that an affiliation with a medical school made good sense. In each case under consideration, the medical schools agreed to provide scientific staffing for the hospitals and to equip and maintain the hospital's laboratories. The Barnes trustees boasted, for instance, that the agreement with Washington University "enables the Hospital to secure the services of the eminent men composing the medical staff of the University, and also insures to the Hospital, without any expense, the use of the magnificent laboratories and equipment of the new medical department of the University."[26] Medical schools and hospitals would no longer be isolated from each other; the scientific talent and resources of the schools would be brought together with the vast clinical facilities of the hospitals. They would work hand-in-hand to expand medical knowledge.

Hospital officials saw a third reason to affiliate with a medical school: such unions were economically mandatory if the hospitals and universities were to do the work they desired. Modern medical technology, necessary for the best medical care, was very expensive. So was the support of laboratories for clinical research. Officials of Children's Hospital admitted that "it is still essentially a struggle to make both ends meet, since with the increased facilities for doing good, come corresponding demands upon the exchequer."[27] Barnes Hospital accumulated a deficit of $36,000 during its first year of operation alone.[28] Even the Peter Bent Brigham Hospital, with over $6,600,000 in assets, complained loudly about expense. The president of the board of trustees warned that "the Corporation, while seemingly well endowed, finds its work always expanding, and the outlook for the future calls for ever-increasing expenditure."[29] In the hospital's first five years of operation (1913–17), the number of patients treated annually rose from 1,370 to 3,674, and yearly expenses escalated from $190,000 to nearly $324,000. During this time annual receipts increased only from $36,000 to $138,000.[30] Henry Christian, the Brigham's physician-in-chief, warned that "growth must cease unless our earnings and endowment funds are increased; in fact retrenchment may be forced upon us on account of the increased cost of almost everything."[31]

Formation of the alliances with medical schools allowed a division of labor that was to everyone's economic advantage. In each case, the hospitals made available to the universities superb teaching facilities that the universities could not have afforded on their own. In return, the universities equipped and maintained the hospitals' laboratories and provided the hospitals with scientifically distinguished medical staffs. The greatest savings were achieved in St. Louis, where the two hospitals and a new medical school plant were built next to each other. Washington University provided Children's and Barnes Hospitals with dispensary buildings, erected a pathological laboratory that served both hospitals, paid the salaries of all the physicians working in the hospitals, and constructed and operated a power plant that supplied the entire complex. Since Children's and Barnes hospitals adjoined each other, they were able to use centralized laundry, kitchen, and ambulance services. If corporations could consolidate resources into larger, more efficient units, then why should hospitals and medical schools not do the same? The consolidation of medical facilities, noted the president of Children's Hospital, was "quite in keeping with the present tendency in the business world—the concentration of energy in one point."[32]

Presbyterian Hospital, Peter Bent Brigham Hospital, Barnes Hospital, and St. Louis Children's Hospital were destined to become teaching hospitals. They each had the basic material prerequisites: large size; modern facilities; a sizable patient base; and impressive financial resources. All had academically prominent medical advisors who continually argued that the hospitals should be genuine educational institutions. The managing boards of these particular hospitals were receptive to that idea, for they wanted their institutions to receive global recognition, and they realized this could be achieved in the twentieth century only by becoming centers of teaching and research. To contribute to the community and the world in the largest possible way, these hospitals saw that they had to add educational and scientific aims to their traditional humanitarian purposes. After decades of rejection of this concept by hospitals across the country, the tide had finally turned.

The Spread of the Teaching Hospital

Although the pioneering mergers were not without troubling details, they ran successfully from the beginning. Very quickly the concerns of those who had opposed them were laid to rest. The benefits to both medical schools and hospitals became clearly apparent, and students were rapidly brought into the hospital routine. After the first year of its affiliation with Columbia, Presbyterian officials concluded that the result has been "eminently satisfactory" to the hospital.[33] Faculty members at Harvard, Columbia, and Washington University rejoiced, for the clerkship and clinical research at their schools had become secure.

The unions in Boston, New York, and St. Louis represented a major turning point in the rise of the teaching hospital. They served as catalysts, helping galvanize sentiment that had been growing nationwide. Across the country dozens of other medical schools soon succeeded in acquiring teaching hospitals under their direct control, either by forming new arrangements with existing hospitals or by influencing state and local governments to build hospitals that would be run as teaching institutions. By 1921, every surviving medical school in the country had established an affiliation with a hospital that it either owned or controlled.[34] Hospitals, once intransigently opposed to medical teaching, now found that they liked the idea, and the public approved as well. In 1916, when the new Municipal Hospital of the University of Cincinnati opened after fourteen years of public skepticism, a local newspaper headline proclaimed: "Now The People Can't Understand Why It Was Not Built Sooner."[35] Medical educators stood incredulous at the rapid acceptance of an idea that had encountered so much resistance only a few years before.

Many similarities existed between the subsequent mergers—as well as the successful lobbying before the legislatures to erect state university hospitals—and the earlier affiliations that started the process. In virtually every case, aggressive medical faculties initiated the negotiations. Physicians approached hospitals and governmental bodies with the same entrepreneurial flair that they manifested in their fund-raising campaigns. To this group of institution-builders, the procurement of teaching hospitals and the establishment of a solid financial base for medical education were equally important tasks. Both were necessary for implementing their long-established goals of providing good medical training and of making academic medicine a viable career. The hospitals that listened to them were of the same kind: large, ambitious, technologically sophisticated institutions that had hopes of achieving international reputations. In case after case, their reasons for becoming a teaching hospital were the same: the belief that teaching hospitals provided the best patient care, and the desire to achieve worldwide recognition through medical education and research. The rise of the teaching hospital represented one more dimension of the widespread pervasion of American life by science during the Progressive Era.

Once underway, the process of transforming hospitals into teaching institutions proceeded very quickly. One merger in a large city would frequently spur similar unions among competitors. In New York, for instance, the affiliation between Columbia and Presbyterian helped inspire an agreement between Cornell Medical School and the New York Hospital. George Rives, the president of the Board of Governors of New York Hospital, in his capacity as chairman of the Board of Trustees of Columbia University had become familiar with the arguments in favor of such arrangements.[36] Likewise, in Boston, the attention given the upstart Peter Bent Brigham Hospital before it had even opened startled the established Boston hospitals (the Massachusetts General Hospital, Boston City Hospital, and Boston Children's Hospital) into forming similar arrangements with Harvard. At the venerable Massachusetts General Hospital, the consternation was the most keenly felt. Without a relationship with Harvard Medical School like that enjoyed by the Brigham, a representative of the hospital was warned by a Harvard official in 1911, the Massachusetts General Hospital "inevitably" will undergo "deterioration," running a "serious risk of losing its very high rank among the hospitals of this country."[37] After the arrival of David Edsall as chief-of-service in 1912—the first "outsider" (that is, non-Bostonian and holding no Harvard degrees) to receive a major clinical appointment at the hospital—the Massachusetts General Hospital agreed to become a true teaching hospital.[38] In 1912, students at last entered its wards as clinical clerks, where they were "now taking part in the actual work of the Hospital and not merely receiving instruction, as in the past."[39]

Although many affiliations were created with private hospitals, a large number were also established with public institutions. Here, the circumstances were generally very similar, with voters and legislative bodies responding to the same arguments advanced to the trustees of private institutions. In 1913, Western Reserve, buoyed by its success with Lakeside Hospital, finally succeeded in persuading the city administration of Cleveland to grant the school the use of City Hospital as a teaching hospital, after years of having had such a request denied.[40] "Every hospital should learn the fact—that efficient teaching of medicine and surgery in its wards is promotive of the best interests and reputation of the hospital,"[41] the medical faculty declared. During World War I, the University of Michigan found that improvements in roads and rails and the development of the automobile industry in nearby Detroit made Ann Arbor a viable location for a medical center. The university president, H. B. Hutchins, influenced the state legislature to appropriate funds to expand University Hospital into a major teaching institution. By 1920, the hospital had grown to approximately 450 beds, and plans were already underway to add an additional 800 beds, each of which was to be available for teaching.[42] In

1917, the Nebraska legislature built a university-owned teaching hospital in Omaha to provide clinical instruction of the modern type.[43]

Particularly in the quest to establish affiliations with municipal hospitals, politics frequently affected the outcome. In some cases, as the example of Cincinnati illustrated, the local political situation facilitated the arrangements. When Charles Dabney was approached to be president of the University of Cincinnati in 1903, he secured a promise from George Cox, the notorious political boss, that there would be no political interference in university affairs should he accept the position, and Cox kept his word.[44] For the next ten years, the medical school's dean, Christian Holmes, worked tirelessly to persuade the voters to erect a municipal hospital for the school. Approaching the task with the dedication of a religious zealot and the adroitness of a professional politician, Holmes hammered away at the consciences of the voters. It "should be made clear to every layman," he told them "that the best interests of the sick are attained when the hospital is a high-class teaching institution."[45] He led three successful campaigns for bond issues to build the hospital, and he negotiated concessions from the local transit company so that car fare to the hospital would be no more than five cents from anywhere in the city, thereby making it accessible to the poor.[46] As the hospital was being built, the Academy of Medicine of Cincinnati lobbied to help insure that control of the hospital would reside with the medical school rather than with the politically-appointed public safety director. The hospital's medical staff should be removed "from the suspicion of political control," one academy representative asserted; with the university in charge, the hospital would not be "the football of politics."[47] Cincinnati's mayor also supported the plan. A great hospital, he said, must always be "a corporate part of the medical school."[48] When Municipal Hospital opened in 1914, it was one of the grandest in the country.

In other places, local politics interfered with the efforts to establish teaching hospitals. Denver was one such example. In the mile-high city, the University of Colorado School of Medicine had been affiliated with Denver City and County Hospital, but according to the medical faculty "this connection is more apparent than real, being one of sufferance only."[49] City officials ran the hospital irrespective of the wishes and needs of the medical school. In 1919 politicians, without apparent reason, even removed the dean of the medical school from the hospital staff.[50] Because of such problems, the state of Colorado ultimately had to build the school a hospital of its own. A similar situation existed in New Orleans, where through the late 1920s the politically-appointed governing board of Charity Hospital refused to grant Tulane any control over appointments or over the teaching at the hospital.[51]

The rise of the teaching hospital proceeded to a large degree independently of the activities of medical education's greatest booster, Abraham Flexner. In his new position with the General Education Board, Flexner spent much more time raising money for medical education and establishing his version of full-time clinical chairs than he did procuring facilities for clinical teaching. In at least two instances, however, Flexner helped arrange new affiliations between hospitals and medical schools. In 1914, he was instrumental in the decision of Wesley Hospital in Chicago to become a teaching hospital of Northwestern University, and between 1914 and 1916 he helped persuade Bellevue Hospital to become a major teaching affiliate of Cornell, Columbia, and New York University.[52] Indirectly, Flexner's influence was far reaching. For instance, his Carnegie report aided Yale University in 1913 in securing an affiliation with New Haven Hospital. While negotiating with the hospital, an officer of Yale had sent a copy of the Flexner report to each of the hospital directors. The report, he later related, "helped us more than any other single factor in bringing about the agreement."[53] The widely read Flexner report, which urged hospitals to participate in teaching and research, undoubtedly influenced trustees of other hospitals as well.

Not every medical school succeeded in obtaining a teaching hospital, and failure to do so was frequently the reason that after 1910 many ambitious medical schools were forced to close. In many instances the obstacles were demographic, for schools in less populated areas were usually unable to find the number and variety of patients needed for good clinical teaching. As early as 1898, it was clear to the president of one rural medical school that "the tendency of medical instruction is in the direction of city schools, where the greatest variety of cases and the highest grade of medical talent is found."[54] As control of an adequate teaching hospital became mandatory for a high ranking from the American Medical Association, rural medical schools came under great pressure. The University of Nebraska, for example, had been dividing its medical instruction between Lincoln and Omaha. In 1914, to avoid a low rating from the AMA, the school moved all its teaching to the more populous Omaha, where the clinical resources were much richer.[55] In tiny Hanover, New Hampshire (1910 population, 1,951), Dartmouth Medical College faced loss of accreditation because its hospital was too small. To maintain its standing with the AMA and the various state licensing boards, the school discontinued the third and fourth years of its medical course and became a two-year school instead.[56] With the rise of the teaching hospital, the geographical face of American medical education irreversibly changed. Once found as much in rural as in urban settings, medical education overwhelmingly moved to the cities.

Other well-intentioned medical schools lacked the money to acquire teaching hospitals. These were usually small private medical schools that had neither a large body of alumni nor a state or city government to turn to for financial assistance. For instance, in 1913 the Drake University College of Medicine in Des Moines, Iowa, found that it had been dropped by the AMA from the highest class of medical schools because it needed to "secure a much larger control of a hospital."[57] Lacking the $3 million needed to build a first-rate teaching hospital, the faculty and Board of Trustees voted to close the school and merge with the State University of Iowa rather than to carry on in an unsatisfactory way.[58] Whatever the obstacle—geographical remoteness or insufficient funds—the lack of a teaching hospital became a death knell for medical schools.

With the rise of the teaching hospital, the long needed improvements in clinical education occurred very rapidly. At a meeting of the Association of American Medical Colleges in 1926, it was proudly announced that ward clerkships "have been instituted in all medical schools."[59] Fears engendered by the presence of medical students in the wards, so common a generation earlier, had virtually disappeared. With the adoption of higher entrance requirements, the average student displayed far more intelligence and better manners than at any time previously. Medical students, given white coats and referred to as "young doctors," came to be accepted in the hospital as a matter of course.[60]

A large number of problems remained, however. By 1930, many schools still had not met their hospital needs, although the facilities they did have were much improved from two decades before. Many educational issues were also unresolved. No uniformity could be found among the schools in the way the clerkship was conducted. There was not even agreement as to where in the curriculum the clerkship belonged. At some schools the hospital rotations were reserved for junior students, with the seniors working in the clinics; at other schools the reverse was true.[61] Few schools allowed clinical clerks a large amount of responsibility. It was unusual for students to be permitted in the wards at night, and even at Columbia students were "in the main, merely observers."[62]

Nevertheless, from the perspective of where clinical education had started, a new system had been implemented—the one still in use today. Subsequent changes were of degree, not of kind—continually adding to the student's work and responsibilities, but not questioning whether students should be given responsibilities in the first place. With the appearance of the teaching hospital, training that in the nineteenth century had been available for only a few students became required of everyone. The modern era of clinical instruction in America had begun.

Meaning of the Teaching Hospital

The emergence of the teaching hospital meant many things for the development of American medicine. Throughout the nineteenth century, the conceptual link between science and medicine had been growing. Nothing symbolized this more than the teaching hospital, which brought science and medicine literally together. Indeed, the unions of the 1910s and 1920s were the beginning of the modern academic medical center, where teaching hospital and medical school have been juxtaposed. It was with total seriousness that the dean of Columbia Medical School wrote in 1910 that the ideal hospital in the future would be constructed on *top* of a medical school.[63] By the late 1920s, a consideration of how to connect hospitals and medical schools was entering books on hospital architecture.[64]

The teaching hospital was also essential to medical education becoming a university endeavor. As the laboratories of the basic scientists were located in medical school buildings, the laboratories of the clinical scientists were usually found within hospitals. At last, clinical investigators possessed the facilities and opportunities for a lifetime of unfettered research and teaching. Without a teaching hospital, no clinical department at any medical school could thrive.

The rise of the teaching hospital also brought about a change in the financing of American hospitals. In the nineteenth century, the hospital belonged more to the welfare than the medical system, and gifts to hospitals were prompted by traditional charitable and religious motives. The Harkness gift to Presbyterian Hospital marked a major turning point. This gift, and many large donations to other teaching hospitals that followed, was contingent upon the hospital being willing to ally itself with a scientifically strong medical school. To compete successfully, hospitals had no choice but to be teaching institutions. John D. Rockefeller, Sr., so munificent in his support of medical research, repeatedly refused to assist nonteaching hospitals outside his home city of New York, for he considered such gifts to be dangerous and unwise charity, not prudent philanthropy.[65] Much money continued to pour into hospitals for traditional humanitarian reasons, but the balance had shifted, particularly for those hospitals seeking the widest recognition.

Relations between hospitals and medical schools were generally cordial, in view of their common purposes. Nevertheless, always lurking close beneath the surface were innumerable tensions that frequently erupted as hospitals and medical schools struggled to maintain their independent identities. Questions concerning such issues as the payment of salaries, the maintenance of facilities, the provision of operating expenses, and the proper allotment of charity and pay beds—not to mention periodic second thoughts about whether medical students really did belong on the wards—continually surfaced. In 1924, a squabble even occurred between Western Reserve and Lakeside Hospital— two institutions that had always enjoyed an unusually close relationship.[66] The traditional conflicts between hospitals and medical schools never vanished, and even today they can be found at every academic medical center in the country.

As a result of their new affiliations with medical schools, the hospitals achieved what they desired: national and international importance. Yet in the process they paid a price: they irreversibly lost control of their own destinies. Hospital trustees, who in the nineteenth century had been responsible for establishing policy and making day-to-day decisions, now found themselves increasingly relegated to the essential but limited role of fund raisers. Instead, policy was determined more and more by the medical boards, whose recommendations the trustees would usually agree to follow. Medical boards were growing in influence at all American hospitals at this time, but nowhere was this change more pronounced than at the teaching hospitals.[67]

Medical education, too, had prospered with the new arrangements, for now the clerkship became universally available. However, some unanticipated consequences quickly became apparent here as well. The line between learning by doing and being economically exploited as a source of cheap labor was a fine one that was frequently trespassed. A student did not have to draw many blood specimens for that act to cease to be of educational value. With so many chores, and with so little time for thinking and sleeping, the clerkship could easily be a dehumanizing experience. And if this problem was severe for students, for interns and residents it was critical.

Finally, what of the patient? Although many medical educators sanctimoniously rationalized the value of the clerkship to good patient care, in actuality the clerkship highlighted the tension between the needs of medical education and those of patient service that had been becoming increasingly apparent since the mid-nineteenth century. One only has to examine the correspondence between the superintendent and physician-in-chief of the Peter Bent Brigham Hospital to appreciate the impositions upon patients that could arise from employing students as clinical clerks. At the Brigham Hospital, students were examining patients during meals and at night; there were many complaints of noise in the wards and of seemingly endless commotion —all the things that nineteenth-century hospital trustees had feared.[68] Medical educators, of course, were not insensitive to the needs of patients and took many important steps to ensure that patient rights would not be infringed.[69] Nevertheless, as one medical faculty stated bluntly: "Patients must clearly understand from the beginning that they are admitted for teaching purposes and that they are to be willing to submit to this when pronounced physically fit."[70] A new balance had clearly been struck. The tension between educational and patient needs had finally been resolved—in favor of education. And for the next sixty years, the public accepted this.

13 State Licensing

IN the broadest perspective, the development of the current system of medical education in the United States involved two distinct processes. One was the creation of the modern medical school. This process, whose beginnings date to the 1850s, culminated during World War I and the 1920s with the creation of a solid financial base, the maturation of academic medicine, and the rise of the teaching hospital. The other, equally important, development involved the elimination of the proprietary schools. This was accomplished in the fifteen years following 1910 by the enactment in all states of stringent licensing laws. By legal force, low-grade schools either had to correct their deficiencies or cease operations.

With the advent of universal state licensing, medical schools came to look very much alike. No two schools offered an identical course of study, but the similarities from school to school vastly outweighed the differences. Standardization of medical education accomplished much good. The public at long last could be assured that every physician entering practice had received excellent training. However, to guarantee uniformity, the licensing laws imposed a rigidity on the course of study with which even the strongest schools could not resist or overcome. Schools that for decades had led the movement for reform now found themselves encumbered by a system they had helped create. Ultimately the constraints lessened, but the question of how much standardization to enforce has perplexed medical educators from the 1920s through the present.

State Licensing and the Rise of the AMA

At the time of the Flexner report of 1910, the era of the proprietary medical school in America was already rapidly coming to an end. From 1906, the peak year, to 1910, the number of medical schools had fallen from 162 to 131, and more closures were on the way. Of the schools in existence in 1910, 37 had total enrollments of fewer than 50 students apiece, and 66 had enrollments of fewer than 100 students.[1] Students were staying away from proprietary schools, which had ceased to be profitable ventures.

Nevertheless, medical schools of low quality still existed in 1910 because of the absence of strong licensing laws. Since the 1870s, licensing boards had been established in most states to certify medical schools and examine applicants for the license to practice, but in general the boards were weak and ineffective, and a few were even corrupt.[2] Abral.am Flexner reported in 1910 that appointments to many state boards were regarded as "political spoils," that some states prohibited medical teachers from serving on the boards, and that many state boards did not execute the tasks legally assigned to them. He felt that "none" of the state boards were "properly constituted, organized, and equipped."[3] As a result, few checks existed on who was allowed to practice medicine. As late as 1906, thirteen states still granted medical licenses to nongraduates.[4] For the situation to be corrected, strong laws had to be enforced, and in every state, not just in some states, because graduates of weak schools could migrate to states with less exacting requirements. Without effective licensing laws, physicians who still thought they could operate medical schools for profit were free to try.

Through 1910, therefore, state licensing laws had been an insignificant factor in the development of American medical education. State laws generally followed rather than preceded changes at the schools. For instance, by the late 1890s, almost all schools had adopted four-year programs, even though very few state boards had yet made that a mandatory requirement.[5] In examining the faculty records of dozens of medical schools, I found almost no mention of state boards in the period prior to the Flexner report.[6] Nevertheless, as Flexner wrote, "the power to examine is the power to destroy."[7] Before 1910 the power of the state boards had not yet been realized, but their potential to destroy undeserving schools was clearly apparent. This was why Flexner called the state boards "the instruments through which the reconstruction of medical education will be largely effected."[8]

In the wake of the Flexner report, an aroused public was finally ready to demand that state boards take their duties seriously. One great muckraking treatise, *The Jungle,* by Upton Sinclair, had played a critical role in the enactment of the Pure Food and Drug Act of 1906. Another great muckraking work, Abraham Flexner's *Medical Education in the United States and Canada,* now had the same effect in prodding the public to demand effective licensing laws. In every state over the next several years, tough new laws were passed or existing laws strengthened. As one requirement of the laws, state boards passed judgment upon the medical schools of the country, and only graduates of "approved" medical schools were permitted to apply for the license to practice medicine. This requirement quickly brought about the demise of weak schools that failed to elevate their standards. Some of these schools were fraudulent; others were well intentioned but lacking in resources. The result, however, was the same for all: they were decapitated by legislative ax.

The enactment of licensing laws was not accomplished painlessly. Many persons, including many who recognized the merits of a scientific medical education, anguished over the thought that governmental regulation would abridge individual freedom. Although recognizing the need for well-trained doctors, they still respected the right of anyone who wished to operate a medical school or of anyone who so desired to practice medicine. The informed citizen could simply patronize the graduates of well-run schools, and no one's rights would be infringed by the big brother of government. Throughout most of the history of the republic, with government's role severely limited, this was the prevailing attitude.

Nevertheless, by the early 1900s broad historical forces were inexorably operating in behalf of rigorous licensing legislation. The country had become vastly more complex since the days of the founding fathers. For decades, the classic concept of laissez-faire had been giving way to the idea that the state and federal governments should take more active roles in the regulation of society's affairs. The creation of a system of tough, universally enforced state licensing laws reflected this changing view toward the responsibilities of government.[9]

No one more directly confronted the lingering doubts about the use of government to regulate medical education than Henry Pritchett and Abraham Flexner. Both recognized that the issue of licensing had to be considered within the larger context of the escalating responsibilities of government that were already taking place. Individuals had rights, but so did individuals collectively have rights in the form of society. The general public, Pritchett wrote, is "profoundly interested" in the training of its doctors. After all, it is the layman "who is to be either made or marred by the medical practitioner."[10] Because the layman had little ability to distinguish among those with medical licenses, and because the medical profession privately had not succeeded in eliminating the inferior schools, society had only one choice: to assume that responsibility itself. State licensing, Flexner admitted, would "abridge the freedom of particular individuals to exploit certain conditions for their personal benefit," but it would "secure for all others more freedom at a higher level." In this way, he argued, licensing involves "the strengthening, not the weakening, of democratic principle."[11] In short, Flexner and Pritchett maintained, the private freedoms lost were less important than the public benefits gained. This was the same justification as that given for the entry of the state into many other spheres of activity at this time.

Acceptance of this new role of government was made easier by the fact that state licensing offered a political solution compatible with the prevailing political ethic of the period. Reformers argued that control of licensing boards should be in the hands of responsible medical educators. State boards should no longer be viewed as political payoffs but should be administered, to use Flexner's words, by "trained experts."[12] "What is needed," Pritchett wrote, "is the closest correlation between the state board of health and the university school of medicine." The medical school should be the board of health's "right hand."[13] In this way, government could be made one step less corrupt, one step more "clean." The licensing movement thus gained force because it incorporated the dominant political values of society. With its emphasis on expertise and scientific management, the movement reflected the enlightened stereotype of the day of what political behavior ought to be.

Licensing laws did not materialize of themselves. Medical educators capitalized on the sentiments described earlier to lobby effectively in their behalf. They had been campaigning for licensing laws for many years, but in the wake of the Flexner report their arguments carried much greater force. Henry Pritchett and Abraham Flexner spoke eloquently on the subject in the public arena. University medical schools collaborated with the licensing boards of their respective states. The Association of American Medical Colleges (AAMC) worked with licensing boards in each of the states, as well as with the Federation of State Medical Boards and the National Board of Medical Examiners. However, the strongest voice was that of the Council on Medical Education of the AMA, whose power in this area was profound. In the period following 1910, judgments by the council regarding the educational merits of the country's medical schools came to have the force of law. State boards decided whether to honor or reject a school's diploma based on the council's assessment of the school's qualifications.

The AMA of the early 1900s was a much different organization from the AMA of the nineteenth century, which had been a weak, ineffectual, provincial society. Based on a scheme of reorganization in which membership in a county society brought with it membership in the state and national organizations, membership in the AMA rose from 8,401 in 1900 to 70,146 in 1910.[14] Contrary to its conservative image of the present, the AMA between 1900 and 1920 supported many liberal causes, including pure food and drug legislation, more extensive public health measures, a federal health department, and compulsory health insurance.[15] In addition, the AMA for the first two decades of the century provided a vehicle for collaboration between practitioners and professors. Indeed, during that time, a number of university medical teachers served as presidents of the organization. This situation prevailed until the 1920s, when professors and practitioners went their separate ways, with academic influence in the AMA remaining only in the university-dominated Council on Medical Education. Thereafter the AMA retained the ascendancy in political and economic affairs of concern to practitioners but not in matters of education and research.[16]

Credit for the AMA's phenomenal growth is generally given to Joseph N. McCormack, a genius at public relations who masterminded the AMA's reorganization.[17] The organizing brilliance of McCormack cannot be dismissed, but he would not have succeeded without broad historical forces working in his favor. As the AMA itself had discovered throughout the nineteenth century, no one's command or persuasion alone could organize the profession. Successful reorganization required an internal consensus—a sense of intellectual unity and collective consciousness—among members of the profession. The growth of scientific medicine provided the basis of integration; it allowed doctors throughout the country to perceive themselves as part of a national community that used similar techniques and methods to accomplish similar purposes. No longer did physicians sharply disagree among themselves over theories of disease causation or over the proper approach to therapeutics and surgery; they spoke a common language and practiced in a common fashion.[18] This interpretation is consistent with the ideas of Robert Wiebe, who has described members of various professional groups, including doctors, as achieving a national identity in the late nineteenth century based on the requirements of their work.[19] Amid these larger changes, McCormack's efforts prevailed.

The AMA's role in the development of American medical education is long overdue for critical evaluation. Conventional wisdom—firmly entrenched in the literature of history, sociology, political science, and medicine—deems the AMA the chief architect of reform. But this mythical view receives no confirmation from the historical facts. In the nineteenth century, as seen earlier, the organization played no role in either the genesis or implementation of the new ideas of how to teach medicine. Indeed, for most of that century, the AMA did not even believe in the importance of the scientific subjects, laboratory teaching, or clinical clerkships. In the early twentieth century, the reports and surveys of the Council on Medical Education undoubtedly contributed to the growing sentiment within the profession in favor of further reform. However, archival records of many dozens of medical schools show faculties going about their work without making even passing reference to the AMA. Only in 1909, when N. P. Colwell, the council's secretary, began inspecting medical schools with Abraham Flexner, do faculty records mention the AMA for the first time. By then the outline of the country's present system of medical education was already firmly in place. The new educational concepts had been enunciated and accepted by the profession at large; universities had usurped control of medical education from the proprietary schools; the educational system had grown enormously and was producing medical students with much better preparation than before; a German-influenced academic elite had established themselves as the leaders of educational reform; and the circumstances had become ripe for an outpouring of medical philanthropy. All this had occurred without any direct contribution from the AMA. It would represent no great error to write a history of American medical education before 1910 that did not mention the AMA at all, except to point out that it was the AMA that persuaded the Carnegie Foundation to conduct its investigation.

It is also difficult to assign the AMA an exclusive role in the developments that occurred after 1910. The final events in creating the modern medical school—the acquisition of reliable sources of funds; the maturation of academic medicine; and the rise of the teaching hospital—proceeded for the most part independently of the AMA. Although the AMA supported those developments and worked vigorously in their behalf, many organizations and persons besides the AMA, as previously discussed, played even larger roles, and public sentiment also shifted firmly in favor of those causes. Indeed, the system that resulted was not entirely what the AMA wished. Had the AMA got its way, strict full-time positions in the clinical departments would never have been created. The General Education Board won that battle; the AMA lost. In short, the role of the AMA in the development of American medical education has been exaggerated even more than that of the Flexner report. The view that the AMA was the force that created the system is a myth.

The origin of this myth would appear to lie in the published reports and addresses of Colwell and Arthur Dean Bevan, the chairman of the Council on Medical Education. Colwell and Bevan continually gave the council credit for changes that archival records of the schools show to be unrelated to the council's work. For instance, Bevan attributed the wave of reform between 1906 and 1910—bad schools closing; good schools improving—to the AMA's first inspection of medical schools.[20] Records of the schools, however, show that these events occurred without any reference to the AMA. In 1928, Bevan maintained that nothing had happened in American medical education prior to the formation of the council in 1904 and that all subsequent changes resulted largely from the council's influence. "This whole movement owed its success primarily to the thorough reorganization of the American Medical Association,"[21] he wrote. From such unsubstantiated pronouncements has come the conventional view of the AMA's role.

Bevan and Colwell may be forgiven. They were zealots for their cause; they lacked a historical sense; they were oblivious to the broad forces that had been shaping medical education for half a century prior to the council's formation. Unfortunately, two generations of writers, including some brilliant scholars, have fostered the myth by studying the history of medical education from the *Journal of the American Medical Association* and the publications of the state medical societies rather than from the archival records of medical schools. In doing so, they have accepted the assertions of AMA officers at face value, without realizing that many of these claims cannot be substantiated by medical school documents. The result has been the perpetuation of a mythical view of the AMA and of how educational reform actually proceeded.[22] In recent years, a healthy counter trend has emerged, as several authors have begun to examine the role of the foundations in providing medicine's endowment. Nevertheless, this counter trend has not shifted much attention away from the AMA as the principal arbiter of reform. The myth has thus survived.

It would be a grave mistake, however, to view the AMA as an insignificant agency. It served medical education in many ways, its most important contribution occurring after 1910 as it helped procure strong state licensing laws. Between 1910 and 1930, its power in this arena was awesome. The AMA could think of the problems of medical education in a national way that even the strongest schools, concerned with their own particular problems, could not. Well organized, well financed, highly respected, and exceptionally adroit in the use of public relations, the AMA became the strongest force for state licensing. Herein lay its great impact on the reform of medical education. It was a role that was profound, even if much more circumscribed than commonly realized.

The Death of the Proprietary School

The AMA participated in medical licensing through its Council on Medical Education. The council, made up of five prominent medical educators from leading schools and a permanent secretary, established a rating system for medical schools: Class A (acceptable), Class B (needing improvements but redeemable), and Class C (in need of complete reorganization).[23] After 1914, schools that were operated for profit were automatically rated as Class C. This ranking system became the basis on which state boards judged medical schools. As early as 1914, Class C institutions were denied recognition in thirty-one states.[24] Similarly, the National Board of Medical Examiners, from its inception in 1915, examined only graduates of Class A schools.[25] Thus, schools that could not receive AMA approval were forced out of existence.

In evaluating medical schools, the Council on Medical Education employed a host of criteria, which were enumerated in its pamphlet "Essentials of an Acceptable Medical College." The council scrutinized every detail of a school's operations, including whether entrance requirements were rigidly enforced, whether school records were properly maintained, whether library and museum facilities were adequate, and whether courses were offered in the proper sequence. In practice, however, Class A ranking depended on three major conditions being met. One was having a large enough endowment. For lack of such, Bowdoin, Fordham, Southwestern, Washburn, Denver and Gross, Drake, and others were denied Class A rankings.[26] A second was the possession of adequate facilities for clinical teaching, preferably a teaching hospital under a school's own control. Dartmouth, Nebraska, Drake, Colorado, and Arkansas, among others, had their Class A ratings threatened or revoked for this reason.[27] The third was the presence of at least six full-time professors in the basic science departments and evidence of an active research program. Many schools lacking in this regard also came under the council's pressure. For instance, Colorado nearly lost its Class A ranking in 1913 for insufficient research, and Georgetown was placed in Class B in 1912 because it did not have full-time teachers.[28] Schools would be scolded for any deficiencies, but only the lack of endowment, teaching hospitals, or full-time faculty engaged in research seriously jeopardized Class A standing.

Of the three major criteria, it was the requirement of full-time faculty conducting research that created the most controversy. By World War I, only the owners of the profit-making schools were justifying the existence of those institutions. For the remaining schools, no one was questioning the wisdom of large endowments or proper hospital facilities. However, some still doubted whether every school needed to be a center of research. The president of Bowdoin, a reputable "practical" school, complained to Henry Pritchett: "I believe that there is room for an institution somewhere between the institutions you criticise and the ideal institutions which you approve. It is possible to overdo the side of research in a practical professional school."[29]

To the university teachers who comprised the Council on Medical Education, however, the time had passed when there was room for "practical" schools like Bowdoin. All schools, in their minds, had to follow the Hopkins model, hiring a minimum number of full-time faculty and making medical research a core activity. It was here that the council, like Abraham Flexner, had its most enduring effect on American medical education. Together, they imposed a single model of medical education on the country. Through the council, the nation's academic elite achieved their ultimate victory. By force of law, their view of how medical schools should be conducted became the national norm.

Amid intense pressure from the council, schools around the country had no choice but to conform to specifications. Most of these schools had been making genuine efforts to improve prior to 1910. The difference afterwards was that there was no longer any margin for failure. References to the AMA, conspicuous for their absence in faculty records prior to Flexner's tour of medical schools, now appeared with monotonous regularity. The Bowdoin faculty noted that "the Council had the power to destroy us" and feared that "it would soon make a hit in our direction."[30] The president of Southern Methodist University declared: "The American Medical Association today absolutely controls medical education. No institution can continue to exist without complying with its requirements."[31] Strong schools at this time still had little to fear from the AMA. Indeed, several of the leading schools—Harvard, Michigan, Pennsylvania, Chicago, Vanderbilt—had supplied the original membership of the council. Such schools had set the standard; they went about their business during World War I unaffected by the council's rankings and the new wave of licensing laws. Weaker schools, however, felt the full brunt of the council's wrath. Those that could not sufficiently improve were forced out of existence. As the president of Southern Methodist noted, "Students are not willing to remain in an institution that is ranked 'C.' "[32] A medical diploma meant very little if its holder was not allowed the license to practice.

Not many schools retired from the field meekly. Except for the diploma mills, almost all schools tried to remedy their deficiencies. For instance, fund-raising drives were launched at Southern Methodist, Washburn, Drake, Bowdoin, Fordham, and many other institutions, which ultimately all went out of existence. The difference between these schools and schools like Nebraska, Colorado, Georgetown, George Washington, Pittsburgh, and Tufts—institutions that were also under AMA pressure—was that the former schools failed, the latter succeeded. Schools in urban areas attached to strong universities stood the greatest chance of attracting the requisite funds and hospital facilities. Schools without those advantages were at much greater risk. They did not differ from the more successful schools in their understanding of how to teach medicine properly or in their desire to do so.

Most schools that closed did so without rancor. Faculties were understandably saddened that they had not acquired the means to remain operational, but they felt that they were better off leaving the work to others than teaching medicine without the proper facilities. For example, the president of the medical school of Washburn University, a school that struggled unsuccessfully to obtain funds, declared, "Washburn does not wish to stand in the light of an institution willing to lower the standards of medical education, and we would prefer to retire from the field rather than to do so."[33] Some colleges and universities associated with weak medical schools actually celebrated at being out of the business of medical education, as a medical school could consume a university's resources. The president of the University of Chattanooga told Henry Pritchett: "You will rejoice with me I am sure in the fact that our trustees at their last meeting decided to discontinue any relationship with the professional schools. We are now committed to the one task of developing a thorough-going College."[34] Only some of the diploma mills protested. For instance, the Bennett Medical College, a flagrantly commercial operation nominally affiliated with Chicago's Loyola University, fought the AMA and the Carnegie Foundation for years before finally being forced into retirement. A school official accused the AMA and Pritchett of hating Catholics.[35] In contrast, Fordham, an underfinanced but honest Catholic medical school that closed gracefully in 1921, did not find any religious prejudice in the low rankings given it by the AMA.[36]

For some schools, consolidation provided an alternative route to survival. The expenses incurred in teaching a class of twenty-five students were little more than if the class numbered seventy-five students, so high were the fixed outlays. It made sound financial sense for two or more weak medical schools to consolidate their resources into one strong institution. The trend toward consolidation had been underway before 1910, but afterwards the council's rankings provided the movement even greater impetus. Thus, in Baltimore, three mediocre schools—the College of Physicians and Surgeons, the University of Maryland (then loosely affiliated with St. John's College in Annapolis), and the Baltimore Medical College—consolidated into the present University of Maryland. In Atlanta, the Atlanta College of Physicians and Surgeons and the Atlanta School of Medicine merged in 1913 to form the Atlanta Medical College; two years later the school was taken over by Emory University. Medical educators knew that the merger of medical schools was just like the merger of any other corporate bodies. In an era in which efficiency had become a popular cult—when businesses everywhere were consolidating resources into large, centralized, efficient units—this approach proved popular.

Consolidation provided a viable solution when schools of equal mediocrity existed in a city large enough to sustain a good medical school. It also succeeded when a strong medical school absorbed a weak competitor, as when Western Reserve absorbed the Cleveland College of Physicians and Surgeons in 1910, or when the University of Colorado absorbed the Denver and Gross College of Medicine in 1911. Attempts at consolidation failed when both parties to the discussions were strong medical schools. Under Henry Pritchett's urgings, the University of California and Stanford considered a merger. In 1915, after five years of talks, negotiations reached an impasse. Stanford wanted equal representation on the new board; the University of California wanted five trustee positions to Stanford's three. Institutional jealousies overcame sound financial thinking and the two schools went their separate ways. Fortunately, each was strong enough to succeed on its own.[37] A similar situation occurred in Philadelphia, where representatives of Jefferson and the University of Pennsylvania held talks about consolidating the two schools. Discussions terminated in 1916 because the Jefferson trustees wanted equal power and representation on the new board, whereas the Pennsylvania trustees demanded majority control.[38] Unlike the common occurrence of strong schools absorbing the weak, no merger ever occurred between two leading schools. Academic rivalries made certain that would not happen.

Even when mergers could be effected, brutal disruptions sometimes occurred. Combining two or more proud, previously independent, faculties was never an easy task. Fierce arguments often ensued over academic rank, responsibilities, and authority. Always there were instructors in the amalgamated schools who felt slighted, if not frankly rejected. In 1913, for instance, two years after the University of Colorado absorbed the Denver and Gross College of Medicine, N. P. Colwell found that "there were many evidences of dissatisfaction or ill-feeling (how shall I describe it?) still remaining following the merger of the two schools." The school lacked an "enthusiastic, pull-together spirit" that kept it from being a "well-arranged, smooth-working machine for the training of medical students."[39] Ultimately tensions abated at Colorado, which was on its way toward becoming an outstanding medical school. Nevertheless, that path was littered—at Colorado and elsewhere—by uncounted persons who became sacrifices to the larger cause.

After 1910, proprietary schools died with amazing rapidity. By 1920, scarcely half a dozen diploma mills remained. By 1930, there were only seventy-six medical schools, all of which were of acceptable quality.[40] The heterogeneity that in 1910 had characterized the country's medical schools no longer existed. A homogeneous system of medical education had been created instead—one in which all schools shared in common the feature of academic excellence. The ideal standard of 1910 had been universally implemented: every school now followed the Hopkins model.

Although the number of medical schools ultimately fell to slightly more than one-half of its 1910 level, the reduction proceeded only half as far as that initially envisioned by Flexner. In 1910, Flexner had suggested that there be thirty-one medical schools serving the United States and Canada. He had not anticipated the degree to which state legislatures would come to the rescue of their medical schools, nor had he foreseen how academic rivalries would prevent consolidations between strong schools. For these reasons, the decrease in the number of medical schools never approached the magnitude he proposed.

In the drive to obtain stringent licensing, the AMA did not work alone. It had the most influential voice, but many groups and organizations also played a role. The most important among these was the AAMC. Others included the Carnegie Foundation, the Southern Medical College Association, and a variety of organizations of state licensing boards. Each of these groups worked in conjunction with one another, producing a strong reform coalition. In 1911, the AAMC began combining its annual meeting with those of the AMA and the Federation of State Licensing Boards.[41] That same year, John A. Witherspoon, a member of the Council on Medical Education, served as president of the AAMC. One medical faculty noted in 1912 how the AMA, the AAMC, and the Carnegie Foundation "play into each others hands."[42] All involved felt that such cooperation was necessary and desirable. Colwell told Pritchett, "Nothing must prevent the various organizations from working together in the utmost harmony."[43]

Nevertheless, the reform coalition contained much internal diversity. A healthy tension always existed among its members—one that still persists today. At times, the organizations appeared jealous of one another, concerned that someone else would receive credit for the changes underway. One medical faculty commented in 1911: "It is interesting to observe that each of these five organizations [Council on Medical Education; AAMC; Carnegie Foundation; National Board of Registration of Physicians and Surgeons; Federation of State Medical Boards] claims the chief credit for the notable advances in medical education of late years."[44] Sometimes they argued violently over the specifics of the reform program: whether evaluations of a particular school were too harsh or too lenient; which schools to aid and which to destroy; how rapidly standards could and should be raised. W. L. Rodman, the secretary of the National Board of Examiners, complained to Pritchett of the Council on Medical Education. "It is surprising how they [the council] insist upon running everything or putting obstacles in the way. They have so long been in the habit of having their own way that they cannot understand how anyone can think of opposing them."[45] Rodman was particularly annoyed with Colwell, who he felt would frequently "sanction and advocate things not in the interest of higher medical education." Rodman thus found pleasing a report that severely criticized Colwell's work.[46]

At one point the reform coalition nearly split apart. This occurred in 1914, when the different groups sharply disagreed over the issue of entrance requirements to medical schools in the South. The Council on Medical Education felt that schools in this region should adhere to the same admission standards as schools in the rest of the country, but the Carnegie Foundation (and later the National Board of Medical Examiners) felt that allowances should temporarily be made because of the much weaker condition of the educational system in the South. A crisis was precipitated when Abraham Flexner, who had already moved to the General Education Board, decided to take matters into his own hands. After visiting the University of Arkansas, apparently on his own initiative, Flexner wrote Arthur Dean Bevan a scathing letter:

> I am once more impressed with the folly and unwisdom of your policy and your complete ignorance of the situation. I have urged Dr. Smith [of the University of Arkansas] to serve summary notice on the Council that he will not ask any higher entrance standard, that he will not introduce a year of science, and that all reference to both these subjects shall be cut out of the medical catalog. ... The Council will either have to change its policy or we will organize a revolt which will practically detach the south from your field of operations at the present.[47]

A furious Bevan chastised Flexner for his "meddlesome interference."[48] Still outraged, Bevan wrote to Pritchett the next day, telling him that Flexner had become "simply impossible, and as far as we are concerned eliminates himself entirely from the situation."[49] A permanent rift might then have occurred, had not the more tactful Pritchett been able to mollify the parties, and had the educational system in the South not improved rapidly enough over the next several years to allow the more stringent admission standards to be met.

The slogan of the reformers had been "fewer and better doctors." Ironically, that never happened. By 1930, there were only fewer medical schools, not fewer doctors. As table 13.1 illustrates, the number of medical students was essentially the same in 1930 as in 1910, despite a temporary drop in enrollment that had occurred during the first decade following the Flexner report.[50] Over this period the proportion of physicians in the population did decrease slightly: from 154 per 100,000 in 1910, to 121 in 1930.[51] It is unlikely that this decline had any tangible effect on the availability of doctors, however, because the telephone, automobile, and good roads allowed the physician of 1930 much greater geographical range than his predecessors of 1910. A generation after the Flexner report, virtually no one feared that the country was not producing enough doctors. Even the socially concerned Commission on Medical Education felt in 1932 that "there is an oversupply of physicians in the country."[52] Only in the 1950s and 1960s, as the social climate changed, did a popular demand for more doctors begin to emerge. This reflected changing mores—the view that health care is a right—rather than any diminution in the number of physicians, for the ratio of doctors in the population was the same in 1958 as it had been twenty years before.[53]

Although the death of the proprietary school did not reduce the number of doctors, it did reduce the opportunities for immigrants, blacks, ethnic minorities, and other underprivileged groups to enter medicine. Admission to the proprietary schools had always been automatic; hence, for capable and dedicated working-class youths who lacked the formal educational qualifications, these schools offered the only opportunity to become doctors. Entrance requirements, which were required for a Class A ranking, effectively excluded most working-class youths. As discussed earlier, the net sociological effect of

TABLE 13.1
Medical Colleges, Students, and Graduates

Year	Number of Colleges	Number of Students	Number of Graduates
1910	131	21,526	4,440
1915	96	14,891	3,536
1920	85	13,798	3,047
1925	80	18,200	3,974
1930	76	21,597	4,565

NOTE: Council on Medical Education and Hospitals, "Medical Education in the United States," *Journal of the American Medical Association* 95 (1930): 504, table 5.

entrance requirements was much smaller than commonly thought. Because of the very high attrition rates that were occurring among poorly prepared students, the lower classes were being kept from the profession already. Nevertheless, the death of the proprietary school formalized this process. The opportunity for most disadvantaged youths to become doctors was revoked, even if few of them were any longer succeeding. Unless formal entrance requirements had been met, the "poor boy" who wished to enter medicine found the admissions door shut.[54]

Of all the oppressed groups, women suffered the most ironic setback. In the wake of the Flexner report, all but one women's medical college closed. Yet Flexner himself had been supportive of women in medicine. He felt that women made excellent physicians and that their place in medicine was "assured."[55] He attacked women's medical schools for the same reasons he opposed all underfinanced schools, but he did not challenge the idea that women should be doctors. To Flexner, the solution was coeducation. However, Victorian mores did not agree. In the years that followed, few schools promoted coeducation vigorously. Accordingly, the representation of women in the medical profession remained very low (table 13.2), until the feminist movement of the early 1970s finally facilitated the entry of women into the profession in larger numbers.[56]

The proprietary school, so despised by the medical reformers, had left behind an honorable tradition. Although it is hard to sympathize with the dishonest schools, the weakest proprietary schools of 1910 were still far better than the best medical schools of 1870. All had expanded their course of instruction to four years, incorporated the scientific subjects, and offered at least a semblance of real scientific training. Moreover, as many medical educators of the period noted, graduates of these schools tended to migrate to rural

TABLE 13.2

Women in Medicine

Year	Number of Women Students	Percentage of All Students	Number of Graduates	Percentage of All Graduates
1904	1,129	4.8	198	3.4
1910	907	4.5	116	2.6
1915	592	4.3	92	2.6
1920	818	6.3	122	4.0
1925	910	5.2	204	5.1
1930	955	4.4	204	4.5

NOTE: Council on Medical Education and Hospitals, "Medical Education in the United States," *Journal of the American Medical Association* 95 (1930): 504, table 6.

areas and small towns, where there was less competition from graduates of prestigious schools—much as foreign medical graduates do today. With the death of the proprietary school, such areas were deprived of physicians' services. This occurred not as a result of anyone's intent but as a consequence of reformers' poor understanding of human nature and their preoccupation with issues that they considered more pressing. Flexner, like many others, had naively assumed that graduates of strong schools would just as readily disperse to rural as to urban areas.[57] He was wrong. They concentrated in the cities, not in the smaller communities. By 1930, the maldistribution of physicians had surfaced as a major public concern. In 1932, the Commission on Medical Education called the distribution of physicians in America "faulty." "Although there is an oversupply of physicians in the country as a whole, there is a relative shortage in certain areas because physicians are concentrated in the larger communities."[58] In the death of the proprietary school, the public had been served by obtaining better doctors, but not by the resultant maldistribution of doctors. Herein lay the origin of the maldistribution crisis of the present.

Although medical educators of 1930 lamented the unequal distribution of physicians, they nonetheless took great pride in what they had accomplished. They had created modern university medical schools, and they had brought about the demise of the proprietary schools. Nevertheless, medical educators had failed to accomplish either of these tasks on their own. Without the assistance of the public, both through the infusion of funds and the enactment of licensing laws, the modern medical school would not have been created, and the proprietary school would not have been exterminated. The medical profession had realized its goals, but it had sacrificed its autonomy. The public, not the profession, gained the ultimate control. The profession's actions the past half century have sometimes suggested that it is oblivious to its public obligations. In this, the profession proceeds at its own risk, however, for an irate public at any time could decide to redress its grievances.

Standardization

Licensing laws had a dual effect on American medical education. They brought about the death of the proprietary school and they also helped standardize medical education at the university schools that remained. In establishing legal requirements, licensing boards followed guidelines prepared by the AMA and AAMC. In this way, medical educators collectively influenced the boards; few of them disagreed with the general principles incorporated into the state laws. Once licensing laws were established, however, schools had to yield to the dictates of the state boards. Even if a school strongly disagreed with the particulars of a state law—or merely thought a particular detail was foolish—it had no choice but to submit. Medical schools thus became bound by the rules of the larger system they had helped create.

During World War I and the 1920s, as today, state laws varied considerably from each other in their details.[59] As a result, a vast number of unimportant differences could be found from school to school. No two schools adhered to identical calendars, provided the same number of hours of instruction in each of the subjects, offered the same proportion of didactic and practical work, preserved identical amounts of time for home study, followed the same examination procedures, or adhered to the same requirements for admission and graduation. Nevertheless, insofar as every state board based its law on a common standard—the recommendations of the AMA and AAMC—the net effect was decidedly in the direction of uniformity. Medical education at every school in the country became very much alike. The numerous differences in details could not obscure the overriding similarities.

Standardization was much needed. In the early twentieth century, demand for physicians' services had been rapidly growing. The successes of scientific medicine and the attendant publicity they had received made the public eager to have doctors readily available. At the same time, society had become much more mobile. With increasing regularity, doctors were practicing in areas other than where they had been trained. This posed a problem: how was the public to know which physicians it could trust? Before the new state licensing laws were passed, the public knew for certain the quality only of physicians who had attended local schools. For instance, residents of Missouri and southern Illinois recognized the difference between graduates of St. Louis University (a good school) and the American Medical College (a very poor school in St. Louis), but inhabitants of other parts of the country were unlikely to understand that distinction.[60] If a medical graduate were to move to a distant community, the knowledge of where he had gone to school would not often be informative concerning his competence and qualifications.

The new licensing laws solved this problem. A medical license now certified a doctor's credentials to a public that might not be familiar with his place of training. Standardization thus allowed doctors to be distributed safely and efficiently to the expanding national market. A doctor trained at any school could now practice almost anywhere in the country with the public's confidence. For this reason, William Osler called the movement toward uniform licensing laws part of the process of "concentration, fusion, and consolidation [that] are welding together various subunits in each nation."[61] Readers of Robert Wiebe will recognize in state licensing another way in which the country was transformed from a society of "island communities" into an integrated, cohesive nation.[62]

Licensing laws engendered trust in a physician's qualifications. All who practiced now carried the imprimatur of the state. Yet licensing laws created problems as well, for they imposed new constraints on the educational activities of the medical schools. Regulations were now ordered, structured, formalized. State boards did not permit exceptions to be made, even for educationally valid reasons. For the sake of uniformity, schools lost the flexibility to deal with the unusual circumstance or to experiment and innovate. Medical schools came to be hindered by the same legislative bureaucracy that they needed to achieve their internal professional goals.

The inflexibility of state boards was particularly conspicuous in four areas. One involved the subject matter of the curriculum. To guarantee competence, state boards specified the minimum number of hours that a school must provide in each subject. However, as medical knowledge continued its phenomenal growth, some subjects became obsolete and others grew in importance, and yet state laws did not permit any reduction in hours below a specified minimum. So that new or growing subjects could be accommodated, the curriculum became even more distended than before. In 1925, scheduled instruction at some schools consisted of as much as 1,200 hours a year, and few schools provided much elective time.[63] The Commission on Medical Education complained bitterly of the situation:

> Faculties and licensing bodies have endeavored to add new subjects and to institute new examinations without deletion of obsolete requirements. The outcome has been great overcrowding of the curriculum and the creation of a body of external regulations which have made it difficult to adapt the training to changing conditions in the community, in the profession, and in education.[64]

Second, and clearly related to the first, schools were not permitted to accommodate the individual needs and interests of their students. Some students aspired to careers in laboratory research, others in surgery or internal medicine, still others in psychiatry, and many were undecided. All were forced to undergo exactly the same training. Franklin Mall had spotted this tendency as early as 1899 and had made it the object of his biting pen. "The great complaint of the good student is coercion. Reared in a free atmosphere, accustomed to great liberty during his college years, he enters the medical school with intellectual slavery staring him in the face."[65] Year-by-year, however, the problem grew worse. One medical educator in 1915 noted the fundamental problems "in attempting to produce four or five types of a marketable product of physicians from a single system of training."[66] William Thayer two years later felt that medical schools were applying "methods designed for school boys to serious-minded men."[67] No one was denying that a future psychiatrist needed a firm scientific foundation or that an aspiring bench worker would benefit from clinical exposure. Rather, they doubted whether all students needed exactly the same preparation. As long as the curriculum was too crowded to permit electives and more latitude of choice, a diversity of educational experiences could not be provided.

The third area pertained to the length of medical training. Not all students were equal in abilities, preliminary education, and interests. A few students were clearly superior; others had difficulty in keeping up with their peers. A four-year program worked for most—but not all. The unusually gifted and well-prepared student might easily complete his studies in three years. The inquisitive student might wish to linger a year or two longer, studying some subject in more depth. As Mall noted, "We all know that students are very unequal in ability, as well as in capacity for work, and why should they all pursue the same course of study?"[68] However, to ensure the competence of everyone, state boards allowed no student to deviate from the standard path. Pennsylvania and Columbia, neither a fraudulent institution, were among the schools that once had established accelerated courses for gifted students, only to be forced by licensing boards to discontinue their programs. Its plan, the dean of Columbia complained, was "an unqualified success from an educational standpoint," but it was "not possible to reduce the time some legislatures deem necessary for the acquisition of a sufficient amount of knowledge to qualify a student for the degree, no matter what his mental ability may be."[69] The first-generation American medical educators who created the system had been inspired by the German ideal of "liberty" in education, but the crowded, rigid program that resulted sometimes seemed more like totalitarianism instead.

Fourth, state boards allowed medical schools no discretion to admit qualified students who had not met the formal entrance requirements, which, by the end of World War I, consisted of two years of college. No medical educator disputed the importance of a proper educational background prior to embarking on medical studies. However, many did believe that entrance requirements should make allowances for the capable student who lacked the standard academic credentials. At a time the school system was still developing, this was not a theoretical issue. A strong preparatory or high school could easily provide a better scientific preparation than many colleges could offer.

Thus, in 1915, even a leading school like Michigan encountered trouble from the state board of Pennsylvania for its practice of admitting students who had done two years of college-equivalent work at a normal school rather than at a university. Michigan, a pioneer of educational reform and a truly great medical school, certainly had no intent to deceive or evade standards, but it was forced by the state board to discontinue that policy.[70] Similarly, the Pennsylvania board in 1914 refused to allow graduates of Tufts to take the licensing examination until the school discontinued its policy of admitting promising students "on condition."[71] On another occasion, Tufts fell under the scrutiny of the Council on Medical Education for admitting a handful of students with unconventional educational backgrounds. After inspection, the council admitted it had no objection to what Tufts had done, but it feared that the students were still "apt to have trouble" when they came before some of the exacting state boards.[72]

Medical educators expressed greater consternation over the rigidity of entrance requirements than over any other legal constraint. In 1914, for instance, A. Lawrence Lowell, Charles Eliot's successor as president of Harvard University, expressed deep reservations over what he termed "excessive formalism" in entrance requirements. The higher standards being enacted were generally desirable, he admitted, but they made no provision for the exceptional "man of power" who had prepared himself differently. Lowell pointed out the results of a study of Harvard College alumni. Performance in medical school correlated with excellence in college work, not with the subjects a student happened to have pursued. *Cum laude* graduates in the humanities performed better at medical school than students with mediocre academic records who had concentrated in the natural sciences. To Lowell, the test for admission should be what a person knows and can do, not what courses he had taken.[73] Nevertheless, pleas such as that of Lowell went unheeded. State boards allowed no deviation from the standard they had established. As the years passed, and as the country's four-tiered educational system matured, entrance requirements as defined by the state boards became immune to challenge.

The constraints imposed by state boards were strongest in the two decades following the Flexner report. In the name of ensuring quality, state boards placed virtual straitjackets on the medical schools, severely restricting their ability to make exceptions or to develop the curriculum. Abraham Flexner complained sharply of this in 1925:

> The desire to stamp out unfit medical schools has also operated to strengthen regimentation. . . . Our present fetters were therefore forged in order to compel wretched schools to give unfit medical students a "better" training.

Now that that end has been measurably accomplished the means have become a fetich, blocking further improvement.[74]

The Commission on Medical Education expressed similar unhappiness with the excessive regimentation in 1932.[75]

Fortunately, an accommodation was already underway. The Federation of State Medical Boards, in response to proddings by the Association of American Medical Colleges, agreed in 1930 to grant the universities greater freedom in all curricular matters. The Federation transferred to the universities responsibility for the details of training, leaving for itself the duties of certifying schools and examining applicants for licensure.[76] This action allowed the schools much greater flexibility in planning their programs, and the decades that followed witnessed a new era of curricular experimentation and innovation.

Nevertheless, flexibility could proceed only so far. Despite their new willingness to allow medical schools the freedom to arrange the curriculum as they wished, state boards could not relinquish their primary function as the public's protector against inadequately trained physicians. Thus, there were limits to how much freedom could be allowed—anatomy could be reduced in hours but not eliminated. The core of the dilemma was that, for all the rhetoric about instilling university methods into medical education, no one could forget that medical schools were professional schools. Medical educators were trapped between their desire to approach medical education as graduate education and the reality that in professional education there are certain things that every doctor needs to know. Students had to learn principles, theories, and methods so that they could acquire the mental tools to be self-learners throughout life. They also had to learn facts of immediate practical importance so that they could practice medicine safely. This constituted the root of the tension between thinking and memorizing, between elective and required courses, and between a flexible and a highly structured curriculum. The tension between graduate and professional goals has never abated. Medical students today are encouraged one moment to take research electives in basic pharmacology; the next moment they are told that they *must* memorize drug dosages in the manner of schoolchildren. The greater freedom medical schools have received from state boards the past half-century has returned responsibility for educational policy back to the schools, but it has provided no resolution of the problem.

14 Modern Medical Education in the United States

BY the 1920s, the modern system of medical education in the United States had fully matured. In subsequent decades, American medical schools would grow dramatically in size and bureaucracy and the curriculum would continually be revised to reflect current knowledge. Nevertheless, these developments would be only modifications of the existing system, not changes in the system itself. American medical education in its main outline was to prove remarkably durable.

Modern medical education in the United States represented a logical response to the growth of scientific medicine. The new scientific subjects and clinical specialties could not be kept out of the curriculum, nor could the laboratory and clinical clerkship be excluded. Nevertheless, the system that developed was not an inevitable one. The decision that medical schools should serve an educational rather than an egalitarian role; the elimination of "practical," teaching-oriented schools; the degree to which research became enthroned; and the transfer of control of medical education from private practitioners to the newly created academic elite represented but a few of the choices made at every step of the process. At no point had there been an absence of alternatives. And with each step that was taken, someone, often unwittingly, paid a price.

The rise of scientific medicine and the creation of the new educational system it demanded were stirring achievements. The system that emerged, however, was far from perfect, and medical educators remained deeply concerned about how difficult the ideals of medical education were to realize in practice. The problems still have not been solved. In the 1980s, medical education has been under attack by many critics, including prominent university and foundation leaders, the Association of American Medical Colleges, the federal government, and the general public—not to mention the self-criticism of medical school officials themselves. What is striking is how little the complaints about medical education heard today have changed from those made by medical educators and informed citizens since the turn of the century. As the system of medical education has been durable, so have been the problems associated with it. If there is to be hope for sensibly addressing these issues, it lies in understanding how our system for training doctors—its positive features as well as its weaknesses—has evolved.

The Corporate Medical School

By the 1920s, the task of institution-building in medical education had been completed. The new scientific and clinical subjects had been introduced at all the schools, as had the laboratory and clerkship. Permanent sources of financial support had been found; new laboratories had been constructed and equipped; teaching hospitals had been acquired; and an army of full-time faculty members had been assembled. In addition, state licensing laws now made certain that no proprietary school would be permitted to survive. Abraham Flexner, the great critic of medical education, acknowledged only ten years after the publication of his report the remarkable changes that had occurred during the preceding decade. "Assuredly things have progressed in this country in the field of medical education much more rapidly than anybody could have supposed possible."[1]

There were many signs that a new era in medical education had started. A good medical education was now available at every school, not just the aristocratic schools. Johns Hopkins, for three decades the preeminent medical school in America, no longer had a monopoly on excellence. Abraham Flexner warned the school in 1921 "to face the problem as to whether the Hopkins was to remain either the first or among the first medical schools of the country, or whether it was in the course of the next decade to sink into an inferior position."[2] Johns Hopkins had not declined; other schools had caught up. In 1928, the Council on Medical Education discontinued its A, B, and C classification of schools. Now that the schools had become universally good, the ranking system had outlived its usefulness. Instead, the council and other medical educators began focusing more and more on the problems of postgraduate medical training (internship, residency, and fellowship). Accordingly, in 1919 the council first published its "Essentials for Approved Internships," and in 1920, it changed its name to the "Council on Medical Education and Hospitals." Work in undergraduate medical education was never viewed as complete, but by the 1920s it was clear to all observers that the task of institution-building had been finished. The system had been created; subsequent work was to be at the level of modifying and adjusting the system as necessary.

What was the nature of this new system? If the production of doctors is likened to the production of any industrial commodity, it becomes apparent that medical education had become mechanized—something that some had thought would never happen. Henry Jacob Bigelow, the Harvard professor of surgery who so violently opposed reform at the school in 1871, told the Massachusetts Medical Society that same year: "You cannot turn out medical men with the uniform perfection of Ames shovels or Springfield muskets."[3] Bigelow was proved wrong. By the 1920s, medical schools, like other modern industries, had adopted standardized methods of production. All schools started with the same raw materials: students with the specified college credentials. The raw material was processed everywhere in the same way: the same courses in the same order, the same techniques of instruction, and approximately the same number of hours devoted to each subject. When production was complete, the state boards applied a final inspection—licensing examinations—which most graduates now passed with ease. Defective products could not entirely be eliminated—the continued existence of medical malpractice proved that point beyond dispute. Nevertheless, the new system was able, in the words of the faculty of the University of Pittsburgh, "to bring forth a product with the fewest failures."[4]

By the end of World War I, the medical school had thus become a factory, in the fullest sense of the term. Like all basic industry, medical education had become capital and labor intensive, requiring laboratories, teaching hospitals, endowments, and a large full-time faculty. The modern medical school bore no more resemblance to the medical school of the Civil War than the modern factory did to the craftman's workshop. The faculty of one medical school observed in 1906 that "the endowed schools, like the trusts in the industrial world, are driving out competition through the special advantages which a large capital gives them."[5] By 1910, proprietary schools had become institutional anachronisms: they were remnants of medical education's pre-industrial age. This was why by the time of the Flexner report they were already terminal. They had been replaced by a new industrial form—the university medical school—capable of churning out uniformly excellent products. As the modern business enterprise, according to Alfred Chandler, Jr., was "the institutional response to the rapid pace of technological innovation and increasing consumer demand . . . during the second half of the nineteenth century,"[6] so was the modern medical school.

The proprietary schools had to be abandoned; because the material requirements of medical education had become so vast, there was no possible way they could continue to compete. In their place, university medical schools with ample funds and facilities were needed, and revolution, not reform of the existing system, was required. The prescient John Shaw Billings recognized this fact as early as 1878: "It is useless to discuss methods of improvement for this [proprietary] class of schools; the only useful reform is one that will put an end to their existence."[7] This observation explains the fundamental paradox of American medical education of the late nineteenth century: why the caliber of medical instruction continued to lag far behind that of Europe, despite the presence since the 1850s of a growing number of American physicians who had studied in Germany and returned to the United States knowledgeable and enthusiastic about scientific medicine. In Germany, institutions capable of properly supporting medical teaching and research were already flourishing in the form of its universities. In the United States, no comparable institutions yet existed. Lasting educational improvements in this country could be made only after the institutions necessary to support them were created—that is, only after medical schools had taken a corporate form.

Nowhere was the corporate transformation of medical schools more apparent than in the emergence of a medical school bureaucracy. As the twentieth century opened, the administrative structure of medical schools was still informal and highly centralized, and authority lay in the hands of the dean and, at university schools, the university president. In the early 1900s, these officials were involved in the minutiae of a medical school's operations to a degree forgotten today. As late as World War I, for instance, faculty members of Western Reserve University thought nothing about asking President Charles Thwing to mediate a dispute regarding the scheduling of classes.[8] Deanships were part-time positions, with holders of that office also involved in teaching, research, and practice. At most schools, the dean's official duties were relatively simple: correspondence; record keeping; registering, seating, and cataloging students; issuing and distributing announcements and school bulletins; attending to matters of discipline; and overseeing examinations.

But if schools were to grow and develop, someone had to take charge of a school's operations, even at the sacrifice of his own scientific or clinical work. At school after school, this duty fell first to the dean. A nascent bureaucracy emerged as the deanship became a full-time office, with responsibility for a school's fund raising, development, faculty recruitment, and administration. By 1920, full-time deans were commonplace, and the positions of vice-deans, associate deans, and assistant deans were being created at many schools as well. To execute their duties, the dean and his staff needed executive skills rather than professional skills. In 1919, while searching for a new dean, the chancellor of the University of Pittsburgh described as the chief requirement for the position "business ability and tact." He thought that it was "more important to find a man who is more proficient in the business end of the thing than on the medical side, in case we cannot find one who is equipped on both sides."[9] In the deanship, entrepreneurship became institutionalized. Some doctors began to spend their full time creating the conditions under which others could work—a far cry from the dean of the 1800s, whose responsibilities represented only minor, annoying diversions from his other professional activities.

Medical schools were never to stop growing in bureaucratic complexity. Even by the 1920s and 1930s, the schools had become much larger and more difficult to run; a dean could no longer properly supervise every aspect of a school's affairs. Important administrative duties began to be performed by the department chairmen. In 1935, the chairman of the department of internal medicine at Cornell complained of this.

> Unless measures are taken to counteract this tendency, the full-time professor who has made his name as a clinician-teacher and investigator will become nothing more than an executive, a sort of hospital superintendent, living on his past reputation. This is far from the idea of a chief who can act as the leader of a highly trained group of younger men.[10]

The rise of medical school bureaucracy, however, was inexorable. Since World War II, medical schools have grown phenomenally, and individual departments have become as large as entire schools had formerly been.[11] As a result, by the 1980s, much administrative responsibility has passed from department heads to division and unit chiefs within the departments. Medical schools are no longer centralized units; they have come to consist of many autonomous departments, each with its own internal rules and procedures. In their governance and administration, not just in their operations, the schools have assumed a corporate form. Medical schools have thus experienced a bureaucratic fate not unlike that of government, business, and other branches of higher education.

Recent Trends

Medical education is never a finished commodity; it is always changing and evolving. In recent decades, three directions in medical education have been especially conspicuous.

The earliest development was the emergence of numerous distinctions and factions within academic medicine. As medical schools grew in size and complexity, a division of labor appeared. In the 1920s, more and more full-time faculty members were choosing careers in clinical practice, teaching, research, or administration. Some, like William Thayer, derived greatest satisfaction from patient care and teaching. Thayer, appointed professor of medicine at Johns Hopkins in 1918, found he did not enjoy executive work and decided to remain in the chair only until a suitable person could be hired to replace him.[12] Others within academic medicine were mostly interested in research, such as the neurosurgeon Walter Dandy, who told officials of Vanderbilt he was not interested in the deanship at any salary because it would take him away from his investigations.[13] Still others, in contrast, sought out administrative positions. For instance, David Edsall, the dean and professor of medicine at Harvard Medical School, resigned his professorship in 1923 to devote his energies exclusively to his work as dean. Between 1918 and 1935, under his leadership, the capital funds of Harvard Medical School increased from $5 million to $17 million.[14] Although most academic physicians continued to pursue clinical practice, teaching, research, and administration in some combination, many faculty members began to emphasize some types of pursuits over others. As they did so, the world of academic medicine, as the world of private practice, became highly differentiated.

The most startling differentiation occurred between the scientific and clinical departments. With the development of clinical science, academically-inclined physicians more and more eschewed the preclinical for the clinical departments. This was understandable. Considering the two clinical years of medical school and the one or two years of hospital internship that physicians routinely took, it would have been astonishing if most of them, influenced by their contact with disease, had not been interested in pursuing more clinically oriented problems. The rapid development of the clinical laboratories provided that opportunity. But at the same time a void was created, and the basic science departments were taken over by those with Ph.D.'s. This phenomenon has been most thoroughly studied in the case of biochemistry but similarly occurred in anatomy, physiology, microbiology, pharmacology, and the other fundamental disciplines.[15]

By the 1920s, a sharp gulf had already come to separate the preclinical from the clinical departments. Clinical and basic scientists had different intellectual orientations: the former investigated questions of disease and therapeutics, while the latter pursued topics of fundamental biology without concern for immediate clinical relevance. In addition, animosities and jealousies added to the gulf. The Ph.D.'s resented the greater income and prestige of the physicians; the clinical scientists strongly resented the arrogance of the Ph.D.'s, who often acted as though they had a monopoly on good research.

However, most of the tension arose from the fact that the scientific and clinical departments had become opponents in a struggle for power. Traditionally, the strength and prestige of American medical schools had resided in the basic science departments. By the 1920s, with the growth of clinical science and the implementation of the full-time system in the clinical disciplines, the clinical departments had gained parity. Clinical departments began to demand —and receive—resources that previously had gone to the basic science departments. The situation at Washington University was typical: one school official told Abraham Flexner in 1928 that "the most urgent need of the Washington University School of Medicine at the present time is the development of the fundamental preclinical departments. The clinical departments of the School have been considerably expanded during the past few years, but the preclinical departments have remained pretty much in *status quo.*"[16] Conflicts between preclinical and clinical departments were inevitable as they battled each other for funds and facilities. At Yale, there was an overt "antagonism of interest between the clinical and pre-clinical halves" of the school.[17] At Harvard, a member of the pathology department feared that the school's plan to develop the clinical departments would create "immediate disaster in the topics of the first two years."[18]

Battles within the modern medical school did not stop at those between the preclinical and clinical departments. Departments of biochemistry and pathology vied for control of preclinical teaching; departments of medicine and surgery likewise struggled for dominance of the clinical curriculum. After World War II, with the proliferation of subspecialization, even more factionalism and internal strife arose. Divisions of general surgery and cardiothoracic surgery competed for influence within a department of surgery. Divisions of cardiology and endocrinology similarly competed within a department of medicine. Within endocrinology divisions, thyroid and diabetes units contended with each other for funds, resources, and opportunities. Weary deans, responsible for the overall integration and direction of a school's affairs, had to struggle, so it sometimes seemed, merely to hold a school together. "Town-gown" disputes were not the only feuds within the medical profession. Also very real were the many quarrels and disputes among the full-time professors themselves.

A second and more recent direction in medical education has been the curriculum experimentation that many medical schools have undertaken since the 1950s. These experiments generally arose in response to medical specialization, which by the 1950s had proceeded far beyond anyone's earlier expectations. The result of specialization was a crowded, highly structured curriculum in which subjects were taught as a series of isolated disciplines rather than as integrated branches of medicine. A particularly great divide separated the preclinical from the clinical teaching, for the scientific courses, now taught primarily by Ph.D.'s, focused on fundamental scientific concepts and seldom drew clinical correlations. Students often did not feel as if they were even in medical school until the third year of study.

Complaints about the fragmentation of the curriculum had been voiced since the turn of the century. It was only in the 1950s, however, that a sense of crisis emerged and that medical schools for the first time made concerted efforts to correct the problem. The most famous of these experiments was the adoption of a novel "integrated" curriculum in the early 1950s by Western Reserve, the story of which has become the subject of a recent book.[19] Other experiments followed, including some highly innovative programs at many of the new medical schools established in the 1960s. The thrust of these various efforts at curriculum reform has been to provide better integration of the laboratory and clinical teaching, greater emphasis on the medical humanities, and more elective time.[20]

A third recent direction in medical education has been the remarkable expansion of biomedical research, which began after World War II. Fueled by the enormous infusion of federal funds, medical schools of the 1980s pursue research to a degree scarcely envisioned even a generation ago, and to accommodate research, medical schools have grown to staggering proportions. The size of the faculties, the number of support personnel (technicians, research assistants, business and administrative staffs), and the physical facilities and equipment earmarked for research have become awesome. Medical schools today are big businesses, with yearly budgets of tens of millions of dollars and large bureaucracies to oversee their operations.

The expansion of the research enterprise has brought with it some impressive achievements. It has allowed academic medicine to grow and thrive to a degree that would have flabbergasted the creators of the system, and it has resulted in an impressive and still growing body of medical knowledge. Indeed, clinical science has begun to repay its debts to the natural sciences from which it sprang, for the pursuit of medical questions has produced many discoveries of fundamental biological importance. The study of inborn errors of metabolism led to an articulation of the one-gene one-enzyme concept; the study of the pneumococcus (the bacterium that produces the most frequent kind of pneumonia) led to the discovery that the "transforming agent" is deoxyribonucleic acid (DNA); investigation of sickle cell anemia and other disorders of the blood protein hemoglobin led to our present understanding of the structure and function of the gene; the pursuit of nutritional diseases resulted in the discovery of the vitamins; and the study of endocrinological diseases led to the identification of many hormones and to our present understanding of how the hormones work. No one could any longer doubt the academic stature of clinical science.[21]

Nevertheless, the enthronement of research has produced many problems. From the beginning of the modern era, a critical question plaguing medical schools has been where and how to draw the line between teaching and research. Since the 1920s, that line has been drawn very far in the direction of research, often to the detriment of good teaching. Yet, not everyone has agreed with that philosophy, and for decades many have continued to argue that research in American medical schools has been overemphasized. Doubts about research have persisted in part because the enterprise itself has grown so large, and in part because medical schools have had new duties to fulfill. In the early twentieth century, the primary responsibilities of medical schools were teaching and research, not patient care. By 1930, with the advent of the teaching hospital, medical schools had expanded their role to include the provision of medical services to the community. However, the enthronement of research contributed to a relatively insular position of the academic medical center that could undermine its efforts to deliver patient care just as it sometimes impeded its efforts to provide good teaching. With research institutionalized, teaching and patient care could both easily be shortchanged. This has been the basis of complaints from the 1920s through the present that academic medical centers are isolated from the conditions of practice and not sufficiently responsive to community needs.[22]

This situation would have come as a shock to the institution-builders who created the modern medical school. The first and second generation medical educators envisioned a university spirit pervading all of a school's activities, but they saw research, teaching, and patient care as closely and harmoniously intertwined. Little did they foresee the degree to which research would come to dominate the American medical school or how semi-autonomous research institutes would be created within the schools. Abraham Flexner, whose view of research was to "work much; publish little," would have been dismayed to learn of the imbalance that has arisen at many schools between teaching, research, and service.[23]

These recent directions—the numerous efforts at curriculum reform; the preoccupation with research; the specialization within academic medicine; and the enormous growth in size of the medical school—have been important indeed. However, all represent an evolution within a system of medical education that was mature by the 1920s; no recent development has fundamentally changed the system itself. Knowledge has grown immensely in the past sixty years, with many new subjects added to and others dropped from the curriculum. But the theory of how medical students should acquire knowledge has not changed in that time. In 1984, the Association of American Medical Colleges released an important and widely publicized report (the "GPEP" report) on training physicians for the twenty-first century. The study concluded that medical education should prepare students "to learn throughout their professional lives rather than simply to master current information and techniques." To accomplish this, students must be "active, independent learners and problem solvers rather than passive recipients of information."[24] These tenets have long been held by medical educators. That the curriculum of the 1980s has lessened the time given to anatomy and that the curriculum of the future might include courses on computers represent needed changes in subject matter, not changes in teaching methods or in our ideas of how medical learning should be conducted.

Similarly, how much research a medical school should accommodate, or which departments or divisions should receive priority in development, are different issues from whether research belongs in a medical school in the first place. Medical schools have grown recently in size, bureaucratic complexity, and resources committed to research, but the institutional structure and values that permitted research to flourish were in place by the 1920s. Revisionism by that time was not only intellectually respectable but central to medical knowledge and practice. Faculty members knew they had the duty to expand knowledge and overturn the fallacies of the past. If the corpus of medical knowledge were not to grow and change, the enterprise would be a dismal failure.

Thus, although these recent trends in medical education have been highly visible, they have represented developments within a mature system, not changes in the system itself. A physician of today would be familiar with the medical school of the 1920s, as well as with the methods of teaching, but he would find the medical school of the 1860s strange and archaic. Conversely, an American physician of the 1860s would be much more at home at a European medical school of centuries ago than he would at a medical school in his own country in the 1920s. The system of medical education of the 1920s is the system that continues to serve the public today. Both the strengths and failings of medical education of the present are legacies from that period. In the 1980s, as perturbations of the American social and economic scene threaten a redefinition of medical practice—who is to enter medicine, who is to pay for medical education, and how and where medical practice is to be conducted—it is important to assess the balance sheet as to how medical education has served its various constituencies.

Successes and Failures

No mid-nineteenth-century American observer would have recognized medical education in his own country a century and a quarter later. Gone was the repressive, stifling grind of instruction by lectures alone. Through laboratories and clinical clerkships, students had been made active participants in their learning. Instruction had been expanded from sessions of sixteen weeks to thirty-four or thirty-six weeks, and from two terms to four. The curriculum had been changed to reflect the profound growth of medical knowledge. All the scientific subjects had been introduced, as had each of the clinical specialties. Medical schools had acquired imposing physical plants. New laboratories had been constructed and equipped; new libraries and museums had been installed; and modern teaching hospitals had been acquired. The faculties had grown enormously in size, and control of medical education had fallen into the hands of a large corps of full-time teachers. With their huge budgets, enormous plants, large staffs, and bureaucratic organizations, medical schools had become big businesses.

Similarly, no nineteenth-century observer would have recognized the place of the medical school in the country's educational system. Medical schools had lost their earlier independent status and, instead, had been integrated into the universities. The multiplicity of paths to a medical career of the nineteenth century—the apprenticeship; the house pupil system; the private summer schools—had all disappeared. Because powerful universities allowed no encroachment on their educational turf, the only alternative path that remained was foreign study. Since World War I, however, this had been an unnecessary and seldom used option for students who could gain admission to an American school.

Medical schools had also become tightly articulated with the other components of the educational system. They stood perched atop a four-tiered system that consisted of grammar schools, high schools, colleges, and graduate and professional schools. Students had formerly entered medical school with a diversity of educational backgrounds; now that fluidity no longer existed. Admission, once a formality, now involved arduous course work at the college level. With high entrance standards, access to medical school became more difficult for the underprivileged, who had less opportunity to receive a good preliminary education. On the other hand, with carefully selected students, medical education became more efficient. The high attrition rates of nineteenth-century medical schools vanished. By the 1970s, attrition rates over the four-year course of study had fallen to less than 1.5 percent.[25] Virtually all who were selected for medical school now became doctors.

American medical education of the twentieth century had become the best in the world. Once subordinate to medical education in Europe, American schools now were internationally envied. Instead of Americans going abroad to receive the best medical training, Europeans came here. This change had become apparent as early as World War I. A quick "dash across the sea for a few weeks" is sometimes worthwhile, Harvard's Richard Cabot explained in 1918. However, he cautioned: "No more of the months and years in German clinics. Today that is a waste scientifically and sometimes harmful in other ways."[26] Decade by decade, American medical schools have grown continually stronger, and today their international leadership remains unchallenged.

American medical research, as American medical education, had also become preeminent. The twentieth-century American medical school, unlike its nineteenth-century predecessor, provided a secure home for original investigation. Some schools have always pursued research more aggressively and successfully than others. Even today, 75 percent of current federal expenditures for medical research are received by only forty schools.[27] Nevertheless, even at the less prestigious institutions research has become a core activity. By 1930, American medical research had ended its colonial subservience to Europe. In 1934, George Whipple, George Minot, and William Murphy were the first American physicians to receive the Nobel Prize in Medicine and Physiology.[28] Since World War II, American medical research has been in a phase of even more rapid development and has become unequalled in both the quantity and quality of work.

As medical education had matured, so had the medical profession. Weak and disorganized in the nineteenth century, the medical profession had become powerful and much more unified by the twentieth. Part of the transformation resulted from the greater cohesiveness of the present-day profession. With the decline of the medical sects, all medical practitioners arose from the same scientific nexus. Long forgotten were the vitriolic public disputes between "regulars" and "sectarians," between medical societies and medical schools, and among individual physicians that tarnished the nineteenth-century medical scene. A more important change, however, was that the profession became heterogeneous as it became cohesive. In the mid-nineteenth century, almost all "regular" physicians were private practitioners. By the twentieth, the profession had differentiated into the worlds of medical practice, academic medicine, hospital administration, and public health, and within each of these broad areas were numerous smaller worlds. At times, the various groups would act in concert with each other and at times not. Feuds between professors and practitioners, medical schools and hospitals, basic scientists and clinical scientists, or general practitioners and medical specialists were no less real for being less publicly visible. Recognition of these internal distinctions and inner tensions is indispensable to understanding the sociological development of the medical profession. To ignore them, portraying the medical profession as a monolith represented by the American Medical Association—as many have done—results in distorted and inaccurate accounts of the profession's development.

In the growth of our present system of medical education, all parts of the medical profession achieved their major goals. For physicians oriented toward academic medicine, career opportunities now existed. The bitter frustrations of the pioneering medical scientists who were routinely denied positions or forced to work under the most deplorable conditions were now a mere memory. The American medical professor of the twentieth century had become just as respected as the German medical professor of the nineteenth century.

Similarly, practitioners had achieved their ambitions. The profession of medicine had captured the prestige, power, and income that had eluded it throughout the nineteenth century. As one manifestation of this change, a career in medicine had become highly sought after. In the nineteenth century, medical schools could easily accommodate all who applied for entrance, but in the twentieth century, demand outstripped supply. By the 1970s, there were three applicants, almost all of whom were academically qualified, for every one position.[29] Students denied admission had to enroll in medical schools abroad if they still hoped to become doctors.

In the development of modern medical education, the public, too, had benefited. In the middle of the nineteenth century, it had little faith in the efficacy of medicine; a century later that situation had dramatically changed. Certainly the public continued to be aware of the limitations of medical practice. There were few definitive therapeutic cures beyond infectious, nutritional, and endocrinological diseases, and many have worried about retaining the art of medicine in a technological era. Nevertheless, the twentieth-century citizen, unlike his nineteenth-century predecessors, could take comfort that medicine had developed objective clinical effectiveness and that where it could not cure it could usually help. In addition, the public could now be confident of the training received by the average physician. In the twentieth century, all who entered medical practice were properly prepared. This contrasted markedly with the situation in the nineteenth century, when a thorough medical education was reserved for the fortunate few who could supplement their medical lectures with other educational experiences such as foreign study or private tutelage.

For all involved, however, the benefits of modern medical education came only at severe costs. A great price was paid by the academic community that developed the system. The modern medical school had been created by a large number of innovative, entrepreneurial persons—deans, department chairmen, prominent professors and investigators—who became slaves to the bureaucracy they had erected. In the fullest sense of the term they became organization men. They had created an institutional structure that provided opportunity and security to academic physicians such as themselves, but in the process they sacrificed their earlier independent spirit. The academic freedom of a university professor is a different type of independence from economic freedom. Medical professors, as all university professors, had to define their positions within an emerging bureaucratic framework. Every professor was now vulnerable to the whims of tenure committees, research foundations, and other academic bodies. Medical professors no longer worked for themselves but for others. They had become subjugated to the institutions they had helped create.

Nowhere was this more apparent than in the quest for funds. For all its power and prestige, the academic establishment had become dependent upon those who supported its activities. From the beginning of the modern era medical scientists had known this and had felt the need to demonstrate to their benefactors that continued patronage was justified. The scientific directors of the Rockefeller Institute for Medical Research, for instance, felt the controlling hand from afar of John D. Rockefeller. In the early years, they issued many sensational press releases hoping to prove to the founder that his investment had been worthwhile.[30] Over the decades, episodes of overt control have been few, but the specter of control has always been present. Any medical grant writer of today who has searched for ways to relate his research to popular crusades like those against cancer or heart disease can testify to this. Medical educators had realized their goal of acquiring funds to pursue their academic interests, but they had irreversibly surrendered the autonomy of medical education to those who paid the bills.

In addition, academic physicians had become the victims of their own success: they had trained their competition. After World War II, medical specialists and subspecialists were turned out at record rates. These doctors began to compete for patients with the academicians who taught them. Today, patients in the suburbs no longer necessarily need to go to teaching hospitals for specialty care; many services formerly available only at teaching hospitals can be obtained at many community hospitals as well. With federal educational subsidies currently declining, patient revenues have become more important than ever to the financial vitality of teaching hospitals, especially those in inner city areas that serve large medically indigent populations. To attract paying patients, some teaching hospitals have begun to resort to aggressive marketing, but so have many of the competing community hospitals. "Town-gown" feuds were formerly matters of ego; now they have become matters of economics as well.

Practitioners of medicine also paid a great price for the modern system of training. They had gained a monopoly on medical practice, but they had lost control of medical education. Leadership in scientific and educational matters now belonged to the academic establishment, which controlled entrance to the medical schools, assembled the curriculum, provided most of the teaching, discovered new knowledge, wrote the textbooks, and dictated to the private practitioners what should be considered "standard medical practice." Although practitioners had acquired social status and economic power, their influence within the medical profession had greatly waned, for professional reputation had become largely a matter of academic accomplishment. The richest and most skillful practitioner with the largest number of patients would seldom be known outside the geographical range of his practice, but a prominent professor of physiology or pediatrics or surgery living in the same community might easily have a name recognized by physicians and medical students around the country, if not the world.

In addition, practitioners, like other new professional groups, quickly

learned that their newfound social position—based on knowledge and expertise rather than land, wealth, and family name—could not be passed on to
their heirs. Physicians, of course, like all well-to-do parents, could provide their
children many advantages, but the children, unlike the children of the traditional aristocracy, ultimately had to succeed on their own. Countless thousands of physicians whose sons and daughters have been denied admission to
medical school have painfully learned this lesson.

Medical students, too, paid a stiff price for the privileges of modern
medical training. Far from being the invigorating experience it was intended
to be, medical education had become brutal in the intellectual and physical
demands it placed upon students. Enormous amounts of material to master;
sleepless nights spent in study or "on call" at the hospital; humiliating treatment by instructors who sometimes made it clear they would much rather not
be with students—all contributed to a demanding and sometimes demeaning
experience that could leave even the strongest student exhausted and cynical.
In 1925, Abraham Flexner expressed concern. "A student staggering under
such a burden cannot, except sporadically, stop to read, work, or think at
random."[31] Flexner's remarks presaged complaints from medical educators of
the present about "angry" and "battered" medical students.[32] Even with
today's more flexible curriculum, the medical course remains rigid and bloated,
and weary students continue to reel under an overwhelming load. The pioneering medical educators who developed the system had never thought that
medical school would be easy, but they had not anticipated how inhumane the
experience would sometimes be.

To make the situation of medical students even worse, it quickly became
apparent that the four-year program could provide only the fundamentals of
medical knowledge. With the continuing proliferation of biomedical information, a medical school education no longer sufficed, even with an overstuffed
curriculum. An evergrowing amount of postgraduate instruction became necessary. During World War I, the average physician took one and one-half years
of internship and entered practice at the age of twenty-eight years.[33] Today,
depending upon the specialty chosen, many physicians do not enter practice
until their mid-thirties. Ever since the 1870s, when the length of the medical
school course was first extended, there has been an ongoing tension between
the need to provide students an adequate corpus of knowledge and technique
and the equally important need to have students finish training at a reasonable
age. In theory, one could study medicine forever; in practice, a physician at
some point must enter the field. With the relentless growth of knowledge, the
former viewpoint has scored every major victory while the latter has suffered
each corresponding defeat. To a twenty-one or twenty-two-year-old youth

beginning the study of medicine today, the road to practice is as long as it is arduous.[34]

The road to practice has also become expensive. Tuition to medical school has been rising at a rate far exceeding the rate of inflation. In the 1982–83 academic year, the average tuition at private medical schools was $10,701, with a high of $19,000 per year. The average cost of tuition plus expenses at those schools was $18,000 annually, with costs running as high as $25,000. The mean debt of medical students who graduated in 1982 was $20,116, and it is estimated that the mean debt of students graduating in 1992 will be $58,000.[35] Traditionally, much has been said about how medicine is bankrupting the country, but the public has heard relatively little about how a medical education is bankrupting students and their families.

These debts will not be easy for physicians to repay. With today's growing surplus of doctors, competition in practice is increasing and physicians' incomes in the future are expected to be relatively lower than in the past. When graduates do begin earning "real" money—only after an additional three to nine years of relatively low pay in postgraduate training programs—fewer of them are likely to have impressive incomes. There is no reason to believe that doctors of the next generation will not earn generous livings, but the halcyon days—at least from the practitioners' standpoint—appear to be over.

Suffering the most from these changes have been students from lower-middle- and middle-income families. Scholarships for medical education have always been few; the rigors of training make part-time employment difficult to pursue; and federally subsidized programs to provide loans to medical students have been markedly reduced.[36] As a result, in the middle 1970s, the proportion of entering medical students from these groups dropped from 21 to 11 percent. These developments have also taken a great toll on the enrollment of minority students. Just when they seemed to be gaining a foothold in the profession—the enrollment of minority students peaked in 1974–75 at 10 percent—high tuition and the decrease in government-subsidized loans caused the proportion of minority medical students to fall.[37] Today, because of high educational costs, equal access into the profession is threatened more than at any time in history, including the period in which high entrance requirements were made mandatory. Medicine is in more danger than ever before of becoming the province of the very wealthy.

The public paid the greatest price of all for modern medical education. It quickly discovered that this was an extremely costly enterprise and that the expenses never stopped rising. Medical schools seemed like bottomless pits. Even in the 1920s, after hundreds of millions of dollars had just been doled out, no medical school felt that it had received enough assistance.

George Eastman, preparing in 1923 to give the University of Rochester School of Medicine another $2.5 million only three years after his initial gift of $5 million, explained: "If I had known his baby was going to grow so fast I should probably have told Flexner to take it back home in the beginning, but it is such a pretty baby that one does not want to give it up now without a struggle to help support it."[38] Would the baby eventually grow to consume its parents? This prospect has loomed increasingly large ever since, for the appetites of medical schools have not lessened. In 1974–75, the operating costs of the 107 medical schools then in existence were $3 billion—more than $28 million per school.[39] A decade later, a yearly budget of $28 million could easily be commanded by a single large department. Yet, no medical school has felt that it has had enough money. Schools have continued to judge their resources, as they have since the turn of the century, relative to their desires and to those of their competitors, not necessarily to their needs. Money has become a relative, not an absolute, scarcity. Small wonder that tuition keeps rising.

Medical schools have not cared where they acquired their money, even if it were at the expense of other branches of the university. As medical schools expanded, their huge technical requirements caused them to absorb disproportionately large amounts of a university's income. In 1972, medical schools, with 0.5 percent of the students, accounted for 10 percent of the expenditures on higher education.[40] To other university branches, this was cause for resentment. Relations between medical schools and other branches of the university were often as hostile as those between "town" and "gown." Medical schools had become university enterprises in the sense that they had adopted university values of scholarship but not always in the sense of becoming part of a harmonious, close-knit family. Indeed, it was the exception for the medical school even to share the university's campus. Here, Welch, Eliot, Flexner, and other creators of the system would have been deeply disappointed. They had envisioned friendly and close associations between university and medical school faculties. They had not foreseen the jealousies and antagonisms that would frequently mar relations between the two.

If the public thought medical schools had become expensive to support, it received an even ruder shock as it discovered how expensive modern health-care services could be. Rising health-care costs were in part related to the country's advanced system of medical education, for it was the research performed in the schools that led to the scientific, technologically-based care that cost so much to provide. Health-care costs had caused a public outcry as early as World War I, when the nation had its first serious flirtation with compulsory health insurance. At that time a week's stay in a hospital cost on the average between $10 and $14—trifling by today's standards, but imposing relative to the average worker's pay of $2 a day.[41] Even greater concern about costs was expressed in 1932, when the Committee on the Costs of Medical Care published a landmark study of the economic aspects of the prevention and care of illness.[42] Year after year, costs have continued inexorably to rise, causing more and more worry and consternation. Today, total health-care costs consume a staggering 10.8 percent of the gross national product, or over $360 billion a year. Medical care has become effective, but increasingly it has become inaccessible to the average person.[43]

The public's concern about medical costs has been accentuated because the return on its investment seems less today than it did a generation ago. Despite countless billions of dollars spent on medical education, medical research, and medical care, no discovery of the past thirty years has rivaled the impact of antibiotics in the 1930s and 1940s or the polio vaccine in the 1950s. Progress against cancer, heart disease, stroke, and degenerative conditions remains slow and frustrating. Much good has continued to come from medical research, but the improvement in the health of the population per dollar of total medical costs has been much less in recent decades than during the first half of the century. In addition, modern medical technology has created troubling ethical dilemmas that the present generation is the first in history to face. It is scarcely a surprise that there is much more public hostility toward medicine in the 1980s than in the 1950s.

Yet the public would be mistaken to blame the problems of health-care costs solely on the medical school or medical profession. In the past generation a political revolution has occurred within society that rivals the research revolution within medicine: the view that health care is a natural right. This dramatic change in public attitude, which continues to fascinate sociologists and political scientists, has resulted in an unprecedented demand for medical services. Thus, despite its complaints about costs, the public has continued to insist upon more medical care rather than less. Health insurance in many instances is no longer insurance in the traditional sense—protection against the economic costs of an unexpected catastrophe—but a type of prepaid medical plan that is expected to cover all medical costs, including those of routine health care.[44] Recent federal proposals to reduce expenditures for Medicare and Medicaid have been hostilely received by persons from almost every point of the political spectrum. The egalitarian streak in the national conscience makes it difficult to allow medical services to be available only to those who can afford them. Many feel that if the very rich can afford kidney dialysis or a heart transplant, then the government should make certain that no one is denied those services. For these reasons, Lester Thurow has pointed out that health-care costs do not represent a problem simply of economics or of rampant technology but a problem of ethics and social priorities.[45]

Future Directions

The discussion of health-care costs brings us to one of the greatest concerns of both medical educators and the public today: how much support should medical schools receive, and who should pay. At a time of record federal budget deficits, historically high interest rates, and government cutbacks in all areas of domestic spending, this is far from an idle question. Medical schools have already been squeezed. Federal support of medical research in recent years has been less generous than in the past, and the government is now proposing a major cut in the "education pass through"—the proportion of Medicare dollars that can be used to reimburse a hospital for expenses relating to teaching and research.[46] From 1970 to 1982, the percentage of all health-care dollars devoted to research and development declined from 3.9 to 2.9 percent, or $9.2 billion for research out of a total health-care budget of $317 billion. By the standard of any industry, this represents a very small investment in research and development.[47] Shock waves have been reverberating throughout academic medicine.

Medical educators, however, have not been passively watching traditional sources of support erode. Some enterprising medical and university entrepreneurs, in the tradition of William Welch and Franklin Mall, have forged new partnerships with industry to establish corporate sponsorship of campus biomedical research. In 1980, Hoechst A.G., a giant West German chemical firm, agreed to spend at least $70 million over ten years to create a department of molecular biology at the Massachusetts General Hospital, a Harvard Medical School affiliate. In 1982, the Monsanto Company agreed to provide Washington University at least $23.5 million over five years to support research on proteins and peptides. Other recent contracts include those between Dupont and Harvard Medical School ($6 million for fundamental genetic research), the Celanese Corporation and Yale ($1.1 million for basic research on enzymes), and Mallinckrodt, Inc. and Washington University ($3.8 million for research on hybridomas, a type of artificially created cell). University scientists are free to publish the results of their research, but the companies can request that work not be submitted for publication until the patent process has been started. The universities involved stand to gain millions of dollars of research support. The sponsoring companies are hoping for commercially applicable discoveries in the explosive area of biotechnology that conceivably could generate billions of dollars of profits.[48]

These contracts have been highly controversial in educational and scientific circles. Each has included numerous safeguards to protect academic freedom, but many observers still fear that major conflicts of interest might arise. At this time the future of corporate-sponsored campus research is uncertain. Nevertheless, as long as federal support remains lukewarm, universities will have strong incentives to pursue the corporations, and if even a portion of the commercial potential is realized, industry will be happy to comply. Thus, it appears very likely that such agreements will flourish and proliferate. If so, the impact on academic medicine will be profound. Potentially, corporate alliances could represent as important a development in medical funding as the advent of the foundations during World War I and the National Institutes of Health after World War II.

Yet, the new corporate-university alliances would only supplement, not replace, the traditional sources of funding, and here the public will have to reconsider how much it values its medical schools. Progress against many chronic illnesses has been distressingly slow, but the only way to make inroads is through further research. At the present this is not mere rhetoric. The startling developments in cell biology and molecular genetics offer genuine hope for eliminating or controlling many chronic diseases through biotechnology. This potential prolongation of life suggests other possible sources for funding. For instance, the life insurance industry—a $130 billion-a-year industry—has contributed very little to medical education and research. Yet, an increase of the average life span by only one week would bring the industry nearly $1 billion a year in additional premiums.[49] To support medical education and research properly is costly, but there are benefits to having the best-trained doctors and the most powerful medical research enterprise in the world, and there are dangers to not having such services widely available. Ultimately, the public will have to decide how much to spend. As with health-care costs, this is a matter of ethics and social priorities, not economics alone.

Regardless of who finances medical schools in the future, or whether research will be supported to the degree academicians believe it should, the present institutional framework of American medical education seems destined to remain intact. This cannot be said of medical practice, which already is changing dramatically. Doctors of today are practicing with more regulation and less autonomy than their predecessors, and it is becoming increasingly common for physicians to be employees rather than self-employed. The most important change in the pattern of practice has been the rise of corporate medicine, as typified by the investor-owned for-profit hospital chains like Hospital Corporation of America, Humana, and American Medical International. Scarcely noticed in 1970, the for-profit chains within a decade have become a conspicuous element of the health-care system. In 1980, Arnold Relman, the editor of the *New England Journal of Medicine,* called them the "most important health-care development of the day." He warned his readers of their dangers, however, for the "new medical-industrial complex" operated in violation of many traditional ethical assumptions underlying the health-care system.[50] Nevertheless, the chains appear likely to grow much larger, and they are considered by Paul Starr to be the most important development in the institutional structure of medical practice since physicians rose to professional sovereignty in the early twentieth century.[51] The chains are already influencing medical practice in that they are interested in hiring more generalists than specialists, and it is likely that corporation doctors in the future will have to undergo a "corporate socialization" so that their style of practice will reflect the policies of management.[52]

The fundamental insight into American medical practice today, therefore, is that it is changing in structure to accommodate the arrival of the corporation. The fundamental insight into American medical education, however, is that it is not changing in structure because by the 1920s it had already taken a corporate form. In the early twentieth century, the university medical school displaced the privately-owned proprietary schools, in a fashion analogous to the displacement of traditional private practice by corporate medicine today. Corporations, as this last chapter has emphasized, is what the university schools indeed are. With their huge plants, facilities, staffs, and financial resources, they could teach medicine employing numerous efficiencies of scale that no proprietary school could hope to match. In addition, they have adopted a corporate organizational structure. Medical schools are run by powerful executive "chiefs"—the department chairmen—whose enormous influence is matched only by their large degree of autonomy. Their role in the medical school is analagous to that of senior executives responsible for major divisions in large businesses. In the modern medical school, as the modern corporation, everyone is salaried. The rewards to employees—the full-time instructors—do not come directly from their contact with patients but from academic promotions—a move up the corporate hierarchy. These observations explain the remarkable constancy of the medical school over the past sixty years, even as the content of medical education and the structure of medical practice have so dramatically changed.

Indeed, the mature American medical school has long done its work amid a variety of settings for medical practice. Early in the century the nature of practice was transformed as the locus of medical care shifted from patients' homes to doctors' offices and as hospitals and dispensaries assumed more prominent roles as places where medical care was delivered.[53] For the past generation, solo practice has been on the decline. In its place has arisen group practice and salaried practice in health maintenance organizations (HMO's). The hospital corporation, important development that it is, is only the latest of many changes in the pattern of practice. The mature medical school has produced doctors to work in each of these settings, as it will continue to do for corporate medicine and for forms of practice that might yet appear. To medical educators, it is not important in which of these settings their products practice medicine, only that the graduates be well trained.

To look at American medicine another way, it is plausible to imagine the United States without private practice as we currently know it, but it is inconceivable to imagine the country without well-trained doctors and strong medical schools. Good doctors will continue to be needed, regardless of the setting in which they ultimately choose (or are forced) to practice medicine. If the physicians of tomorrow work for proprietary concerns rather than for themselves, they will still need to be knowledgeable, compassionate, skillful in the art of cost-effective medicine, and capable of remaining up-to-date once out of training. The challenge to the medical schools—as it long has been—is to produce such doctors. There is much work to be done to improve the schools, but no one is proposing abandoning them or trading them in for something else.[54]

Thus, the problems of producing good doctors today remain the traditional ones. The great scientific achievements that have revolutionized theory and practice have led to a bloated curriculum, a surfeit of facts, an emphasis on rote memory, and an inattention to the patient as person. There is so much technical material for students to master immediately that there is little time left for conceptualization and learning about the psychological and social aspects of illness. In the report on medical education recently released by the Association of American Medical Colleges, these were the issues that received the most detailed consideration.[55]

These problems are not new. In 1909, Eli H. Long, the president of the Association of American Medical Colleges, pointed out that "the greatest deficiency in the conduct of the medical course to-day" was "the failure to train the student to think and reason out matters for himself." Medical education, he explained, should "make our graduates thinking and reasoning men rather than encyclopedic men."[56] In 1918, Richard Cabot complained about "what is ordinarily left out of medical preparation." By this he meant "the *preparedness for treating a human being as if he possessed a mind, affections, talents, vices and habits good and bad,* as well as more or less diseased organs."[57] For over a century, the goal of medical education has been to produce thinking physicians, scientifically competent, who are sensitive to the emotional as well as the medical condition of the patient. Medical educators of each successive generation have reaffirmed their belief in that ideal. The problem has not been the validity of the ideal but the great difficulty of achieving it in practice. That most physicians are as good as they are is a tribute to the men and women themselves, for the system that prepared them is far from perfect.

How should these problems be addressed? If we are to produce thinking doctors, the lesson of history is that modifications of the curriculum matter very little. Proper organization and presentation of the material is indispensable. Yet to adjust the amounts of biochemistry and physiology, to decide whether to teach the scientific subjects sequentially or in conjunction with one another, to increase the amount of elective time, or to add new subjects in response to changes in medical knowledge—such approaches do not address the central task of developing students who are thinkers rather than memorizers. Other factors matter much more. One is that students be carefully chosen for the qualities of independence and critical capacity, not just for their ability to earn high grades. Medical schools have always been limited by the quality of students they admit. This remains true today, even though the students are incomparably better than those of a century ago. In its report, the Association of American Medical Colleges emphasized this point. The study concluded that scores on the Medical College Admission Test should be used only for screening applicants. Final selection decisions should be made on the basis of students' abilities "to learn independently" and "to acquire critical analytical skills."[58] As indicated earlier in the book, this is no easy task. It is much easier for an admissions committee to look at the grade point average than to assess an applicant's capacity for critical thought. Nevertheless, it is vital that the effort continue to be made.

To produce thinking doctors, history also points out that medical schools must value education vis-à-vis their many other functions such as research, obtaining grants, providing patient care, and running fellowship and residency programs. To become critical thinkers, students need careful supervision, a large amount of personalized attention, and instructors with the time and ability to engage in Socratic dialogues. These can be provided only if a school makes a real commitment to teaching. Consider the decisions made every day by assistant professors of pediatrics or surgery or internal medicine on how to spend their time. In the afternoon, after obligatory morning patient rounds have been completed, they can either work in the laboratory or return to the wards for discussions with students and house officers. Incentive to do the latter is markedly reduced when faculty members know that peer recognition and institutional promotion depend on their productivity in research. Instilling habits of thought in students is an arduous and time-consuming task; far simpler for instructors to ignore the students for more academically rewarding activities in the laboratory. As the GPEP report observed, the priority given to other activities at many schools has "militated against the education of medical students."[59] Stated bluntly, a medical school can revise the curriculum as much as it wishes, but all is for naught if it does not value and reward good teaching. For teaching to flourish, schools must be willing to promote and pay high salaries to good teachers, not just to good researchers. Some schools may complain of the expense or argue that money is better spent on research, but they must realize that if they do not consider the training of students to be a high enough financial priority, then no amount of juggling of courses will compensate.[60]

Finally, if medical schools are to produce caring doctors, history again forces us to recognize the limitations of formal instruction. In recent decades, many schools have begun to offer courses in the medical humanities. Such courses have represented a sincere response to a genuine problem, and few would deny the desirability of doctors being well rounded. Nevertheless, it must be remembered that compassion is not so much learned knowledge as it is a personal characteristic that can be nurtured in the proper environment. To think otherwise is to make the ultimate acquiescence to pedagogy—to believe that even caring can be taught. For this reason, medical educators for many years have contended that the way to instill the art of medicine lies less in course work than in the careful selection of students for their personal qualities and in making certain that students are exposed to clinicians who reinforce those attributes. They maintain that if empathetic teachers and practitioners are held in esteem by medical schools and offered to students as role models, then students are more likely to internalize those values. This is why the GPEP report placed so much emphasis on selecting students with the right "values and attitudes" for medicine and on establishing "mentor relationships" between faculty members and students.[61]

Today, medical education faces its most imposing challenge ever: the specter of science and technology running rampant. If the onslaught of information was great a century ago, it is overwhelming now. New technologies and tests are presently proliferating at an unfathomable rate. Perceptive writers such as Herbert Marcuse and Jacques Ellul have written cogently about the problems modern society is facing from uncontrolled technology. They have warned that technology is gaining a life and identity of its own, that it is threatening to act as society's master rather than as its servant.[62]. Nowhere are their observations more true than in the area of medicine. The problem of learning how to use technology properly, as Stanley Reiser has pointed out, is the greatest conceptual challenge facing physicians of the present and future.[63]

The proliferation of medical technology is a pressing concern for the public, not just for doctors. This is because the misuse of technology can, and does, result in depersonalized and exorbitantly expensive care. One must remember that doctors practice medicine the way they are taught. Whether physicians of the future will retain the personal touch and whether they will provide care in a cost-effective fashion depend very much on the quality of their training. In the end, many of today's greatest problems of medical practice become problems of medical education.

It is precisely because the practice of medicine has become so technologically dominated that the ideals of medical education developed over a century ago have become more important than ever today. As Charles Eliot, Henry Bowditch, William Pepper, Victor Vaughan, John Shaw Billings, Franklin Mall, William Welch, and William Osler spent their careers preaching, medical education should have a procedural rather than a substantive emphasis, thereby producing physicians who are thinkers rather than memorizers. The thinking physician, as they used the term, is the one who in the practice of medicine asks not "what is there to do?" but "should it be done?" This type of physician realizes that many techniques and procedures have limited applicability, that others have no role at all, and that in the great majority of cases the most reliable information is still obtained from the patient. The thinking physician thus orders fewer tests rather than more and thereby practices a type of medicine that is less costly and less hazardous for the patient. The "rule-of-thumb" practitioner, in contrast, practices "protocol medicine," ordering tests because they are there, not necessarily because they are needed, and thereby generates more costs and subjects his patients to greater risks and discomfort. He is deluded into believing he has mastered technology because he is using it, whereas the thinking physician who employs fewer tests actually understands the uses and limitations of technology much more. Critical thinking, in short, offers the way to keep science and technology in harness. Critical thinking is an elusive ideal—one that has frustrated medical educators in their attempts to impart it to students for over a hundred years. Nonetheless, it has become more relevant to medical education today than ever before. Medical educators have often failed, sometimes miserably, in achieving this ideal, but it is absolutely essential that they not abandon the effort.

Notes

Introduction

1. Such themes would not seem out of place to the growing number of writers who have been calling for the history of medicine to be interpreted in a broad cultural context. Many of these writers are cited in the notes.

2. The "Reed report" was intended to have the same effect on legal education as the Flexner report did on medical education, but that goal was never achieved. Both reports were sponsored by the Carnegie Foundation for the Advancement of Teaching. See Alfred Z. Reed, *Training for the Public Profession of the Law* (New York: Carnegie Foundation for the Advancement of Teaching, 1921). Useful analyses of the Reed report are found in Ellen Condliffe Lagemann, *Private Power for the Public Good: A History of the Carnegie Foundation for the Advancement of Teaching* (Middletown, Conn.: Wesleyan University Press, 1983), 75–84; William R. Johnson, *Schooled Lawyers: A Study in the Clash of Professional Cultures* (New York: New York University Press, 1978), 156–57; and Jerold S. Auerbach, *Unequal Justice: Lawyers and Social Change in Modern America* (New York: Oxford University Press, 1976), 102–29.

Chapter 1

1. Statistics of Joseph Jones, cited in H. H. Cunningham, *Doctors in Gray: The Confederate Medical Service*, 2nd ed. (Baton Rouge: Louisiana State University Press, 1960), 4. There is reason to believe that Jones's statistics underestimated the true incidence of illness and death. This was because many sick soldiers were discharged—often to die at home—and others tried to treat themselves in the camps. See George Worthington Adams, *Doctors in Blue: The Medical History of the Union Army in the Civil War* (New York: Henry Schuman, 1952), 222–23.

2. Adams, *Doctors in Blue*, 199–203.

3. Ibid., 135, 136; Richard Shryock, "A Medical Perspective on the Civil War," in Richard Shryock, *Medicine in America: Historical Essays* (Baltimore: The Johns Hopkins University Press, 1966), 92.

4. Cunningham, *Doctors in Gray*, 234; Adams, *Doctors in Blue*, 129.

5. "Minutes of Fourteenth Annual Meeting of the American Medical Association," *Transactions of the American Medical Association* 14 (1864): 32; Adams, *Doctors in Blue*, 38–41.

6. "Report of the Committee on Medical Education," *Transactions of the American Medical Association* 16 (1866): 589.

7. Accounts of American medical schools at mid-century are provided by William F. Norwood, *Medical Education in the United States Before the Civil War* (Philadelphia: University of Pennsylvania Press, 1944); Martin Kaufman, *American Medical Education: The Formative Years, 1765–1910* (Westport, Conn.: Greenwood Press, 1976); and William G. Rothstein, *American Physicians in the Nineteenth Century: From Sects to Science* (Baltimore: The Johns Hopkins University Press, 1972), 85–121.

8. N. S. Davis, *Contributions to the History of Medical Education and Medical Institutions in the United States of America, 1776–1876* (Washington, D.C.: Government Printing Office, 1877), 41.

9. Charles Eliot, "Public Health Service," *Harvard Alumni Bulletin,* 29 Jan. 1925, 527.

10. Report of committee on extending the length of the winter term of lectures, medical faculty meeting minutes, University of Pennsylvania School of Medicine, 15 Nov. 1880, University of Pennsylvania Archives.

11. On "mental discipline" as an educational philosophy of the nineteenth-century American college, see Laurence R. Veysey, *The Emergence of the American University* (Chicago: The University of Chicago Press, 1965), 21–56; and John S. Brubacher and Willis Rudy, *Higher Education in Transition: A History of American Colleges and Universities, 1636–1976,* 3rd ed. (New York: Harper & Row, 1976), 287–92.

12. Eliot, "Public Health Service," 527.

13. University of Michigan, *President's Annual Report* (1872), 12.

14. "Report of the Committee on Medical Education," *Transactions of the American Medical Association* 4 (1851): 420–23.

15. Harvard University, *Annual Report of the President and Treasurer of Harvard College* (1879–80), 33.

16. "Address of William O. Baldwin, M.D., President of the Association," *Transactions of the American Medical Association* 20 (1869): 70.

17. Martin Kaufman, *Homeopathy in America: The Rise and Fall of a Medical Heresy* (Baltimore: The Johns Hopkins University Press, 1971), 142.

18. Faculty meeting minutes, Western Reserve University School of Medicine, 28 March 1916, and 5 May 1916, Case Western Reserve University Archives.

19. Statutes of the Medical School of Maine (Records of the Medical Faculty), 31 March 1876, Special Collections, Bowdoin College Library.

20. Minutes of the Alumni Association of the Medical Department of Western Reserve College (1872–1915), 15 June 1910, Howard Dittrick Museum of Historical Medicine, Cleveland Health Sciences Library.

21. On disciplinary problems at nineteenth-century American colleges, see Veysey, *Emergence of the American University,* 32–40; Brubacher and Rudy, *Higher Education in Transition,* 123; and Frederick Rudolph, *The American College and University: A History* (New York: Random House, 1962), 96–99, 104–8.

22. A useful discussion of "black medicine" in the old South is found in Todd L. Savitt, *Medicine and Slavery: The Diseases and Health Care of Blacks in Antebellum Virginia* (Urbana, Ill.: University of Illinois Press, 1978), 171–84. Much needed is a definitive history of medical education for blacks.

23. On women in medicine see Mary Roth Walsh, *"Doctors Wanted: No Women Need Apply." Sexual Barriers in the Medical Profession, 1835–1975* (New Haven: Yale University Press, 1979); Barbara Harris, *Beyond Her Sphere: Women and the Professions in American History* (Westport, Conn.: Greenwood Press, 1978); and Richard Shryock, "Women in American Medicine," in Shryock, *Medicine in America,* 177–99. For an overview of the literature on women in the professions in America, see Joan Jacobs Brumberg and Nancy Tomes, "Women in the Professions: A Research Agenda for American Historians," *Reviews in American History* 10 (1982): 275–96.

24. "Address of Alfred Stillé, M.D., President of the Association," *Transactions of the American Medical Association* 22 (1871): 94.

25. "Address of D. W. Yandell, M.D., President of the Association," *Transactions of the American Medical Association* 23 (1872): 103.

26. Eleanor M. Tilton, *Amiable Autocrat: A Biography of Dr. Oliver Wendell Holmes* (New York: Henry Schuman, 1947), 295.

27. Henry Jacob Bigelow to W. Chayet, 10 March 1862, Dean's Office Files, c. 1839–

1900, Folder, "Committee on Examinations and Replies of Professors, 1862," Countway Library, Harvard Medical School.

28.   Henry Jacob Bigelow, *Medical Education in America* (Cambridge, Mass.: Welch, Bigelow, 1871), 79.

29.   Examples included the University of Pennsylvania and the College of Physicians and Surgeons (New York) in 1847. See Martin Kaufman, "American Medical Education," in *The Education of American Physicians: Historical Essays,* ed. Ronald L. Numbers (Berkeley: University of California Press, 1980), 14.

30.   "Report of the Committee on Medical Education," *Transactions of the American Medical Association* 22 (1871): 130.

31.   Norwood, *Medical Education in the United States Before the Civil War,* 432.

32.   William Osler, "The Fixed Period," in William Osler, *Aequanimitas with other Addresses to Medical Students, Nurses and Practitioners of Medicine,* 3rd ed. (Philadelphia: Blakiston, 1932), 387.

33.   "Report of the Committee on Medical Education," *Transactions of the American Medical Association* 23 (1872): 120; and John Shaw Billings, "Medicine in the United States, and Its Relations to Cooperative Investigation," *The Medical News* 49 (1886): 172.

34.   University of Michigan, *President's Annual Report* (1875), 9–10.

35.   William Welch, "Medical Education in the United States," in William Welch, *Papers and Addresses,* vol. 3 (Baltimore: The Johns Hopkins University Press, 1920), 121.

36.   On Redman, see Whitfield J. Bell, Jr., "John Redman, Medical Preceptor (1722–1808)," in Whitfield J. Bell, Jr., *The Colonial Physician and Other Essays* (New York: Science History Publications, 1975), 27–39.

37.   "Report of the Committee on Medical Education," *Transactions of the American Medical Association* 17 (1867): 364.

38.   Davis, *Contributions to the History of Medical Education,* 46. Evidence exists, however, that the apprenticeship continued into the twentieth century. At the Drake University College of Medicine, for example, students spent a full year in a doctor's office until a fourth year, designed to add greater clinical instruction, was added to the curriculum in 1903 (Drake University, *Bulletin* [June 1903]: 153).

39.   On the extramural schools, see Dale C. Smith, "The Emergence of Organized Clinical Instruction in the Nineteenth Century American Cities of Boston, New York and Philadelphia" (Ph.D. diss., University of Minnesota, 1979), 112–48.

40.   Cincinnati Hospital, *Annual Report* (1884), 8, History of Health Sciences Library and Museum, University of Cincinnati.

41.   Arch I. Carson, "Register of Internes of the Cincinnati Hospital, 1830–1900," p. 5, Cincinnati General Hospital Collection, Box M. 9. 1, Special Collections, University Libraries, University of Cincinnati.

42.   Charles B. Porter et al. to the Trustees of the Massachusetts General Hospital, 25 April 1892, File, "House Officers, History of," Massachusetts General Hospital Archives.

43.   Russell M. Jones, ed., *The Parisian Education of an American Surgeon: Letters of Jonathan Mason Warren (1832–1835)* (Philadelphia: American Philosophical Society, 1978), 2, 4.

44.   On the Parisian experience, see *The Parisian Education of an American Surgeon;* Russell M. Jones, "American Doctors and the Parisian Medical World, 1830–1840," *Bulletin of the History of Medicine* 47 (1973): 40–65, 177–204; Russell M. Jones, "American Doctors in Paris, 1820–1861: A Statistical Profile," *Journal of the History of Medicine and Allied Sciences* 25 (1970): 143–57; William Osler, "The Influence of Louis on American Medicine," in William Osler, *An Alabama Student and Other Biographical Essays* (New York: Oxford University Press, 1908), 189–210; and Walter R. Steiner, "Some Distinguished American Medical Students of Pierre-Charles-Alexandre Louis of Paris," *Bulletin of the History of Medicine* 7 (1939): 783–93.

45.   For a detailed look at one such school, see Edward C. Atwater, "The Protracted Labor and Brief Life of a Country Medical School: The Auburn Medical Institution, 1825," *Journal of the History of Medicine and Allied Sciences* 34 (1979): 334–52.

46.   Report of the Committee of the Medical Department of the University of Pennsylvania, Board of Trustee meeting minutes, 7 June 1859, University of Pennsylvania; and medical faculty meeting minutes, 25 April 1859, University of Pennsylvania School of Medicine.

47.   The major reward of being a medical professor was intangible: the recognition and

distinction of being a professor, as well as the calls to medical consultation that resulted from such status. Medical professors earned the predominant part of their income from private practice.

48. "Address of William O. Baldwin," 73.

49. The Northampton convention is discussed in Kaufman, *American Medical Education*, 79–82. Drake's essays, originally published in the *Western Journal of the Medical and Physical Sciences*, were collected in a book, *Practical Essays on Medical Education and the Medical Profession in the United States* (Cincinnati: Roff & Young, 1832). The reports of the American Medical Association on medical education appeared in various issues of *Transactions of the American Medical Association*.

50. "Address of Henry Miller, M.D., President of the Association," *Transactions of the American Medical Association* 13 (1860): 68.

51. Norwood, *Medical Education in the United States*, 344–45; Kaufman, *American Medical Education*, 127–28; Lesley B. Arey, *Northwestern University Medical School, 1859–1959* (Evanston, Ill.: Northwestern University Press, 1959), 32–70.

52. Edward Atwater has recently brought attention to the New Orleans School of Medicine in his essay, "Internal Medicine," in Numbers, *The Education of American Physicians*, 164–66. See also A. E. Fossier, "History of Medical Education in New Orleans from Its Birth to the Civil War," *Annals of Medical History*, n.s., 6 (1934): 427–47; and Norwood, *Medical Education in the United States*, 368–71, 401–2. E. D. Fenner's original descriptions of the school's clinical teaching are found in his "Introductory Lecture," *New Orleans Medical News and Hospital Gazette* 3 (1856): 577–600; and "Remarks on Clinical Medicine," *New Orleans Medical News and Hospital Gazette* 4 (1857): 458–72.

53. William W. Keen, "Medical Education," in William W. Keen, *Addresses and Other Papers* (Philadelphia: W. B. Saunders, 1905), 195.

54. On the Thomsonian movement, see Rothstein, *American Physicians in the Nineteenth Century*, 125–51; and Joseph F. Kett, *The Formation of the American Medical Profession: The Role of Institutions, 1780–1860* (New Haven: Yale University Press, 1968), 97–131. In the early nineteenth century a state-issued medical license was necessary to practice medicine in the United States. To receive a license, medical graduates had to pass an examination, which was usually administered by the state medical society. After 1820, the licensing requirements were gradually abandoned; by 1870, licensing laws had been repealed in virtually every state. Possession of a medical school diploma, however easily obtained, now sufficed to practice medicine. See Richard Shryock, *Medical Licensing in America, 1650–1965* (Baltimore: The Johns Hopkins University Press, 1967), 3–42; Kett, *The Formation of the American Medical Profession;* and Robert C. Derbyshire, *Medical Licensure and Discipline in the United States* (Baltimore: The Johns Hopkins University Press, 1969), 1–6.

55. Bigelow to Chayet, 10 March 1862.

56. On the Paris clinical school of the first half of the nineteenth century, see Erwin H. Ackerknecht, *Medicine at the Paris Hospital, 1794–1848* (Baltimore: The Johns Hopkins University Press, 1967); and Michel Foucault, *The Birth of the Clinic: An Archaeology of Medical Perception*, trans. A. M. Sheridan Smith (New York: Pantheon, 1973). In an important recent study, Toby Gelfand shows the continuity of nineteenth-century French medicine with its eighteenth-century antecedents. See Gelfand, *Professionalizing Modern Medicine: Paris Surgeons and Medical Science and Institutions in the 18th Century* (Westport, Conn.: Greenwood Press, 1980).

57. Walter B. Cannon, *The Way of an Investigator: A Scientist's Experiences in Medical Research* (New York: Norton, 1945), 32.

58. Quoted in Ackerknecht, *Medicine at the Paris Hospital*, 90.

59. Ibid., 126.

60. On the reception of the germ theory of disease in the United States, see Phyllis Allen Richmond, "American Attitudes Toward the Germ Theory of Disease (1860–1880)," *Journal of the History of Medicine and Allied Sciences* 9 (1954): 428–54. Although the antivivisection movement has been most thoroughly studied in England, some consideration of American attitudes on the subject is contained in James Turner, *Reckoning with the Beast: Animals, Pain, and Humanity in the Victorian Mind* (Baltimore: The Johns Hopkins University Press, 1980).

61. Oliver Wendell Holmes, *Teaching from the Chair and at the Bedside* (Boston: David Clapp, 1867), 20.

62. John Ware, Jacob Bigelow, and Oliver Wendell Holmes, "The Views of the Medical Faculty of Harvard University, relative to the extension of the Lecture Term," *Transactions of the American Medical Association* 2 (1849): 356.

63. Holmes, *Teaching from the Chair*, 7.

64. Brown-Séquard, born and trained in France, received the appointment of professor of physiology and pathology of the nervous system at Harvard Medical School in 1864. For three years he conducted experimental studies in physiology, maintaining his laboratory at his own expense, until poor health forced him to resign his position. See C. E. Brown-Séquard to George Shattuck, 17 March 1865, and 28 April 1865, Dean's Office Files, Folder, "Letters to and from Professor Brown-Séquard," Harvard Medical School.

65. Quoted in Ernest Earnest, *S. Weir Mitchell: Novelist and Physician* (Philadelphia: University of Pennsylvania Press, 1950), 54.

66. Quoted in Anna Robeson Burr, *Weir Mitchell: His Life and Letters* (New York: Duffield, 1929), 119.

67. Quoted in Simon Flexner and James T. Flexner, *William Henry Welch and the Heroic Age of American Medicine* (New York: Viking, 1941), 112–13.

68. "Report of the Committee on Medical Literature," *Transactions of the American Medical Association* 1 (1848): 287.

69. Richard Shryock, "American Indifference to Basic Science during the Nineteenth Century," in Shryock, *Medicine in America*, 71–89; Nathan Reingold, "American Indifference to Basic Research: A Reappraisal," in *Nineteenth-Century American Science, A Reappraisal*, ed. George H. Daniels (Evanston: Northwestern University Press, 1972), 38–62. On early nineteenth-century American science, see also George H. Daniels, *American Science in the Age of Jackson* (New York: Columbia University Press, 1968).

70. Sally G. Kohlstedt, *The Formation of the American Scientific Community: The American Association for the Advancement of Science, 1848–1860* (Urbana, Ill.: University of Illinois Press, 1976).

71. Richard Shryock, "The American Physician in 1846 and 1946: A Study in Professional Contrasts," in Shryock, *Medicine in America*, 149–76; Paul Elliot Starr, *The Social Transformation of American Medicine: The Rise of a Sovereign Profession and the Making of a Vast Industry* (New York: Basic Books, 1982).

72. "Minutes of the First Annual Meeting of the American Medical Association," *Transactions of the American Medical Association* 1 (1848): 7.

73. "Report of the Committee on Medical Education," *Transactions of the American Medical Association* 22 (1871): 114.

74. "Report of the Special Committee appointed to prepare 'A Statement of the Facts and Arguments which may be adduced in favour of the prolongation of the Courses of Medical Lectures to six months,'" *Transactions of the American Medical Association* 2 (1849): 359.

75. "Address of Thomas M. Logan, M.D., President of the Association," *Transactions of the American Medical Association* 24 (1873): 87.

76. The Warren family of Boston comprised one of America's great medical and social dynasties. See Rhoda Truax, *The Doctors Warren of Boston: First Family of Surgery* (Boston: Houghton Mifflin, 1968).

Chapter 2

1. I have been influenced in my choice of the term "infrastructure" by Alfred D. Chandler, Jr., who used the term in describing how the mid-nineteenth century revolution in transportation and communications underlay the transformation of the organization of American business that occurred later in the century. See Chandler, *The Visible Hand: The Managerial Revolution in American Business* (Cambridge, Mass.: Harvard University Press, 1977), 79–205. For a brief, theoretical discussion of how sudden historical change tends to be rooted in the past from which it comes, see George Rosen, "Critical Levels in Historical Process. A Theoretical Explanation Dedicated to Henry Ernest Sigerist," *Journal of the History of Medicine and Allied Sciences* 13 (1958): 179–85.

2. Erwin H. Ackerknecht, *Medicine at the Paris Hospital, 1794–1848* (Baltimore: The Johns Hopkins University Press, 1967); Michel Foucault, *The Birth of the Clinic: An Archaeology of Medical Perception*, trans. A. M. Sheridan Smith (New York: Pantheon, 1973).

3. William Osler, "The Influence of Louis on American Medicine," in William Osler, *An Alabama Student and Other Biographical Essays* (New York: Oxford University Press, 1908), 189–210; Walter R. Steiner, "Some Distinguished American Medical Students of Pierre-Charles-Alexandre Louis of Paris," *Bulletin of the History of Medicine* 7 (1939): 783–93. See also Russell M. Jones, "American Doctors and the Parisian Medical World, 1830–1840," *Bulletin of the History of Medicine* 47 (1973): 40–65, 177–204; Russell M. Jones, "American Doctors in Paris, 1820–1861: A Statistical Profile," *Journal of the History of Medicine and Allied Sciences* 25 (1970): 143–57; and James H. Cassedy, *American Medicine and Statistical Thinking, 1800–1860* (Cambridge: Harvard University Press, 1984), 60–67.

4. Ackerknecht, *Medicine at the Paris Hospital*, 121–27, 123 (quotation). A valuable overview of French higher education in the nineteenth century, with a particularly bleak portrayal of medical education, is Theodore Zeldin, *France 1848–1945*, vol. 2 (Oxford: Oxford University Press, 1977), 316–45.

5. William Coleman, *Biology in the Nineteenth Century: Problems of Form, Function, and Transformation* (New York: John Wiley, 1971), 48–49; Thomas N. Bonner, *American Doctors and German Universities: A Chapter in International Intellectual Relations, 1870–1914* (Lincoln: University of Nebraska Press, 1963), 15.

6. Helpful sources on the development of medical science in the nineteenth century include Richard Shryock, *The Development of Modern Medicine: An Interpretation of the Social and Scientific Factors Involved*, 2nd ed. (New York: Alfred A. Knopf, 1947); Erwin H. Ackerknecht, *A Short History of Medicine*, 2nd ed. (New York: Ronald Press, 1968); and Charles Singer, *A Short History of Medicine* (New York: Oxford University Press, 1928).

7. Coleman, *Biology in the Nineteenth Century*, 160–66.

8. Much has been written about experimental medicine in France; see especially John E. Lesch, *Science and Medicine in France: The Emergence of Experimental Physiology, 1790–1855* (Cambridge: Harvard University Press, 1984); and Frederic L. Holmes, *Claude Bernard and Animal Chemistry* (Cambridge, Mass.: Harvard University Press, 1974). Ironically, as noted in chapter 1, France boasted many great scientists in the laboratory fields that were closely related to medicine, but none of these persons ever held a professorship in a French medical school—a startling fact that illustrated, according to Ackerknecht, "the superb disdain in which French medicine held medical science" (*Medicine at the Paris Hospital*, 126).

9. On German scholarship in nonmedical areas, see Jurgen Herbst, *The German Historical School in American Scholarship: A Study in the Transfer of Culture* (Ithaca, N.Y.: Cornell University Press, 1965); Carl Diehl, *Americans and German Scholarship, 1770–1870* (New Haven: Yale University Press, 1978); and Fritz K. Ringer, *The Decline of the German Mandarins: The German Academic Community, 1890–1933* (Cambridge, Mass.: Harvard University Press, 1969).

10. Quoted in W. Bruce Fye, "Why a Physiologist?—The Case of Henry P. Bowditch," *Bulletin of the History of Medicine* 56 (1982): 23.

11. Ibid., 24–25.

12. Bonner, *American Doctors and German Universities*, 23.

13. Of great interest is how German scientific medicine moved east as well as west. See John Z. Bowers, *When the Twain Meet: The Rise of Western Medicine in Japan* (Baltimore: The Johns Hopkins University Press, 1980).

14. Bonner, *American Doctors and German Universities*, 13–14, 157.

15. Henry Hun, *A Guide to American Medical Students in Europe* (New York: William Wood, 1883), 3.

16. Bonner, *American Doctors and German Universities*, 23–30.

17. Ibid., 69–106. For a detailed look at medical education in Vienna, see Erna Lesky, *The Vienna Medical School of the 19th Century*, trans. L. Williams and I. S. Levij (Baltimore: The Johns Hopkins University Press, 1976).

18. George Rosen, "Carl Ludwig and his American Students," *Bulletin of the History of Medicine* 4 (1936): 609–50.

19. William Welch to his sister, 18 June 1876, William H. Welch Papers, Alan Mason Chesney Medical Archives, Johns Hopkins Medical Institutions.

20. "A Perfect Period of Study," comments by Simon Flexner on Welch's film address made in his 82nd year, 20 Aug. 1936, William H. Welch Papers.

21. William H. Welch, "On Some of the Humane Aspects of Medical Science," in William H. Welch, *Papers and Addresses,* vol. 3 (Baltimore: The Johns Hopkins University Press, 1920), 6.

22. Franklin P. Mall, "What Is Biology?" *The Chautauquan* 18 (1894): 412.

23. Walter B. Cannon, *The Way of an Investigator: A Scientist's Experiences in Medical Research* (New York: Norton, 1945), 32.

24. William Welch to Frederic Dennis, 5 Dec. 1877, William H. Welch Papers.

25. Quoted in Florence Rena Sabin, *Franklin Paine Mall: The Story of a Mind* (Baltimore: The Johns Hopkins University Press, 1934), 64.

26. Frederic Dennis to W. S. Walcott, 14 March 1884, William H. Welch Papers.

27. William Welch, "Some of the Advantages of the Union of Medical School and University," in *Papers and Addresses,* 32.

28. George W. Corner, *An Anatomist at Large: An Autobiography and Selected Essays* (New York: Basic Books, 1958), 32.

29. Fye, "Why a Physiologist?" 23–27.

30. Lillian E. Prudden, *Biographical Sketches and Letters of T. Mitchell Prudden, M.D.* (New Haven: Yale University Press, 1927), 54, 107–9.

31. Warren Lombard, "Notes for Report to Secretary of Harvard Class of 1878," n.d., Folder 1, Box 1, Warren Plimpton Lombard Papers, Michigan Historical Collections, Bentley Historical Library, University of Michigan.

32. "Copy of a Letter Written by Dr. John J. Abel to Dr. C. W. Edmunds, May 24, 1937, in regard to his Early Work in Pharmacology at the University of Michigan," Michigan Historical Collections, Bentley Historical Library, University of Michigan.

33. Daniel J. Kevles, *The Physicists: The History of a Scientific Community in Modern America* (New York: Alfred A. Knopf, 1977), 31, 37–38.

34. Charles Eliot, "Inaugural Address," in *Charles Eliot: The Man and His Beliefs,* vol. 1, ed. William Allan Neilson (New York: Harper & Brothers, 1926), 25.

35. Laurence R. Veysey, *The Emergence of the American University* (Chicago: University of Chicago Press, 1965), 174–75. On late nineteenth-century American scholarship, see Alexandra Oleson and John Voss, eds., *The Organization of Knowledge in Modern America, 1860–1920* (Baltimore: The Johns Hopkins University Press, 1979).

36. Illustrating the deleterious effect of pragmatic Jacksonian culture on medical research was a well-known episode involving James Jackson, Jr., one of the American students of Louis. In 1832, Louis wrote to Jackson's father urging him to permit his son to have four or five years of uninterrupted research. The elder Jackson vetoed the request and stated his reasons unequivocally: in the United States such a course "would have been so singular, as in a measure to separate him from other men. We are a business doing people. We are new. We have, as it were, but just landed on these uncultivated shores; there is a vast deal to be done; and he who will not be doing must be set down as a drone" (James Jackson, *A Memoir of James Jackson, Jr.* [Boston: I. R. Butts, 1835], 55).

37. The most valuable source on the development of higher education in the United States is Veysey, *The Emergence of the American University.* Other helpful works include Robert A. McCaughy, "The Transformation of American Academic Life: Harvard University 1821–1892," *Perspectives in American History* 8 (1974): 239–332; John S. Brubacher and Willis Rudy, *Higher Education in Transition: A History of American Colleges and Universities, 1636–1976,* 3rd ed. (New York: Harper & Row, 1976); Frederick Rudolph, *The American College and University* (New York: Alfred A. Knopf, 1962); Richard Hofstadter and Walter P. Metzger, *The Development of Academic Freedom in the United States* (New York: Columbia University Press, 1955); Richard Hofstadter and C. DeWitt Hardy, *The Development and Scope of Higher Education in the United States* (New York: Columbia University Press, 1952); Richard J. Storr, *The Beginnings of Graduate Education in America* (Chicago: The University of Chicago Press, 1953); and Burton J. Bledstein, *The Culture of Professionalism: The Middle Class and the Development of Higher Education in America* (New York: Norton, 1976).

38. The view of the antebellum college presented here, derived from sources in the preceding footnote, represents the standard portrayal of that institution. In recent years, a revisionist current of scholarship has depicted a much more optimistic picture of the old-time

college, suggesting that those institutions were much more intellectually respectable than previously thought. See, for instance, David Allmendinger, *Paupers and Scholars* (New York:. St. Martin's Press, 1975); Stanley M. Guralnick, *Science and the Ante-bellum American College* (Philadelphia: American Philosophical Society, 1975); and David B. Potts, "Curriculum and Enrollments: Some Thoughts on Assessing the Popularity of Antebellum Colleges," *History of Higher Education Annual* 1 (1981): 88–109.

39. Welch, "On Some of the Humane Aspects of Medical Science," 6.

40. William Welch, "The Advancement of Medical Education," in Welch, *Papers and Addresses*, 43.

41. Ibid., 43.

42. Eliot, "Inaugural Address," 3.

43. Welch, "Some of the Advantages of the Union of Medical School and University," 37.

44. Bowdoin College, *President's Report* (1898–99), 33.

45. University of Michigan, *President's Annual Report* (1882), 10–11.

46. Welch, "Some of the Advantages of the Union of Medical School and University," 28.

47. University of Michigan, *President's Annual Report* (1873), 12.

48. University of Michigan, *President's Annual Report* (1874), 18.

49. University of Michigan, *President's Annual Report* (1876), 11–12.

50. Ibid., 12.

51. Much controversy has arisen concerning the growth of the country's educational system. Writers of the previous generation tended to view the school system as a liberating instrument that promoted social mobility and individual opportunity, the essence of democracy. Recent revisionist interpretations have emphasized the class, racial, ethnic, and sex biases of the leaders of the public school movement, and these scholars have viewed the movement as fostering social control, not social mobility. To such writers, the primary function of the schools has been to provide workers for a capitalist economy and to promote "proper" middle-class values that would keep the workers attached to the system. For a review of this topic, see Laurence Veysey, "The History of Education," *Reviews in American History* 10 (1982): 281–91.

52. Brubacher and Rudy, *Higher Education in Transition*, 160.

53. Ibid., 257; and Bledstein, *The Culture of Professionalism*, 271.

54. Between 1890 and 1910, the number of students and teachers in American high schools increased more than fourfold, and by 1920 more than doubled again. By 1920, 8 percent of the country's college-aged youths were enrolled in some form of institution of higher learning, though of course many never graduated. See Robert H. Wiebe, *The Search for Order, 1877–1920* (New York: Hill and Wang, 1967), 119; and Brubacher and Rudy, *Higher Education in Transition*, 257.

55. Bowdoin College, *President's Report* (1891–92), 3–10; University of Michigan, *President's Annual Report* (1872), 10; Western Reserve University, *Reports of the President and Faculties* (1892–93), 5–6; and University of Nebraska, *Biennial Reports of the Board of Regents to the Governor* (1905), 8.

56. James Whorton, "Chemistry," in *The Education of American Physicians: Historical Essays*, ed. Ronald L. Numbers (Berkeley: University of California Press, 1980).

57. George W. Webster, "Report on the Curricula of American Medical Colleges," *New York Medical Journal and Philadelphia Medical Journal* 80 (1904): 207.

58. Kevles, *The Physicists*, 78.

Chapter 3

1. Major secondary sources on the history of Harvard Medical School are Henry Beecher and Mark Altschule, *Medicine at Harvard: The First 300 Years* (Hanover, N.H.: University Press of New England, 1977); Thomas Harrington, *The Harvard Medical School*, vols. 1–3 (New York: Lewis, 1905); Frederick C. Shattuck and J. Lewis Bremer, "The Medical School, 1869–1929," in *The Development of Harvard University since the Inauguration of President Eliot, 1869–1929*, ed. Samuel Eliot Morison (Cambridge, Mass.: Harvard University Press, 1930), 555–94; and Kenneth Ludmerer, "Reform at Harvard Medical School, 1869–1909," *Bulletin of the History of Medicine* 55 (1981): 343–70.

2. Harrington, *Harvard Medical School*, vol. 3, 1309; and Charles Eliot, "Public Health Service," *Harvard Alumni Bulletin* (29 Jan. 1925): 527.

3. Beecher and Altschule, *Medicine at Harvard*, 87.

4. The two best studies of Eliot are Hugh Hawkins, *Between Harvard and America: The Educational Leadership of Charles Eliot* (New York: Oxford University Press, 1972); and Henry James, *Charles W. Eliot: President of Harvard University 1869–1909*, vols. 1–2 (Boston: Houghton Mifflin, 1930).

5. *Annual Report of the President and Treasurer of Harvard College* (1869–70), 18.

6. *Annual Report of the President and Treasurer of Harvard College* (1870–71), 25.

7. James Clarke White (unsigned editorials), "Medical Education–New Professorships in the Medical Department of Harvard University," *Boston Medical and Surgical Journal* 74 (1866): 63–65; "Election in Harvard University," *Boston Medical and Surgical Journal* 74 (1866): 508–9; "Censorial Duties—Medical Education," *Boston Medical and Surgical Journal* 75 (1866): 105–7; "The Past and Present School of Paris," *Boston Medical and Surgical Journal* 75 (1866): 389–90.

8. White, "The Past and Present School of Paris," 390.

9. Ibid., 389, 390.

10. Henry Jacob Bigelow, *Medical Education in America* (Cambridge, Mass.: Welch, Bigelow, 1871); Oliver Wendell Holmes, *Teaching from the Chair and at the Bedside* (Boston: David Clapp, 1867).

11. Walter L. Burrage, "Henry Jacob Bigelow," in *Dictionary of American Medical Biography: Lives of Eminent Physicians of the United States and Canada, from the Earliest Times*, ed. Howard A. Kelly and Walter L. Burrage (Boston: Milford House, 1928), 95–97.

12. Hawkins, *Between Harvard and America*, 3–14. On the dedication to socially worthy causes among many Northern intellectuals of the patrician class after the Civil War, see George M. Fredrickson, *The Inner Civil War: Northern Intellectuals and the Crisis of the Union* (New York: Harper & Row, 1965).

13. No Harvard president had ever attended meetings of the medical faculty, much less assumed the chair. But Eliot chaired virtually every medical faculty meeting from his inauguration as president in 1869 until his retirement in 1909. His presence is documented in Harvard University Medical Faculty, Minutes of Meetings, Countway Library, Harvard Medical School.

14. Descriptions of these exchanges have been provided elsewhere. See Beecher and Altschule, *Medicine at Harvard*, chap. 5; Harrington, *Harvard Medical School*, vol. 3, chaps. 33–35; Shattuck and Bremer, "Medical School," 557–62; James, *Eliot*, vol. 1, 278–90; and Samuel Eliot Morison, *Three Centuries at Harvard, 1636–1936* (Cambridge: Harvard University Press, 1936), 338–41.

15. This episode is recounted in Hawkins, *Between Harvard and America*, 61.

16. Charles Eliot, "Inaugural Address," in *Charles W. Eliot: The Man and His Beliefs*, vol. 1, ed. William Allan Neilson (New York: Harper, 1926), 6.

17. Ibid., 6.

18. "Address of Dr. Bowditch," *Old Penn*, 11 June 1904, 3.

19. Ibid., 3.

20. Charles Eliot, "The New Education," *Atlantic Monthly* 23 (1869): 215–16.

21. Eliot, "Inaugural Address," 7–8.

22. Eliot, "The New Education," 216.

23. Harrington, *Harvard Medical School*, vol. 3, 1309–10.

24. During the 1874–75 academic session, the medical school of Syracuse University instituted a three-year graded curriculum with nine-month terms. From what I have been able to determine, however, the reforms were less radical than the others discussed in this chapter, since the lecture and recitation remained the primary teaching devices (*Annual Announcement and Catalogue of Physicians and Surgeons of the Syracuse University* [1874–75], 6–9). I have been unable to locate archival material from this period that might further illuminate the early reforms at Syracuse.

25. Report of the Committee of the Medical Department of the University of Pennsylvania, in Board of Trustees meeting minutes, 7 June 1859, University of Pennsylvania Archives, University of Pennsylvania.

26. Medical faculty meeting minutes, University of Pennsylvania School of Medicine, 20 Jan. 1866, University of Pennsylvania Archives.

27. Prior to 1877, opportunities for dissection were available, but dissection was not required.

28. Following the reforms, salaries for full professors ranged from $2,000 a year in physiology, materia medica, and morbid anatomy, to $3,300 a year in anatomy. These figures were approximately equal to what professors were receiving previously, when the average value of a chair was about $2,500 per annum. Medical faculty meeting minutes, University of Pennsylvania School of Medicine, 28 June 1879, and 25 April 1859, University of Pennsylvania Archives.

29. Medical faculty meeting minutes, University of Pennsylvania School of Medicine, 26 April 1864, University of Pennsylvania Archives.

30. Folder, "Robert Empie Rogers," Alumni Records Collection, University of Pennsylvania, University of Pennsylvania Archives; William Osler, "William Pepper," in William Osler, *An Alabama Student and Other Biographical Essays* (New York: Oxford University Press, 1908), 219.

31. William Pepper, *Higher Medical Education, the True Interest of the Public and of the Profession. Two Addresses Delivered Before the Medical Department of the University of Pennsylvania, on October 1, 1877, and October 2, 1893* (Philadelphia: J. B. Lippincott, 1894), 61.

32. James Tyson to the Faculty of the Medical Department, 1 Jan. 1873, in medical faculty meeting minutes, 28 Feb. 1873, University of Pennsylvania School of Medicine, University of Pennsylvania Archives.

33. See, for instance, C. H. Benns to William Pepper, 15 Aug. 1877, and William M. Ord to William Pepper, 15 Sept. 1877, William Pepper Papers, Rare Book Room, University of Pennsylvania Library, University of Pennsylvania. That Pepper displayed thorough familiarity with medical education in Europe is apparent in Pepper, *Higher Medical Education,* 5–59.

34. For instance, in 1876 the faculty had declared itself "ready to co-operate cordially in any needed forward movement, when such becomes practicable by the assurance of necessary endowment" (Letter from Medical Faculty to the Committee of the Board of Trustees on the Medical Department, 19 Feb. 1876, in medical faculty meeting minutes, University of Pennsylvania School of Medicine, 18 Feb. 1876, University of Pennsylvania Archives.

35. Report of Special Committee on the Medical Department, in Board of Trustee meeting minutes, University of Pennsylvania, 28 March 1876, pp. 3, 5 (quotation).

36. George Corner, *Two Centuries of Medicine. A History of the School of Medicine, University of Pennsylvania* (Philadelphia: J. B. Lippincott, 1965), 147; Pepper, *Higher Medical Education,* 70; *Annual Report of Provost and Treasurer of the University of Pennsylvania* (1883), 27.

37. Figures were obtained from the course listings in *Catalogue of the Trustees, Officers, and Students of the University of Pennsylvania* (1877–78), 58.

38. Ibid., 56–57.

39. Report of Special Committee on the Medical Department, 8.

40. "The Provost's Letter of Resignation," *Annual Report of Provost and Treasurer of the University of Pennsylvania* (1894), 36.

41. Wilfred B. Shaw, ed., *The University of Michigan: An Encyclopedic Survey,* vol. 2 (Ann Arbor: University of Michigan Press, 1942), 797; Folder, "Reports of various departments of the Medical School regarding the work completed during the years, 1880–1882," Box 72, Records of the Medical School of the University of Michigan, Michigan Historical Collections, Bentley Historical Library, University of Michigan.

42. University of Michigan, *President's Annual Report* (1878), 13.

43. University of Michigan, *President's Annual Report* (1883), 13; *President's Annual Report* (1890), 90; and *President's Annual Report* (1891), 16.

44. University of Michigan, *President's Annual Report* (1891), 27–29.

45. University of Michigan, *President's Annual Report* (1882), 9.

46. Victor C. Vaughan, *A Doctor's Memories* (Indianapolis: Bobbs-Merrill, 1926), 199, 210–11.

47. Ibid., 223.

48. The standard history of the early period of the Johns Hopkins Medical School is Allan M. Chesney, *The Johns Hopkins Hospital and the Johns Hopkins University School of Medicine: A Chronicle,* vol. 1 (Baltimore: The Johns Hopkins University Press, 1943).

49. Ibid., 1–6.

50.   Gert H. Brieger, "The California Origins of the Johns Hopkins Medical School," *Bulletin of the History of Medicine* 51 (1977): 339–52.
51.   A. McGehee Harvey, "John Shaw Billings: Forgotten Hero of American Medicine," *Perspectives in Biology and Medicine* 21 (1977): 35–57.
52.   Quoted in Fielding H. Garrison, *John Shaw Billings: A Memoir* (New York: G. P. Putnam's Sons, 1915), 393.
53.   Billings later recounted his medical school experiences at a meeting of the Harvard Medical Alumni Association: "In those two years I did not attend the systematic lectures very regularly. I found that by reading the text-books, I could get more in the same time and with very much less trouble. I practically lived in the dissecting-room and in the clinics, and the very first lecture I heard was a clinical lecture." He felt that "what has remained [of my medical school training] is what I got in the dissecting-room and in the clinics" (John Shaw Billings, "Speech at Meeting of the Harvard Medical Alumni Association," *Boston Medical and Surgical Journal* 131 [1894]: 141).
54.   John Shaw Billings, "Medical Education in Germany" (unpublished notes), Box 34, John Shaw Billings Papers, New York Public Library. The title appended to the notes is misleading, for the notes contain descriptions of medical education in all of the major European centers.
55.   John Shaw Billings, "Hospital Construction and Organization," in *Hospital Plans. Five Essays Relating to the Construction, Organization & Management of Hospitals* (New York: William Wood, 1875), 1–46; Billings, *Johns Hopkins Hospital. Reports and Papers Relating to Construction and Organization*, no. 1 (Baltimore: n.p., 1876); Billings, *Medical Education. Extract from Lectures Delivered Before the Johns Hopkins University, Baltimore, 1877–8* (Baltimore: William K. Boyle, 1878); Billings, "On the Plans for the Johns Hopkins Hospital at Baltimore," *Medical Record* 12 (1877): 129–33, 145–48; and Billings, "A Review on Higher Medical Education," *American Journal of the Medical Sciences* 76 (1878): 174–89.
56.   William Welch to Franklin Mall, spring 1893, quoted in Florence Sabin, *Franklin Paine Mall: The Story of a Mind* (Baltimore: The Johns Hopkins University Press, 1934), 113–14.
57.   William Osler, "The Fixed Period," in *Aequanimitas with other Addresses to Medical Students, Nurses and Practitioners of Medicine*, 3rd ed. (Philadelphia: Blakiston, 1932), 386.
58.   Chesney, *The Johns Hopkins Hospital*, 95–97, 193–221.
59.   Mary Roth Walsh, *"Doctors Wanted: No Women Need Apply." Sexual Barriers in the Medical Profession, 1835–1975* (New Haven: Yale University Press, 1977), 178–206.
60.   The delay in the opening of the Johns Hopkins Medical School allowed early faculty members like William Welch to cultivate their scientific associations at the university and instill a scientific spirit at the hospital while they were waiting for the medical school to open. Donald Fleming feels that this sequence of events contributed to the broad scientific spirit that pervaded the medical school from its inception. See Donald Fleming, *William H. Welch and the Rise of Modern Medicine* (Boston: Little, Brown, 1954), 81–82.
61.   William Osler, "The Hospital as a College," in *Aequanimitas*, 319, 325.
62.   "Address of D. W. Yandell, M.D., President of the Association," *Transactions of the American Medical Association* 23 (1872): 95.
63.   "Address of T. G. Richardson, M.D., President of the Association," *Transactions of the American Medical Association* 29 (1878): 94. The myth that the AMA contributed to the early reforms has been perpetuated by writers such as Morris Fishbein, who attributed Eliot's reforms at Harvard in 1871 to a desire to comply with AMA recommendations. See Fishbein, *A History of the American Medical Association 1847–1947* (Philadelphia: W. B. Saunders, 1947), 10.
64.   Alfred Stillé to Calvin Ellis, 30 May 1871, Dean's Office Files, c. 1839–1900, Box 1, Folder, "Letters April–July 1871," Countway Library, Harvard Medical School. Although Stillé indicated in this letter that he had learned of the reforms only through the school's advertisements and through editorials in the *Boston Medical and Surgical Journal*, he nonetheless called Harvard's new program another of "the trophies . . . for the reform movement which has been fostered & kept alive by the American Med. Association."
65.   N. P. Colwell, "Progress in Medical Education," in U.S. Department of the Interior, Bureau of Education, *Report of the Commissioner of Education* (Washington, D.C.: Government Printing Office, 1913), 33.
66.   Dean Smiley, "History of the Association of American Medical Colleges 1876–

1956," *Journal of Medical Education* 32 (1957): 512–14; and Ward Darley, "AAMC Milestones in Raising the Standards of Medical Education," *Journal of Medical Education* 40 (1965): 321.

67. Bigelow, *Medical Education in America,* 17.

68. Ibid., 14.

69. Franklin P. Mall, "The Anatomical Course and Laboratory of the Johns Hopkins University," *Bulletin of the Johns Hopkins Hospital* 7 (1896): 86.

70. William Sydney Thayer, "Self-Education Under Guidance," in William Sydney Thayer, *Osler and Other Papers* (Baltimore: The Johns Hopkins University Press, 1931), 228–46.

71. Billings, *Johns Hopkins Hospital,* 2.

72. John Shaw Billings, "The National Board of Health," *The Plumber and Sanitary Engineer* 3 (1880): 47.

73. John Shaw Billings, "Schools" (unpublished lecture), Box 41, John Shaw Billings Papers, New York Public Library.

74. John Shaw Billings, *Waste* (Oxford, Ohio: n.p., 1895), 9.

75. Osler, "The Hospital as a College," 315.

76. John Shaw Billings, "The Medical Journals of the United States," *Boston Medical and Surgical Journal* 100 (1879): 1–2; Wilburt C. Davison, "Reflections on the Medical Book and Journal Situation," *Bulletin of the History of Medicine* 11 (1942): 182–200.

77. Victor Vaughan, "The Medical School During the Administration of President Hutchins from October 1909 to June 1920" (typed report), n.d., Box 8, Records of the Medical School of the University of Michigan, Michigan Historical Collections, Bentley Historical Library, University of Michigan. As late as 1876, the Michigan medical library subscribed to only one French and one German medical journal.

78. William T. Porter, "The Teaching of Physiology in Medical Schools," *Boston Medical and Surgical Journal* 139 (1898): 652.

79. William Osler, "After Twenty-Five Years," in *Aequanimitas,* 201.

80. Burton J. Bledstein, *The Culture of Professionalism: The Middle Class and the Development of Higher Education in America* (New York: Norton, 1976), 47.

81. William Osler, "Unity, Peace, and Concord," in Osler, *Aequanimitas,* 431.

82. William Welch, "On Some of the Humane Aspects of Medical Science," in William Henry Welch, *Papers and Addresses,* vol. 3 (Baltimore: The Johns Hopkins University Press, 1920), 5.

83. John Shaw Billings, "Valedictory Address" (unpublished lecture), n.d., Box 44, John Shaw Billings Papers, New York Public Library.

84. William Thayer, "Teaching and Practice," in *Osler,* 191.

85. Mall, "Anatomical Course," 85.

86. Osler, "After Twenty-Five Years," 201–2.

87. William H. Welch, "The Evolution of Modern Scientific Laboratories," *Bulletin of the Johns Hopkins Hospital* 7 (1896): 22.

88. Morton White, *Social Thought in America: The Revolt against Formalism* (Boston: Beacon Press, 1957).

89. Ibid., esp. chaps. 7, 9, 10, 12, 13.

90. Many accounts of Dewey's views exist. A useful brief introduction to his ideas may be found in Merle Curti, *The Social Ideas of American Educators,* 2nd ed. (Paterson, N.J.: Pageant Books, 1959), 499–541. A standard treatment of Dewey is Morton G. White, *The Origin of Dewey's Instrumentalism* (New York: Columbia University Press, 1943). Dewey's most complete statement of his views on education is found in John Dewey, *Democracy and Education* (New York: Macmillan, 1916).

91. Oscar Handlin, *John Dewey's Challenge to Education: Historical Perspectives on the Cultural Context* (New York: Harper, 1959).

92. Franklin P. Mall, "The Value of Research in the Medical School," *Michigan Alumnus* 8 (1904): 396, 395.

93. Ibid., 396.

94. Sabin, *Franklin Paine Mall,* 118–99, 155–56 (baby in bath water anecdote); George W. Corner, *Anatomist at Large: An Autobiography and Selected Essays* (New York: Basic Books, 1958), 20–22; George W. Corner, *The Seven Ages of a Medical Scientist: An Autobiography*

(Philadelphia: University of Pennsylvania Press, 1981), 38–40; Fleming, *William H. Welch*, 107–8.

95. Osler, "The Hospital as a College," 315.
96. Osler, "The Fixed Period," 389.
97. Ibid., 389.
98. Charles Newman, *The Evolution of Medical Education in the Nineteenth Century* (London: Oxford University Press, 1957), 118–20.
99. Toby Gelfand, *Professionalizing Modern Medicine: Paris Surgeons and Medical Science in the 18th Century* (Westport, Conn.: Greenwood Press, 1980), 148; Erwin H. Ackerknecht, *Medicine at the Paris Hospital 1794–1848* (Baltimore: The Johns Hopkins University Press, 1967), 37–38.
100. Thomas Neville Bonner, *American Doctors and German Universities: A Chapter in International Intellectual Relations 1870–1914* (Lincoln: University of Nebraska Press, 1963), 150, 158; Sabin, *Franklin Paine Mall*, 150–53; William Welch to Frederic S. Dennis, 7 Nov. 1876, William H. Welch Papers, Alan Mason Chesney Medical Archives, Johns Hopkins Medical Institutions.
101. Osler, "The Hospital as a College," 313–14.
102. Mall, "On the Value of Research in the Medical School," 396.
103. Sabin, *Franklin Paine Mall*, 138–39.
104. Corner, *Anatomist at Large*, 22.
105. Sabin, *Franklin Paine Mall*, 139.
106. John F. Fulton, *Harvey Cushing: A Biography* (Springfield, Ill.: Charles C Thomas, 1946), 75–77.
107. William S. Thayer, "Scholarship in Medicine," in Thayer, *Osler*, 220.
108. "A Report from the Committee of Graduates and Undergraduates upon the Course of Study at the Harvard Medical School," 1899, Countway Library, Harvard Medical School.

Chapter 4

1. David S. Fairchild, "History of the Growth of Drake University College of Medicine, and the Changes in the Methods of Medical Education During that Time," 1905 address, College of Medicine Folder, Special Collections Division, Cowles Library, Drake University.
2. Faculty meeting minutes, 31 March 1885, College of Medicine of the University of Southern California, Norris Medical Library, University of Southern California, Los Angeles.
3. Carl W. Rand, *Joseph Pomeroy Widney: Physician and Mystic* (Los Angeles: Salerni Collegium and University of Southern California School of Medicine, 1970), 41.
4. "Report on Entrance Examinations," in College of Physicians and Surgeons faculty meeting minutes, 7 April 1887, Office of the Dean, College of Physicians and Surgeons, Columbia University.
5. Faculty meeting minutes, 20 March 1893, Office of the Dean, College of Physicians and Surgeons, Columbia University.
6. Yale University, *President's Report* (1890), 44–45.
7. Dean F. Smiley, "History of the Association of American Medical Colleges, 1876–1956," *Journal of Medical Education* 32 (1957): 515.
8. "The Present Status of Medical Education in the United States," *Journal of the American Medical Association* 20 (1893): 24.
9. *Annual Report of Provost and Treasurer of the University of Pennsylvania* (1894), 26–27, University of Pennsylvania Archives.
10. William Pepper, *Higher Medical Education, The True Interest of the Public and of the Profession* (Philadelphia: J. B. Lippincott, 1894), 74.
11. Richard H. Shryock, *The Unique Influence of the Johns Hopkins University on American Medicine* (Copenhagen: Ejnar Munksgaard, 1953), 62.
12. Ibid., 63.
13. William H. Welch to Franklin P. Mall, 25 June 1900, William H. Welch Papers, Alan Mason Chesney Medical Archives, Johns Hopkins Medical Institutions.

14. Thomas Neville Bonner, *American Doctors and German Universities: A Chapter in International Intellectual Relations, 1870–1914* (Lincoln: University of Nebraska Press, 1963), 70.

15. Robert P. Hudson, "Patterns of Medical Education in Nineteenth Century America" (Master's thesis, Johns Hopkins University, 1966), 223.

16. The chronology of the development of the germ theory is familiar to historians, but the complexities of its reception and applications have yet to be definitively evaluated. Also still to be written is a comprehensive account of the development of bacteriology. For example, relatively little has been written about the backward steps in the development of bacteriology, such as Robert Koch's premature claim in 1890 of a cure for tuberculosis, or of the resistance that the germ theory encountered in the 1880s in many quarters. Some sense of the complexities of the assimilation of bacteriology into medicine is provided in Russell Maulitz's perceptive article, " 'Physician versus Bacteriologist': The Ideology of Science in Clinical Medicine," in *The Therapeutic Revolution: Essays in the Social History of American Medicine*, ed. Morris J. Vogel and Charles E. Rosenburg (Philadelphia: University of Pennsylvania Press, 1979), 91–107. An excellent account of the spontaneous generation controversy is in John Farley, *The Spontaneous Generation Controversy from Descartes to Oparin* (Baltimore: The Johns Hopkins University Press, 1977).

17. University of Minnesota, *Biennial Report of the Board of Regents* (1901–1902), 137, University of Minnesota Archives.

18. "A Perfect Period of Study," comments by Simon Flexner on Welch's film address made in his 82nd year, 20 Aug. 1936, William H. Welch Papers.

19. Quoted in Benjamin Spector, *A History of Tufts College Medical School* (Boston: Tufts College Medical Alumni Association, 1943), 172.

20. N. P. Colwell, "Medical Education, 1915," in U.S. Department of the Interior, Bureau of Education, *Report of the Commissioner of Education* (Washington, D.C.: Government Printing Office, 1915), 191.

21. The development of many diagnostic technologies, with attention to their potential misuse as well as use, is discussed in Stanley Reiser's insightful *Medicine and the Reign of Technology* (Cambridge: Cambridge University Press, 1978).

22. The best known of these works are Thomas McKeown, *The Role of Medicine: Dream, Mirage, or Nemesis?* (Princeton, N.J.: Princeton University Press, 1979), and Thomas McKeown, *The Modern Rise of Population* (New York: Academic Press, 1976).

23. William Welch, "Present Position of Medical Education, Its Development and Great Needs for the Future," in William Welch, *Papers and Addresses*, vol. 3 (Baltimore: The Johns Hopkins University Press, 1920), 112.

24. On the early history of the Washington University Medical School, see Ruth Werner Steele, "Origin and History of the Medical Department of Washington University, 1891–1914" (Master's thesis, Washington University, 1944); and Marjorie Fox, "History of Washington University School of Medicine" (MS, 1949–52), Washington University School of Medicine Archives, St. Louis, Missouri.

25. Accounts of some of these schools are provided in E. J. Goodwin, *A History of Medicine in Missouri* (St. Louis: W. L. Smith, 1905), chap. 8; and Max Goldstein, ed., *One Hundred Years of Medicine and Surgery in Missouri* (St. Louis: St. Louis Star, 1900), chap. 14.

26. Fox, "History of Washington University School of Medicine," chap. 2; Steele, "Origin and History of the Medical Department of Washington University," chap. 3; *Bulletin of the Medical Department of Washington University* (1904), 29.

27. Fox, "History of Washington University School of Medicine," chap. 2; Steele, "Origin and History of the Medical Department of Washington University," chap. 3. The medical school bulletins of the period record the expansion of both clinical and scientific instruction.

28. *Quarterly Bulletin of the Medical Department of Washington University* 3 (1904): 126.

29. Course descriptions are taken from the 1903, 1904, and 1905 *Bulletin of the Medical Department of Washington University*, Washington University School of Medicine Archives.

30. Winfield Chaplin to W. K. Bixby, 8 August 1904, Chancellor's Records, Washington University, Washington University Archives.

31. *Bulletin of the Medical Department of Washington University* (1904), 43.

32. Several of these schools began with two-year programs, teaching the basic science subjects only.

33. Cornell University Medical College, *Announcement* (1909–10), 22; "Cornell's New Building is Formally Opened," The Brooklyn *Eagle*, 29 Dec. 1900, Medical Archives, New York Hospital-Cornell University Medical Center.

34. Cornell University Medical College Preliminary Announcement, 1898–1899, in faculty meeting minutes, 20 May 1898, Cornell University Medical College, Medical Archives, New York Hospital-Cornell University Medical Center. As an example of this approach in practice, in the pathology course there were eighty-four hours of laboratory work and sixty-four hours of recitation (Faculty meeting minutes, 18 Nov. 1898, Cornell University Medical College).

35. Yale University, *President's Report* (1890), 46.

36. "The Course of Medical Instruction. The Improvements Needed," *The Hospital Bulletin of the University of Maryland* 5 (1909): 130.

37. "Clinical Notebooks of George Dock, 1899–1908," 27 Sept. 1907, Michigan Historical Collections, Bentley Historical Library, University of Michigan. See also session of 30 Sept. 1904.

38. Ronald L. Numbers, ed., *The Education of American Physicians: Historical Essays* (Berkeley: University of California Press, 1980).

39. Quoted in John Harley Warner, "Physiology," in Numbers, *The Education of American Physicians*, 67.

40. Donald Fleming, "Émigré Physicists and the Biological Revolution," *Perspectives in American History* 2 (1968): 152–89. This group consisted of Erwin Schrödinger, Leo Szilard, Max Delbrück, and Salvador Luria. Note that Luria was trained as a biologist.

41. Faculty biographical information was obtained from the following sources. Tufts: Spector, *A History of Tufts College Medical School*, 71–95. Washington: Goodwin, *History of Medicine;* Goldstein, *One Hundred Years;* and Howard A. Kelly and Walter L. Burrage, eds., *American Medical Biographies* (Boston: Milford House, 1928). Bowdoin: Various faculty biographical materials are available at Special Collections, Bowdoin College Library. Minnesota: Folder, "Old Faculty History," Miscellaneous Long Box 1, University of Minnesota Medical School, Papers, University of Minnesota Archives. The numbers in the text refer to faculty members for whom biographical information could be found. For instance, in 1900 there were forty-six members of the Washington University faculty. The number thirty refers to those about whom I could find information. It is likely that the majority of those who were not listed in the sources consulted did not study in Europe.

42. Walter B. Cannon, *The Way of an Investigator: A Scientist's Experiences in Medical Research* (New York: Norton, 1945), 88–89.

43. Faculty meeting minutes, 18 Nov. 1898, Cornell University Medical College.

44. B. C. Hirsh to John Marshall, 25 May 1899, in medical faculty meeting minutes, 6 June 1899, University of Pennsylvania School of Medicine.

45. Faculty meeting minutes, 6 Dec. 1904, College of Medicine of the University of Nebraska, University of Nebraska-Lincoln Archives.

46. Howard M. Hanna to Charles Thwing, 26 March 1907, Box 20, Charles Franklin Thwing Office Files, Case Western Reserve University Archives.

47. Faculty meeting minutes, 5 Feb. 1908, 9 April 1908, and 17 May 1908, Western Reserve University School of Medicine, Case Western Reserve University Archives.

48. "Administration and Organization of American Medical Schools," in Folder, "University of Pittsburgh School of Medicine History 1908–1914," Historical Materials of the University of Pittsburgh, Falk Library, University of Pittsburgh.

49. "Department of Medicine," in *Annual Report of Provost and Treasurer of the University of Pennsylvania* (1887), 88–89.

50. Arthur T. Cabot to Charles Eliot, 31 May [1893–1903], Folder 43, Box 104, Charles Eliot Papers, Harvard University Archives. The periodical, *The Journal of Experimental Medicine*, ultimately went to the Rockefeller Institute.

51. Faculty meeting minutes, 17 Jan. 1910, College of Physicians and Surgeons, Columbia University.

52. "State Board Statistics for 1909," *The Hospital Bulletin of the University of Maryland* 6 (1910): 73.

53. University of Minnesota, *Biennial Report of the Board of Regents* (1889–90), 14.

54. *Annual Report of the Provost and Treasurer of the University of Pennsylvania* (1902), 13.

55. Columbia University, *Annual Report* (1902), 61–62.

56. Faculty meeting minutes, 20 April 1908, College of Physicians and Surgeons, Columbia University. From 1902–3 to 1907–8, the total enrollment at the school fell from 797 to 304.

57. *Annual Report of the President of Tufts College* (1907–08), 40; "The Medical School," in University of Minnesota, *President's Report* (1914–15), 71; Victor C. Vaughan, "The Medical School During the Administration of President Hutchins from October 1909 to June 1920," Box 8, Records of the Medical School of the University of Michigan, Michigan Historical Collections, Bentley Historical Library, University of Michigan; Victor C. Vaughan, "Report of the Dean of the Medical School," Sept. 1915, Box 2, Records of the Medical School of the University of Michigan; "A Brief History of the School of Medicine of the University of Pittsburgh," and "Report of the Special Committee on the Medical School," Folder, "University of Pittsburgh School of Medicine Faculty Council c. 1910," Historical Materials of the University of Pittsburgh; and Abraham Flexner, "Reminiscences of Dr. Welch," 16 May 1934, File, "William Welch," Abraham Flexner Papers, Library of Congress.

58. Elias P. Lyon, "Annual Statement of the Condition of the St. Louis University Medical School," 22 May 1909, File, "St. Louis University," Abraham Flexner Papers, Library of Congress.

59. Faculty meeting minutes, 20 Oct. 1899, Cornell University Medical College.

60. "To the Trustees of Columbia College," in File, "College of Physicians and Surgeons, 5 Manuscripts, Documents Relating to Consolidation with Columbia College," College of Physicians and Surgeons, Papers, Butler Library, Columbia University.

61. Minutes of the Alumni Association of the Medical Department of Western Reserve College (1872–1915), 16 June 1909, Howard Dittrick Museum of Historical Medicine, Cleveland Health Sciences Library.

62. Minutes of the College of Medicine of the University of Southern California, 5 May 1885, and 3 July 1908. In addition, the faculty created two nonprofit corporations, the Hospital Building Association and the Los Angeles College Clinic Association, whose purpose was to raise funds for school operations and for the erection of a teaching hospital. The faculty donated large amounts of their own money to these organizations. Minutes of the corporations are at the Biomedical Library, University of California, Los Angeles.

63. Tufts had a building fund, to which faculty members contributed 10 percent of their income. Maryland also had such a fund, and between 1893 and 1906 the faculty expended $270,000 to purchase property and erect and equip buildings. The Washington University faculty established the Medical Fund Society to help raise a permanent endowment for the school. Faculty members at Dartmouth and Nebraska routinely made private contributions to offset their schools' deficits. See Faculty meeting minutes, 6 July 1898, and 6 June 1899, Tufts College Medical School, Tufts University Archives; Randolph Winslow, "The University of Maryland in 1871 and 1906," *The Hospital Bulletin of the University of Maryland* 2 (1906): 52–53; Robert J. Terry, "Recalling Some Events in the History of the Medical Fund Society," *Washington University Medical Alumni Quarterly* 13 (1950): 127–30, 133; William J. Tucker to William T. Smith, 24 Dec. 1900, in faculty meeting minutes, 25 Feb. 1901, Records of the Medical Faculty of Dartmouth College, Dartmouth College Archives; and University of Nebraska, *Biennial Report of the Board of Regents to the Governor* (1911), 17.

64. Faculty meeting minutes, 4 Aug. 1893, Georgetown University School of Medicine, Georgetown University Archives.

65. Faculty meeting minutes (Dean's Book), 1 May 1886, and 15 Feb. 1893, Medical Department of Columbian College, Special Collections Division, Gelman Library, George Washington University.

66. Faculty meeting minutes, 19 Oct. 1899, Miami Medical College, in Faculty Minutes, April 1881–July 1909, Medical History Collection—Medical Schools, Special Collections, University Libraries, University of Cincinnati.

67. "Memorandum for President Pritchett in relation to Washburn College and its Medical Department," 10 Jan. 1910, Frank Knight Sanders Papers, Washburn University Library, Topeka, Kansas.

68. Events at Pennsylvania provided an example of this mechanism at work. In 1905 the school obtained "a great deal of information" from visits of faculty members to other schools, and this information proved "very helpful and useful" to the school in arranging its courses in

medicine and surgery (Medical faculty meeting minutes, 22 May 1905, University of Pennsylvania School of Medicine).

69. The AAMC was extremely self-conscious that its membership included many of the weaker schools, while many of the leading schools would not join. See, for instance, E. Fletcher Ingals to W. H. Howell, ?8 Dec. 1899; E. Fletcher Ingals to W. H. Howell, 8 Jan. 1900; and E. Fletcher Ingals to William Osler, 8 Dec. 1899; all in Miscellaneous Historical Documents, Association of American Medical Colleges Archives, Washington, D.C.

70. Faculty meeting minutes, 23 April 1891, Western Reserve University School of Medicine; Faculty meeting minutes, 8 April 1905, Miami Medical College, in Faculty Minutes, April 1881–July 1909; Executive faculty meeting minutes, 8 Sept. 1907, University of Colorado School of Medicine, Denison Memorial Library, University of Colorado Health Sciences Center.

71. Another standard curriculum, prepared by a committee of one hundred medical educators for the American Medical Association in 1909, appears in Council on Medical Education of the American Medical Association, "Report on Medical Curriculum," *Journal of the American Medical Association* 52 (1909): 1521–22.

72. George Webster, "On the Curricula of American Medical Colleges," *New York Medical Journal and Philadelphia Medical Journal,* 80 (1904): 145–50, 205–9.

73. "The Minutes of an Informal Conference of Some University Medical Schools Held in Chicago, June 3, 1908," in Folder, "Conference of University Medical Schools, 1908–July 6, 1909," Miscellaneous Box 1, University of Minnesota Medical School, Papers, University of Minnesota Archives.

74. Medical faculty meeting minutes, 23 April 1906, University of Pennsylvania School of Medicine; "Report of the Dean of the Medical School," in Columbia University, *Annual Report* (1911), 78–79; "Report of Committee on Medical Education," in Proceedings of the Seventeenth Annual Meeting of the Association of American Medical Colleges, 6 May 1907, p. 17, Association of American Medical Colleges Archives.

75. *Annual Report of the Provost and Treasurer of the University of Pennsylvania* (1887), 20.

76. "Address at the Opening of Day Classes at the Medical Department of Georgetown University," 30 Sept. 1895, Box "Medicine 1880–1916," Medical Faculty Correspondence, Georgetown University, Georgetown University Archives; Faculty meeting minutes, 18 June 1895, Georgetown University School of Medicine.

77. Steele, "Origin and History of the Medical Department of Washington University," chap. 2.

78. *Annual Report of the President and Treasurer of Harvard College* (1879–80), 33.

79. "Report of Committee on Extending the Length of the Winter Term of Lectures," in Medical faculty meeting minutes, 15 Nov. 1880, University of Pennsylvania School of Medicine; "Report of the Medical Faculty," in Minutes of the Board of Trustees, 1884–1914, 6 March 1889, Case Western Reserve University Archives; University of Michigan, *President's Annual Report* (1893), 17.

80. Laurence R. Veysey, *The Emergence of the American University* (Chicago: The University of Chicago Press, 1965), 178.

81. William Osler, "After Twenty-Five Years," in William Osler, *Aequanimitas with other Addresses to Medical Students, Nurses and Practitioners of Medicine,* 3rd ed. (Philadelphia: Blakiston, 1932), 199.

82. Ibid., 200.

83. Mention of these committees and their work appears from time to time in the faculty meeting minutes of the various schools.

84. Records of the annual meetings of the organization are at the Association of American Medical Colleges Archives.

85. George Hoxie, "Principles of Medical Education," President's Address, in Proceedings of the Twentieth Annual Meeting of the Association of American Medical Colleges, March 21–22, 1910, p. 15, Association of American Medical Colleges Archives.

86. University of the City of New York, Medical Department, *Annual Announcement of Lectures and Catalogue* (1883), 6.

87. Washington University School of Medicine executive faculty meeting minutes, 22 Sept. 1910, Washington University School of Medicine Archives; David Houston to Robert Brookings, 4 Feb. 1911, Chancellor's Records, Washington University, Washington University

Archives; David Houston to Robert Brookings, 22 Nov. 1909, Chancellor's Records, Washington University Archives; David Houston to Willard Bartlett, 15 Oct. 1910, Chancellor's Records, Washington University Archives; "Report of the Committee on the Organization of the Medical School, December 16, 1909," in Minutes of Meetings of Washington University Board of Directors, 1853–1925, 17 Dec. 1909, Washington University Archives; Faculty meeting minutes, 8 June 1908, and 31 May 1909, Medical Department of Washington University, September 1882–June 1909, Washington University School of Medicine Archives.

88. "Statement of W. Jarvis Barlow to faculty of College of Medicine," in Minutes of the College of Medicine of the University of Southern California, 10 June 1909.

89. Ibid.

90. Hill M. Bell to David S. Fairchild, 6 April 1905, and David S. Fairchild to Hill M. Bell, 13 April 1905, in College of Medicine Folder, Special Collections Division, Cowles Library, Drake University; "Memorandum for President Pritchett in relation to Washburn College and its Medical Department;" Box 1, "Denver University Medical School Letters, 1898–1902," Gross Medical College Collection, Western Historical Collections, University of Colorado-Boulder Library (contains twenty-three letters written between November 1901 and April 1902 by Dean Henry Sewall, chiding faculty members for having missed teaching assignments).

91. "Minutes of the Second Informal Conference of University Medical Schools, Atlantic City, June 9, 1909," in Folder, "Conference of University Medical Schools, 1908–July 6, 1909," Miscellaneous Box 1, University of Minnesota Medical School, Papers.

92. "The Present Status of Medical Education in the United States," 24.

93. Not surprisingly, the courses varied in length, intent, and quality. The Nebraska course, for example, lasted one week and was designed as "a brief survey of recent advances in medicine, particularly in the laboratory fields." The course offered by the Miami Medical College lasted a full month and emphasized practical work in the laboratory and medical school clinics ("Report of the Dean of the College of Medicine," in University of Nebraska, *Biennial Report of the Board of Regents to the Governor* [1909], 85; Miami Medical College, *Course for Practitioners, April–May 1896*, Box 1, Medical History Collection—Medical Schools). In addition to these courses, a number of postgraduate medical schools were created in the 1880s to serve a similar purpose. On these schools, see the excellent article by Steven J. Peitzman, " 'Thoroughly Practical': America's Polyclinical Medical Schools," *Bulletin of the History of Medicine* 54 (1980): 166–87.

94. Martin Kaufman, *Homeopathy in America: The Rise and Fall of a Medical Heresy* (Baltimore: The Johns Hopkins University Press, 1971); and William G. Rothstein, *American Physicians in the Nineteenth Century: From Sects to Science* (Baltimore: The Johns Hopkins University Press, 1972).

95. Richard H. Shryock, *Medical Licensing in America, 1650–1965* (Baltimore: The Johns Hopkins University Press, 1967).

96. Richard H. Shryock, "The American Physician in 1846 and in 1946: A Study in Professional Contrasts," in Richard H. Shryock, *Medicine in America. Historical Essays* (Baltimore: The Johns Hopkins University Press, 1966), 149–76; Paul Starr, *The Social Transformation of American Medicine: The Rise of a Sovereign Profession and the Making of a Vast Industry* (New York: Basic Books, 1982), 79–144.

97. Robert J. Terry to David Houston, 17 June 1909, Chancellor's Records, Washington University. The physiological chemistry course was likewise overcrowded. See Faculty meeting minutes, 21 Sept. 1903, Medical Department of Washington University, September 1882–June 1909.

98. "Preliminary Report of the Curriculum Committee," c. 1911, Box 8, Yale Medical School, Dean's Files, Yale University Archives.

99. *Annual Report of Provost and Treasurer of the University of Pennsylvania* (1899), 26–32.

100. George W. Corner, *A History of the Rockefeller Institute, 1901–1953, Origins and Growth* (New York: Rockefeller Institute Press, 1964), 53.

101. Abraham Flexner, *Medical Education in the United States and Canada* (New York: Carnegie Foundation for the Advancement of Teaching, 1910), 6.

102. George Hoxie, "Medicine as a University Discipline" [an appeal to the alumni of the University of Kansas], 27 Dec. 1909, Collections of Articles on the History of the University of Kansas Medical Center, Logan Clendening Library of the History of Medicine, University of Kansas Medical Center.

103. "University of Michigan Laboratory Course in Physiology, 1904–1905" [mimeographed copy], Folder 51, Box 2, Warren Plimpton Lombard Papers, Michigan Historical Collections, Bentley Historical Library, University of Michigan.

104. Robert Levy to A. T. Blachly, 6 Jan. 1902, "Copies of Letters, 1900–1903," Box 1, Gross Medical College Collection, Western Historical Collections, University of Colorado-Boulder Library.

105. Faculty meeting minutes, 19 March 1903, Georgetown University School of Medicine. Cheating did not occur at weak schools only. For example, the problem caused concern at the University of Minnesota, which considered establishing an honor system to combat the situation (Executive faculty meeting minutes, 8 June 1911, Volume 27, College of Medicine and Surgery, University of Minnesota Medical School, Papers). Many other good schools also occasionally encountered this problem. The point at issue in the text was the magnitude of cheating and student disorder, and whether teaching efforts were thereby compromised.

106. Flexner, *Medical Education in the United States and Canada*, 235–36, 239.

107. Faculty meeting minutes, 12 Sept. 1901, and 18 Dec. 1901, College of Physicians and Surgeons, Minute Book, 1894–1904, Special Collections, University of Maryland Health Sciences Library; "The New College Building," *Journal of the Alumni Association of the College of Physicians and Surgeons, Baltimore* 2 (1899): 33–34.

108. Faculty meeting minutes, 25 Aug. 1903 (research club), and 21 April 1904 (rejected applicant), College of Physicians and Surgeons, Minute Book, 1894–1904.

109. "Report of Judicial Council," in Minutes of the Fifteenth Annual Meeting of the Association of American Medical Colleges, 10 April 1905, p. 27, Association of American Medical Schools Archives.

110. Edward G. Jones to Abraham Flexner, 5 May 1910, Abraham Flexner Papers, Library of Congress.

111. Hillard Wood to Abraham Flexner, 30 Jan. 1910, Abraham Flexner Papers, Library of Congress.

112. William Welch to Franklin Mall, 25 June 1900, William H. Welch Papers, Johns Hopkins.

113. William Osler, "The Fixed Period," in Osler, *Aequanimitas*, 387.

114. Eli H. Long, "Functions of the Medical School," President's Address, Proceedings of the Nineteenth Annual Meeting of the Association of American Medical Colleges, March 15–16, 1909, p. 3, Association of American Medical Colleges Archives.

115. For instance, see M. Allen Starr, "Medical Education in New York," *Columbia University Quarterly* 9 (1907): 147.

116. Bonner, *American Doctors and German Universities*, 139–56. On the growing stature of American medical schools in the eyes of European physicians, see also Erna Lesky, "American Medicine as Viewed by Viennese Physicians, 1893–1912," *Bulletin of the History of Medicine* 56 (1982): 368–76.

117. Ernest Earnest, *S. Weir Mitchell: Novelist and Physician* (Philadelphia: University of Pennsylvania Press, 1950), 215.

118. Flexner, *Medical Education in the United States and Canada*, 12.

119. William W. Keen, "Medical Education," in William W. Keen, *Addresses and Other Papers* (Philadelphia: W. B. Saunders, 1905), 200.

120. *Annual Report of Provost and Treasurer of the University of Pennsylvania* (1892), 17.

121. "Report of the Dean of the Medical College," in Western Reserve University, *Report of the President and Faculties (1903–04)*, 61. See also "Report of Committee on Advertising," in Faculty meeting minutes, 10 Feb. 1899, Western Reserve University School of Medicine.

122. Carey K. Fleming to Robert Levy, 7 Aug. 1902, "Copies of Letters, 1900–1903," Box 1, Gross Medical College Collection, Western Historical Collections, University of Colorado-Boulder Library; Faculty meeting minutes, 3 June 1902, Georgetown University School of Medicine; Faculty meeting minutes, 6 May 1902, College of Physicians and Surgeons, Minute Book, 1894–1904; Faculty meeting minutes (Dean's Book), 3 Oct. 1903, Medical Department of Columbian College, George Washington University.

123. N. P. Colwell, "Progress in Medical Education," in U.S. Department of the Interior, Bureau of Education, *Report of the Commissioner of Education* (Washington, D.C.: Government Printing Office, 1913), 33, 35.

124. Annual Report, Board of Overseers of the Medical Department, 4 June 1901, in

Minutes of the Overseers of the Medical Department of Washington University, June 1891–November 1905, Washington University School of Medicine Archives.

125. "Report of the Department of Medicine," in Yale University, *President's Report* (1906), 139.

Chapter 5

1. Victor Vaughan, "The Functions of a State University Medical School," n.d., manuscript, p. 3, File, "University of Michigan," Abraham Flexner Papers, Library of Congress.

2. Bruce Kuklick, *The Rise of American Philosophy: Cambridge, Massachusetts, 1860–1930* (New Haven: Yale University Press, 1977).

3. Mary Furner, *Advocacy and Objectivity: A Crisis in the Professionalization of American Social Science, 1865–1905* (Lexington: University Press of Kentucky, 1975); Thomas Haskell, *The Emergence of Professional Social Science: The American Social Science Association and the Nineteenth-Century Crisis of Authority* (Urbana: University of Illinois Press, 1977).

4. Daniel Kevles, *The Physicists: The History of a Scientific Community in Modern America* (New York: Alfred A. Knopf, 1977).

5. Faculty meeting minutes, 16 Feb. 1900, Tufts College Medical School, Tufts University Archives.

6. Simon Flexner and James Thomas Flexner, *William Welch and the Heroic Age of American Medicine* (New York: Viking, 1941), 242–50.

7. That Johns Hopkins in the 1890s prodded even leading schools like Harvard to support research much more vigorously was admitted by no less an authority than Charles Eliot. See Richard Shryock, *The Unique Influence of the Johns Hopkins University on American Medicine* (Copenhagen: Ejnar Munksgaard, 1953), 8.

8. N. P. Colwell, "Progress in Medical Education," in U.S. Department of the Interior, Bureau of Education, *Report of the Commissioner of Education* (Washington, D.C.: Government Printing Office, 1913), 44–45. Moreover, within medical schools the amount of research was increasing. For instance, from 1870 to 1916 the faculty of Harvard Medical School published 1,191 articles, with more articles appearing in the last ten of those years than in the preceding thirty-six. (Charles Eliot to Wallace Buttrick, 15 Dec. 1916, Folder 6487, Box 613, Series I, General Education Board Papers, Rockefeller Archive Center, North Tarrytown, New York).

9. On the development of medical research in the United States see Richard Shryock, *American Medical Research: Past and Present* (New York: Commonwealth Fund, 1947).

10. William H. Welch, "In Acceptance of a Medallion," in William Welch, *Papers and Addresses*, vol. 3 (Baltimore: The Johns Hopkins University Press, 1920), 363.

11. Walter B. Cannon to Charles Eliot, 28 Oct. 1904, Box 205, Charles Eliot Papers, Harvard University Archives.

12. Robert Kohler, *From Medical Chemistry to Biochemistry: The Making of a Biomedical Discipline* (Cambridge: Cambridge University Press, 1982), 176–82.

13. Henry P. Bowditch to A. T. Cabot, 28 Feb. 1907, Box 3, Henry P. Bowditch Papers, Countway Library, Harvard Medical School.

14. The standard reference on the Rockefeller Institute is George W. Corner, *A History of the Rockefeller Institute, 1901–1953, Origins and Growth* (New York: Rockefeller Institute Press, 1964). On research institutes, see also John Blake's helpful article, "Scientific Institutions since the Renaissance: Their Role in Medical Research," *Proceedings of the American Philosophical Society* 101 (1957): 31–62.

15. Corner, *A History of the Rockefeller Institute*, vi–vii, 26–29, 39–43, 329–30, 537–38, 540–42.

16. Quoted in Edith Gittings Reid, *The Great Physician: A Short Life of Sir William Osler* (London: Oxford University Press, 1931), 230–31.

17. William Osler, "The Student Life," *Medical News* 87 (1905): 626.

18. Quoted in Florence Rena Sabin, *Franklin Paine Mall: The Story of a Mind* (Baltimore: The Johns Hopkins University Press, 1934), 181.

19. Welch, "Present Position of Medical Education," *Papers and Addresses*, 118.

20. Lewellys F. Barker, *Time and the Physician* (New York: G. P. Putnam's Sons, 1942), 120.

21. Colwell, "Progress in Medical Education," 44.

22. "Report of the Special Committee on the Medical School," Folder, "University of Pittsburgh School of Medicine Faculty Council c. 1910," Historical Materials of the University of Pittsburgh, Falk Library, University of Pittsburgh.

23. Report of ad hoc committee to the Faculty of Medicine of the University of Pennsylvania, 21 Jan. 1901, Medical faculty meeting minutes, 21 Jan. 1901, University of Pennsylvania School of Medicine, University of Pennsylvania.

24. Edward H. Nichols to J. Collins Warren, n.d., File October 1902, Box 119, Charles Eliot Papers.

25. Henry Pritchett to W. J. Curtis, 18 June 1910, File, "Bowdoin College," Carnegie Foundation Archives, Carnegie Corporation, New York.

26. Shryock, *Unique Influence of Johns Hopkins,* 61.

27. Bowdoin College, *President's Report* (1909–10), 22, 23.

28. Franklin P. Mall, "The Anatomical Course and Laboratories of the Johns Hopkins University," *Bulletin of the Johns Hopkins Hospital* 7 (1896): 85.

29. George Blumer to Yandell Henderson, 29 Aug. 1918, File, "1918—Reorganization of the School," Box 7, Dean's Files, Yale Medical School, Yale University Archives.

30. Roy L. Moodie to Victor Vaughan, 23 Nov. 1915, Box 2, Records of the Medical School of the University of Michigan, Michigan Historical Collections, Bentley Historical Library, University of Michigan.

31. Albert R. Baker, "Evolution of the American Medical College," President's Address, in Transactions of the Association of American Medical Colleges, *Bulletin of the American Academy of Medicine* 5 (1901): 499.

32. Statutes of the Medical School of Maine (faculty meeting minutes), 15 Oct. 1917, Special Collections, Bowdoin College Library; and William DeWitt Hyde to William L. Putnam, 9 June 1910, Folder, "Correspondence with Putnam," Box 2, Bowdoin College Medical School, Miscellaneous Records, Special Collections, Bowdoin College Library.

33. Frederick Waite, *Western Reserve University: Centennial History of the School of Medicine* (Cleveland: Western Reserve University Press, 1946), 197–99.

34. Quoted in Rosemary Stevens, *American Medicine and the Public Interest* (New Haven: Yale University Press, 1971), 41.

35. The presence of these men at the faculty meetings is documented in the minutes of the medical faculty meetings of the various schools.

36. Statement of Charles Eliot, Harvard University medical faculty meeting minutes, 1 May 1909, Countway Library, Harvard Medical School.

37. "Report of Financial Committee," in Faculty meeting minutes, 8 April 1896, Western Reserve University School of Medicine, Case Western Reserve University Archives.

38. "The Medical School," in University of Minnesota, *President's Report* (1927–28), 198.

39. Seth Low to James W. McLane, 18 Dec. 1890, in Faculty meeting minutes, 18 Dec. 1890, College of Physicians and Surgeons, Office of the Dean, College of Physicians and Surgeons, Columbia University.

40. "College of Physicians and Surgeons. Receipts and expenditures from July 1, 1891 to July 1, 1902," College of Physicians and Surgeons, Papers, Butler Library, Columbia University.

41. Henry Pritchett to S. B. McCormick, 15 Feb. 1910, Historical Materials of the University of Pittsburgh. On the reorganization, see also Thomas Arbuthnot to C. C. Guthrie, Sept. 1909, and Thomas Arbuthnot to Oscar Klotz, 2 Sept. 1909, both in Historical Materials of the University of Pittsburgh.

42. Faculty meeting minutes, 17 Jan. 1910, College of Physicians and Surgeons, Columbia University.

43. Theodore Janeway, "Outside Professional Engagements by Members of Professional Faculties," *Educational Review* 55 (1918): 219.

44. "Minutes of a meeting . . . of University Medical Schools, . . . June 19, 1913," in Folder, "Conference of University Medical Schools, 1913–1915," Miscellaneous Box 2, University of Minnesota Medical School, Papers, University of Minnesota Archives.

45. Franklin Mall, "Reorganization of the Department of Anatomy of Cornell University Medical College, New York City" (unsigned editorial), *Anatomical Record* 5 (1911): 415.

46. University of Minnesota, *Biennial Report of the Board of Regents* (1909–10), 29–30.
47. University of Minnesota, *Biennial Report of the Board of Regents* (1895–96), 48. On entrance requirements, see Gert Brieger's excellent essay, " 'Fit to Study Medicine': Notes for a History of Pre-Medical Education in America," *Bulletin of the History of Medicine* 57 (1983): 1–21. A full history of premedical education is sorely needed.
48. Henry Pritchett to Frederick W. Hamilton, 25 Feb. 1910, File, "Tufts College," Abraham Flexner Papers, Library of Congress.
49. N. P. Colwell to Henry Pritchett, 8 April 1914, File, "Vanderbilt University 1905–1915," Carnegie Foundation Archives, Carnegie Corporation.
50. *Annual Report of Provost and Treasurer of the University of Pennsylvania* (1907), 20.
51. For representative statements that the essentials of premedical training lay in the natural science courses rather than in the bachelor's degree per se, see John M. Baldy to the Tufts College Medical School, 3 Dec. 1914, "Medical Correspondence, 1908–1917," Tufts University Archives; John Rogers to Mr. Hoy, 3 July 1909, File, "Cornell University," Abraham Flexner Papers, Library of Congress; Victor Vaughan to Abraham Flexner, 13 April 1909, File, "University of Michigan," Abraham Flexner Papers, Library of Congress; and "Report of the Dean of the Faculty of Medicine," in *Annual Report of Provost and Treasurer of University of Pennsylvania* (1905), 113–14.
52. Faculty meeting minutes, 20 Oct. 1899, Cornell University Medical College, Medical Archives, New York Hospital-Cornell Medical Center.
53. University of Minnesota, *Biennial Report of the Board of Regents* (1895–96), 48.
54. Events at Columbia illustrated this process. Samuel Lambert, dean of the medical school, returned from a meeting of the American Medical Association's Council on Medical Education in 1908 with the following observation: "If any conclusion can be drawn from this conference it is that all the best schools will require one year and at least half the schools two years of college work in physics, chemistry and biology with the class entering in 1910." The implication was clear. Schools desiring to remain in the academic forefront had no choice but to establish entrance requirements, or their competition would pass them by (Faculty meeting minutes, 20 April 1908, College of Physicians and Surgeons, Columbia University).
55. W. David Baird, *Medical Education in Arkansas, 1879–1978* (Memphis: Memphis State University Press, 1979), 117; and Martin Kaufman, *The University of Vermont College of Medicine* (Hanover, N.H.: University of Vermont College of Medicine, 1979), 134.
56. Henry Pritchett to F. C. Waite, 21 Dec. 1914, and 24 Dec. 1914, File, "Medical Education"; Henry Pritchett to N. P. Colwell, 11 April 1914, File, "Vanderbilt University 1905–1911"; and Brown Ayres to Henry Pritchett, 14 June 1913, File, "University of Tennessee." All of these references are at the Carnegie Foundation Archives, Carnegie Corporation. To illustrate the severity of the problem, in the entire state of Georgia in 1909 there were only 642 male high school graduates and 267 male college graduates. After the Atlanta College of Physicians and Surgeons started to require a high school diploma for admission, the size of the first-year class fell from 141 to 65 (W. F. Westmoreland, "A Report on the Colleges and Secondary Schools of Georgia," 1910–11, in Folder, "Atlanta College of Physicians and Surgeons 1898–1913. Budget 1910–1913"; and W. S. Elkin to Board of Trustees, 3 May 1913, Folder, "Atlanta College of Physicians and Surgeons 1898–1913. Annual Report, 1907–1913"; in History Files, A. W. Calhoun Medical Library, Emory University School of Medicine).
57. Columbia University, *Annual Report* (1908), 31.
58. Colwell, "Medical Education," 195.
59. "Report of Committee on Medical Education," in Proceedings of the Seventeenth Annual Meeting of the Association of American Medical Colleges, 6 May 1907, p. 17, Association of American Medical Colleges Archives.
60. Faculty meeting minutes, 21 Oct. 1907 and 18 Oct. 1909, College of Physicians and Surgeons, Columbia University.
61. *Annual Report of Provost and Treasurer of the University of Pennsylvania* (1897), 35.
62. "Report of the Dean of the Medical School," Columbia University, *Annual Report* (1904), 96.
63. "Report of the Dean of the Medical School," *Annual Report of the President of Tufts College* (1913–14), 29.
64. Cornell University Medical College, *Announcement* (1909–10), 28.

65. For instance, the University of Minnesota Medical School had a "Six-Year Medical Course Committee" which controlled the premedical curriculum at the university and had the responsibility of ensuring there would be no duplication of courses between the college and the medical school. For records of this committee, see University of Minnesota, Six-Year Medical Course Committee, "Record Book, 1903–11," University of Minnesota Archives.

66. Minutes of business meetings of the Council on Medical Education and Hospitals, 1907–17, 27 Nov. 1915, pp. 214–15, American Medical Association Archives, Chicago.

67. "The Minutes of an Informal Conference of Some University Medical Schools Held in Chicago, June 3, 1908," in Folder, "Conference of University Medical Schools, 1908–July 6, 1909," Miscellaneous Box 1, Papers, University of Minnesota Archives.

68. Franklin P. Mall, "The Value of Research in the Medical School," *The Michigan Alumnus* 8 (1904): 397.

69. Abraham Flexner, *Medical Education in the United States and Canada* (New York: Carnegie Foundation for the Advancement of Teaching, 1910), 37–38.

70. John Rogers to Mr. Hoy, 3 July 1909, File, "Cornell University," Abraham Flexner Papers, Library of Congress.

71. Statistics on these medical schools were compiled from their annual catalogs.

72. University of Minnesota, *Biennial Report of the Board of Regents* (1895–96), 49–50.

73. See, for instance, Edwin R. Axtell to George Hubbard, 16 Aug. 1898, Folder, "Denver University Medical School Letters, 1898–1902," Box 1, Gross Medical College Collection, Western Historical Collections, University of Colorado-Boulder Library; and Letter from N. S. Darr's secretary, 29 July 1897, Folder 1, Box 1, Gross Medical College Collection, University of Colorado-Boulder Library.

74. See, for instance, Robert Levy to Hiram Johnson, 18 Oct. 1902, and Robert Levy to Walter Rendtorff, 12 Nov. 1902, in Folder, "Copies of Letters, 1900–1903," Box 1, Gross Medical College Collection, University of Colorado-Boulder Library.

75. Robert Levy to W. B. Parkinson, 20 May 1903, Folder, "Copies of Letters, 1900–1903," Box 1, Gross Medical College Collection, University of Colorado-Boulder Library.

76. Data obtained from Denver and Gross College of Medicine, *Annual Announcement* (1902–03), 43–44, and (1905–06), 43. The graduating class of 1905 was larger than sixteen because it included transfer students.

77. Faculty meeting minutes, 11 Oct. 1906, Georgetown University School of Medicine, Georgetown University Archives.

78. Executive Committee meeting minutes (beginning October 1906), 14 April 1909, Medical Department of Washington University, Washington University School of Medicine Archives.

79. Martin Kaufman, *American Medical Education: The Formative Years, 1765–1910* (Westport, Conn.: Greenwood Press, 1976), 160.

80. Statistics cited in Magali Larson, *The Rise of Professionalism: A Sociological Analysis* (Berkeley: University of California Press, 1977), 284 n. 81.

81. "How To Study Medicine," *The Hospital Bulletin of the University of Maryland* 6 (1910): 150.

82. *Annual Report of the President of Tufts College* (1912–13), 12.

83. Harvard University medical faculty meeting minutes, 13 Feb. 1909, Countway Library, Harvard Medical School; "Report of the Department of Medicine," in Yale University, *President's Report* (1903), 124–25; Lewis H. Weed to Abraham Flexner, 12 March 1925, Folder 6271, Box 589, Series I, General Education Board Papers, Rockefeller Archive Center.

84. "Report of the Special Committee on the Medical School," University of Pittsburgh.

85. Steven Jonas, *Medical Mystery: The Training of Doctors in the United States* (New York: Norton, 1978), 274.

Chapter 6

1. Medical faculty meeting minutes, 16 Nov. 1903, University of Pennsylvania School of Medicine, University of Pennsylvania Archives.

2. N. P. Colwell, "Progress in Medical Education," in U.S. Department of the Interior, Bureau of Education, *Report of the Commissioner of Education* (Washington, D.C.: Government Printing Office, 1913), 43.

3. *The General Education Board. An Account of its Activities 1902–1914* (New York: General Education Board, 1915), 164.

4. "Report of the Department of Medicine," in Yale University, *President's Report* (1900), 63.

5. Samuel Avery to Harold Gifford, 28 Sept. 1909, Record Group 2/9/4, Chancellor Samuel Avery Papers, University of Nebraska-Lincoln Archives.

6. George Dock to George Blumer, n.d., File, "Full Time System," Box 39, Dean's Files, Yale Medical School, Yale University Archives.

7. Faculty meeting minutes, 18 Feb. 1895, College of Physicians and Surgeons, Office of the Dean, College of Physicians and Surgeons, Columbia University, New York.

8. List of Faculty Salaries, Harvard University, Academic Year 1907–08, Furnished to Carnegie Foundation, File, "Harvard University 1904–1917," Carnegie Foundation Archives, Carnegie Corporation, New York.

9. Faculty meeting minutes, 16 Jan. 1899, College of Physicians and Surgeons, Columbia University.

10. John F. Fulton, *Harvey Cushing: A Biography* (Springfield, Ill.: Charles C Thomas, 1946), 330–31.

11. Joseph Erlanger to Thomas S. Arbuthnot, 30 May 1909, Historical Materials, Falk Library, University of Pittsburgh.

12. For biographies of Welch, see Simon Flexner and James Thomas Flexner, *William Henry Welch and the Heroic Age of American Medicine* (New York: Viking, 1941); and Donald Fleming, *William H. Welch and the Rise of Modern Medicine* (Boston: Little, Brown, 1954).

13. Fleming, *William H. Welch*, 133.

14. William H. Welch to Emma Welch Walcott, 27 Feb. 1903, William H. Welch Papers, Alan Mason Chesney Medical Archives, Johns Hopkins Medical Institutions.

15. Biographical sketches of members of the society are provided in A. McGehee Harvey, *The Interurban Clinical Club (1905–1976): A Record of Achievement in Clinical Science* (Philadelphia: W. B. Saunders, 1978).

16. A. McGehee Harvey, *Science at the Bedside: Clinical Research in American Medicine, 1905–1948* (Baltimore: The Johns Hopkins University Press, 1981), 98.

17. Florence Rena Sabin, *Franklin Paine Mall: The Story of a Mind* (Baltimore: The Johns Hopkins University Press, 1934), 264.

18. James Turner, *Reckoning with the Beast: Animals, Pain, and Humanity in the Victorian Mind* (Baltimore: The Johns Hopkins University Press, 1980), 107–21. The antivivisection movement mobilized British medical scientists in the same way. See Richard D. French, *Antivivisection and Medical Science in Victorian Society* (Princeton, N.J.: Princeton University Press, 1975).

19. William H. Welch, "Formal Opening of the Peter Bent Brigham Hospital," in William H. Welch, *Papers and Addresses*, vol. 3 (Baltimore: The Johns Hopkins University Press, 1920), 156.

20. "Report of the Department of Medicine," in Yale University, *President's Report* (1901), 91.

21. Robert H. Wiebe, *The Search for Order 1877–1920* (New York: Hill and Wang, 1967).

22. William S. Thayer, "Scholarship in Medicine," *Boston Medical and Surgical Journal* 176 (1917): 521. Of note, the same differentiation of the profession into professors and practitioners occurred in law as in medicine. In the late nineteenth century, a group of lawyers appeared whose primary concern was research and teaching. This movement first became apparent at Harvard Law School in 1870, when Christopher Columbus Langdell became dean; over the next two generations it spread to university law schools elsewhere. To Langdell, law was a science and the library the legal scholar's laboratory. He and others like him saw themselves as law professors, not practicing attorneys, and they viewed the university as their natural milieu. It was this group of law professors that was primarily responsible for the great reforms in legal education of the period. On legal education, see William R. Johnson, *Schooled Lawyers: A Study in the Clash of Professional Cultures* (New York: New York University Press, 1978); Jerold S. Auerbach, *Unequal*

Justice: Lawyers and Social Change in Modern America (New York: Oxford University Press, 1976), 74–129; Jerold S. Auerbach, "Enmity and Amity: Law Teachers and Practitioners, 1900–1922," *Perspectives in American History* 5 (1971): 551–601; and Robert Stevens, "Two Cheers for 1870: The American Law School," *Perspectives in American History* 5 (1971): 405–548.

23.   William Clarence Boteler to Thomas H. Hawkins, 31 Dec. 1895, Folder 1, Box 1, Gross Medical College Collection, Western Historical Collections, University of Colorado-Boulder Library.

24.   Russell C. Maulitz, " 'Physician versus Bacteriologist': The Ideology of Science in Clinical Medicine," in *The Therapeutic Revolution: Essays in the Social History of American Medicine*, ed. Morris J. Vogel and Charles E. Rosenberg (Philadelphia: University of Pennsylvania Press, 1979), 91–107.

25.   This episode is related in Fleming, *William H. Welch*, 72.

26.   Franklin P. Mall, "The Value of Research in the Medical School," *The Michigan Alumnus* 8 (1904): 397.

27.   "A Report on the Medical Department of Washington University," with Abraham Flexner to Henry Pritchett, 15 Nov. 1909, File, "Henry Pritchett 1909–1910," Box 17, Abraham Flexner Papers, Library of Congress.

28.   Sabin, *Franklin Paine Mall*, 161.

29.   Turner, *Reckoning with the Beast*, 95, 98.

30.   Walter B. Cannon to Charles Eliot, 5 April 1902, Box 205, Charles Eliot Papers, Harvard University Archives.

31.   Harvey, *Science at the Bedside*, 183. This book provides a valuable account of the development of clinical science in America.

32.   Ibid., 83.

33.   Ibid., 66–67, 135–36; George W. Corner, *A History of the Rockefeller Institute, 1901–1953, Origins and Growth* (New York: Rockefeller Institute Press, 1964), 92–93.

34.   Harvey, *Science at the Bedside*, 117.

35.   Sidney Fine, *Laissez Faire and the General-Welfare State: A Study of Conflict in American Thought, 1865–1901* (Ann Arbor: University of Michigan Press, 1956).

36.   Richard Malmsheimer, "From Rappaccini to Marcus Welby: The Evolution of an Image" (Ph.D. diss., University of Minnesota, 1978), 228.

37.   For biographies of Osler, see Harvey Cushing, *The Life of Sir William Osler*, 2 vols. (Oxford: Clarendon Press, 1925); and Edith Gittings Reid, *The Great Physician: A Short Life of Sir William Osler* (London: Oxford University Press, 1931).

38.   This interpretation of the twentieth-century heroes was made by Professor Donald Fleming, Lectures on "American Intellectual History, 1900 to the Present," Harvard University.

39.   William Sydney Thayer, "The Heart of the Library," in William Sydney Thayer, *Osler and Other Papers* (Baltimore: The Johns Hopkins University Press, 1931), 44.

40.   Reid, *The Great Physician*, 124.

41.   Quoted in C. N. B. Camac, ed., *Counsels and Ideals from the Writings of William Osler*, 2nd ed. (Boston: Houghton Mifflin Company, 1921), 343.

42.   Ibid., 72, 73.

43.   Mark R. Everett, *Medical Education in Oklahoma: The University of Oklahoma School of Medicine and Medical Center 1900–1931* (Norman: University of Oklahoma Press, 1972), 155–56.

44.   W. David Baird, *Medical Education in Arkansas, 1879–1978* (Memphis: Memphis State University Press, 1979), 136.

45.   Harvey, *The Interurban Clinical Club*, 186.

Chapter 7

1.   Richard Shryock, *American Medical Research, Past and Present* (New York: Commonwealth Fund, 1947), 49.

2.   William W. Keen, "Medical Education," in William W. Keen, *Addresses and Other Papers* (Philadelphia: W. B. Saunders, 1905), 197.

3.   Henry Ward, "Address of the President," in Proceedings of the Eighteenth Annual

Meeting of the Association of American Medical Colleges, March 16–17, 1908, p. 34, Association of American Medical Colleges Archives, Washington, D.C.

4. *Annual Report of the President and the Treasurer of Harvard College* (1899–1900), 20.

5. Medical faculty meeting minutes, 18 Nov. 1875; R. E. Rogers to the Committee of the Board of Trustees of the Medical Department, Dec. 1875, in Medical faculty meeting minutes, 1 Dec. 1875; and Letter from Medical Faculty to the Committee of the Board of Trustees on the Medical Department, 19 Feb. 1876, in Medical faculty meeting minutes, 18 Feb. 1876. All of these references are in the University of Pennsylvania School of Medicine Collection, University of Pennsylvania Archives.

6. Faculty meeting minutes, 5 May 1887, College of Physicians and Surgeons, Office of the Dean, College of Physicians and Surgeons, Columbia University.

7. "Debt of the College of Physicians and Surgeons," in File, "College of P & S, 1878–1892, 6 documents . . . regarding financial matters of the college," in College of Physicians and Surgeons, Papers, Butler Library, Columbia University.

8. Abraham Flexner, *Medical Education in the United States and Canada* (New York: Carnegie Foundation for the Advancement of Teaching, 1910), 133.

9. Henry Pritchett to James R. Day, 19 April 1910, File, "Syracuse University 1905–1938," Carnegie Foundation Archives, Carnegie Corporation.

10. University of Michigan, *President's Annual Report* (1896), 13.

11. Flexner, *Medical Education*, 133.

12. Statutes of the Medical School of Maine (faculty meeting minutes), 19 June 1909, Special Collections, Bowdoin College Library.

13. Flexner, *Medical Education*, 140, 185–319, appendix. The number of schools (131) in 1910, referred to earlier in the book, is less than the number cited here (148) because Flexner's survey included postgraduate schools. In some instances, Flexner obtained actual budgetary statistics; in other instances he knew only the resources available to the school. In the latter cases the figures cited here are likely to be high because faculties at many of the lesser schools kept part of the tuition income for personal dividends.

14. "Annual Statement of the Condition of the St. Louis University Medical School, May 22, 1909," File, "St. Louis University," Abraham Flexner Papers, Library of Congress.

15. "Report of Financial Committee," Faculty meeting minutes, 8 April 1896, Western Reserve University School of Medicine, Case Western Reserve University Archives.

16. *Annual Report of Provost and Treasurer of the University of Pennsylvania* (1902), 21.

17. See, for example, University of Michigan, *President's Annual Report* (1899), 9–10; University of Minnesota, *Biennial Report of the Board of Regents* (1901–02), 137. For Pennsylvania and Western Reserve, see the ensuing discussion in text.

18. Medical faculty meeting minutes, 26 Oct. 1908, University of Pennsylvania School of Medicine.

19. Ibid.

20. See, for instance, "Report of the Dean of the Medical School," in Western Reserve University, *Report of the President and Faculties* (1894–95), 40; "Report of Committee on Advertising," Faculty meeting minutes, 10 Feb. 1899, Western Reserve University School of Medicine; "Report of the Dean of the Medical College," in Western Reserve University, *Report of the President and Faculties* (1901–02), 76.

21. Western Reserve University, *Report of the President and Faculties* (1909–10), 37 (plea for endowment), 36 (quotation).

22. Memorandum of Nicholas Murray Butler, in Faculty meeting minutes, 17 Jan. 1910, College of Physicians and Surgeons, Columbia University.

23. Columbia University, *Annual Report* (1903), 35.

24. Ibid., 34–38.

25. Columbia University, *Annual Report* (1908), 33.

26. Yale University, *President's Report* (1890), 44–47.

27. See, for instance, "Report of the Department of Medicine," in Yale University, *President's Report* (1905), 144–45.

28. "Report of the Department of Medicine," in Yale University, *President's Report* (1901), 91 (endowment needs); "Report of the Department of Medicine," in Yale University, *President's Report* (1909), 198 (quotation).

29. Annual Report, Board of Overseers of the Medical Department, 4 June 1901, in Minutes of the Overseers of the Medical Department of Washington University, June 1891–November 1905, Washington University School of Medicine Archives.

30. "Report of the Special Committee on the Medical School," Folder, "University of Pittsburgh School of Medicine Faculty Council c. 1910," Historical Materials, Falk Library, University of Pittsburgh; "Report of the Dean of the College of Medicine," in University of Cincinnati, *Annual Report of the Board of Directors* (1904), 51; "Extracts from Argument in favor of proposed merger of the University College of Medicine with the Medical College of Virginia, July 1906," File, "University College of Medicine, Richmond, Virginia," Abraham Flexner Papers, Library of Congress.

31. *Annual Report of the President of Tufts College* (1905–06), 12.

32. "Tufts College Medical School," in N. P. Colwell to Hermon C. Bumpus, 10 June 1915, Medical Correspondence, 1908–17, Tufts University Archives.

33. "Report of the Dean of the College of Medicine," in University of Nebraska, *Biennial Report of the Board of Regents to the Governor* (1903), 43.

34. Statutes of the Medical School of Maine (faculty meeting minutes), 19 June 1909, Bowdoin College Library; Bowdoin College, *President's Report* (1910–11), 22–26; William J. Tucker to William T. Smith, 24 Dec. 1900, in Meeting of 25 Feb. 1901, Records of the Medical Faculty of Dartmouth College, Dartmouth College Archives; "A Needed Improvement in Medical Teaching in America," File, "Fordham University," Abraham Flexner Papers, Library of Congress; "Needs and Remedies," *The Hospital Bulletin of the University of Maryland* 6 (1910): 129–30; "Annual Statement of the Condition of the St. Louis University Medical School, May 22, 1909," File, "St. Louis University," Abraham Flexner Papers, Library of Congress; Drake University *Bulletin* (June 1903): 154; Brown Ayres to Henry Pritchett, 29 March 1909, File, "University of Tennessee," Carnegie Foundation Archives, Carnegie Corporation; W. S. Leathers to Henry Pritchett, 21 April 1910, File, "University of Mississippi," Abraham Flexner Papers, Library of Congress; J. T. Kingsbury to Henry Pritchett, 23 April 1910, File, "University of Utah," Abraham Flexner Papers, Library of Congress; meeting of 13 Feb. 1909, and statement of W. Jarvis Barlow to faculty of College of Medicine, in meeting of 10 June 1909, in Minutes of the College of Medicine of the University of Southern California, Norris Medical Library, University of Southern California, Los Angeles.

35. "Memorandum for President Pritchett in relation to Washburn College and its Medical Department," 10 Jan. 1910, Frank Knight Sanders Papers, Washburn University Library, Topeka, Kansas.

36. Edward A. Balloch to Wilbur P. Thirkield, 16 May 1910, File, "Howard University," Carnegie Foundation Archives, Carnegie Corporation.

37. Paul Bartsch to Henry Pritchett, 14 April 1919, File, "Howard University," Carnegie Foundation Archives, Carnegie Corporation.

38. "Medical Education for Negroes," report of N. P. Colwell to Council on Medical Education, with N. P. Colwell to Henry Pritchett, 12 March 1918, File, "American Medical Association 1915–39," Carnegie Foundation Archives, Carnegie Corporation.

39. *Annual Report of Provost and Treasurer of the University of Pennsylvania* (1899), 26.

40. Faculty meeting minutes, 22 Feb. 1898, New York University School of Medicine, New York University School of Medicine Archives.

41. Kenneth M. Ludmerer, "Reform at Harvard Medical School, 1869–1909," *Bulletin of the History of Medicine* 55 (1981): 360–63.

42. Susan R. Barton to William Pepper, 17 Sept. 1877, p. 230, William Pepper Papers, University of Pennsylvania Library, Philadelphia.

43. Henry C. Lea to William Pepper, 31 Oct. 1889, p. 621, Pepper Papers; Board of Trustee meeting minutes, 21 May 1891, University of Pennsylvania, University of Pennsylvania Archives.

44. Albert R. Lamb, *The Presbyterian Hospital and the Columbia-Presbyterian Medical Center 1868–1943* (New York: Columbia University Press, 1955), 72–73.

45. Western Reserve University, *Report of the President and Faculties* (1892–93), 63–64, 65.

46. Bellevue Hospital Medical College and Carnegie Laboratory, *Circular*, Spring 1886, New York University School of Medicine Archives.

47. Andrew Carnegie, *Address to the Graduating Class of Medical Students of Bellevue Hospital, New York* (New York: C. G. Burgoyne, 1885), 5–9.

48. Eric Larrabee, *The Benevolent and Necessary Institution: The New York Hospital 1771–1971* (Garden City, N. Y.: Doubleday, 1971), 289.

49. Cornell University Medical College, *Announcement* (1906–1907), 22; "Cornell's New Building is Formally Opened," The Brooklyn *Eagle*, 29 Dec. 1900, Volume of Memorabilia, Cornell University Medical College, 1891–1903, Medical Archives, New York Hospital-Cornell University Medical Center; Faculty meeting minutes, 21 Nov. 1908, Cornell University Medical College, Medical Archives, New York Hospital-Cornell University Medical Center.

50. Ludmerer, "Reform at Harvard Medical School," 363–70.

51. More will be said of medical philanthropy in chapter 10.

52. On the funding of American science in the nineteenth century, see Howard S. Miller, *Dollars for Research: Science and Its Patrons in Nineteenth-Century America* (Seattle: University of Washington Press, 1970).

53. Columbia University, *Annual Report* (1911), 6.

54. Minutes of the Alumni Association of the Medical Department of Western Reserve College (1872–1915), 16 June 1909, Howard Dittrick Museum of Historical Medicine, Cleveland Health Sciences Library; University of Michigan, *President's Annual Report* (1905), 34.

55. "The College of Medicine and Surgery," in University of Minnesota, *The President's Report* (1911–12), 117–18.

56. Flexner, *Medical Education*, 136.

57. J. T. Kingsbury to Henry Pritchett, 23 April 1910, File, "University of Utah," Abraham Flexner Papers, Library of Congress.

58. Henry Pritchett to J. C. Branner, 29 Nov. 1913, File, "Stanford University," Carnegie Foundation Archives, Carnegie Corporation.

59. Henry Pritchett to Theodore Hough, 29 Nov. 1920, File "Henry Pritchett 1920–30," Abraham Flexner Papers, Library of Congress.

60. Drake University *Bulletin* (June 1903), 154.

61. A splendid study of the Rockefeller Sanitary Commission for the Eradication of Hookworm Disease is John Ettling, *The Germ of Laziness: Rockefeller Philanthropy and Public Health in the New South* (Cambridge: Harvard University Press, 1981).

62. Correspondence on this matter is found in Box 255, Charles Eliot Papers, Harvard University Archives.

63. Robert Brookings to Henry Pritchett, 29 Dec. 1909, in Marjorie Fox Grisham, "Research Notes," manuscript, Washington University Archives.

64. See correspondence in File, "Gifts 1890–1906," George Blumer Papers, Yale University Medical School Library.

65. George Blumer to Doctor Howland, 23 April 1909, File, "1909—J. M. Flint's Budget," Blumer Papers; "Report of the Department of Medicine," in Yale University, *President's Report* (1905), 145.

66. "Report of the Dean of the Medical School," in Western Reserve University, *Report of the President and Faculties* (1902–03), 50.

67. "Report of the Department of Medicine," in Yale University, *President's Report* (1910), 191.

68. "The Success of the Harvard Medical School," *Boston Medical and Surgical Journal* 88 (1873): 632.

Chapter 8

1. Graham Lusk to Phillip Shaffer, 5 April 1911, Folder, "1911," Box 12, Phillip A. Shaffer Papers, Washington University School of Medicine Archives.

2. Western Reserve University, *Reports of the President and Faculties* (1908–09), 47.

3. "Communication addressed to Dr. Wm. J. Mayo," 1914, Folder, "Miscellaneous Correspondence, 1883–1948," Miscellaneous Box 3, University of Minnesota Medical School, Papers, University of Minnesota Archives.

4. Secondary literature on clinical teaching in America is scanty. The most thorough discussions are contained in the essays on clinical subjects in Ronald L. Numbers, ed., *The Education of American Physicians: Historical Essays* (Berkeley: University of California Press, 1979). Clinical instruction is also discussed in Edward C. Atwater, " 'Making Fewer Mistakes': A History of Students and Patients," *Bulletin of the History of Medicine* 57 (1983): 165–87; Kenneth M. Ludmerer, "Reform of Medical Education at Washington University," *Journal of the History of Medicine and Allied Sciences* 35 (1980): 149–73; and Kenneth M. Ludmerer, "Reform at Harvard Medical School, 1869–1909," *Bulletin of the History of Medicine* 55 (1981): 343–70. The interested reader would be well advised to consult Abraham Flexner's account of clinical teaching in *Medical Education in the United States and Canada* (New York: Carnegie Foundation for the Advancement of Teaching, 1910), 91–125.

5. William Welch, "The Relation of the Hospital to Medical Education and Research," in William Welch, *Papers and Addresses*, vol. 3 (Baltimore: The Johns Hopkins University Press, 1920), 135.

6. For a description of the clerkship and its advantages over other methods of clinical teaching, see William Osler, "The Hospital as a College," in William Osler, *Aequanimitas with other Addresses to Medical Students, Nurses and Practitioners of Medicine*, 3rd ed. (Philadelphia: Blakiston, 1932), 311–25.

7. William Osler, "The Fixed Period," in Osler, *Aequanimitas*, 389.

8. Faculty meeting minutes, 22 May 1902, School of Medicine, Georgetown University, Georgetown University Archives.

9. Cornell University Medical College, *Announcement* (1906–07), 43.

10. "Report of the Dean of the Medical School," in Columbia University, *Annual Report* (1909), 65–66.

11. Frederic A. Washburn, *The Massachusetts General Hospital: Its Development, 1900–1935* (Boston: Houghton Mifflin, 1939), 169–70.

12. The outpatient clinic was widely used for clinical teaching in the latter nineteenth and early twentieth centuries. For a discussion of the dispensary, see Charles Rosenberg, "Social Class and Medical Care in 19th-Century America: The Rise and Fall of the Dispensary," *Journal of the History of Medicine and Allied Sciences* 29 (1974): 32–54.

13. "Report of the Dean of the Medical School," in Columbia University, *Annual Report* (1906), 105–7; "The Clinic in Medical Instruction," *Columbia University Quarterly* 9 (1907): 179.

14. Faculty meeting minutes, 7 Dec. 1910, Western Reserve University School of Medicine, Case Western Reserve University Archives. See also Faculty meeting minutes, 8 July 1909, Case Western Reserve University Archives.

15. This discussion is not meant to deny the value of outpatient instruction, but merely to indicate its limitations when used as the exclusive method of clinical teaching. Medical educators of the early 1900s acknowledged these limitations. For instance, see Columbia University, *Annual Report* (1903), 38–39.

16. For instance, in 1900 a committee of medical students at Harvard forcefully expressed its dissatisfaction with the educational limitations of outpatient instruction. See "A Report from the Committee of Graduates and Undergraduates upon the Course of Study at the Harvard Medical School," 1899, p. 80, Countway Library, Harvard Medical School.

17. William Welch, "Present Position of Medical Education, Its Development and Great Needs for the Future," in Welch, *Papers and Addresses*, 113.

18. Flexner, *Medical Education*, 105.

19. William Osler to Henry Bowditch, 20 June 1886, Henry P. Bowditch Papers, Countway Library, Harvard Medical School; Harvey Cushing to Arthur Hadley, 30 April 1906, Series I, Box 27, Arthur Hadley Letters, Yale University Archives. As it happened, many prominent hospital positions were occupied by outstanding, dedicated teachers. However, this would occur strictly by chance; the system was not designed to find and reward such persons.

20. "Report of the Dean of the Medical School," in Columbia University, *Annual Report* (1909), 65.

21. Welch, "Present Position of Medical Education," 114; Welch, "Formal Opening of the Peter Bent Brigham Hospital," in Welch, *Papers and Addresses*, 155.

22. Welch, "Present Position of Medical Education," 114.

23. Flexner, *Medical Education,* 108.

24. David Riesman, "Clinical Teaching in America, With Some Remarks on Early Medical Schools," *Transactions and Studies of the College of Physicians of Philadelphia,* 3d ser., 7 (1939): 91–95; Edward D. Churchill, "The Development of the Hospital," in *The Hospital in Contemporary Life,* ed. Nathaniel W. Faxon (Cambridge: Harvard University Press, 1949), 29–30; Richard H. Shryock, *The History of Nursing* (Philadelphia: W. B. Saunders, 1959), 213–14.

25. Francis R. Packard, *History of Medicine in the United States* (New York: Hafner, 1931), 322–25, 327; William H. Williams, *America's First Hospital: The Pennsylvania Hospital, 1751–1841* (Wayne, Pa.: Haverford House, 1976), 108. Similarly, the original rules of the Massachusetts General Hospital permitted students in the hospital only at the appointed hours on the appointed days. Students were not allowed to walk freely about the wards or to converse with patients or nurses. They could examine patients only when specifically instructed to do so because "it must be obvious that the greatest inconveniences must arise, if such examinations were commonly made by the pupils" ("Massachusetts General Hospital," statement written by James Jackson and John C. Warren, May 1824, File, "Medical Education," Massachusetts General Hospital Archives).

26. Trustee meeting minutes, 6 Sept. 1907, Peter Bent Brigham Hospital, Administrative Office, Peter Bent Brigham Hospital, Boston. Such indignities were commonplace. At Charity Hospital of Cleveland in 1884, Western Reserve students were not permitted in the main hall of the building. At Boston City Hospital in 1892, Harvard students were permitted to walk the wards with their professors, but only under jeopardy of being banned from the hospital for even the slightest disturbance (Faculty meeting minutes, 8 Sept. 1884, Western Reserve University School of Medicine; G. H. M. Rowe to C. P. Worcester, 18 June 1892, Folder, "Letters, 1892," Box 2, Harvard Medical School, Dean's Office Files, c. 1839–1900, Countway Library, Harvard Medical School).

27. Lawrence D. Longo, "Obstetrics and Gynecology," in Numbers, *The Education of American Physicians,* 220. Learning obstetrics by doing in the unsupervised setting of the home was not necessarily a satisfactory experience for students or patients. This point was illustrated in 1917, when tragedy struck during a complicated delivery attended by two unsupervised third-year students of the University of Colorado. A thirteen-pound baby was delivered stillborn, dead from asphyxiation, the cord being wrapped tight around its neck. The students had been present for over ten hours without calling for help. During this time, they had administered anesthesia as well as an agent to hasten labor. The fault lay with both the students, who exercised poor judgment in not calling for help, and with the faculty, whose administrative laxity in not clearly defining what students were permitted to do by themselves allowed the situation to happen. Even with a faculty member present, the same outcome might have occurred, but the incident clearly illustrated the problems that could arise from poor student supervision (Executive faculty meeting minutes, 7 Feb. 1917, University of Colorado School of Medicine, Denison Memorial Library, University of Colorado Health Sciences Center, Denver).

28. The history of the hospital in America remains to be written, but attention should be drawn to Charles Rosenberg's seminal articles, "And Heal the Sick: The Hospital and the Patient in 19th Century America," *Journal of Social History* 10 (1977): 428–47; and "Inward Vision and Outward Glance: The Shaping of the American Hospital, 1880–1914," *Bulletin of the History of Medicine* 53 (1979): 346–91. Also very helpful are Morris J. Vogel, *The Invention of the Modern Hospital: Boston, 1870–1930* (Chicago: The University of Chicago Press, 1980); Harry F. Dowling, *City Hospitals: The Undercare of the Underprivileged* (Cambridge: Harvard University Press, 1982); David Rosner, *A Once Charitable Enterprise: Hospitals and Health Care in Brooklyn and New York 1885–1915* (Cambridge: Cambridge University Press, 1982); and Churchill, "The Development of the Hospital."

29. Flexner, *Medical Education,* 299–300.

30. Ibid., 239.

31. Ibid., 209; R. H. Whitehead to Henry Pritchett, 7 Nov. 1909, File, "State University of Iowa 1905–1914," Carnegie Foundation Archives, Carnegie Corporation, New York; Frank Strong to My dear Doctor, 17 Oct. 1910, Frank Knight Sanders Papers, Washburn University Library, Topeka, Kansas; "The Medical School," in University of Minnesota, *The President's Report* (1912–13), 75; (1913–14), 99; and (1914–15), 71.

32. "The Medical School," in University of Minnesota, *The President's Report* (1912–13), 72; "Communication addressed to Dr. Wm. J. Mayo," University of Minnesota Archives (quotation).

33. Flexner, *Medical Education*, 194 (quotation), 196; Henry Pritchett to David Starr Jordan, 22 May 1911, File, "Stanford University," Carnegie Foundation Archives, Carnegie Corporation.

34. Dock's teaching exercises were transcribed and preserved in a remarkable set of volumes, "Clinical Notebooks of George Dock, 1899–1908," Michigan Historical Collections, Bentley Historical Library, University of Michigan. It is apparent from these records that Michigan students were given responsibility for patient care. At the start of each rotation, Dock would inform the students that "the patient is under your care as part of your duties." He would instruct them "to follow up the case as long as the patient is in the hospital, seeing the patient at least once or twice a day." Students were required to make "daily visits and observations and notes" (sessions of 30 Sept. 1904 and 27 Sept. 1907). For another detailed description of the sophisticated methods of clinical teaching employed at the University of Michigan, see C. L. Ford to the Editor of *Medical News*, n.d., Folder, "Correspondence & Miscellaneous Material, 1902–1903 and Undated," Box 72, Records of the Medical School of the University of Michigan, Michigan Historical Collections, Bentley Historical Library, University of Michigan.

35. Reuben Peterson to Victor C. Vaughan, 25 Feb. 1899, Folder 2, Box 1, Reuben Peterson Papers, Michigan Historical Collections, Bentley Historical Library, University of Michigan.

36. Ibid. On the needs of the University of Michigan Hospital, see also Reuben Peterson to The Honorable Board of Regents, 15 Feb. 1900, University of Michigan, Folder 2, Box 1, Reuben Peterson Papers.

37. University of Michigan, President's *Annual Report* (1895), 14; "Clinical Notebooks of George Dock," session of 27 Sept. 1901.

38. Victor Vaughan to Honorable Harry C. Bulkley, 1 Dec. 1916, and Victor Vaughan to Walter H. Sawyer, 6 Dec. 1916, Box 4, Records of the Medical School of the University of Michigan.

39. Marjorie Fox, "History of Washington University School of Medicine" (Unpublished manuscript, 1949–52), chap. 2, pp. 8–10, Washington University School of Medicine Archives; Winfield Chaplin to W. K. Bixby, 8 Aug. 1904, Chancellor's Records, Washington University, Washington University Archives.

40. Statement of Samuel Lambert to the faculty, in Faculty meeting minutes, 16 Oct. 1905, College of Physicians and Surgeons, Office of the Dean, College of Physicians and Surgeons, Columbia University; *Annual Report* (1903), 36–37; and "Report of the Dean of the Medical School," in Columbia University, *Annual Report* (1908), 84.

41. Wendy N. Jacobson, "American Medicine in Transition: The Case of the Yale Medical School, 1900–1920," (Senior honors thesis, Department of History, Wesleyan University, 1976), 50.

42. E. W. Hooper to Frederick Shattuck, 8 Feb. 1892, in James Clarke White, File, "Committee on Improved Clinical Facilities, 1889–1892," Countway Library, Harvard Medical School.

43. By virtue of its close affiliation with the Mary Hitchcock Memorial Hospital, Dartmouth was able to employ advanced methods of clinical instruction. Students would examine patients at the bedside, assist in operations, administer ether, perform dressing changes, conduct tests of blood and urine, follow the daily progress of patients assigned to them, and discuss the diagnosis, prognosis, and course of their patients with their instructors. However, the value of this experience was greatly diminished by the few patients that were seen. A cottage hospital of only forty beds, Mary Hitchcock in 1909–10 received only 826 admissions. Of these, a mere 159 were cases in internal medicine, which was universally considered the backbone of clinical teaching.

The situation was much better at Western Reserve, where, in an arrangement facilitated by overlapping boards of trustees, the medical school had enjoyed a true teaching affiliation with Lakeside Hospital since 1898. However, Western Reserve's clinical teaching was handicapped by the school's weak financial position. Its clinical instructors served the school without any remuneration, making their university work, in the words of President Charles Thwing, "an unprofitable side-line." Other high grade schools with whom Western Reserve competed—Harvard, Pennsylvania, Columbia, Cornell, Johns Hopkins, New York University, Michigan, Minnesota, California —paid their clinical professors from $1,500 to $7,500 a year, making it much easier for instructors at those schools to find the time to teach students individually and conduct research. For this reason Thwing felt that the improvement of the clinical departments was "a much more serious need of the school" than improvement of the laboratory departments, which already had salaried instructors. He viewed the endowment of the clinical departments as the school's urgent need "if this is to remain a university school in fact as well as in name." The faculty, too, acknowledged that despite the school's hospital advantages, its clinical material was "not being used to the maximum of efficiency." See Dartmouth College Medical School, *Catalogue* (1910–11), 7; Western Reserve University, *Report of the President and Faculties* (1908–09), 47; and "Report of the Dean of the Medical School," in Western Reserve University, *Report of the President and Faculties* (1900–01), 166; (1906–07), 48–58; and (1907–08), 45–60. Also Faculty meeting minutes, 8 Nov. 1910, Western Reserve University School of Medicine.

44. Osler, "The Hospital as a College," 320.

45. Faculty meeting minutes, 14 May 1906, College of Physicians and Surgeons, Columbia University; Faculty meeting minutes, 11 April 1908, Cornell University Medical College, Medical Archives, New York Hospital-Cornell University Medical Center.

46. Society of the New York Hospital, *Annual Report* (1910), 45.

47. White, File, "Committee on Improved Clinical Facilities."

48. "The Need of a Hospital for the Harvard Medical School," *Boston Medical and Surgical Journal* 155 (1906): 352.

49. Yale University, *President's Report* (1912), 23; "A Statement of Interest and Importance to Every Friend of Yale University," with Starr Murphy to Wallace Buttrick, 19 Feb. 1914, Folder 6661, Box 635, Series I, General Education Board Papers, Rockefeller Archive Center, North Tarrytown, New York; Minutes of the Meetings of the Faculty Council, 2 Oct. 1916, Historical Materials, Falk Library, University of Pittsburgh; "Report of the Special Committee on the Medical School," in Folder, "University of Pittsburgh School of Medicine Faculty Council c. 1910," Historical Materials, Falk Library, University of Pittsburgh; "Administration and Organization of American Medical Schools," in Folder, "University of Pittsburgh School of Medicine History 1908–14," Historical Materials, Falk Library, University of Pittsburgh; Minutes of the Meetings of the Faculty Council, 2 Oct. 1916, Historical Materials, Falk Library, University of Pittsburgh; Charles L. Greene to Victor Vaughan, 27 Jan. 1915, Box 1, Records of the Medical School of the University of Michigan; Petition of the Executive Faculty to the President and Board of Regents of the University of Colorado, in Executive faculty meeting minutes, 8 Feb. 1919, University of Colorado School of Medicine; Executive faculty meeting minutes, 2 March 1918, University of Colorado School of Medicine; "Statement of W. Jarvis Barlow to faculty of College of Medicine," in Minutes of the College of Medicine of the University of Southern California, 10 June 1909, Norris Medical Library, University of Southern California.

50. F. W. Evans to C. C. Bass, 6 June 1925, and John H. Musser to Richard M. Pearce, 3 March 1925, in Folder 7247, Box 706, Series I, General Education Board Papers, Rockefeller Archive Center. See also Musser to Pearce, 17 Jan. 1925, Bass to Abraham Flexner, 19 June 1925, and Abraham Flexner, "Notes on Tulane University," December 1924, in Folder 7247, Box 706, Series I, General Education Board Papers, Rockefeller Archive Center. In addition, see C. C. Bass and Wickliffe Rose, meeting of 9 May 1924, Wickliffe Rose Diary, General Education Board Papers, Rockefeller Archive Center; and Frank H. Watson to Henry A. Christian, 9 April 1908, Volume 1, Henry A. Christian Papers, Countway Library, Harvard Medical School.

51. Columbia University, *Annual Report* (1910), 31.

52. For histories of the College of Physicians and Surgeons, Columbia University, see Willard C. Rappleye, *The Current Era of the Faculty of Medicine, Columbia University, 1910–1958* (New York: Columbia University Press, 1958); Albert R. Lamb, *The Presbyterian Hospital and the Columbia-Presbyterian Medical Center 1868–1943* (New York: Columbia University Press, 1955); and Frederic Lee, "The School of Medicine," in *A History of Columbia University, 1754–1904* (New York: Columbia University Press, 1904), 307–34.

53. "Report of the Dean of the Medical School," in Columbia University, *Annual Report* (1905), 84.

54. For a history of Roosevelt Hospital, see New York [City] Roosevelt Hospital, *The Roosevelt Hospital, 1871–1957* (New York: Roosevelt Hospital, 1957).

55. Roosevelt Hospital, *Annual Report* (1908), 32.
56. Information concerning the negotiations between Roosevelt Hospital and Columbia Medical School, if not otherwise specified, has been taken from Files 112a and 112b, Dean's Office Files, College of Physicians and Surgeons, Office of the Dean, College of Physicians and Surgeons, Columbia University; and Faculty meeting minutes, 1905–1910, College of Physicians and Surgeons, Columbia University.
57. Lambert interned at Bellevue Hospital in 1885–86.
58. Samuel Lambert to James W. McLane et al., 10 April 1908, File 112b, Dean's Office Files, College of Physicians and Surgeons, Columbia University.
59. Columbia University, *Annual Report* (1908), 34.
60. Samuel Lambert to W. Emlen Roosevelt, 25 Nov. 1910, File 112a, Dean's Office Files, College of Physicians and Surgeons.
61. Ibid.
62. William Darrach to Samuel Lambert, 1910, File 112a, Dean's Office Files, College of Physicians and Surgeons, Columbia University.
63. Samuel Lambert to W. Emlen Roosevelt, 3 Nov. 1910, File 112a, Dean's Office Files, College of Physicians and Surgeons, Columbia University.
64. Maurice J. Lewi to Honorable Andrew S. Draper, 31 Jan. 1911, File 196, Dean's Office Files, College of Physicians and Surgeons, Columbia University.
65. Samuel Lambert to W. Emlen Roosevelt, 16 Feb. 1912, File 112a, Dean's Office Files, College of Physicians and Surgeons, Columbia University.
66. Roosevelt Hospital, *The Roosevelt Hospital*, 78–80; Lamb, *The Presbyterian Hospital and the Columbia-Presbyterian Medical Center*, 74.
67. James W. McLane et al. to the Faculty of the College of Physicians and Surgeons, 6 Dec. 1910, with Faculty meeting minutes, 19 Dec. 1910, College of Physicians and Surgeons, Columbia University.
68. Joseph A. Blake to George L. Rives, 17 April 1909, File 112b, Dean's Office Files, College of Physicians and Surgeons, Columbia University.
69. Ibid.
70. Biographical information on McLane has been obtained from "James Wood McLane" in *Cyclopedia of American Physicians and Surgeons*, ed. John Shrady (New York: Hershey, 1903). For a record of some of his gifts to the school, see James W. McLane to Dear Doctor, 25 Oct. 1872, in College of Physicians and Surgeons, Papers, Butler Library, Columbia University; Faculty meeting minutes, 6 June 1887, College of Physicians and Surgeons, Columbia University.
71. Lamb, *The Presbyterian Hospital and Columbia-Presbyterian Medical Center*, 74.

Chapter 9

1. "Clinical Notebooks of George Dock, 1899–1908," session of 23 Feb. 1906, Michigan Historical Collections, Bentley Historical Library, University of Michigan.
2. Gerald E. Markowitz and David Rosner have reminded us of the primacy of these motives among many practitioners in their article, "Doctors in Crisis: A Study of the Use of Medical Education Reform to Establish Modern Professional Elitism in Medicine," *American Quarterly* 25 (1973): 83–107.
3. Abraham Flexner, *Medical Education in the United States and Canada* (New York: Carnegie Foundation for the Advancement of Teaching, 1910), 36–37.
4. Frank K. Sanders to Henry Pritchett, 31 Jan. 1910, File, "Washburn College," Carnegie Foundation Archives, Carnegie Corporation, New York.
5. Bowdoin College, *President's Report* (1909–10), 23.
6. Some records of the Federation have been preserved in Miscellaneous Boxes 1 and 2, University of Minnesota Medical School, Papers, University of Minnesota Archives. As a sign of the weakness of the Association of American Medical Colleges, Flexner found in 1910 that thirty-five of the fifty member colleges were not meeting the Association's minimal standards, and only in 1914 did the Association drop the first member school for not conforming to minimal requirements ("History of Minimum Standards and Accreditation and the Role of the American

Association of Medical Colleges," Miscellaneous Historical Documents, Association of American Medical Colleges Archives, Washington, D.C.).

7. Rosemary Stevens, *American Medicine and the Public Interest* (New Haven: Yale University Press, 1971), 386–87.

8. Arthur Dean Bevan, "Cooperation in Medical Education and Medical Service," *Journal of the American Medical Association* 90 (1928): 1173–77.

9. On the cooperation between the Council and the Carnegie Foundation, see Minutes of Business Meetings of the Council on Medical Education and Hospitals, 1907–17, 28 Dec. 1908, American Medical Association Archives, Chicago; and correspondence in File, "American Medical Association 1909–1914," Carnegie Foundation Archives, Carnegie Corporation. From the Council meeting of 28 Dec. 1908, the following record appears:

> He [Pritchett] agreed with the opinion previously expressed by members of the Council that while the Foundation would be guided very largely by the Council's investigations, to avoid the usual claims of partiality no more mention should be made in the report of the Council than any other source of information. The report would therefore be, and have the weight of an independent report of a disinterested body, which would then be published far and wide. It would do much to develop public opinion.

10. On Pritchett's life, see Abraham Flexner, *Henry Pritchett: A Biography* (New York: Columbia University Press, 1943).

11. Henry Pritchett to Mr. Wister, 3 Jan. 1908, File, "Carnegie Foundation for the Advancement of Teaching, 1908–1913," Box 8, Henry Pritchett Papers, Library of Congress. On Pritchett's interest in promoting original research, see also Henry Pritchett to Andrew Carnegie, 14 Jan. 1902, and Henry Pritchett to Andrew Carnegie, 21 Jan. 1908, File, "Andrew Carnegie," Box 2, Pritchett Papers, Library of Congress.

12. An insightful history of the Carnegie Foundation is Ellen Condliffe Lagemann, *Private Power for the Public Good: A History of the Carnegie Foundation for the Advancement of Teaching* (Middletown, Conn.: Wesleyan University Press, 1983). Still useful is Howard J. Savage, *Fruit of an Impulse: Forty-Five Years of the Carnegie Foundation 1905–1950* (New York: Harcourt, Brace, 1953).

13. Lagemann, *Private Power*, 67.

14. Henry Pritchett to J. Norris Myers, 6 Jan. 1925, File, "Medical Education," Carnegie Foundation Archives. This quotation also appeared on the dustjacket to another book by Abraham Flexner, *Medical Education: A Comparative Study* (New York: Macmillan, 1925).

15. Biographical information has been obtained from Abraham Flexner, *I Remember: The Autobiography of Abraham Flexner* (New York: Simon and Schuster, 1940).

16. Daniel Fox, "Abraham Flexner's Unpublished Report: Foundations and Medical Education, 1909–1928," *Bulletin of the History of Medicine*, 54 (1980): 475–96.

17. Flexner, *I Remember*, 110.

18. Abraham Flexner, "Reminiscences of Dr. Welch," 16 May 1934, File, "William Welch," General Correspondence, Abraham Flexner Papers, Library of Congress.

19. Flexner, *I Remember*, 111.

20. Lawrence Cremin, *The Transformation of the School: Progressivism in American Education 1876–1957* (New York: Alfred A. Knopf, 1961), 280 n. 7.

21. Abraham Flexner, *A Modern College and A Modern School* (Garden City, N.Y.: Doubleday, Page & Company, 1923), 100.

22. Flexner, *I Remember*, 52.

23. Flexner, *Medical Education in the United States and Canada*, 53.

24. Ibid., 62.

25. Ibid., 63.

26. Ibid., 92.

27. Ibid., 92.

28. Ibid., 53.

29. Ibid., 62.

30. Ibid., 53.

31. Ibid., 117, 60, 61.

32. Ibid., 68–69.

33. Ibid., 98.
34. Ibid., 84.
35. Ibid., 97.
36. Ibid., 99.
37. Ibid., 55.
38. Ibid., 69.
39. Ibid., 68 n. 2.
40. Abraham Flexner, *Medical Education in Europe* (New York: Carnegie Foundation for the Advancement of Teaching, 1912), 168.
41. On the Lincoln School see Cremin, *Transformation of the School*, 280–91.
42. Ibid., 280.
43. Flexner, *I Remember*, 250.
44. Flexner, *Medical Education in the United States and Canada*, 24 (quotation), 20–27.
45. Ibid., 22.
46. Ibid., 22.
47. Ibid., 26.
48. Ibid., 48.
49. Ibid., 59.
50. Ibid., 56.
51. Ibid., 56.
52. Ibid., 56.
53. Ibid., 14.
54. Ibid., 17, 15.
55. Ibid., 89.
56. Ibid., 88.
57. Ibid., 88.
58. Ibid., 124.
59. Ibid., 173.
60. Ibid., 19.
61. Ibid., 89.
62. Flexner, "Reminiscences of Dr. Welch."
63. Records of the Carnegie Corporation note that "for the first eight years of the Corporation's history, and until the time of his death, Mr. Carnegie himself remained the president of the board, and the conduct of the Corporation was, in these years, under his personal direction and authority." With the exception of a $1 million grant to Vanderbilt Medical School in 1913, the Carnegie Corporation's involvement in medical education postdated Carnegie's death (Minutes of Meetings of the Board of Trustees, 1922, Carnegie Corporation Archives).
64. Minutes of Business Meetings of the Council on Medical Education and Hospitals, 28 Dec. 1910, American Medical Association Archives.
65. Victor Vaughan to Henry Pritchett, 7 Nov. 1912, File, "University of Michigan," Carnegie Foundation Archives, Carnegie Corporation.
66. Saul Jarcho, "Medical Education in the United States, 1910–1956," *Journal of the Mount Sinai Hospital* 26 (1959): 339–85; H. David Banta, "Abraham Flexner—A Reappraisal," *Social Science and Medicine* 5 (1971): 655–61; Robert P. Hudson, "Abraham Flexner in Perspective: American Medical Education, 1865–1910," *Bulletin of the History of Medicine* 46 (1972): 545–61; Carleton B. Chapman, "*The Flexner Report* by Abraham Flexner," *Daedalus* 103: (Winter 1974): 105–17; Stephen J. Kunitz, "Professionalism and Social Control in the Progressive Era: the Case of the Flexner Report," *Social Problems* 22 (1974): 16–27; Howard S. Berliner, "A Larger Perspective on the Flexner Report," *International Journal of Health Services* 5 (1975): 573–92; Howard S. Berliner, "New Light on the Flexner Report: Notes on the AMA-Carnegie Foundation Background," *Bulletin of the History of Medicine* 51 (1977): 603–9; Lester S. King, "The Flexner Report of 1910," *Journal of the American Medical Association* 251 (1984): 1079–86.
67. Steven Jonas, *Medical Mystery: The Training of Doctors in the United States* (New York: Norton, 1978); Michael J. Lepore, *Death of the Clinician: Requiem or Reveille?* (Springfield, Ill.: Charles C Thomas, 1982); Irving J. Lewis and Cecil G. Sheps, *The Sick Citadel: The*

American Academic Medical Center and the Public Interest (Cambridge, Mass.: Oelgeschlager, Gunn & Hain, 1983).

68. Harvard University, *The President's Report* (1982–83), 7.
69. Flexner, *Medical Education in the United States and Canada*, 26.
70. Ibid., 67–68.
71. Ibid., 26.
72. Ibid., 77.
73. Ibid., 76.
74. Ibid., 76.
75. Flexner, *Medical Education: A Comparative Study*, 18. This important but seldom cited book is well worth the reading. It sharply criticized American medical schools of 1925 for their crowded and rigid curricula and for placing too great an emphasis on rote learning. American medical education, to Flexner, had not yet fulfilled its promise.
76. Although this generalization is true, Flexner's condescending attitude toward blacks merits notice. See his comments on medical education for blacks in *Medical Education in the United States and Canada*, 180–81, and the discussion of his relations with Howard University in Kenneth R. Manning, *Black Apollo of Science: The Life of Ernest Everett Just* (New York: Oxford University Press, 1983), 128–29. Like so many "liberal" whites of the period, Flexner was not immune from expressing racial slurs. Nevertheless, his racism was relatively tame, compared with the malignant variety seen among extremists like the Ku Klux Klan and the eugenicists. Manning described him as a "paternalistic segregationist" and feels that despite his flaws, Flexner was "without doubt . . . one of the best allies a black could find among whites of that era" (Manning, *Black Apollo*, 128).
77. Flexner, *Medical Education in the United States and Canada*, 42.
78. Flexner, *I Remember*, 106.
79. Ibid., 106.
80. Ibid., 75.
81. Ibid., 3.
82. Flexner, *Medical Education in the United States and Canada*, 43.
83. Thomas Haskell, *The Emergence of Professional Social Science: The American Social Science Association and the Nineteenth-Century Crisis of Authority* (Urbana: University of Illinois Press, 1977).
84. Samuel P. Hays, *The Response to Industrialism, 1885–1894* (Chicago: The University of Chicago Press, 1957), 22.
85. Flexner, *Medical Education in the United States and Canada*, 143.
86. Flexner, *I Remember*, 131.
87. For instance, conditions at the Indiana University School of Medicine were no better than at some schools Flexner treated very harshly, but he told the dean, "I want to deal just as lightly with the defects of Indiana University as I conscientiously can." Schools that Flexner felt should be exterminated did not receive such charitable consideration (Abraham Flexner to B. D. Myers, 19 Feb. 1910, File, "Indiana University," Abraham Flexner Papers, Library of Congress).
88. Hans Zinsser, *As I Remember Him: The Biography of R. S.* (Boston: Little, Brown, 1940), 131.
89. Henry Pritchett to John L. Heffron, 18 June 1910, File, "Syracuse University 1905–1938," Carnegie Foundation Archives, Carnegie Corporation.
90. C. R. Bardeen to Abraham Flexner, 26 April 1910, File, "University of Wisconsin," Abraham Flexner Papers, Library of Congress; W. S. Carter to Abraham Flexner, 19 April 1910, File, "University of Texas," Abraham Flexner Papers, Library of Congress; Egbert Le Fevre to Henry Pritchett, 28 March 1910, File, "New York University," Abraham Flexner Papers, Library of Congress; A. Grant Evans to Henry Pritchett, 22 April 1910, File, "University of Oklahoma," Abraham Flexner Papers, Library of Congress.
91. Columbia University, *Annual Report* (1910), 31–32.
92. Joseph Bennett to Henry Pritchett, 5 April 1910, File, "Boston College of Physicians and Surgeons," Abraham Flexner Papers, Library of Congress; Charles F. Bevan to Henry Pritchett, 8 April 1910, File, "College of Physicians and Surgeons, Baltimore," Abraham Flexner Papers, Library of Congress; Henry Buchtel to Henry Pritchett, 23 Feb. 1910, File, "University

of Denver," Abraham Flexner Papers, Library of Congress; Frank L. Wilmeth to P. F. Collier and Son, 20 June 1910, File, "Collier's Magazine," Abraham Flexner Papers, Library of Congress.

93. William DeWitt Hyde to Henry Pritchett, 13 June 1910, File, "Bowdoin College," Carnegie Foundation Archives, Carnegie Corporation.

94. A. W. Harris to Henry Pritchett, 14 March 1910, File, "Northwestern University," Abraham Flexner Papers, Library of Congress.

95. Charles Dabney to Abraham Flexner, 5 May 1910, File, "University of Cincinnati," Abraham Flexner Papers, Library of Congress.

96. James R. Day to Henry Pritchett, 28 Feb. 1910, File, "Syracuse University 1905–1938," Carnegie Foundation Archives, Carnegie Corporation.

97. John L. Heffron to Henry Pritchett, 15 June 1910, File, "Syracuse University 1905–1938," Carnegie Foundation Archives, Carnegie Corporation.

98. William Charles White to Henry Pritchett, 25 Feb. 1915, File, "University of Pittsburgh 1905–1919," Carnegie Foundation Archives, Carnegie Corporation.

99. Flexner, *I Remember*, 131.

100. Henry Pritchett to William Halsted, 1 Nov. 1910, File, "The Johns Hopkins University," Carnegie Foundation Archives, Carnegie Corporation.

101. Frank L. Wilmeth to P. F. Collier and Son, 20 June 1910, File, "Collier's Magazine," Abraham Flexner Papers, Library of Congress.

102. J. H. Kirkland to Henry Pritchett, 11 Feb. 1913, File, "Vanderbilt University 1905–1915," Carnegie Foundation Archives, Carnegie Corporation. Curiously, many of the schools that sought the help of Pritchett or Flexner had initially been quite angered by the report. Pritchett told Flexner a few months after the report's release: "I am having at this time a most interesting time with a number of the medical schools which were hard hit by our criticisms of last June. Quite a number of these gentlemen who were ready with their defenses in June are coming to me in the quiet to consult as to what they can really do" (Henry Pritchett to Abraham Flexner, 27 Oct. 1910, File, "Henry Pritchett 1909–10," Flexner Papers, Library of Congress).

103. Flexner, *Medical Education in the United States and Canada*, 105, 123.

104. Henry Pritchett to Arthur D. Bevan, 21 March 1914, File, "American Medical Association 1909–1914," Carnegie Foundation Archives, Carnegie Corporation.

105. David E. Rogers, "Some Musings on Medical Education: Is It Going Astray?" *The Pharos* 45 (Spring 1982): 11–14.

106. Ibid., 13, 14.

107. Richard Hofstadter, *Anti-Intellectualism in American Life* (New York: Alfred Knopf, 1963), 323–58.

108. Cremin, *Transformation of the School*, vii.

Chapter 10

1. Richard H. Shryock, *American Medical Research, Past and Present* (New York: Commonwealth Fund, 1947), 79.

2. Ibid., 81.

3. Robert H. Bremner, *American Philanthropy* (Chicago: The University of Chicago Press, 1960).

4. Anson Phelps Stokes, Jr., to Herbert E. Smith, 24 June 1910, File, "1910–11 Administration," Box 10, Yale Medical School, Dean's Files, Yale University Archives; Yale University, *President's Report* (1911), 24; and Yale University, *President's Report* (1912), 24.

5. "Important Steps in the Development of the Yale University School of Medicine," in Folder, "1918—Reorganization of the School," Box 7, Yale Medical School, Dean's Files, Yale University Archives; George Day to Wallace Buttrick, 22 April 1920, Folder 6663, Box 635, Series I, General Education Board Papers, Rockefeller Archive Center, North Tarrytown, New York; Anson Phelps Stokes, Jr., to General Education Board, 10 May 1920, in General Education Board meeting minutes, Series III, 27 May 1920, General Education Board Papers, Rockefeller Archive Center.

6. Shryock, *American Medical Research*, 132.

7. E. Richard Brown, *Rockefeller Medicine Men: Medicine and Capitalism in America* (Berkeley: University of California Press, 1979), 178.

8. N. P. Colwell to Clyde Furst, 18 Dec. 1912, File, "American Medical Association 1909–1914," Carnegie Foundation Archives, Carnegie Corporation, New York.

9. Raymond P. Fosdick, *Adventure in Giving: The Story of the General Education Board* (New York: Harper & Row, 1962), 172.

10. Untitled memorandum on activities of the General Education Board, dated March 1928, Folder 3542, Box 337, Series I, General Education Board Papers, Rockefeller Archive Center.

11. The most important example of this was the General Education Board's $5 million grant to the University of Rochester in 1920 for the founding of the medical school. Abraham Flexner of the General Education Board conceived the idea of the project and brought it to the university's attention. The university liked the idea and applied to the Board for a grant. The application was accepted, and the medical school came into existence. However, in the official statement on the founding of the school, Rush Rhees, president of the University of Rochester, "was careful not to indicate that the initial suggestion for this development came from a report of the General Education Board knowing the long established policy of that Board to make grants in response to the request of institutions" (Memorandum, "University of Rochester," n.d., Folder 7276, Box 708, Series I, General Education Board Papers, Rockefeller Archive Center).

12. Fosdick, *Adventure in Giving*, 168. However, all the schools selected by the General Education Board "were either in the process of establishing some degree of full-time teaching or were at least working earnestly in that general direction" (Ibid., 168).

13. Jerome Greene to Abraham Flexner, 20 Feb. 1920, Folder 7226, Box 702, Series I, General Education Board Papers, Rockefeller Archive Center.

14. General Education Board, "Notice to the Press," n.d., Folder 3569, Box 345, Series I, General Education Board Papers, Rockefeller Archive Center. See also Raymond N. Ball to Charles W. Dodge, 5 Jan. 1927, Folder 7275, Box 708, Series I, General Education Board Papers, Rockefeller Archive Center.

15. Fosdick, *Adventure in Giving*, 168.

16. Andrew Carnegie to J. H. Kirkland, 20 May 1913, in Executive Committee meeting minutes, 21 May 1913, Carnegie Corporation of New York, Carnegie Corporation Archives, New York. For a record of the Carnegie Corporation's activities in medical education, see Howard J. Savage to Walter A. Jessup, 19 Jan. 1934, File, "Medical Education," Carnegie Foundation Archives, Carnegie Corporation.

17. Quoted in General Education Board, *Annual Report* (1919–20), 36.

18. Abraham Flexner to Henry Pritchett, 27 March 1919, Folder 1406, Box 152, Series I, General Education Board Papers, Rockefeller Archive Center. Information on the General Education Board's grant to Vanderbilt is found in this letter as well as in General Education Board, *Annual Report* (1919–20), p. 34–36; and Memorandum on General Education Board's Gift to Vanderbilt University, 7 Nov. 1919, Folder 1406, Box 152, Series I, General Education Board Papers, Rockefeller Archive Center.

19. John D. Rockefeller, Jr., and Frederick T. Gates, "Suggestions Regarding Methods of Procedure," 12 June 1903, with office memorandum of 21 July 1948, Folder 3486, Box 331, Series I, General Education Board Papers, Rockefeller Archive Center.

20. Frederick T. Gates to the General Education Board, 30 June 1905, Folder 3569, Box 345, Series I, General Education Board Papers, Rockefeller Archive Center. The most complete account of the General Education Board's activities is Fosdick, *Adventure in Giving*. Although written as an "in-house" history, the book contains much valuable information and remains useful. The best discussion of Gates is in John Ettling, *The Germ of Laziness: Rockefeller Philanthropy and Public Health in the New South* (Cambridge: Harvard University Press, 1981), esp. 49–72. This book also offers considerable insight into the General Education Board and other Rockefeller philanthropies.

21. In that tragedy, a strike at the Rockefeller-controlled Colorado Coal and Fuel Corporation in Ludlow, Colorado, was ended when forty-five workers and civilians were killed by United States militia acting as strikebreakers.

22. Quoted in Bremner, *American Philanthropy*, 119.

23. Carnegie Corporation of New York, *Report of the President and of the Treasurer* (1924), 6.

24. Board of Trustees meeting minutes, 9 Jan. 1918, Carnegie Corporation of New York, Carnegie Corporation Archives.

25. "Report of Special Committee," in General Education Board meeting minutes, 22 Oct. 1914, Series I, General Education Board Papers, Rockefeller Archive Center.

26. Fosdick, *Adventure in Giving;* Abraham Flexner, *I Remember: The Autobiography of Abraham Flexner* (New York: Simon and Schuster, 1940), esp. 264, 275–76, 343.

27. Henry Pritchett to Abraham Flexner, 23 Dec. 1910, Folder 7212, Box 701, Series I, General Education Board Papers, Rockefeller Archive Center.

28. Henry Pritchett to Wallace Buttrick, 11 Nov. 1919, Folder 7189, Series I, Box 697, General Education Board Papers, Rockefeller Archive Center.

29. Jerome Greene to Henry A. Christian, 30 Nov. 1914, Folder 6486, Box 613, Series I, General Education Board Papers, Rockefeller Archive Center.

30. Thomas Neville Bonner, *The Kansas Doctor: A Century of Pioneering* (Lawrence: University of Kansas Press, 1959), 181.

31. Quoted in Allan Nevins, *Study in Power: John D. Rockefeller, Industrialist and Philanthropist,* vol. 2 (New York: Scribner's, 1953), 199.

32. Frederick T. Gates to Frank Chadwick, 29 May 1905, Vol. 351, Subseries G, Series L, Record Group 1, Rockefeller Family Papers, Rockefeller Archive Center; Frederick T. Gates to Harriet Lynch, 19 Jan. 1903, Vol. 349, Subseries G, Series L, Record Group 1, Rockefeller Family Papers, Rockefeller Archive Center.

33. Ernest D. Burton, "Memorandum of Conversation with Mr. Abraham Flexner and Mr. Trevor Arnett in New York, Monday, May 28, 1923," Folder 7190, Box 698, Series I, General Education Board Papers, Rockefeller Archive Center. Even the furious opposition of Frederick T. Gates could not persuade the Board of Trustees to disallow a recommendation of the officers that a grant be made to the University of Iowa College of Medicine. Gates objected to the proposal because of his strong belief that private support should never go to public schools. To the end of his days, Gates fumed over this episode, complaining of "bureaucratic officers, usurping the power of the Board" (Fosdick, *Adventure in Giving,* 166–67).

34. Frederick T. Gates to John D. Rockefeller, 6 June 1905, Vol. 351, Subseries G, Series L, Record Group 1, Rockefeller Family Papers, Rockefeller Archive Center.

35. Alfred D. Chandler, Jr., *The Visible Hand: The Managerial Revolution in American Business* (Cambridge, Mass.: Belknap Press of Harvard University, 1977). This point is also made in Daniel M. Fox, "Abraham Flexner's Unpublished Report: Foundations and Medical Education, 1909–1928," *Bulletin of the History of Medicine* 54 (1980): 475–96.

36. Martin Fischer, *Christian R. Holmes: Man and Physician* (Springfield, Ill.: Charles C Thomas, 1937), 23; Frank Billings to Henry Pratt Judson, 11 Jan. 1917, Folder 7188, Box 697, Series I, General Education Board Papers, Rockefeller Archive Center.

37. Ruth C. Maszkiewicz, *The Presbyterian Hospital of Pittsburgh: From its Founding to Affiliation with the University of Pittsburgh* (Pittsburgh: Presbyterian-University Hospital, 1978), 80–82.

38. Data on the 1910 budget are from Abraham Flexner, *Medical Education in the United States and Canada* (New York: Carnegie Foundation for the Advancement of Teaching, 1910), 329. A discussion of the 1912 appropriation is in Henry Pritchett to J. C. Branner, 11 Dec. 1913, File, "Stanford University," Carnegie Foundation Archives, Carnegie Corporation.

39. Flexner, *Medical Education,* 331; Meeting of 30 Oct. 1916, Folder, "Committee on Budget, Appointments, and Promotions, April 28, 1916–May 17, 1917," Miscellaneous Box 1, University of Minnesota Medical School, Papers, University of Minnesota Archives,

40. Mark R. Everett, *Medical Education in Oklahoma: The University of Oklahoma School of Medicine and Medical Center 1900–1931* (Norman: University of Oklahoma Press, 1972), 180.

41. W. David Baird, *Medical Education in Arkansas 1879–1978* (Memphis: Memphis State University Press, 1979), 110, 143.

42. David Houston to Robert Brookings, 4 Jan. 1910, Chancellor's Records, Washington University, Washington University Archives.

43. Christian R. Holmes, "The New Cincinnati General Hospital and The New University Medical School," 22 May 1911, in Vol. 3, Christian R. Holmes Scrapbooks, Special Collections, University of Cincinnati Libraries.

44. Quoted in Fosdick, *Adventure in Giving,* 169.

45. Trevor Arnett, memorandum on the University of Colorado, 24 March 1922; George

Norlin to Wallace Buttrick, 27 March 1922; George Norlin to Abraham Flexner, 23 Feb. 1924; and George Norlin to Abraham Flexner, 8 March 1924, in Folder 7261, Box 706, Series I, General Education Board Papers, Rockefeller Archive Center.

46. George W. Corner, *A History of the Rockefeller Institute, 1901–1953, Origins and Growth* (New York: Rockefeller Institute Press, 1964), 31.

47. Ettling, *The Germ of Laziness.*

48. Brown, *Rockefeller Medicine Men;* Howard S. Berliner, "Philanthropic Foundations and Scientific Medicine (D.Sc. diss., The Johns Hopkins University, 1977).

49. Frederick T. Gates, *Chapters in My Life* (New York: Free Press, 1977), 182.

50. *Biographical Sketches and Letters of T. Mitchell Prudden, M.D.* (New Haven: Yale University Press, 1927), 174.

51. On philanthropy, see Bremner, *American Philanthropy;* Merle Curti and Roderick Nash, *Philanthropy in the Shaping of American Higher Education* (New Brunswick, N.J.: Rutgers University Press, 1965); and, for a radical critique, see Robert F. Arnove, ed., *Philanthropy and Cultural Imperialism: The Foundations at Home and Abroad* (Boston: G. K. Hall, 1980).

52. Frederick T. Gates to John D. Rockefeller, Jr., 7 May 1924, Register 59, Box 3, Frederick T. Gates Papers, Rockefeller Archive Center.

53. See, for instance, Gates's discussion of this example in Frederick T. Gates, "Fundamental Principles of Mr. Rockefeller's Philanthropies," memorandum dated 7 Oct. 1908, Register 26, Box 2, Frederick T. Gates Papers, Rockfeller Archive Center.

54. No individual or foundation stated this viewpoint more clearly than the Carnegie Corporation. In 1922, announcing its recent decision to provide aid to medical schools, the corporation declared:

> The basis of medical education in the sciences of chemistry, physics, biology, and the like, has been made perfectly clear. The development of the science of medical practice has likewise been greatly clarified. It has, therefore, been more evident in the field of medical education than in almost any other field of university endeavor that the appropriation of definite sums of money could accomplish important and fruitful results. (Carnegie Corporation of New York, *Report of the President and of the Treasurer* [1922], 10)

55. Frederick T. Gates, "Notes on Homeopathy," Nos. 1–5, Register 33, Box 2, Frederick T. Gates Papers, Rockefeller Archive Center.

56. Frederick T. Gates to John D. Rockefeller, 20 Jan. 1911, Register 33, Box 2, Frederick T. Gates Papers, Rockefeller Archive Center.

57. Frederick T. Gates to John D. Rockefeller, Jr., 28 April 1923, Register 36, Box 2, Frederick T. Gates Papers, Rockefeller Archive Center.

58. Frederick T. Gates, "Notes on Homeopathy," 1911, No. 4, Register 33, Box, 2, Frederick T. Gates Papers, Rockefeller Archive Center.

59. *Annual Report of Provost and Treasurer of the University of Pennsylvania* (1901), 19–20.

60. General Education Board, *Annual Report* (1919–20), 28.

61. Henry Pritchett, "The Medical School and the State," *Journal of the American Medical Association* 63 (1914): 648.

62. Brown, *Rockefeller Medicine Men,* 251, n. 40.

63. Gates, *Chapters in My Life,* 187 (theological seminary), 188 (rest of quotation).

64. Florence Sabin, *Franklin Paine Mall: The Story of a Mind* (Baltimore: The Johns Hopkins University Press, 1934), 2.

65. Victor Vaughan to Walter H. Sawyer, 29 March 1917, Box 5, Records of the Medical School of the University of Michigan, Michigan Historical Collections, Bentley Historical Library, University of Michigan.

66. Flexner, *I Remember,* 290.

67. Flexner's activities as a fund raiser are recounted in ibid., 176–84, 257–311.

68. Paul Starr, *The Social Transformation of American Medicine: The Rise of a Sovereign Profession and the Making of a Vast Industry* (New York: Basic Books, 1982), 13–17.

69. Charles P. Howland to Abraham Flexner, 4 Feb. 1924, and Wallace Buttrick to Abraham Flexner, 17 Jan. 1924, in Folder 3485, Box 331, Series I, General Education Board Papers, Rockefeller Archive Center.

70. Quoted in Flexner, *I Remember,* 177.

71. Quoted in James E. Gifford, Jr., *The Evolution of a Medical Center: A History of Medicine at Duke University to 1941* (Durham: Duke University Press, 1972), 42.

72. Information on these applications is found in Folder 7242, Box 704 (St. Louis University); Folder 7227 and Folder 7228, Box 702 (Albany); Folder 7229, Box 702, and Folder 7330, Box 703 (Baylor); Folder 7263, Box 706 (Georgia); and Folder 7254, Box 705 (Arkansas); in Series I, General Education Board Papers, Rockefeller Archive Center. Maryland's application is discussed in General Education Board meeting minutes, 29 April 1921, and that of Illinois is in General Education Board meeting minutes, 2 December 1920, Series I, General Education Board Papers, Rockefeller Archive Center. Material on George Washington University's application is in Meeting with Archibald Hopkins, 4 May 1925, Wickliffe Rose Diary, General Education Board Papers, Rockefeller Archive Center.

73. Material on Harvard's unsuccessful grant application is in Box 613, Series I, General Education Board Papers, Rockefeller Archive Center.

74. William Welch, "Present Position of Medical Education, Its Development and Great Needs for the Future," in William Welch, *Papers and Addresses*, vol. 3 (Baltimore: The Johns Hopkins University Press, 1920), 113.

Chapter 11

1. Columbia University, *Annual Report* (1910), 84.

2. Simon Flexner and James Thomas Flexner, *William Henry Welch and the Heroic Age of American Medicine* (New York: Viking, 1941), 277.

3. Titles in the first issue of the *Journal of Clinical Investigation* included "On the Relation Between Conductivity and Chloride in the Urine," "Blood Reaction and Blood Gases in Pneumonia," "A Method for the Determination of the Amount of Oxygen and Carbon Dioxide in the Mixed Venous Blood of Man," and "Evidence that Digitalis Influences Contraction of the Heart in Man." Over the years, the journal became a journal of applied biochemistry.

4. Hans Zinsser to Abraham Flexner, 21 April 1921, Folder 7289, Box 711, Series I, General Education Board Papers, Rockefeller Archive Center, North Tarrytown, New York.

5. On the development of clinical science, see A. McGehee Harvey, *Science at the Bedside: Clinical Research in American Medicine 1905–1945* (Baltimore: The Johns Hopkins University Press, 1981). See also Lester King, "Clinical Science Gets Enthroned," *Journal of the American Medical Association* 250 (1983): 1169–72, 1847–50; and Ellen R. Brainard, "History of the American Society for Clinical Investigation," *Journal of Clinical Investigation* 38 (1959): 1784–95.

6. George Blumer to Abraham Flexner, 9 March 1920, Folder 6663, Box 635, Series I, General Education Board Papers, Rockefeller Archive Center; see also George Blumer to Yandell Henderson, 29 Aug. 1918, File, "1918—Reorganization of the School," Box 7, Yale Medical School, Dean's Files, Yale University Archives.

7. Abraham Flexner to James H. Kirkland, 13 Feb. 1920, Folder 1407, Box 152, Series I, General Education Board Papers, Rockefeller Archive Center.

8. A. McGehee Harvey, *The Interurban Clinical Club (1905–1976): A Record of Achievement in Clinical Science* (Philadelphia: W. B. Saunders, 1978), 391.

9. Lewellys F. Barker, "Medicine and the Universities," *Journal of the American Medical Association* 4 (1902): 143–47.

10. Steven Jonas, *Medical Mystery: The Training of Doctors in the United States* (New York: Norton, 1978), 244.

11. Donald Fleming, *William H. Welch and the Rise of Modern Medicine* (Boston: Little, Brown, 1954), 179, 178. Osler later supported the strict full-time system at McGill.

12. Jerome Greene to David Edsall, 25 Nov. 1914, Folder 6486, Box 613, Series I, General Education Board Papers, Rockefeller Archive Center. Harvard's application to the General Education Board for a grant to support its clinical departments was denied because the school intended to employ a system of geographical full time and because it used several different hospitals. Materials relating to this episode are in Box 613, Series I, General Education Board Papers, Rockefeller Archive Center.

13. Harvey, *Interurban Clinical Club*, 113–14.

14. See, for instance, Gerald L. Geison, "Divided We Stand: Physiologists and Clinicians in the American Context," in *The Therapeutic Revolution: Essays in the Social History of American Medicine*, ed. Morris J. Vogel and Charles E. Rosenberg (Philadelphia: University of Pennsylvania Press, 1979), 76.

15. Arthur Dean Bevan to Henry Pritchett, 5 Oct. 1921, File, "American Medical Association 1915–39," Carnegie Foundation Archives, Carnegie Corporation, New York.

16. Jerome D. Greene to Henry A. Christian, 24 Nov. 1914, Folder 6486, Box 613, Series I, General Education Board Papers, Rockefeller Archive Center.

17. Arthur Dean Bevan, "Medical Education in the United States; The Need of a Uniform Standard," *Journal of the American Medical Association* 51 (1908): 568.

18. Victor Vaughan to E. P. Lyon, 16 Aug. 1915, Box 2, Records of the Medical School of the University of Michigan, Michigan Historical Collections, Bentley Historical Library, University of Michigan.

19. William H. Welch to Eugene Opie, 17 March 1915, William H. Welch Papers, Alan Mason Chesney Medical Archives, Johns Hopkins Medical Institutions.

20. Edith Gittings Reid, *The Life and Convictions of William Sydney Thayer* (London: Oxford University Press, 1936), 182.

21. Harvey, *Science at the Bedside*.

22. Ellen Cangi, "Abraham Flexner's Philanthropy: The Full-Time System in the Department of Surgery at the University of Cincinnati College of Medicine, 1910–1930," *Bulletin of the History of Medicine* 56 (1982): 161.

23. Abraham Flexner, "Anecdote of Dr. Welch," 26 March 1935, File, "William Welch," Abraham Flexner Papers, Library of Congress.

24. Barker, "Medicine and the Universities," 145.

25. Victor Vaughan, "The Functions of a State University Medical School" (unpublished manuscript, n.d.), p. 2, in File, "University of Michigan," Abraham Flexner Papers, Library of Congress.

26. Sally Kohlstedt, *The Formation of the American Scientific Community: The American Association for the Advancement of Science 1848–1860* (Urbana: University of Illinois Press, 1976); Thomas Haskell, *The Emergence of Professional Social Science: The American Social Science Association and the Nineteenth-Century Crisis of Authority* (Urbana: University of Illinois Press, 1977).

27. Fosdick, *Adventure in Giving*, 172. By contrast, in 1961 nearly three of four preclinical faculty members held full-time appointments (Ibid., 172).

28. Abraham Flexner, "Comments on Dr. Darrach's Manuscript," September 1919, Folder 7210, Box 700, Series I, General Education Board Papers, Rockefeller Archive Center.

29. J. Arthur Myers, *Masters of Medicine: An Historical Sketch of the College of Medical Sciences University of Minnesota 1888–1966* (St. Louis: Warren H. Green, 1968), 95–97. Several of the essays in Owen H. Wangensteen, ed., *Elias Potter Lyon: Minnesota's Leader in Medical Education* (St. Louis: Warren H. Green, 1981), also discuss the "massacre." Although the faculty was completely reorganized in 1913, the first full-time clinical appointments were not made until 1915.

30. E. A. Weiss to Thomas Arbuthnot, 6 Oct. 19—, Historical Materials of the University of Pittsburgh, Falk Library, University of Pittsburgh.

31. W. F. R. Phillips to Henry Pritchett, 14 June 1909, File, "George Washington University," Carnegie Foundation Archives, Carnegie Corporation.

32. Robert Wiebe, *The Search for Order 1877–1920* (New York: Hill and Wang, 1967); Robert Wiebe, *The Segmented Society: An Introduction to the Meaning of America* (New York: Oxford University Press, 1975).

33. Joseph C. Aub and Ruth K. Hapgood, *Pioneer in Modern Medicine: David Linn Edsall of Harvard* (Cambridge: Harvard Medical Alumni Association, 1970), 106.

34. John B. Youmans, "Vanderbilt—Yesterday, Today and Tomorrow," *Journal of the Tennessee Medical Association* 59 (1966): 45–46.

35. "The Development of the Yale Medical School and the New Haven Hospital" (unpublished report, 1919), in File, "Reports, Studies, Memos," Box 7, Yale Medical School, Dean's Files, Yale University Archives; Wendy Jacobson, "American Medicine in Transition. The Case

of the Yale Medical School, 1900–1920" (Senior honors thesis, Department of History, Wesleyan University, 1976), 52–54.

36. Unsigned statement to Isaac M. Ullman, 25 Feb. 1919, File, "Medical Board 1919–22," Box 33, Yale Medical School, Dean's Files, Yale University Archives.

37. Harvey, *Science at the Bedside,* 349.

38. Meeting with Dr. Simon Flexner, 3 Oct. 1923, Wickliffe Rose Diary, General Education Board Papers, Rockefeller Archive Center.

39. C. Canby Robinson to James H. Kirkland, 23 Dec. 1923, Folder 1409, Box 152, Series I, General Education Board Papers, Rockefeller Archive Center.

40. "Report of the Special Committee on the Medical School as desired by the Board of Trustees, University of Pittsburgh" (manuscript, n.d.), Folder, "University of Pittsburgh School of Medicine Faculty Council c. 1910," Historical Materials of the University of Pittsburgh.

Chapter 12

1. Charles Rosenberg, "And Heal the Sick: The Hospital and the Patient in 19th Century America," *Journal of Social History* 10 (1977): 428–47; Charles Rosenberg, "Inward Vision and Outward Glance: The Shaping of the American Hospital, 1880–1914," *Bulletin of the History of Medicine* 53 (1979): 346–91; and Morris J. Vogel, *The Invention of the Modern Hospital: Boston, 1870–1930* (Chicago: The University of Chicago Press, 1980).

2. Statutes of the Medical School of Maine (records of the medical faculty), 13 March 1912, Special Collections, Bowdoin College Library, Brunswick, Maine.

3. An agreement between Presbyterian Hospital and the College of Physicians and Surgeons was initially reached in December 1910. This agreement was modified slightly, and the final contract was signed in April 1911.

4. Kenneth M. Ludmerer, "Reform of Medical Education at Washington University," *Journal of the History of Medicine and Allied Sciences* 35 (1980): 149–73.

5. Board of Managers meeting minutes, 25 Jan. 1912, and 7 Feb. 1912, Administrative Office, St. Louis Children's Hospital; Robert Brookings to Bishop E. R. Hendrix, 16 Sept. 1912, Chancellor's Records, Washington University, Washington University Archives; address of Bishop E. R. Hendrix in Barnes Hospital, *Proceedings Attending the Laying of the Corner Stone, October 11, 1912* (St. Louis: n.p., 1912), 15; and address of Robert Brookings in Barnes Hospital, *Addressed Delivered at the Dedication of Barnes Hospital, October 27, 1914* (St. Louis: n.p., 1914), 14–15.

6. Joseph A. Blake to Samuel Lambert, 8 Jan. 1910, File 57, Dean's Office Files, College of Physicians and Surgeons, Office of the Dean, College of Physicians and Surgeons, Columbia University; Samuel Lambert to James W. McLane et al., 10 April 1908, File 112b, Dean's Office Files, College of Physicians and Surgeons, Columbia University; and "Report of the Dean of the Medical School," in Columbia University, *Annual Report* (1910), 85.

7. The six were Henry P. Walcott, Arthur T. Cabot, Charles T. Adams II, Henry P. Bowditch, John Collins Warren, and William L. Richardson.

8. Donna Munger, "Robert Brookings and the Flexner Report. A Case Study of the Reorganization of Medical Education," *Journal of the History of Medicine and Allied Sciences* 23 (1968): 356–71. In addition, two other members of the Washington University Board of Directors, B. D. Lee and Edward Mallinckrodt, had wives who were on the Board of Managers of Children's Hospital.

9. On Brookings's relationship with Cupples, see Robert Brookings, "Autobiographical Manuscript" (manuscript, 1932), 9–10, Robert S. Brookings Papers, Washington University Archives.

10. Ibid., 9; Minutes of the Trustees of Barnes Hospital, 1905–16, Administrative Office, Barnes Hospital, St. Louis.

11. Memorandum, John Shaw Billings to Trustees of the Peter Bent Brigham Hospital, n.d., Folder, "Peter Bent Brigham Hospital," Box 68, John Shaw Billings Papers, New York Public Library.

12. Board of Managers meeting minutes, 10 June 1913, The Presbyterian Hospital in the

City of New York, Administrative Office, Presbyterian Hospital, New York. Some record of Billings's activities as secretary of Presbyterian Hospital's building committee is found in Folder, "Presbyterian Hospital," Box 68, Billings Papers, New York Public Library.

13. Henry A. Christian to Charles Eliot, [late January or early February] 1908, Vol. 1, Henry A. Christian Papers, Countway Library, Harvard Medical School.

14. Barnes Hospital, *Proceedings Attending the Laying of the Corner Stone*, 15; and E. R. Hendrix to Robert Brookings, 16 Sept. 1912, Chancellor's Records, Washington University.

15. Board of Managers meeting minutes, 13 Dec. 1910, Presbyterian Hospital, New York.

16. Ibid.

17. *First Annual Report of the Barnes Hospital, Saint Louis, 1915–1916* (St. Louis: H. S. Collins, 1918), 5–6.

18. Borden S. Veeder, "The Relation of the Children's Hospital to the Community," in St. Louis Children's Hospital, *Annual Report* (1914), 46.

19. For instance, these points were made by Brookings in *Addresses Delivered*, 15–16.

20. Board of Managers meeting minutes, 13 Dec. 1910, Presbyterian Hospital, New York.

21. Joseph A. Blake to John S. Billings, 28 Feb. 1909, and Joseph A. Blake to George L. Rives, 17 April 1909, in File 112b, Dean's Office Files, College of Physicians and Surgeons, Columbia University; Henry A. Christian to John Collins Warren, 31 Jan. 1911, Vol. 1, Henry A. Christian Papers, Harvard Medical School.

22. Henry A. Christian to Frederick S. Lee, 19 March 1913, Vol. 1, Henry A. Christian Papers, Harvard Medical School. Cannon was offered "general oversight of the routine physiological methods of studying patients." He was invited to "make occasional rounds in the wards with the Visiting Staff to keep in touch with the type of patients and to make suggestions in regard to the physiological points of view," and he was given the "freedom to conduct physiological investigations upon patients himself or indirectly through his assistants." His salary came from the medical school rather than the hospital. Arrangements for Folin and Councilman were similar.

23. Address of Eugene Opie, in *The Dedication of the New Buildings of Washington University Medical School, April 28, 29, and 30, 1915* (St. Louis: n.p., 1915), 19–20.

24. Peter Bent Brigham Hospital, *Annual Report* (1916), 1.

25. Henry A. Christian to John P. Reynolds, 4 March 1911, Vol. 5, Henry A. Christian Papers, Harvard Medical School.

26. *First Annual Report of the Barnes Hospital*, 6.

27. St. Louis Children's Hospital, *Annual Report* (1903), 5.

28. *First Annual Report of the Barnes Hospital*, 16.

29. Peter Bent Brigham Hospital, *Annual Report* (1914), 3.

30. Figures are taken from several issues of Peter Bent Brigham Hospital, *Annual Report.*

31. Peter Bent Brigham Hospital, *Annual Report* (1916), 105.

32. St. Louis Children's Hospital, *Annual Report* (1910), 8.

33. The Presbyterian Hospital in the City of New York, *Annual Report* (1912), 18.

34. Saul Jarcho, "Medical Education in the United States, 1910–1956," *Journal of the Mount Sinai Hospital* 26 (1959): 356.

35. Unidentified newspaper clipping, 14 March 1916, Vol. 5, Christian R. Holmes Scrapbooks, Special Collections, University of Cincinnati Libraries.

36. Documents pertaining to the affiliation between Cornell Medical College and the New York Hospital are located in the Faculty Minutes, Cornell University Medical College, and the Board of Governors Papers, Society of the New York Hospital, both of which are in the Medical Archives, New York Hospital-Cornell University Medical Center, New York.

37. Henry A. Christian to John Collins Warren, 4 Jan. 1911, Vol. 1, Henry A. Christian Papers, Harvard Medical School.

38. Discussion of Edsall's role in forging a new relationship between the Massachusetts General Hospital and Harvard Medical School is found in Joseph A. Aub and Ruth K. Hapgood, *Pioneer in Modern Medicine: David Linn Edsall of Harvard* (Cambridge: Harvard Medical Alumni Association, 1970), 124–36. Later, as dean of Harvard Medical School, Edsall also helped strengthen relations with Boston City Hospital (Ibid., 220).

39. Massachusetts General Hospital, *Annual Report* (1913), 108.

40. Faculty meeting minutes, 14 June 1909, 6 March 1912, and 21 Nov. 1913, Western Reserve University School of Medicine, Case Western Reserve University Archives.

41. Faculty meeting minutes, 6 March 1912, Western Reserve University School of Medicine, Case Western Reserve University Archives.

42. Victor Vaughan, "The Medical School During the Administration of President Hutchins from October 1909 to June 1920" (manuscript, n.d.), Box 8, Records of the Medical School of the University of Michigan, Michigan Historical Collections, Bentley Historical Library, University of Michigan.

43. University of Nebraska, *Biennial Reports of Regents to the Governor* (1917), 16, and (1919), 21.

44. Reginald C. McGrane, *The University of Cincinnati: A Success Story in Urban Higher Education* (New York: Harper & Row, 1963), 194.

45. University of Cincinnati, "Installation of Dr. Christian R. Holmes as Dean of the Medical College and Conference on Premedical Education, January 16–17, 1914," p. 15, in Box 1, Medical History Collection—Miscellany, Special Collections, University of Cincinnati Libraries.

46. Ibid., 7; unidentified newspaper clippings of 1 Oct. 1902, and 8 Feb. 1903, Vol. 1, Christian R. Holmes Scrapbooks, University of Cincinnati Libraries.

47. "University May Have Charge of Hospital," clipping from Cincinnati *Times Star*, 16 Oct. 1913, Vol. 4, Christian R. Holmes Scrapbooks, University of Cincinnati Libraries.

48. Quoted in Christian R. Holmes, "Hospitals and their Relation to Medical Colleges and the Training of Interns," *Journal of the American Medical Association* 62 (1914):831.

49. Petition of the Executive Faculty to the President and Board of Regents of the University of Colorado, in Executive faculty meeting minutes, 8 Feb. 1919, University of Colorado School of Medicine, Denison Memorial Library, University of Colorado Health Sciences Center, Denver.

50. Ibid. See also the discussion of the situation at the county hospital at the meeting of 13 Sept. 1913.

51. Detailed information on the situation at Charity Hospital is found in Folders 7247, 7248, and 7249, Box 706, Series I, General Education Board Papers, Rockefeller Archive Center.

52. Draft, James Deering to the Trustees of the Medical Department of Northwestern University and the Trustees of Wesley Hospital, 18 Feb. 1914, File, "Henry Pritchett 1911–1914," Abraham Flexner Papers, Library of Congress; Abraham Flexner to James Deering, 19 March 1914, File, "Henry Pritchett 1911–1914," Abraham Flexner Papers, Library of Congress; Bellevue and Allied Hospitals, City of New York, *Annual Report* (1916), 29, (1914), 31, and (1915), 42; Abraham Flexner to John D. Rockefeller, Jr., 2 July 1915, Folder 7183, Box 697, Series I, General Education Board Papers, Rockefeller Archive Center.

53. Anson Stokes to Abraham Flexner, 29 May 1913 ,Folder 6661, Box 635, Series I, General Education Board Papers, Rockefeller Archive Center.

54. Bowdoin College, *President's Report* (1897–98), 18–19.

55. University of Nebraska, *Biennial Reports of the Board of Regents to the Governor* (1911), 17, (1913), 28, and (1915), 13; Irving S. Cutter to Samuel Avery, 15 July 1914, Record Group 2/9/3, Chancellor Samuel Avery Papers, University of Nebraska-Lincoln Archives.

56. N. P. Colwell to Ernest Fox Nichols, n.d., in meeting of 11 Feb. 1910; Arthur Dean Bevan to George S. Graham, n.d., in meeting of 19 Jan. 1913; and report of John M. Gile, in meeting of 10 March 1913; in Records of the Medical Faculty of Dartmouth College, Dartmouth College Archives. Also, meeting of 26 April 1913, Records of the Trustees of Dartmouth College, Dartmouth College Archives; and statement of president Edward Fox Nichols to the Alumni of Dartmouth Medical School, 30 April 1913, in Folder 39, Correspondence 1912–14, Ernest Fox Nichols Papers, Dartmouth College Archives.

57. N. P. Colwell to H. M. Bell, 23 Jan. 1913, College of Medicine Folder, Special Collections Division, Cowles Library, Drake University.

58. Ibid. Also, T. P. Shorts to the Board of Trustee of Drake University, 30 Jan. 1913; Ferdinand J. Smith to the Board of Trustees of Drake University, 4 Feb. 1913; Hill M. Bell to the Board of Trustees of Drake University, 5 Feb. 1913; and meeting of medical faculty, 10 Feb. 1913; in College of Medicine Folder, Drake University.

59. John Walker Moore, "Clinical Clerkships in Medicine: Student Unit System," *Bulletin of the Association of American Medical Colleges* 2 (1927):136.

60. N. P. Colwell, "The Hospital's Function in Medical Education," *Journal of the Ameri-*

can Medical Association 88 (1927):781–84. Whether the higher entrance requirements "practically eliminated buffoonery and rowdyism from the medical student body" as Colwell claimed (p. 781) was subject to interpretation, but few observers doubted the higher academic credentials and greater sense of dedication of the average medical student of the 1920s.

61. Moore, "Clinical Clerkships in Medicine," 136.

62. *A Medical Center for New York* (New York: The Presbyterian Hospital, 1924), 23.

63. "Report of the Dean of the Medical School," in Columbia University, *Annual Report* (1910), 87.

64. See, for instance, Edward F. Stevens, *The American Hospital of the Twentieth Century* (New York: F. W. Dodge, 1928), 382.

65. Frederick T. Gates had the duty of providing the unhappy news to many who unsuccessfully appealed to Rockefeller for support of their local hospitals. Gates would inform them that Rockefeller believed that the care of the sick was the responsibility of the community itself. It was Rockefeller's feeling, Gates explained, that "he who from outside of your community assists you, does your community and your cause not a service, but a distinct disservice." See Frederick T. Gates to C. F. Huth, 13 May 1904; Frederick T. Gates to Emma L. Chapin, 10 March 1904; and Frederick T. Gates to Lizabeth L. Jackson, 22 March 1904; in Vol. 349, Subseries G, Series L, Record Group I, Rockefeller Family Papers, Rockefeller Archive Center.

66. One point of contention was the question of how much of a clinical professor's salary should be paid by the medical school and how much by the hospital. Another was the matter of determining the percentage of pay and charity beds. The medical school favored increasing the number of charity beds, so that the hospital might be even more a teaching institution, but the Lakeside trustees demurred, worried that the hospital's revenues would fall too steeply. See Lakeside Hospital Board of Trustees and Executive Committee meeting minutes, 15 Jan. 1924, Hospital Archives, University Hospitals of Cleveland.

67. Ultimately still another group rose to authority in hospital affairs: the hospital administrators.

68. On the disruptions caused by students in the wards of the Peter Bent Brigham Hospital, see the correspondence between superintendent H. B. Howard and physician-in-chief Henry A. Christian, in Vol. 6, Henry A. Christian Papers, Harvard Medical School.

69. See, for instance, George Dock's exhortations to clinical clerks at Michigan to treat patients with respect and dignity ("Clinical Notebooks of George Dock, 1899–1908," [sessions of 27 Sept. 1901, 30 Sept. 1904, and 28 Sept. 1908], Michigan Historical Collections, Bentley Historical Library, University of Michigan).

70. "A Needed Improvement in Medical Teaching in America," in File, "Fordham University," Abraham Flexner Papers, Library of Congress.

Chapter 13

1. Abraham Flexner, *Medical Education in the United States and Canada* (New York: Carnegie Foundation for the Advancement of Teaching, 1910), 151.

2. A definitive history of medical licensing awaits to be written. Until then, the reader may profitably consult Richard Shryock, *Medical Licensing in America, 1650–1965* (Baltimore: The Johns Hopkins University Press, 1967); Robert Derbyshire, *Medical Licensure and Discipline in the United States* (Baltimore: The Johns Hopkins University Press, 1969); Joseph F. Kett, *The Formation of the American Medical Profession: The Role of Institutions 1780–1860* (New Haven: Yale University Press, 1968); William Rothstein, *American Physicians in the Nineteenth Century: From Sects to Science* (Baltimore: The Johns Hopkins University Press, 1972), 63–84, 305–10; Samuel Baker, "Physician Licensure Laws in the United States, 1865–1915," Journal of the History of Medicine and Allied Sciences 39 (1984):173–97; and Flexner, *Medical Education in the United States and Canada,* 167–73.

3. Flexner, *Medical Education in the United States and Canada,* 170–71.

4. "Secretary's Report," *Journal of the American Medical Association* 48 (1907):1706.

5. Baker, "Physician Licensure Laws," 190.

6. Only in the records of a few laggard schools did I find even passing reference to licensing

boards. One state board in particular—the Illinois board, under the leadership of John H. Rauch —has frequently been praised in the secondary literature for issuing a series of reports between 1877 and 1891 in which it urged educational reform. It is probable that these reports helped heighten awareness of modern educational methods among the profession at large, but I found no mention of them in the faculty records I examined.

7. Flexner, *Medical Education in the United States and Canada,* 169.

8. Ibid., 167.

9. This change in the role of government has been widely discussed, but attention should still be drawn to Sidney Fine's classic treatise, *Laissez Faire and the General-Welfare State: A Study of Conflict in American Thought, 1865–1901* (Ann Arbor: University of Michigan Press, 1956).

10. Henry Pritchett, "The Medical School and the State," *Journal of the American Medical Association* 53 (1914):648.

11. Flexner, *Medical Education in the United States and Canada,* 155.

12. Ibid., 49.

13. Pritchett, "The Medical School and the State," 649.

14. James Burrow, *AMA: Voice of American Medicine* (Baltimore: The Johns Hopkins University Press, 1963), 49.

15. Ibid., 67–151; James Burrow, *Organized Medicine in the Progressive Era: The Move Toward Monopoly* (Baltimore: The Johns Hopkins University Press, 1977); Ronald Numbers, *Almost Persuaded: American Physicians and Compulsory Health Insurance, 1912–1920* (Baltimore: The Johns Hopkins University Press, 1978).

16. Rosemary Stevens, *American Medicine and the Public Interest* (New Haven: Yale University Press, 1971), 210, 386–87; Shryock, *Medical Licensing,* 92–94.

17. Burrow, *Organized Medicine,* 16–28.

18. The reader will understand that the common conceptual framework of modern doctors still leaves considerable room for disagreement in areas of "medical judgment."

19. Robert Wiebe, *The Search for Order 1877–1920* (New York: Hill and Wang, 1967); Robert Wiebe, *The Segmented Society: An Introduction to the Meaning of America* (New York: Oxford University Press, 1975).

20. Arthur Dean Bevan, "Cooperation in Medical Education and Medical Service," *Journal of the American Medical Association* 90 (1928):1175.

21. Ibid., 1173.

22. Exceptions would be a number of well-done histories of individual medical schools, which have skillfully used archival records of those institutions. However, these studies have not examined medical education in a national perspective and thus have had little impact on our general conception of the AMA.

23. This rating system had been in use since the Council's first inspection in 1906, but it was after 1910 that state boards began refusing to recognize Class C schools.

24. Martin Kaufman, *American Medical Education: The Formative Years, 1765–1910* (Westport, Conn.: Greenwood Press, 1976), 177.

25. Shryock, *Medical Licensing in America,* 78–79.

26. For space considerations, specific citations will not be given, but this information was obtained from faculty minutes, official correspondence, and other archival records of the respective schools.

27. Ibid.

28. N. P. Colwell to W. A. Jayne, 11 Sept. 1913, in Executive faculty meeting minutes, 13 Sept. 1913, University of Colorado School of Medicine, Denison Memorial Library, University of Colorado Health Sciences Center, Denver; N. P. Colwell to George M. Kober, 19 July 1912, in Faculty meeting minutes, 6 Aug. 1912, Georgetown University School of Medicine.

29. William DeWitt Hyde to Henry Pritchett, 13 June 1910, File, "Bowdoin College," Carnegie Foundation Archives, Carnegie Corporation, New York.

30. Statutes of the Medical School of Maine (faculty meeting minutes), 14 March 1914, Special Collections, Bowdoin College Library, Brunswick, Maine.

31. Statement of R. S. Hyer, in Board of Trustees meeting minutes, 30 June 1913, Southern Methodist University, President's Office, Southern Methodist University, Dallas.

32. Ibid.

33. Frank K. Sanders to N. P. Colwell, 19 June 1911, Frank Knight Sanders Papers, Washburn University Library, Topeka, Kansas.

34. John H. Race to Henry Pritchett, 23 June 1910, File, "University of Chattanooga," Carnegie Foundation Archives, Carnegie Corporation.

35. See the many angry exchanges between H. S. Spalding, representing Bennett, and Pritchett, in File, "Loyola University," Carnegie Foundation Archives, Carnegie Corporation.

36. Articles and newspaper clippings pertaining to Fordham's closure are in the Fordham University Archives, Fordham University, New York. The school's chief problem was the lack of money. Numerous fund-raising efforts fell far short of their mark, and the school was forced to close.

37. Information pertaining to these negotiations is found in Files, "Stanford University" and "University of California," Carnegie Foundation Archives, Carnegie Corporation.

38. Henry Pritchett to William Potter, 11 July 1916, and Henry Pritchett to William Potter, 31 July 1916, in File, "University of Pennsylvania," Carnegie Foundation Archives, Carnegie Corporation.

39. N. P. Colwell to W. A. Jayne, 11 Sept. 1913, in Executive faculty meeting minutes, 13 Sept. 1913, University of Colorado School of Medicine. At that meeting, the Executive Faculty concurred with Colwell's assessment.

40. Ten of these schools offered the first two years of instruction only.

41. "History of the AAMC Annual Meetings," Miscellaneous Historical Documents, Association of American Medical Colleges Archives.

42. Meeting of 13 March 1912, Statutes of the Medical College of Maine.

43. N. P. Colwell to Henry Pritchett, 16 Jan. 1915, File, "American Medical Association 1915–39," Carnegie Foundation Archives, Carnegie Corporation.

44. Meeting of 21 March 1911, Statutes of the Medical College of Maine.

45. W. L. Rodman to Henry Pritchett, 11 Dec. 1915, File, "National Board of Medical Examiners," Carnegie Foundation Archives, Carnegie Corporation.

46. W. L. Rodman to Henry Pritchett, 29 March 1915, File, "National Board of Medical Examiners," Carnegie Foundation Archives, Carnegie Corporation.

47. Abraham Flexner to Arthur Dean Bevan, 7 March 1914, File, "American Medical Association 1909–1914," Carnegie Foundation Archives, Carnegie Corporation.

48. Arthur Dean Bevan to Abraham Flexner, 9 March 1914, File, "American Medical Association 1909–1914," Carnegie Foundation Archives, Carnegie Corporation.

49. Arthur Dean Bevan to Henry Pritchett, 10 March 1914, File, "American Medical Association 1909–1914," Carnegie Foundation Archives, Carnegie Corporation.

50. It should be noted that enrollment in 1910 had already declined from enrollment in 1904, the peak year, when there were 28,142 students and 5,747 graduates in the United States. See Council on Medical Education and Hospitals, "Medical Education in the United States," *Journal of the American Medical Association* 95 (1930):504.

51. Shryock, *Medical Licensing in America*, 84.

52. *Final Report of the Commission on Medical Education* (New York: Office of the Director of the Study, 1932) 386.

53. In 1958, there was one doctor for 740 persons in America, compared to a ratio of one to 763 in 1938 (Shryock, *Medical Licensing in America*, 98). On the other hand, in the 1980s popular sentiment has changed again, and the cry once more is to produce fewer doctors. This has occurred because the reduction of medical costs has become medicine's paramount social and political issue. Doctors are expensive to train and even more expensive to support. The decision of how many doctors to produce is thus seen for what it is: a political rather than an educational question. Historians like Charles Rosenberg, Ronald Numbers, and David Rosner, who have contended that medical practices and institutions need to be understood in the broad cultural context, are seen to be right. For views that the country now has a surplus of doctors, see Robert Petersdorf, "The Doctors' Dilemma," *New England Journal of Medicine* 299 (1978):628; and Alvin Tarlof, "Shattuck Lecture—The Increasing Supply of Physicians, The Changing Structure of the Health-Services System, and the Future Practice of Medicine," *New England Journal of Medicine* 308 (1983):1235–44.

54. To the exclusion of the working classes must be added the implementation of quotas on the admission of Jews and Roman Catholics in the period between the two world wars—one

of the truly shameful episodes in the history of American medical education. See Saul Jarcho, "Medical Education in the United States, 1910–1956," *Journal of the Mount Sinai Hospital* 26 (1959):357–59; and George Rosen, *The Structure of American Medical Practice 1875–1941*, ed. Charles E. Rosenberg (Philadelphia: University of Pennsylvania Press, 1983), 68–69.

55. Flexner, *Medical Education in the United States and Canada*, 178. Flexner's views on the medical education of women appear here, pp. 178–79.

56. From 1973–74 to 1983–84, the proportion of women among medical graduates rose from 11.1 to 28.3 percent. See Anne E. Crowely, Sylvia I. Etzel, and Edward S. Petersen, "Undergraduate Medical Education," *Journal of the American Medical Association* 252 (1984):1529.

57. Flexner, Medical Education in the United States and Canada, 44–46.

58. *Final Report of the Commission on Medical Education*, 387, 120.

59. The diversity of state laws, it should be noticed, created difficulties for physicians already in practice who sought to move to another state. Gradually, however, much confusion was eliminated from the state laws, and a system of reciprocity began to take form.

60. Assessment of a doctor in this way was just an approximation, for not all graduates of deficient schools were dangerous, and not all graduates of reputable schools were skilled.

61. William Osler, "Unity, Peace, and Concord," in William Osler, *Aequanimitas with other Addresses to Medical Students, Nurses and Practitioners of Medicine*, 3rd ed. (Philadelphia: Blakiston, 1932), 433.

62. Wiebe, *The Search for Order*.

63. Abraham Flexner, *Medical Education: A Comparative Study* (New York: Macmillan, 1925), 141.

64. *Final Report of the Commission on Medical Education*, 390–91.

65. Franklin P. Mall, "Liberty in Medical Education," *Philadelphia Medical Journal* 3 (1899):723.

66. William Charles White to Henry Pritchett, 23 Feb. 1915, File, "University of Pittsburgh 1905–1919," Carnegie Foundation Archives, Carnegie Corporation.

67. William Sydney Thayer, "Scholarship in Medicine," in William Sydney Thayer, *Osler and Other Papers* (Baltimore: The Johns Hopkins University Press, 1931), 221.

68. Mall, "Liberty in Medical Education," 721.

69. "Report of the Dean of the Medical School," in Columbia University, *Annual Report* (1908), 82. On Pennsylvania, see Medical faculty meeting minutes, 23 April 1906, University of Pennsylvania School of Medicine, University of Pennsylvania Archives.

70. Victor Vaughan to John M. Baldy, 2 July 1915, Box 2; Victor Vaughan to John M. Baldy, 9 March 1915, Box 1; and John M. Baldy to Victor Vaughan, 26 Feb. 1915, Box 1; in Records of the Medical School of the University of Michigan, Michigan Historical Collections, Bentley Historical Library, University of Michigan.

71. John M. Baldy to the Tufts College Medical School, 3 Dec. 1914, Medical Correspondence, 1908–1917, Tufts University Archives.

72. Letters, N. P. Colwell to Frank G. Wren, 14 Jan. 1918 (quotation), and 22 Dec. 1917; and Frank G. Wren to N.P. Colwell, 10 Jan. 1918, and 17 Jan. 1918; Medical Correspondence, 1908–1917, Tufts University Archives.

73. A. Lawrence Lowell, "The Danger to the Maintenance of High Standards from Excessive Formalism," *Journal of the American Medical Association* 62 (1914):823–26.

74. Flexner, *Medical Education: A Comparative Study*, 142.

75. *Final Report of the Commission on Medical Education*, 390.

76. *Final Report of the Commission on Medical Education*, 166–67, 391.

Chapter 14

1. Abraham Flexner to G. Canby Robinson, 15 Oct. 1920, Folder 1407, Box 152, Series I, General Education Board Papers, Rockefeller Archive Center, North Tarrytown, New York.

2. Abraham Flexner to Wallace Buttrick, 7 May 1921, Folder 3171, Box 303, Series I, General Education Board Papers, Rockefeller Archive Center.

3. Henry J. Bigelow, *Medical Education in America* (Cambridge, Mass.: Welch, Bigelow, 1871), 13.

4. "Report of the Special Committee on the Medical School," Folder, "University of Pittsburgh School of Medicine Faculty Council c. 1910," Historical Materials of the University of Pittsburgh, Falk Library, University of Pittsburgh.

5. "Editorial," *The Hospital Bulletin* 2 (1906):110. This journal was an unofficial publication of the University of Maryland School of Medicine.

6. Alfred D. Chandler, Jr., *The Visible Hand: The Managerial Revolution in American Business* (Cambridge, Mass.: Belknap Press of Harvard University Press, 1977), 12. I have learned much about the develoment of modern medical schools from studying the development of modern corporations. Chandler's book has been an especially useful source.

7. John Shaw Billings, "A Review on Higher Medical Education," *Bulletin of the History of Medicine* 6 (1938):304.

8. H. Milton Brown to Charles F. Thwing, 2 May 1917, Box 18, Charles Franklin Thwing Office Files, Case Western Reserve University Archives.

9. Samuel B. McCormick to T. S. Arbuthnot, 17 May 1919, Folder, "University of Pittsburgh School of Medicine. Search for Dean, 1919," Historical Materials of the University of Pittsburgh.

10. Quoted in A. McGehee Harvey, *Science at the Bedside: Clinical Research in American Medicine 1905–1945* (Baltimore: The Johns Hopkins University Press, 1981), 244.

11. In 1984, in the author's own department of internal medicine at Washington University, there were 145 full-time faculty members with the rank of instructor or higher. The department had eleven divisions, with cardiology, the largest, containing twenty members. In 1960, in contrast, there were 155 full-time faculty members in the entire school.

12. Lewellys F. Barker, *Time and the Physician* (New York: G. P. Putnam's Sons, 1942), 218.

13. James H. Kirkland to G. Canby Robinson, 25 May 1920, Folder 1407, Box 152, Series I, General Education Board Papers, Rockefeller Archive Center.

14. Meeting with Dr. David Edsall, 26 April 1923, Wickliffe Rose Diary, General Education Board Papers, Rockefeller Archive Center; Henry K. Beecher and Mark D. Altschule, *Medicine at Harvard: The First Three Hundred Years* (Hanover, N.H.: University Press of New England, 1977), 207.

15. On biochemistry, the seminal studies of Robert Kohler are an invaluable source. See his book, *From Medical Chemistry to Biochemistry: The Making of a Biomedical Discipline* (Cambridge: Cambridge University Press, 1982), and his article, "Medical Reform and Biochemical Sciences: Biochemistry—a Case Study," in *The Therapeutic Revolution: Essays in the Social History of American Medicine*, ed. Morris J. Vogel and Charles E. Rosenberg (Philadelphia: University of Pennsylvania Press, 1979), 27–66. On the other basic science disciplines, see the articles by John Blake on anatomy, James Whorton on chemistry, and David Cowen on materia medica and pharmacology in *The Education of American Physicians: Historical Essays*, ed. Ronald C. Numbers (Berkeley: University of California Press, 1980).

16. W. McKim Marriott to Abraham Flexner, 10 Jan. 1928, Folder 7100, Box 689, Series I, General Education Board Papers, Rockefeller Archive Center.

17. Yandell Hendersen to the Committee on Reorganization of the Medical School, 27 Dec. 1918, File, "1918—Reorganization of the School," Box 7, Yale Medical School, Dean's Files, Yale University Archives.

18. E. E. Southard to Henry A. Christian, 18 March 1913, Volume 1, Henry A. Christian Papers, Countway Library, Harvard Medical School.

19. Greer Williams, *Western Reserve's Experiment in Medical Education and Its Outcome* (New York: Oxford University Press, 1980).

20. See, for instance, Peter V. Lee, *Medical Schools and the Changing Times: Nine Case Reports on Experimentation in Medical Education, 1950–1960* (Evanston, Ill.: Association of American Medical Colleges, 1962); Vernon W. Lippard and Elizabeth Purcell, eds., *The Changing Medical Curriculum* (New York: The Josiah Macy, Jr., Foundation, 1972); Vernon W. Lippard and Elizabeth Purcell, eds., *Case Histories of Ten New Medical Schools* (New York: The Josiah Macy, Jr., Foundation, 1972).

21. On the contributions to basic science that have resulted from the study of medical

problems, see Henry K. Beecher, ed., *Disease and the Advancement of Basic Science* (Cambridge, Mass.: Harvard University Press, 1960).

22. Thus, in 1927 the superintendent of the University of Minnesota Hospital complained of the tendency of the modern teaching hospital "to emphasize its educational functions, more than its relation to the people as a service institution." See "The Medical School," University of Minnesota, *President's Report* (1926–27), 141. For a recent criticism of the academic medical center's relations to the community, see Irving J. Lewis and Cecil G. Sheps, *The Sick Citadel: The American Academic Medical Center and the Public Interest* (Cambridge, Mass.: Oelgeschlager, Gunn & Hain, 1983).

23. Flexner states his belief in this credo, which he acquired from Daniel Gilman, in Abraham Flexner, *I Remember: The Autobiography of Abraham Flexner* (New York: Simon and Schuster, 1940), 51. So, too, would Flexner have been appalled by scientific cheating, which has received a great deal of notoriety the past few years. For a journalistic account of this subject, see William Broad and Nicholas Wade, *Betrayers of the Truth: Fraud and Deceit in the Halls of Science* (New York: Simon and Schuster, 1983).

24. *Physicians for the Twenty-First Century. The GPEP Report. Report of the Panel on the General Professional Education of the Physician and College Preparation for Medicine* (Washington, D.C.: Association of American Medical Colleges, 1984), 9, 12.

25. Robert H. Ebert, "Medical Education in the United States," in *Doing Better and Feeling Worse: Health in the United States*, ed. John H. Knowles (New York: Norton, 1977), 180.

26. Richard C. Cabot, *Training and Rewards of the Physician* (Philadelphia: J. B. Lippincott, 1918), 39.

27. David R. Perry, David R. Challoner, and Robert J. Oberst, "Research Advances and Resource Constraints. Dilemmas Facing Medical Education," *New England Journal of Medicine* 305 (1981):320–24.

28. In 1912, the French-born and educated Alexis Carrel won the Nobel Prize in Medicine and Physiology for studies of vascular suture and organ transplantation performed at the Rockefeller Institute in New York. Some would consider this the first Nobel Prize for the United States. In 1930, Karl Landsteiner of the Rockefeller Institute received the prize for his discovery of human blood groups. However, this work was done in Vienna between 1900 and 1903, more than two decades before he moved to America.

29. Ebert, "Medical Education in the United States," 180.

30. George W. Corner, *A History of the Rockefeller Institute, 1901–1953, Origins and Growth* (New York: Rockefeller Institute Press, 1964), 158–59.

31. Abraham Flexner, *Medical Education: A Comparative Study* (New York: Macmillan, 1925), 141.

32. Carl V. Moore, "The Angry Medical Student and the Changing Face of Medical Education," *The Pharos* 29 (July 1966):72–77; Henry K. Silver, "Medical Students and Medical School," *Journal of the American Medical Association* 247 (1982):309–10. For studies of the socialization of medical students, see Robert K. Merton, George G. Reader, and Patricia L. Kendall, *The Student-Physician: Introductory Studies in the Sociology of Medical Education* (Cambridge, Mass.: Harvard University Press, 1957); Howard S. Becker, *Boys in White: Student Culture in Medical School* (Chicago: The University of Chicago Press, 1961); and Robert H. Coombs, *Mastering Medicine: Professional Socialization in Medical School* (New York: Free Press, 1978).

33. Arthur Dean Bevan to Henry Pritchett, 23 Jan. 1917, File, "American Medical Association 1915–1939," Carnegie Foundation Archives, Carnegie Corporation, New York.

34. This is not to say that there have been no compromises along the way. Today, for instance, some schools allow selected students to enter accelerated programs in which they receive the A.B. and M.D. degrees in six or seven years after graduation from high school rather than the customary eight. However, such programs have not altered the general trend, which has been decidedly toward a later and later age at which physicians finally enter practice.

35. John I. Sandson, "A Crisis in Medical Education: The High Cost of Student Financial Assistance," *New England Journal of Medicine* 308 (1983):1286.

36. Here it might be mentioned that the lower cost of education at the old proprietary schools had nothing to do with tuition, which was often higher than at the university schools.

Rather, with easier entrance requirements, students could begin their medical training at an earlier age and thus earn a living from practice that much sooner. In addition, since the course of study tended to be much less rigorous, students who wished could more readily hold part-time jobs while pursuing their studies.

37. Sandson, "A Crisis in Medical Education," 1287–88.

38. George Eastman to Rush Rhees, 13 July 1923, File 7/11/23–10/21/23, Box "Correspondence between Rush Rhees and George Eastman, 1908–1932," Rush Rhees Papers, Department of Rare Books, Manuscripts, and Archives, University of Rochester Library, Rochester, New York.

39. Steven Jonas, *Medical Mystery: The Training of Doctors in the United States* (New York: Norton, 1978), 291.

40. Ibid., 291.

41. Ronald L. Numbers, *Almost Persuaded: American Physicians and Compulsory Health Insurance, 1912–1920* (Baltimore: The Johns Hopkins University Press, 1978), 2. On the debate over compulsory health insurance during World War I, in addition to this volume, see James G. Burrow, *AMA: Voice of American Medicine* (Baltimore: The Johns Hopkins University Press, 1963), 132–51; and Paul Starr, *The Social Transformation of American Medicine: The Rise of a Sovereign Profession and the Making of a Vast Industry* (New York: Basic Books, 1982), 235–57.

42. *Medical Care for the American People: The Final Report of the Committee on the Costs of Medical Care* (Chicago: The University of Chicago Press, 1932).

43. Rosemary Stevens has focused on the dilemma of making medical services available to everyone in her classic study of the health care system, *American Medicine and the Public Interest* (New Haven: Yale University Press, 1971). In this book, Stevens examined issues of medical manpower and distribution as well as costs.

44. A perceptive essay making this point is Arthur D. Silk, "American Medical Care—Is It Worth It?," *New England Journal of Medicine* 307 (1982):117.

45. Lester Thurow, "Learning to Say 'No'," *New England Journal of Medicine* 311 (1984):1569–72.

46. C. Ronald Kahn, "A Proposed New Role for the Insurance Industry in Biomedical Research Funding," *New England Journal of Medicine* 310 (1984):257–58.

47. With the decline in federal educational subsidies and with the public's growing concern for containing medical costs, teaching hospitals, not just medical schools, have been financially squeezed. See Arnold Relman, "Who Will Pay for Medical Education in our Teaching Hospitals?," *Science* 226(1984):20–23; and Arnold Relman, "Are Teaching Hospitals Worth the Extra Cost?," *New England Journal of Medicine* 310 (1984):1256–57. Financial pressures have already led one teaching hospital, University (of Louisville) Hospital, to allow itself to be bought by Humana Inc., a for-profit hospital chain. At this writing no other teaching hospital has been acquired by a proprietary chain, and the results of the Louisville experiment are not yet known. Clearly, however, the Louisville experiment could be the beginning of a momentous development in medical education, especially at the postgraduate (house staff and fellowship) level.

48. "Corporate Links Worry Scholars," *New York Times*, 17 Oct. 1982, p. F–4; "Allies in the Laboratory," *Washington University Magazine* (Summer 1983):18–23.

49. Kahn, "A Proposed New Role for the Insurance Industry," 257.

50. Arnold S. Relman, "The New Medical-Industrial Complex," *New England Journal of Medicine* 303 (1980):963–70. The rise of the investor-owned hospitals has recently been analyzed by Paul Starr in an important book that has already become a classic. See Starr, *The Social Transformation of American Medicine*, 420–49.

51. Starr, *The Social Transformation of American Medicine*, 428.

52. Ibid., 444–49; Steve A. Friedman, "Megacorporate Health Care: A Choice for the Future," *New England Journal of Medicine* 312(1985):579–82.

53. George Rosen, *The Structure of American Medical Practice 1875–1941*, ed. Charles E. Rosenberg (Philadelphia: University of Pennsylvania Press, 1983).

54. Predictions of the stability of the corporate medical school assume the stability of the large corporation in America. The reader will note that a few have forecast the demise of the large corporation, or at least its breakup into smaller, more manageable units. See Eli Ginzberg and George Vojta, *Beyond Human Scale: The Large Corporation at Risk* (New York: Basic Books, 1985).

55. *Physicians for the Twenty-First Century.*

56. Eli H. Long, "Functions of the Medical School," President's Address, Proceedings of the Nineteenth Annual Meeting of the Association of American Medical Colleges, March 15–16, 1909, pp. 13, 14, Association of American Medical Colleges Archives.

57. Cabot, *Training and Rewards of the Physician,* 42.

58. *Physicians for the Twenty-First Century,* 7.

59. Ibid., xv.

60. Measuring good teaching is a difficult, subjective task, and many schools are leery about promoting faculty members for contributions that are hard to evaluate. Yet, measuring good research can also be very difficult, which is why some departments at some schools assess a faculty member's research solely on the basis of number of publications. Today, most medical schools, like other institutions of higher learning, value research much more than they value teaching. The larger impediment to improving the quality of instruction is not the difficulty of evaluating good teaching but that of persuading medical schools to reward good teaching more generously.

61. *Ibid.,* 7, 22. Some medical educators would also caution that the public's expectations of doctors in this regard are sometimes too high. They maintain that it is all very well to say that doctors should be caring, as long as doctors are not expected to be immune from human frailty.

62. Herbert Marcuse, *One-Dimensional Man: Studies in the Ideology of Advanced Industrial Society* (Boston: Beacon Press, 1964); Jacques Ellul, *The Technological Society* (New York: Alfred A. Knopf, 1964).

63. Stanley Reiser, *Medicine and the Reign of Technology* (Cambridge: Cambridge University Press, 1978).

Index

335

Index

Clinical education: control of, 214

Clinical science: development of, 132–33, 209, 210, 260–61, 263

Clinical scientists, 209–11, 261

Clinical teaching, 152, 309n4; *see also* Clerkship

Coeducation, 60, 248

Cohn, Alfred, 209

Cohnheim, Julius, 128

College degree: as entrance requirement, *see* Bachelor's degree

College of Physicians and Surgeons (Baltimore), 101, 158, 186, 243–44; educational quality at, 97t, 98; faculty, 98

College of Physicians and Surgeons (Boston), 186

College of Physicians and Surgeons (New York), 37, 74, 147, 161, 140–41, 220, 283n 29; *see also* Columbia University Medical School

Colleges, *see specific colleges*

Columbia University Medical School, 74, 81, 82, 85, 86, 111, 116, 117, 159, 185, 222, 229, 230, 296n56, 302n54; alliance with Presbyterian Hospital, 223; educational quality at, 96, 97t; entrance requirements, 85–86; faculty, 40; faculty salaries, 126; financial problems, 144; fund raising, 149; hospital affiliations of, 227; philanthropic contributions to, 193, 198, 208; teaching hospital negotiations and, 159, 162–63; *see also* College of Physicians and Surgeons (New York)

Columbian College Medical Department, 86; faculty dividends at, 101

Colwell, N. P., 106, 239, 240, 244

Commission on Medical Education, 251, 254

Committee on the Costs of Medical Care, 273

Competition among medical schools, 15, 84–86, 218

Continuing education, 94, 136, 298n93; *see also* Postgraduate instruction

Cornell University Medical College, 81–82, 86, 117, 119, 159, 229; and affiliation with New York Hospital, 227; benefactors, 198; clerkships, 154; curriculum changes at, 84, 295n34; entrance requirements, 115; faculty, 33; fund raising, 148, 193

Corporate sponsorship: of biomedical research, 274–75

Council on Medical Education, *see* American Medical Association

Councilman, William, 170, 223, 324n22

Courses, *see* Curriculum

Cox, George, 228

Cremin, Lawrence, 173, 177, 190

Crocker, George, 208

Cupples, Samuel, 221, 323n9

Curriculum, 41, 50, 107; crowded, 70–71, 89, 182, 189, 251, 271, 316n75; experimentation, 262; four-year, 89, 90t, 106, 270; Harvard, 47–48; "integrated," 262; laboratory work in, 69, 107; in mid-nineteenth century, 11–12; reform, 20–24, 50, 51, 63, 264; sequence of, 53–54; standardization of, 88–89, 250; three-year, 88; variations in, 89, 250, 298n93

Curtis, Charles P., 223

Cushing, Harvey, 71, 98, 126, 204

Cushny, Arthur, 57

Dabney, Charles, 40, 110, 186, 228

Dandy, Walter, 260

Dartmouth Medical College, 81, 86, 145, 159, 229, 241, 296n63, 311–12n43

Davis, Nathan Smith, 16, 20

Deanship, 258–59

Dennis, Frederic, 35, 36

Denver and Gross College of Medicine: absenteeism and teaching at, 93; academic attrition and, 119; and consolidation with University of Colorado, 244; faculty dividends at, 101; reforms at, 81; student research at, 98

Denver City and County Hospital, 228

Dewey, John, 64, 67, 167, 176, 292n90; *see also* Progressive medical education

Diagnosis of disease: refinement of lab testing and, 77–78

Didactic instruction, 12, 51–52, 175; abandonment of, 55–56, 63–64, 72

Diploma mill scandals of 1880–81, 13

"Diploma relations," 45

Diplomas: buying of, 13

Disciplinary problems, 13–14, 282n12

Disease: bacteriologic origins of, 77t; natural history of, 22

Dock, George, 82, 125, 168, 209, 311n34, 326 n69

Index

235–36; medical school budgets and, 143*t*, 306*n*13; prelude to, 168–73

Folin, Otto, 104, 223, 324*n*22

Fordham Medical School, 81, 145, 185, 241, 243, 328*n*36

For-profit hospital chains, 275–76, 277, 332*n*47, 332*n*50

Four-year program, 53, 54, 56, 57, 63, 72, 74, 89, 235, 270

Fosdick, Raymond, 193

Fox, Daniel, 172

France: attitudes toward experimental research in, 23, 286*n*8; medical education in, 18, 29–30, 47, 49, 59, 283*n*44, 284*n*56; and impact of medical science on America, 22, 130

Frazier, Charles, 170

Freer, Paul, 57

Full-time system, 207–13, 217

Fund raising, 203, 205–6, 242–43, 272; early efforts toward, 146–51; and entrepreneurial efforts of medical educators, 203, 205–6

Gamble, James, 209

Gates, Frederick T., 194, 197, 200, 202, 205, 319*n*33, 326*n*65

General Education Board, 20; Abraham Flexner and, 229, 318*n*11; administrative procedures of, 193–94, 197, 319*n*33; faculty salary negotiations and, 208, 210; full-time clinical department system and, 210, 211, 239, 318*n*12, 321*n*12; fund raising and, 203, 204, 205; interference with medical school operations by, 195, 196; philanthropic contributions of, 192, 193–94, 199

Geneva Medical College, 14

George Washington University, 81, 86, 206, 215, 243

Georgetown University: clinical clerkships at, 154; educational quality at, 97*t*, 98; faculty dividends, 101; grading and promotion standards, 119–20; lack of research at, 241; night school, 91; reforms, 81, 86, 92; success of, 243

Gerhard, William, 26

Germ theory of disease, 76, 130, 201, 284*n*60, 294*n*16

Germany, 258; cost of medical education in, 32–33; and influence on American medical education, 83–84, 93–94, 105, 124; and influence on American medicine, 110; medical education in, 43, 47, 49, 59; medical science in, 30–38; medical system in, 69, 70; postgraduate study in, 75; and scholarship in nonmedical areas, 286*n*9

Gilman, Daniel Coit, 58, 59, 110, 173, 331*n*23

GPEP report, 264, 278, 279

Greene, Jerome, 211, 212

Hadley, Arthur, 110

Halifax Medical School, 179

Halsted, William, 59, 75, 104, 127

Hammond, William Alexander, 11

Handlin, Oscar, 68

Harkness, Edward, 220, 231

Harper, William Rainey, 110

Harriet Lane Home, 221

Harris, A. W., 186

Harrison, Charles, 116–17

Harvard University Medical School, 11, 47, 63, 82, 85; and affiliation with Peter Bent Brigham Hospital, 220, 223; changes in, 113; corporate sponsorship of, 274; curriculum of, 14, 47–48, 71; educational quality at, 96, 97*t*, 98; during Eliot administration, 21, 41, 51–53, 109, 113; entrance requirements of, 12, 113, 121; establishment of biological chemistry department at, 104; faculty, 33, 37, 40, 104, 125; fund raising, 146, 148, 150, 193, 206, 211, 321*n*12; history, 288*n*1; hospital affiliations, 159, 227; introduction of laboratory instruction at, 74; reforms, 57, 61, 72, 73; research at, 23–24, 25, 103, 107; salaries of full professors at, 126*t*; under David Edsall, 260

Harvey, A. McGehee, 58, 133, 212

Haskell, Thomas, 183–84

Health-care costs, rising, 272–74

Health maintenance organizations (HMO's), 277

Herter, Christian, 204

High schools: and establishment of "diploma relations," 45

Higher education: development of, in United States, 287*n*37, 288*n*54; *see also* University

Holmes, Christian, 83, 228

Holmes, Oliver Wendell, 23–24, 26, 49, 67

Holt, L. Emmett, 135, 204

339

Index

Index

Physical diagnosis, 17, 22, 65

Physician-patient ratio, 178, 247, 328n53

Physicians: and distinction between scholarship and practice, 6, 129–30; quality of, 278–79; resident, 17; socially elite, 28

Physiology laboratory, 83

Politics: and interference in establishment of teaching hospitals, 228

Porter, William, 65, 98

Postgraduate instruction, 257, 270

"Practical schools," 141, 166, 169, 187; elimination of, 7–8; versus scientific, 108

Practitioners: and dislike of professors, 124–31, 215–16; and establishment of entrance requirements, 118; and rapprochement with professors, 131–38, 216–17; subordination of, 213–17; as teachers, 123, 208, 217; twentieth-century, 269, 270

Preceptors, 16, 61

Preclinical versus clinical departments, 260–61

Premedical training, 302n51

Presbyterian Hospital, 163, 220–23, 225, 231

Pritchett, Henry, 111, 141, 149–50, 170, 171, 187–89, 199, 244, 246–47, 314n9, 317n102; and criticism of General Board of Education, 195–96; Flexner report and, 187–89; government regulation of medical education and, 236–37; views of, on scientific teaching, 107

Privatdocenten, 94

Professors of medicine, 92, 101; appointed to run clinical departments, 214; and dependence on student fees, 22; and differentiation from practitioner, 5–6, 129–30, 212–13; and effect on ranking, 241–42; first physiology, 37; full-time, 6, 35, 93, 123; part-time, 93; and placement on salary, 50; practitioners and, 124–38, 213–17; salaries of, 125, 126, 126t, 208, 283–84n47, 290n28, 311–12n43, 326n66; *see also* Full-time system

Progressive Education Association, 190

Progressive Era, 5, 106, 108; and emphasis on scientific method, 79; and rise of teaching hospital, 226

Progressive medical education, 5, 63–72, 105, 167, 176–77, 189, 190; and "learning by doing," 64, 65, 71, 81; origins of, 64–65; *see also* Dewey, John

Proprietary medical schools, 80; commercialism of, 15, 99; creation of, 3, 11; death of,

5, 241–49, 258; differences in, 98–99; elimination of, 187, 234; in mid-nineteenth century, 14, 19, 47; proliferation of, 95

Prudden, T. Mitchell, 37

Public concerns: about medical costs, 273

Pyemia, 10

Quinine, 10

Rauch, John H., 327n6

Redman, John, 16

"Reed report," 281n2; *see also* Legal education

Reform movement in medical education, 47–63, 73–79; AMA and, 27–28; early efforts of, 20–24; German medical science and, 29–38; national growth of, 87–93; pioneers of, 47–63; spread of, 72–101; as umbrella for many groups, 168–69

Reiser, Stanley, 279

Relman, Arnold, 276

Research, 8, 26–27, 34, 38, 102, 300n8, 333n60; biomedical, expansion of, 262; careers, 37; careers in, 35–36; corporate sponsorship of, 274–75; cost of, 139; development of, 7; and effect on ranking, 241–42; enthronement of, 217–18, 263, 264, 278–79; federal support of, 274; and financial burden on medical schools, 106–7; financial constraints and, 151; full-time positions in, 124; funding of, 207; and opening of Johns Hopkins, 103, 300n7; positions, 25–26; skepticism toward, 23–24; teaching and, 102–8; twentieth-century, 266–67; *see also* Academic medicine; Clinical science; Full-time system

Research institutes, 104–5; *see also specific institutes*

Residency, 17; *see also* House pupil system

Revolt against formalism, 67

Rivalry, medical school, 15, 84–86, 218

Rives, George, 227

Robinson, C. Canby, 218

Rockefeller, John D., Jr., 197, 202

Rockefeller, John D., Sr., 148, 150, 193, 197, 200, 201, 202, 231, 269, 326n65

Rockefeller Foundation, 192

Index

Thinking, critical, 280

Thomsonian movement, 22, 284n54

Three-year medical course, 50, 53, 56, 72, 74, 88

Thurow, Lester, 273

Thwing, Charles, 40, 110, 258, 311–12n43

Thyroid extract, 77

Toledo Medical College, 97t

"Town-gown" disputes, 123–24, 130–31, 138, 215–16, 269

Tremont Street Medical School, 113

Tufts University, 81, 117, 119, 145, 185, 243, 296n63; admissions, 253; benefactors, 198; class size limitations at, 86; curriculum committee, 92; medical faculty, 83, 86; quality of education at, 97t; research status of, 103

Tuition, 54, 141–42, 271, 331–32n36

Tulane Medical School, 81, 160, 193, 228

Typhoid fever, 76–77

Tyson, James, 54

University: emergence of, 38–43, 287–88n38; funding of medical schools in, 272; growth of enrollment in, 44–45; medical school as part of, 5, 7, 48, 50, 52–53, 55, 56, 57, 58, 63; medicine enters, 108–13; objectivity and universality in, 52

University affiliation, 14–15, 38–43, 108–13; financial advantages of, 86–87, 149–50, 206; financing of medical education and, 86–87, 149–50, 206

University of Arkansas, 116, 137, 199, 206, 241, 246

University of California, 81, 198, 217, 244

University of Chattanooga, 243

University of Chicago, 193, 196; benefactors, 198

University of Cincinnati, 81, 87, 97t, 144, 198, 228

University of Colorado School of Medicine, 81, 88, 97t, 160, 193, 199, 228, 241, 243, 244, 310n27

University of Georgia, 206

University of Illinois, 108, 158, 206

University of Iowa, 158, 193, 230, 319n33

University of Kansas, 81, 158, 196

University of Maryland School of Medicine, 82, 85, 86, 120, 145, 158, 185, 206, 243–44

University of Michigan, 47, 82, 91, 143, 198, 217, 227; class size limitations at, 86; clinical clerkship at, 154, 311n34; educational quality at, 96, 97t; and emulation of reforms, 21, 61, 72, 73; enrollment, 141; entrance requirements, 12–13, 44, 253; faculty, 33; fund raising, 149; Hospital, 157, 158; introduction of laboratory instruction at, 74; medical literature and, 65, 292n77; reforms, 56–57, 63, 72; research status of, 103

University of Minnesota, 81, 85, 92, 111, 112–13, 119, 143, 160, 217, 298n93; benefactors, 198; class size limitations at, 86; educational quality at, 96, 97t; entrance requirements, 115, 303n65; faculty, 83; fund raising, 149, 198; honor system at, 299n105; teaching hospital, 158; "Vincent's massacre," 214, 322n29

University of Mississippi Medical School, 81, 145

University of Nebraska College of Medicine, 81, 84, 86, 92, 145, 228, 229, 241, 243, 296n63, 298n93; faculty salaries at, 125

University of Oklahoma School of Medicine, 81, 137, 185, 199

University of Oregon, 193

University of Pennsylvania, 11, 12, 25, 47, 61, 84–85, 91, 95, 283n29; clinical clerkship at, 154; consolidation discussions at, 244; curriculum changes at, 84; educational background of students at, 114, 114t; and emulation of reforms, 72, 73, 106, 140, 296–97n68; enrollment, 100, 116, 141; entrance requirements, 85; faculty salaries at, 19, 125, 290n28; financial problems, 143, 146; four-year rule at, 74; fund raising, 146–47; Hospital, 157; introduction of laboratory instruction at, 74; reforms, 53–54, 55–56, 63, 72, 290n34; research status of, 103

University of Pittsburgh, 81, 84, 86, 111, 122, 128, 144, 159, 198, 214–15, 218, 243, 259

University of Rochester School of Medicine, 193, 198, 199, 204, 272, 318n11

University of Southern California in Los Angeles: College of Medicine, 73–74, 81, 86, 93, 97t, 145, 160, 296n62

University of Tennessee, 99, 145

University of Texas, 143t, 185

University of Utah, 81, 145, 149

University of Vermont, 109, 116

University of Virginia, 144, 193

University of Wisconsin, 81, 185, 198, 217